D1564846

Daily Feast

MEDITATIONS FROM
FEASTING ON THE WORD®

❧ YEAR B ❧

Daily Feast

MEDITATIONS FROM
FEASTING ON THE WORD®

❧ YEAR B ❧

EDITED BY
Kathleen Long Bostrom
Elizabeth F. Caldwell

WESTMINSTER
JOHN KNOX PRESS
LOUISVILLE · KENTUCKY

First edition
Published by Westminster John Knox Press
Louisville, Kentucky

11 12 13 14 15 16 17 18 19 20—10 9 8 7 6 5 4 3 2

Book design by Drew Stevens
Cover design by Dilu Nicholas

Library of Congress Cataloging-in-Publication Data

Daily feast : meditations from Feasting on the Word / Kathleen Long
Bostrom and Elizabeth Caldwell, editors. — 1st ed.
    p. cm. — (Daily feast)
Includes index.
ISBN 978-0-664-23797-4 (Year B : alk. paper) 1. Bible—Meditations.
2. Devotional calendars. 3. Common lectionary (1992) I. Bostrom,
Kathleen Long. II. Caldwell, Elizabeth, 1948- III. Feasting on the Word.
BS491.5.D35 2011
242'.2—dc23

2011023555

Most Westminster John Knox Press books are available at special quantity
discounts when purchased in bulk by corporations, organizations, and special-interest
groups. For more information, please e-mail SpecialSales@wjkbooks.com.

Contents

ix   Introduction

xi   A Note from the Publisher

1   First Sunday of Advent

10   Second Sunday of Advent

19   Third Sunday of Advent

28   Fourth Sunday of Advent

37   Christmas Eve

42   Christmas Day

47   First Sunday after Christmas Day

56   Second Sunday after Christmas Day

65   Epiphany of the Lord

74   Baptism of the Lord
(First Sunday after the Epiphany)

83   Second Sunday after the Epiphany

92   Third Sunday after the Epiphany

101   Fourth Sunday after the Epiphany

110   Fifth Sunday after the Epiphany

119   Sixth Sunday after the Epiphany

128   Seventh Sunday after the Epiphany

137   Eighth Sunday after the Epiphany

146   Ninth Sunday after the Epiphany

155   Last Sunday after the Epiphany
(Transfiguration Sunday)

164   First Sunday in Lent

167   Ash Wednesday

176   Second Sunday in Lent

185   Third Sunday in Lent

194   Fourth Sunday in Lent

203   Fifth Sunday in Lent

212   Palm/Passion Sunday

222   Holy Week
        Monday of Holy Week   222
        Tuesday of Holy Week   223
        Wednesday of Holy Week   224
        Maundy Thursday   225
        Good Friday   226
        Holy Saturday   227
        The Resurrection of the Lord (Easter Day)   228

231   Second Sunday of Easter

240   Third Sunday of Easter

249   Fourth Sunday of Easter

258   Fifth Sunday of Easter

267   Sixth Sunday of Easter

276   Ascension of the Lord

285   Seventh Sunday of Easter

294   Pentecost

303   Trinity Sunday

312   Proper 3

321   Proper 4

330   Proper 5

339   Proper 6

348   Proper 7

357   Proper 8

366   Proper 9

375   Proper 10

384   Proper 11

393   Proper 12

402   Proper 13

411   Proper 14

420   Proper 15

429   Proper 16

438   Proper 17

447   Proper 18

456   Proper 19

465   Proper 20

474   Proper 21

483   Proper 22

492   Proper 23

501   Proper 24

510   Proper 25

519   All Saints' Day

524   Proper 26

533   Proper 27

542   Proper 28

551   Proper 29 (Reign of Christ)

560   List of Contributors

569   Scripture Index

Introduction

When we opened the first volume of Feasting on the Word: Preaching the Revised Common Lectionary and began reading, we knew that the contents were consistent with the title. As teachers and preachers, to have four perspectives on the lectionary in one volume truly satisfied our hunger for rich engagement with biblical texts. With the publication of each additional volume in the twelve-volume series, we became excited about the possibilities for the ways these essays could be resources for other spiritual practices.

This book is designed to give you a chance to step back and focus on a smaller piece from some of the essays from the Feasting on the Word commentaries. Whether you are a pastor, educator, church member, or lay leader, let these reflections on biblical texts be a daily feast for your continuing formation in the life of the Christian faith.

Consider the ways that *Daily Feast* might be used:

- ⇢ **Daily meditation**: Begin or end your day with a reading and reflection on one of the texts for the week.
- ⇢ **Journaling**: As you read, think, and pray, journal in response to the thoughts that are evoked for you. Some find that journaling with words works best. Others find that using markers, crayons, or watercolors invites a different kind of imaging in response to text.
- ⇢ **Preparing for preaching or worship leadership**: Have a copy of this available to give to liturgists and choir directors, all those involved in worship leadership. As staff or worship teams work on liturgy and prepare for worship leadership, this book can become a resource for meditation and prayer, and may even be adapted for use in worship.
- ⇢ **Preparing for teaching**: Use in your own meditation during the week as you prepare your heart and mind to teach all ages of God's children.

- → **Reaching out beyond the church**: Use in a variety of settings where a pastoral presence is invited to participate, such as social agencies, health-care facilities, hospitals, prisons, mission trips.
- → **Beginning or concluding an adult class in the church school**: Read a selection and a prayer as a time of centering.
- → **In committee meetings or staff meetings**: Use a *Daily Feast* selection as an opening meditation.

Note that portions of the texts for each Sunday are presented, beginning on the previous Monday, so that you can spend the week reflecting on the Scripture passages for the coming Sunday. Each weekday and Saturday will feature reflections on one of the four passages—Old Testament, Psalm, Epistle, and Gospel—along with a response and a prayer. Sundays and special days such as Christmas Eve and Holy Week will contain reflections on all four of the texts. (See "A Note from the Publisher" for more information about the Revised Common Lectionary and an explanation of how Feasting on the Word follows the lections during Ordinary Time.)

Included here are brief excerpts from each of the Scripture readings, but we encourage you to have a Bible handy so you can read the complete passage.

As we have read texts and the reflections on these texts from the four perspectives, we found ourselves slowing down, taking time to read Scripture, and connecting with these essays in new ways. We anticipate that the variety and depth of the perspectives on biblical texts of the authors of the essays will enrich your own spiritual practices.

We hope that our experience will be yours. So take some time. Read the text. Read the reflection. Consider your response, and be in prayer. May this resource be a daily feast for you.

Kathleen Bostrom and Lib Caldwell

A Note from the Publisher

This devotional is a part of the series Feasting on the Word: Preaching the Revised Common Lectionary, a twelve-volume commentary series for preaching and teaching. The uniqueness of the approach in the Feasting commentaries is in providing four perspectives on each preaching occasion from the Revised Common Lectionary. The theological, pastoral, exegetical, and homiletical dimensions of each biblical passage are explored with the hope that preachers will find much to inform and stimulate their preparations for preaching from this rich "feast" of materials.

Feasting on the Word follows the readings in the Revised Common Lectionary (RCL) as developed by the Consultation on Common Texts, an ecumenical consultation of liturgical scholars and denominational representatives from the United States and Canada. The RCL provides a collection of readings from Scripture to be used during worship in a schedule that follows the seasons of the church year. In addition, it provides for a uniform set of readings to be used across denominations or other church bodies.

The RCL provides a reading from the Old Testament, a Psalm response to that reading, a Gospel, and an Epistle for each preaching occasion of the year. It is presented in a three-year cycle, with each year centered around one of the Synoptic Gospels. Year A is the year of Matthew, Year B is the year of Mark, and Year C is the year of Luke. John is read each year, especially during Advent, Lent, and Easter. The RCL offers two tracks of Old Testament texts for the Season after Pentecost or Ordinary Time: a semicontinuous track, which moves through stories and characters in the Old Testament, and a complementary track, which ties the Old Testament texts to the theme of the Gospel texts for that day. Some denominational traditions favor one over the other. For instance, Presbyterians and Methodists generally follow the semicontinuous track, while Lutherans and Episcopalians generally follow the complementary track. To appeal to an ecumenical audience, the readings in this devotional follow the complementary track for Year A, are split between the complementary and semicontinuous tracks for Year B, and cover the semicontinuous stream for Year C.

Because not all lectionary days are used in a given year, depending on how the calendar falls, you may not need some of the readings here until a subsequent lectionary cycle. Check the official RCL Web site at http://lectionary.library.vanderbilt.edu for a list of readings for the current year.

Originally designed to be a twelve-volume set of preaching commentaries, the series has now grown to include several other related projects in addition to this devotional. A full church school curriculum program is now available at www.feastingontheword.net/curriculum. A three-volume set of worship resources to complement the commentaries is now in development, as is a guide for preaching the children's sermon. A major new undertaking using the four-perspective approach, Feasting on the Gospels, a seven-volume series of commentaries on the entirety of the Gospels, will be published, beginning in 2013. Information about these projects can be found on the Feasting on the Word Web site, www.feastingontheword.net.

Finally, we would like to thank all who were involved in the original Feasting on the Word series, including our partner, Columbia Theological Seminary; general editors David L. Bartlett and Barbara Brown Taylor; editorial board members Charles L. Campbell, Carlos Cardoza-Orlandi, Gary W. Charles, Allen Hilton, Cynthia A. Jarvis, E. Elizabeth Johnson, Thomas G. Long, Kathleen M. O'Connor, Marcia Y. Riggs, George W. Stroup, Emilie M. Townes, Richard F. Ward; project manager Joan Murchison; and project compiler Mary Lynn Darden.

❦ *First Sunday of Advent* ❦

Isaiah 64:1–9

From ages past no one has heard,
  no ear has perceived,
no eye has seen any God besides you,
  who works for those who wait for him. (v. 4)

Psalm 80:1–7, 17–19

O Lord God of hosts,
  how long will you be angry with your people's prayers?
. . . .
Restore us, O God of hosts;
  let your face shine, that we may be saved. (vv. 4, 7)

1 Corinthians 1:3–9

God is faithful; by him you were called into the
fellowship of his Son, Jesus Christ our Lord. (v. 9)

Mark 13:24–37

Heaven and earth will pass away, but my words
will not pass away. But about that day or hour no one
knows, neither the angels in heaven, nor the Son, but
only the Father. Beware, keep alert; for you do not
know when the time will come. (vv. 31–33)

✢ MONDAY ✦

Isaiah 64:1–9

REFLECTION

The coming of Advent jolts the church out of Ordinary Time with the invasive news that it's time to think about fresh possibilities for deliverance and human wholeness.

PATRICIA E. DE JONG

We cannot create peace through selfishness, but by opening ourselves to hope. Hope is what is left when your worst fears have been realized and you are no longer optimistic about your future. Hope is what comes with a broken heart willing to be mended.

PATRICIA E. DE JONG

At Advent, God's people summon the courage and the spiritual strength to remember that the holy breaks into the daily. In tiny ways, we can open our broken hearts to the healing grace of God, who opens the way to peace.

PATRICIA E. DE JONG

RESPONSE

How has a broken heart brought you to a place of hope?

PRAYER

Grant me the hope I long for, so that the broken places in my heart might be healed. Amen.

✣ TUESDAY ✣

Isaiah 64:1–9

REFLECTION

"Waiting for God" is no passive endeavor; it involves painful longing and bold allegiance, in short, a passionate patience.

WILLIAM P. BROWN

The season of Advent has always held in tension the combination of God's judgment and God's promise.

DONALD BOOZ

Advent affords us the opportunity to look at how God interacts with humankind from ages past to the present day.

DONALD BOOZ

To hear the voice of Isaiah is to proclaim that Advent is more than a time to hear promises about God. Advent becomes a season of attentiveness to the presence of God already among us.

DONALD BOOZ

RESPONSE

Name one specific way in which you are waiting for God.

PRAYER

Startle me out of my complacency, God, this and every day. Amen.

✦ WEDNESDAY ✦

Psalm 80:1–7, 17–19

REFLECTION

The NRSV's "angry" is an interpretation of a metaphor; the Hebrew asks how long God will "fume" against the prayers of the people. Certainly to "fume" frequently means to be furious, and to show it outwardly. Perhaps our psalmist envisions the prayers of God's people never quite penetrating through a thick haze of divine indifference to the suffering of God's people. The psalmist calls for God to "shine forth" (v. 1), and to "let your face shine, that we may be saved" (vv. 3, 7, 19). This divine light, a symbol of transcendent power throughout the religions of the ancient Near East, cuts through the smoke, whether of anger or indifference, restoring God's beneficent interest and unleashing power to save.   PAUL D. BRASSEY

RESPONSE

Do you think that God is indifferent to the suffering of the world? To your suffering?

PRAYER

If I have done something to anger you, bring me to awareness that I might seek your forgiveness. Amen.

✦ THURSDAY ✦

1 Corinthians 1:3–9

REFLECTION

There is a theological conviction at the heart of the apostle's gratitude: Paul trusts God to complete in the church what God has initiated in the death and resurrection of Jesus.

E. ELIZABETH JOHNSON

Paul's approach to thanksgiving, however, is carefully chosen. He does not simply celebrate the human efforts of the community. In fact, he does just the opposite. Everything for which Paul gives thanks is a gift of God's grace in Jesus Christ. His opening word of greeting in this text sets the tone: "grace" (v. 3).

CHARLES L. CAMPBELL

RESPONSE

What does "grace" mean to you?

PRAYER

I long to be a person who knows and shows grace. Amen.

✤ FRIDAY ✦

1 Corinthians 1:3–9

REFLECTION

The futurity of resurrection and the reality of death make right
ethical relations essential in the church.

E. ELIZABETH JOHNSON

The grace of Jesus Christ encompasses the entirety of the
community's life—past, present and future—not simply as the
forgiveness of sins, but as the power for faithful living.

CHARLES L. CAMPBELL

Grace here has radical social implications; it is not simply a
word spoken to individuals or a power at work in individuals.
Grace creates a new kind of community—one in which the
divisions and hierarchies of the world no longer function
because the grace of Jesus Christ, not human accomplishment
or status, is the source of the community's life.

CHARLES L. CAMPBELL

RESPONSE

Where have you seen grace in action this week?

PRAYER

O Christ, may your grace and peace truly be with us this
Advent season! Amen.

✢ SATURDAY ✢

Mark 13:24–37

REFLECTION

By contrast, of course, those who lived before the birth of
Jesus did not know the day or the hour of his arrival, so they
needed to live in a continual state of watchfulness. The birth of
the Messiah could only be celebrated as a surprise party that
could take place on any day, at any moment. By anticipating
the return of the Son of Man here, at the beginning of Advent,
we wait in the same way those who lived before Jesus was born
waited, not knowing the day or the hour when the Messiah
would appear. We also join them in hearing—and needing—
the same exhortation to be watchful and to keep awake.

MARTIN B. COPENHAVER

Jesus does not intend for us to predict when he will return.
Rather, he is urging us to live as if his return were just around
the corner.   MARTIN B. COPENHAVER

RESPONSE

If you knew for certain that Christ's return would happen
within the next twenty-four hours, what would you do?

PRAYER

I pray, dear God, to be one who waits for you actively and with
great joy! Amen.

✦ SUNDAY ✦

Isaiah 64:1–9

REFLECTION

God "hides" in order to deconstruct a distorted set of beliefs and practices, thereby opening Israel to receive again (as gift and event) their calling to be God's people. Hiding is a form of divine judgment that ultimately serves divine mercy, a "No" that clears the ground for a more profound "Yes."

SCOTT BADER-SAYE

This is not a season for passive waiting and watching. It is a season of wailing and weeping, of opening up our lives and our souls with active anticipation and renewed hope. . . . And so we do not lose heart; rather, we live with our hearts broken open so that compassion, caring, and God's reckless love can find a way into our hearts and the heart of the world.   PATRICIA E. DE JONG

Psalm 80:1–7, 17–19

REFLECTION

God's energizing radiance brings not only illumination or the assurance of favor, but life itself.   CHARLES M. WOOD

Psalm 80 is an incredible confession, not of sin, but of faith. It confesses the people's trust in a God who is big enough to hear their hurt, strong enough to handle their anger and pain. It also identifies the congregation as a people who, even in their suffering, have the courage to call on the Lord God of hosts to help them . . . while we may look back, God always looks ahead.

TALITHA ARNOLD

In lamentation the people and their leaders maintain a dialogue with God. That dialogue is always better than giving up on God.

CHARLES L. AARON JR.

1 Corinthians 1:3–9

REFLECTION

Unlike a tangent to a circle, the grace of God in and through Jesus Christ flows not only between God and the Christian community, but also in the Christian community's daily experience and history. CARLOS F. CARDOZA-ORLANDI

When we tend to the task of blessing, to first words and last words, a benediction becomes so much more than familiar words intoned by rote. Such a moment is laden with possibility. God's presence can become palpably present.

MARTIN B. COPENHAVER

Mark 13:24–37

REFLECTION

While the world's busyness may seem to be pointed toward Christmas, it is seldom pointed toward the coming Christ child. As Advent progresses, the number of shopping days left before the big day offers a countdown that stresses us out and keeps us up late. LILLIAN DANIEL

We may not be physically asleep; quite the opposite. But in our wakefulness to worldly ways, we fall asleep to the spiritual season, and so we need a wake-up call. LILLIAN DANIEL

Jesus reminds us now, as he reminded them then, that he will come again. We need not get lost in the details. Better to concentrate on being ready. JUDY YATES SIKER

RESPONSE

What resolution do you make as this year begins?

PRAYER

May I stay awake to the possibilities of this Advent. Amen.

❧ *Second Sunday of Advent* ❦

Isaiah 40:1–11

He will feed his flock like a shepherd;
   he will gather the lambs in his arms. (v. 11)

Psalm 85:1–2, 8–13

Steadfast love and faithfulness will meet;
   righteousness and peace will kiss each other. (v. 10)

2 Peter 3:8–15a

The Lord is not slow about his promise, as some
think of slowness, but is patient with you, not wanting
any to perish, but all to come to repentance. (v. 9)

Mark 1:1–8

"See, I am sending my messenger ahead of you,
   who will prepare your way;
the voice of one crying out in the wilderness:
   'Prepare the way of the Lord,
   make his paths straight.'" (vv. 2–3)

✦ MONDAY ✦

Isaiah 40:1–11

REFLECTION

On one hand, God will come with might and God's arm will rule; on the other hand, God will feed this flock like a shepherd. Both are pastoral words to a people whose long exile has found them questioning both God's power and God's love.

CYNTHIA A. JARVIS

Though everything else fails, God's word endures forever, and God comes to lead them home. KATHLEEN M. O'CONNOR

God wills comfort and consolation to those in the very depths of despair and depends upon human as well as divine agency to bring that message from God's royal realm. RICHARD F. WARD

RESPONSE

Are you more inclined to find your consolation from God or from other people?

PRAYER

Let my hope be in your Word, which never fades. Amen.

✢ TUESDAY ✢

Psalm 85:1–2, 8–13

REFLECTION

Both Bethlehem's manger and Calvary's cross are signs of
salvation for us. But so is the life lived in between, in all
the ways Jesus made flesh those words of love, faithfulness,
righteousness, and peace. Moreover, for Christians, salvation
is not just believing in Jesus Christ, but embodying what he
embodied in this world. When steadfast love and faithfulness
meet in our lives, when righteousness and peace embrace in our
business practices, our family relations, or our nation's policies,
God's salvation is near at hand. When we work for justice, we
make way for God in our world.   TALITHA ARNOLD

Salvation never happens in a vacuum; it is always salvation
from something.   CHARLES L. AARON JR.

RESPONSE

From what do you need to be saved?

PRAYER

As I live between the manger and the cross, may the Word
made flesh dwell in my spirit. Amen.

✦ WEDNESDAY ✦

Psalm 85:1–2, 8–13

REFLECTION

The shalom that humans desire depends upon their truthful
faithfulness to the steadfast love and righteous justice of
God. . . . The image of truthful faithfulness springing forth from
the earth would indicate that humanity's obligation toward God
demands faithful and righteous stewardship of the earth, as well
as truth and justice in all our affairs.   PAUL D. BRASSEY

Similarly, to be true shalom—meaning not just the absence
of conflict but the fullness of life—peace needs righteousness
(*tsedeq*). Not the puffed-up morality the word has come to
connote, but righteousness in its original meaning, that is,
right relations, be they with God, with others, in our families,
or among nations. Sometimes we call it justice. But for that
righteousness or justice to be more than legalistic fairness, it
needs the breadth of vision found in God's shalom.

TALITHA ARNOLD

RESPONSE

When you practice stewardship of the earth, do you think about
how you are bringing God's shalom into being?

PRAYER

God of justice, fill me to overflowing with your shalom. Amen.

→ THURSDAY ←

2 Peter 3:8–15a

REFLECTION

In the meantime, we have to rename the meantime. This is not the time of despair, but the time of waiting (v. 14). This is not the time of our frustration, but of God's patience (v. 15). This is, thank God, not yet the fire next time. Because this is the time of God's patience, this is—still—the time of our salvation. . . . What seems to be a long delay in Christ's return is really God's gracious way of saying to us, from generation to generation, it is not too late. Wait in penitence and hope.   DAVID L. BARTLETT

RESPONSE

How does the thought of Advent as a time of God's patience change the way you view this season?

PRAYER

Be patient with me, God, and give me patience as I wait for you. Amen.

✦ FRIDAY ✦

Mark 1:1–8

REFLECTION

By starting with an adult John awaiting an adult Jesus, Mark reminds us that Jesus grew up.

It is an important reminder for such a time, when it is a temptation to linger too long at the manger. A baby can be demanding, but in the case of this baby, the adult he will become is infinitely more so.   MARTIN B. COPENHAVER

Had John not prepared the way, and then admitted it, Advent would be a season not of waiting but of mistakenly believing it has all been accomplished by the latest guru.   LILLIAN DANIEL

RESPONSE

Imagine a conversation between John and Jesus. What do you think they would talk about upon meeting as adults for the first time?

PRAYER

When I tend to linger at the manger, nudge me forward to a deeper understanding of the demands you make upon my life. Amen.

✢ SATURDAY ✢

Mark 1:1–8

REFLECTION

The Holy Spirit is a gift to anticipate even at the beginning of the liturgical year, because it is the culmination of the whole story. In his own life and ministry, Jesus also pointed beyond himself to one who is to come—in this instance, to the Spirit who will follow and be a continuing presence in the world and among the people of God.   MARTIN B. COPENHAVER

Clearly, this is not the birth story of Matthew or Luke. No manger scenes derive from this Gospel. Yet, here in the opening lines of Mark we have a "birth story" of sorts. On this second Sunday in Advent, it is good to tell of new beginnings, to tell about a God who breaks into our time with good news. In this Advent season he comes. Perhaps not as might be expected; perhaps not in the time frame desired—but he comes.

JUDY YATES SIKER

RESPONSE

Have you ever considered the opening lines of Mark to be the birth story of Jesus?

PRAYER

Thank you for the gift of the Holy Spirit. May the Spirit be born anew in all the world. Amen.

☙ SUNDAY ☙

Isaiah 40:1–11

REFLECTION

God's mighty arm is not that of an arbitrary tyrant but that of a gentle shepherd who carries her flock in her bosom. Her gentle nurture is indeed mighty, and her might is her gentle nurture. This is no ordinary shepherd. GEORGE W. STROUP

God's strength appears in the barely thinkable power of gentleness, in tender and caring presence, in intimacy such as a shepherd expresses when gathering the wounded, scattered flock. KATHLEEN M. O'CONNOR

In the face of derision and indifference, we are to speak of this God whose fierce compassion and care for humankind trumps the power of the other "gods" who seem to enjoy sovereignty in human relationships. RICHARD F. WARD

Psalm 85:1–2, 8–13

REFLECTION

Our joy in God and in creation is a mirroring of the joy and delight of the Father in the Word and the Spirit and in their shared life. CHARLES M. WOOD

The basis for salvation is blessing, not terror of divine judgment. . . . Salvation is more than deliverance from one's enemies or release from captivity. It is the presence of God . . . an active presence, one that defines salvation as a dynamic process, not a one-shot "I've-been-saved" experience. Steadfast love and faithfulness don't just coexist; they meet.

TALITHA ARNOLD

2 Peter 3:8–15a

REFLECTION

There is a reason that God has delayed the final act of the cosmic drama. The reason is to allow time for repentance. What looks like tardiness is really mercy. DAVID L. BARTLETT

Good news needs to be proclaimed during Advent. It is more than some hindrance or slowdown before the real season begins. W. C. TURNER

Mark 1:1–8

REFLECTION

As in the past, Jesus may shock us when he comes and shows us who we really are before God. CHRISTOPHER R. HUTSON

Waiting for the savior is humbling. It forces us to admit that the world does not operate on our schedule. LILLIAN DANIEL

Repentance and confession entail facing the truth about ourselves and changing the direction of our lives. And who wants to do either of those things? So the good news can often sound like bad news, at least at first. Repentance and confession both require a searching and honest look back. There are no shortcuts. MARTIN B. COPENHAVER

RESPONSE

Look in the mirror—not to criticize or praise your own reflection; instead, think about how you mirror God's creative power and love when you are faithful to Christ.

PRAYER

I am sometimes afraid to be your messenger, God. Peel away that fear. Let me proclaim your good news with joy. Amen.

❧ *Third Sunday of Advent* ❦

Isaiah 61:1–4, 8–11

The spirit of the Lord GOD is upon me,
  because the LORD has anointed me;
he has sent me to bring good news to
      the oppressed,
  to bind up the brokenhearted,
to proclaim liberty to the captives,
  and release to the prisoners. (v. 1)

Psalm 126

May those who sow in tears
  reap with shouts of joy.
Those who go out weeping,
  bearing the seed for sowing,
shall come home with shouts of joy,
  carrying their sheaves. (vv. 5–6)

1 Thessalonians 5:16–24

Rejoice always, pray without ceasing, give
thanks in all circumstances; for this is the will
of God in Christ Jesus for you. (vv. 16–18)

John 1:6–8, 19–28

"I am the voice of one crying out in the
      wilderness,
'Make straight the way of the Lord,'"
as the prophet Isaiah said. (v. 23)

✦ MONDAY ✦

Isaiah 61:1–4, 8–11

REFLECTION

So long as Christians live as divided people, known to the world as those who judge, fight, and exclude, the church will fail to be missional, no matter how much money it gives and how many missionaries it sends.   SCOTT BADER-SAYE

Mission is not primarily something that goes out from God's people—by sending money or sending missionaries—but something that defines God's people, as existing for the sake of the oppressed, brokenhearted, imprisoned, and mournful.

SCOTT BADER-SAYE

RESPONSE

In what ways has your life aided or diminished the work of the church?

PRAYER

Have I been a hindrance to your work, O God? If so, give me the courage to make the changes I need to make. Amen.

☙ TUESDAY ☙

Psalm 126

REFLECTION

The psalm looks for signs of God's promise in dark and difficult times. It first finds them in the remembrance of things past, in the joy and the laughter the people knew when God brought them home from exile and even their neighbors acknowledged God's mighty deeds on their behalf (vv. 1–3).

TALITHA ARNOLD

But Psalm 126 is not an exercise in nostalgia. The remembrance of things past has a present purpose. Recalling God's deliverance long ago leads directly to the call for God to use that same transforming power now.

TALITHA ARNOLD

The weeping sowers weep, let us suppose, because they are afraid. They are putting the seed into the ground under quite unpromising circumstances, not knowing what to expect. God will turn their tears to laughter, we might then imagine, not because they have been properly penitent or properly diligent (this is not a fable about ants), nor because they have grown spiritually through adversity, but because they are needy creatures and because God is God.

CHARLES M. WOOD

RESPONSE

What past memory brings you joy when you are struggling with dark and difficult times?

PRAYER

May the actions of today become a joyful memory in the future. Amen.

→ WEDNESDAY ←

Psalm 126

REFLECTION

The natural power of God to turn seeds into grain would
be miracle enough. But Psalm 126 makes an even greater
statement. The seeds are not ordinary seeds, but seeds of
sorrow. The fruit they bear is not grain or wheat, but shouts
of joy.   TALITHA ARNOLD

This is no jingle-bells joy bought with a swipe of a credit card.
The seeds of this joy have been planted in sadness and watered
with tears. This is the honest joy that often comes only after
weeping has tarried the night.   TALITHA ARNOLD

RESPONSE

Where and in what ways have you planted seeds of sorrow?
Seeds of joy?

PRAYER

Turn my sorrows into joy; and let me do that for someone else
this week. Amen.

⇝ THURSDAY ⇜

1 Thessalonians 5:16–24

REFLECTION

It is telling that verse 18b, "this is the will of God in Christ Jesus for you," is without fail applied only to negative and disheartening life events— illness, death, and so on—so that the exhortation in verse 18a, "Give thanks [*eucharisteite*] in all circumstances," is seen as a challenging demand rather than a gracious invitation. Paul, a masterful rhetorical craftsman, knew exactly what he was doing by beginning, "Rejoice always!" Sometimes, believe it or not, the good things in life are God's will too.   WILLIAM BROSEND

On the one hand, the church is called to live in full expectancy of the Lord's return. This is what keeps us ready, busy, on the post of duty. The expectation has the world and all to do with the urgency in ministry and mission, or lack thereof. . . . On the other hand, the church must live as if the Lord is depending on it indefinitely. For its ongoing life it must care for matters that are mundane, like seeing to it that the servants receive their care, that the altar is tended to, that property is kept up, that schedules are made and observed. No one fit of piety, emotion, or sincerity takes the place of such vigilance.   W. C. TURNER

RESPONSE

Make a short list of the good things that are happening in your life right now.

PRAYER

I give thanks to you, O God, with my whole heart! Amen.

1 Thessalonians 5:16–24

REFLECTION

Imagine using Paul's vision of openness based on the triad of faith, hope, and love to speak to a fearful member of the congregation. Imagine painting a scene of the Christian life balanced like a three-legged stool. First, we might say to those we are called to serve that if we can express thankfulness in all things, then we can say yes to whatever Is, and we can embrace the reality of our lives rather than live in conflict with it. Second, if we can accept the notion that God uses everything, then we can enter into the now. Third, we discover in this process that God makes all things new. LEE W. BOWMAN

Paul addresses and implicitly raises again for the reader the question of what life lived out in response to the gospel, "a life worthy of God" (1 Thess. 2:12), looks like. For Paul such life is joyous, prayerful, eucharistic (in the multiple meanings of that word), Spirit-filled, prophetic, and tested. How that looks for each brother and sister will differ. Asking the question is the important thing, and it is a question too rarely asked.

WILLIAM BROSEND

RESPONSE

Is there a word of comfort you need to speak to a family member, neighbor, or friend?

PRAYER

Use me, Lord, use even me, to bring your presence into the now. Amen.

⁂ SATURDAY ⁂

John 1:6–8, 19–28

REFLECTION

The pastoral temptation of Advent is to turn from attention to our waiting for *Christ* and to focus instead on *our* waiting for Christ. Are we sufficiently prepared for the events of the days ahead? Are we sufficiently content to enjoy them? Faithful anticipation can turn quickly into frenzied activity and anxious self-examination. Advent turns from waiting to scurrying. Just when we should be looking forward to the manger, we are looking inward, taking our own spiritual temperature.

DAVID L. BARTLETT

Deep into Advent, this Gospel text does not offer images of a young family on a holy trek to Bethlehem. Readers will see no shepherds and hear no cantatas in the fields. There are no villainous innkeepers and no sage magi in John's prologue. In fact, there is little in today's text or the entire prologue that supports a tendency in the church to obscure Advent and romanticize Christmas. On the contrary, John 1:6–8 is a signature Advent text, as it reminds careful readers that the first witness to Jesus arrived on the earthly scene before Jesus did. He arrived not to get everything decorated and everyone ready for Christmas, but to "prepare the way of the LORD" (Isa. 40:3). He came to "bear witness" to the coming Light of God, reminding all who would listen that the darkest forces in the world are not finally as powerful as they appear.

GARY W. CHARLES

RESPONSE

What activity could you cut out of your life to ease the stress that often fills this pre-Christmas time?

PRAYER

Christ of Advent, slow me down. Slow me down. Amen.

⇥ SUNDAY ⇤

Isaiah 61:1–4, 8–11

REFLECTION

If salvation is not another place and time but the reality of this world as it should be (what Christians have come to call the "reign of God"), then Isaiah asks us to think about how we might participate in ushering in what is, theologically speaking, the "real world." Being missional, in light of this passage, means profoundly challenging all forms of cultural Christianity that would make "church" an end in itself, a community of the saved devoted to maintaining a building, a set of programs, and a fellowship of the like-minded.   SCOTT BADER-SAYE

Psalm 126

REFLECTION

The connection between the two (tears and joy) in this case is simply the steadfast love of God. It is a sense of human vulnerability that is evoked by the image of the sowers' weeping (and if there is anything behind the hints of ancient rituals of seedtime associated with these verses in some commentaries, it may be just the reality of human vulnerability before the uncertainties and mysteries of our existence); and it is that same vulnerability, that mere need, which is addressed here by the psalmist's final confident avowal, which might also be taken as God's promise.   CHARLES M. WOOD

1 Thessalonians 5:16–24

REFLECTION

It is in this sense that we better understand the call for unceasing joy, prayer, and thanksgiving—not as hyperbole or temporal impossibility, but as unrestrained action. We are to rejoice, pray, and give thanks (*eucharisteite*) (5:18) unreservedly and absolutely, just as the whole of our being, spirit and soul and body, are to be unblemished. The shape of the Christian life is not contoured in measured apportionment—one part work to one part prayer, or some other recipe for spiritual fulfillment—but in unreserved and all-consuming self-giving.

WILLIAM BROSEND

John 1:6–8, 19–28

REFLECTION

Like John we are to witness to the light of Christ as a voice in the wilderness of twenty-first-century consumerism. As voices in the wilderness, we must make a countercultural claim that dislocates the consumption of things, even when we offer these things as Christmas gifts. . . . As we testify to the light, we also embody that light as believers who reveal the life of Christ anew in the world this Advent season. To embody the light and reveal the life of Christ anew means that we are to live so as to nurture our humanity—especially the capacity to love our enemies— and to act humanely, offering compassionate and restorative justice.

MARCIA Y. RIGGS

The separation between "evangelical" and "mainline" or "old-line" Christians is entirely artificial. All of us are Christians because we have been evangelized— have heard and believed the gospel. All of us are under orders to bear witness to others.

DAVID L. BARTLETT

RESPONSE

What would you say if asked to describe who Jesus is "not"?

PRAYER

Lead me not into the temptation to trivialize the incredible good news of your birth into the world, O Christ. Amen.

❧ *Fourth Sunday of Advent* ☙

2 Samuel 7:1–11, 16

Your house and your kingdom shall be
made sure forever before me; your throne
shall be established forever. (v. 16)

Luke 1:47–55

My soul magnifies the Lord,
  and my spirit rejoices in God my Savior,
for he has looked with favor on the lowliness
  of his servant. (vv. 46b–48a)

Romans 16:25–27

To the only wise God, through Jesus Christ, to
whom be the glory forever! Amen. (v. 27)

Luke 1:26–38

Then Mary said, "Here am I, the servant of the Lord;
let it be with me according to your word." (v. 38)

✦ MONDAY ✦

2 Samuel 7:1–11, 16

REFLECTION

When we speak of an uncontained God from well-contained
places, an electing God from seats of power, a graceful God
from positions of plenty—we don't miss the point of the gospel
that inheres in these things so much as we miss some of its
power.   MARK DOUGLAS

It may be easy for Christians, worshiping on this Sunday, to
see how the promise of a house for David and a kingdom that
will be forever has been fulfilled in a surprising way by the gift
of God in Christ. Far more challenging—and perhaps of more
benefit to those as familiar with the Christmas story as were
David and Nathan with the story of Israel—would be to wonder
where today God is moving ahead of us and acting in ways that
will catch us by surprise.   EUGENE C. BAY

RESPONSE

How has God caught you by surprise?

PRAYER

Light of the world, find a home within me, but even more, let
me find a home within you. Amen.

✦ TUESDAY ✦

Luke 1:47–55

REFLECTION

The content of the new work of God is not given in lofty theological images but as the ethic of a changed world order. In concrete and specific terms, Mary sings in the language of revolution (a turning around) to record her understanding of the great reversals that have unfolded, albeit, we must add, in a hidden way.   ANDREW PURVES

Through her song of justice, Mary calls us to be change agents for a better world for all.   TRISHA LYONS SENTERFITT

We need one another's affirmation, just as Mary needed Elizabeth's, to live into God's plan for the world.

                                        TRISHA LYONS SENTERFITT

RESPONSE

What gift do you offer to help those who are oppressed?

PRAYER

Make me an instrument of change in some small way; and grant me the courage to think in grander terms. Amen.

→ WEDNESDAY ←

Luke 1:47–55

REFLECTION

All of us, men and women, are included in Mary's and
Elizabeth's times of expectancy, calling us together in
partnership with God in God's plan for this world. This
song addresses all the ways we set ourselves apart from one
another, which is the excuse we need to set us over and against
one another. We are all uniquely made in the image of God,
meaning that we are to see God in one another and are called to
say yes to justice for all.   TRISHA LYONS SENTERFITT

One has to explore whether liberation of one group has to be
predicated on the oppression of another group. Would not a
theology of relinquishment, where those who benefit from
the oppression relinquish the privileges that come from sinful
social orders, serve better as a model?   RANDALL C. BAILEY

RESPONSE

What excuses do you use to keep from risking your own
security for the sake of someone else?

PRAYER

Dispel my tendency to hide from the need of the world. Amen.

✥ THURSDAY ✥

Romans 16:25–27

REFLECTION

The wonder of Christmas includes the humbling recognition that God came to humanity (and continues to come) in weakness as a vulnerable child. Nothing is more amazing than the gift of unmerited grace. Therefore, whatever gifts are brought to the manger in thankful obedience, whatever sacrifices are made for the Lord, whatever praise is uttered, no human responses to God can compare to the gift of God's grace that redeems human beings, adopts us into God's family, reconciles us to God and one another, and atones for our sin, enabling and empowering us to faithful obedience.

DONALD W. MUSSER

God continues to be astonishingly inclusive; and we have learned to read and reread our Bible in light of the evidence of God's Spirit breaking out in the lives we assumed were not qualified. God's goal is unchanging: that all should join in the "obedience of faith," that all should experience a being-redeemed way of life.

SALLY A. BROWN

RESPONSE

If you had to sum up your expression of gratitude for the wonder of the incarnation in one word, what would that word be?

PRAYER

I am shocked beyond words with the thought of your magnificent love. Amen.

✦ FRIDAY ✦

Romans 16:25–27

REFLECTION

It is important not to confuse joy and happiness. The New Testament says a great deal about joy and very little about happiness. The root of the word happiness is "hap," which means "chance" (as in "happenstance"). Happiness is a mood, an emotion that changes as circumstances around us change. It is like a thermometer that goes up and down as it interprets the events around us, making us vulnerable to happiness one minute and despair the next. Joy, on the other hand, sets the temperature of our environment, rather than responding to it.

CATHY F. YOUNG

"Glory" is an attribute of God (Rom. 3:7, 23; 9:23) and virtually the power or force by which God accomplishes God's aims, including the raising of Jesus from the dead (6:4).

SUSAN R. GARRETT

RESPONSE

How do you define the difference between joy and happiness?

PRAYER

I praise you with a happy and joyful heart! Amen.

✣ SATURDAY ✣

Luke 1:26–38

REFLECTION

The best discussions of Mary's response recognize the pitfalls inherent in rendering Mary either a passive participant, who has no choice but to submit to God's will, or an autonomous individual, who can choose differently than to bear God to the world. The doctrine of Christian vocation offers clarity. Mary's obedience is neither optional nor forced. Mary acts freely when she offers herself as a servant of the Lord. To embrace her identity as the Mother of God is the only choice that is true to her calling, because it is consistent with who she actually is.

CYNTHIA L. RIGBY

The selection of Mary to be the mother of Jesus is an occasion to spur Christians to exit the realm of predictability and open themselves up to the unexpected and the unimaginable.

ASHLEY COOK CLEERE

RESPONSE

Are there certain characteristics of Mary that you most admire?

PRAYER

Turn the tables of my expectations upside down, and let me be an active participant in your grace. Amen.

✦ SUNDAY ✦

2 Samuel 7:1–11, 16

REFLECTION

Where in the world, where in our life as a congregation, where in one's personal life, may God be wanting to do something that is being blocked by human aspirations and agendas, however seemingly noble? How receptive are we to the God who will not be confined or enshrined but retains and cherishes the freedom to surprise us—as in the coming of Christ down the back stairs of Bethlehem, to be born of Mary, grow up in the hick town of Nazareth, spend his time with the least, the lowly, and the lost, and, most surprising of all, become "obedient to the point of death—even death on a cross"? Could that same God be leading the church in new and unthought-of directions?

EUGENE C. BAY

We may not be kings, but we too are tempted to make our plans without God, even on a holiday that celebrates God taking flesh. We need the history lesson as much as David. We too need to be reminded where God found us and what we would be without God's grace. We too need to be reminded that God saved more than just us, but is reconciling the world to God's self.

BETH LANEEL TANNER

Luke 1:47–55

REFLECTION

For years Mary has been portrayed as submissive because of her yes to God at the annunciation. Today it is time to recognize that this prophetic woman also says no to all that negates God's purposes in human history. First, Mary celebrates the greatness of God, and then she proclaims God's liberating compassion for the poor. Mary sings the joy that she is feeling and sings blessing for the oppressed, whether that oppression comes from being underprivileged or overprivileged.

TRISHA LYONS SENTERFITT

Romans 16:25–27

REFLECTION

Advent is a season of hopeful anticipation, but it begins with the acknowledgment of human despair. We are all sinners in need of a Savior. Left to our own devices, we find life unbearable. Yet gradually, Advent prepares us for the gift of Emmanuel—God-with-us. Because of all God did, and continues to do, in and through Jesus Christ, life today can yield abundance and assure our future. CATHY F. YOUNG

Luke 1:26–38

REFLECTION

Luke tells us that not only is redemption possible; it has already happened. Because of the birth, life, death, and resurrection of Christ, the holy continues to break into our lives, to bring us closer to the completion of creation and the already-and-not-yet reign of God. KIMBERLY BRACKEN LONG

RESPONSE

As Advent winds to a close, reflect on how this season has truly been a time of preparing for the coming of Christ into the world.

PRAYER

Instead of always thinking about what I need, remind me of what I already have. Amen.

❧ *Christmas Eve* ❧

*(These reflections are to be used between the
Fourth Sunday of Advent and Christmase Eve.)*

Isaiah 9:2–7

The people who walked in darkness
    have seen a great light;
those who lived in a land of deep darkness—
    on them light has shined. (v. 2)

Psalm 96

O sing to the LORD a new song;
    sing to the LORD, all the earth. (v. 1)

Titus 2:11–14

He it is who gave himself for us that
he might redeem us from all iniquity and purify
for himself a people of his own who are
zealous for good deeds. (v. 14)

Luke 2:1–14

Then an angel of the Lord stood before them, and the
glory of the Lord shone around them, and they were terrified.
But the angel said to them, "Do not be afraid; for see—I am
bringing you good news of great joy for all the people; to you
is born this day in the city of David a Savior, who is the
Messiah, the Lord." (vv. 9–11)

Isaiah 9:2–7

REFLECTION

The advent of the kingdom that comes with the incarnation of God turns not on our skills, talents, efforts, or luck. Instead, God brings about the kingdom. That, in itself, could feel uplifting, refreshing, and hopeful for those whose feelings of filthiness and hopelessness are the product of their fear that they have failed to establish a better world and gotten dirty in the process.   MARK DOUGLAS

"Light" is a metaphor suggestive of the presence of God, the approach of God's grace, mercy, and peace. Isaiah refers to "a great light" (v. 2). The preacher may want to suggest that the light of Christ, while "great" indeed for those who have seen and welcomed it, was not "great" at its coming, in the sense of being a blazing or blinding light, and is not "great" in that sense now. It was and is now a gentle, modest light that Christ brings, so as not to overwhelm or coerce.   EUGENE C. BAY

This passage from Isaiah challenges us to push a few inches beyond the comfortable picture of the nativity tableau. The child whose birth we attend tonight was born into a world painted not in pastels but in dust and blood. This incarnation is not a spiritual, otherworldly concept, but the mystery of God present in a real human child, welcomed into a real world with all its agonies and ambiguities and challenges and joys.

LINDA LEE CLADER

Psalm 96

REFLECTION

The response of faith to such a divine and universal kingship is not arrogance, or pride, or any kind of violence toward those of other religions. The response is worship, and it is worship of a sort that invites all others to participate. The Lord's glory is to be declared among the nations (v. 3), so all people can sing a new song to the Lord (v. 1).   ANDREW PURVES

The rhythms of the psalm flow back and forth, rocking the ear like a newborn baby. There is a sense of urgency not unlike that of a woman panting in labor: "Sing to the Lord, sing to the Lord, sing to the Lord—bless, tell, declare—ascribe, ascribe, ascribe—bring, come, worship, tremble. Say, 'The Lord is King!'"
TRISHA LYONS SENTERFITT

But be forewarned: the newness of the song reaches beyond the usual strains of Christmas Eve! It leads us from the quiet awe of Bethlehem, our captivation with the infant, even our astonished reverence before the mystery of Incarnation, to embrace the nations—"all the peoples" and indeed "all the earth." It tells of God's glory expressed in "marvelous works," not manifested only through Israel's history, but through the stories we bring to the manger as well.   GAIL A. RICCIUTI

Titus 2:11–14

REFLECTION

Titus's theological excursus reminds us of the holy hush that constitutes so much of Christmas Eve worship. Amidst the rush of preparation and the fervor of expectations, the lights are dimmed and silence takes hold of us, our frantic fussing stilled. Weary and pensive we sit; eyes closed, dazzled by the glitter of holiday festivities. Our vision inexplicably clears, and things previously unseen are brought into focus. We are embraced by the overwhelming impossibility that the Center of Ultimacy has come, in love, to us. Out of that silence wells a joy that transcends our doubts, fears, and ambiguities.

DONALD W. MUSSER

It is not enough to hear the glorious music of this holy day and retell the Christmas story. God calls us to be transformed by grace and wonder. The divine love that God pours out to us expands as it is shared with others. We seek to do what is good because of God's goodness.   CATHY F. YOUNG

The bottom line for the author of this letter is that our families and our churches are to testify to the grace of God through Jesus Christ, who has freed us from the powers that rule the world and transformed us into his own people, who strive always to do what is good. Christ gave himself for us in order that we might resist the dominant yet ungodly passions or spirits of the age—spirits of anger, hatred, and divisiveness, for example, or spirits of acquisitiveness and idolatry—and bear communal witness to a better way.   SUSAN R. GARRETT

Luke 2:1–14

REFLECTION

There is something theologically correct about our nostalgic portrayals of the nativity: the happy family and guests huddled 'round the manger made of straw, a warm brown cow looking on, softly chewing. What is right about this is that there is a home—a home whose hearth is Jesus Christ himself. He is the center of Mary and Joseph's life, the song of the angels, the mission of the shepherds. Where the Christ child lays, the story tells us, is home. This child is born for "all the people." He is our Savior, our Messiah, the one in whom our unsettledness gives way to great joy and peace.   CYNTHIA L. RIGBY

The woe attached to a mobile society that scatters close relatives across the continent exists in tandem with a blessing. Unlikely acquaintances become intimately involved in one another's lives. Local churches frequently find themselves innately adept at facilitating these essential relationships, as they pray for and with one another and share meals together.

Amid a populace that exhibits tentative hospitality toward atypical families, congregations celebrate the Lord's Supper, a sacrament that models what it means to be welcoming. The inclusive communion table invites and accepts persons of disparate backgrounds, illustrating the value of a broadened sense of family and making the church a "conspicuous family" in a world that is inclined to judge the stranger and exclude the other.   ASHLEY COOK CLEERE

That the shepherds greet God incarnate not only in a barn but in the animals' trough points us to the table—Luke does not show Jesus resting on a pile of quilts in the corner, but in the feeding place. This baby, resting in a manger on the night of his birth, will be "the bread of God . . . which comes down from heaven and gives life to the world," the very "bread of life" (John 6:33, 35). Each time the community gathers around the table, it remembers this mystery: that though it is beyond our comprehension, God took on human form, lived among us, suffered for us, died and was raised, that we might know true life, in this world and the next.   KIMBERLY BRACKEN LONG

RESPONSE
How is God Emmanuel—"with us"—in this time and place?

PRAYER
Jesus Christ, Emmanuel, Light of the World, Savior of all, we welcome you! We welcome you. Amen.

❧ *Christmas Day* ❧

Isaiah 52:7–10

How beautiful upon the mountains
 are the feet of the messenger who announces peace,
who brings good news,
 who announces salvation,
 who says to Zion, "Your God reigns." (v. 7)

Psalm 98

The Lord has made known his victory;
 he has revealed his vindication in the sight of the nations.
He has remembered his steadfast love and faithfulness
 to the house of Israel.
All the ends of the earth have seen
 the victory of our God. (vv. 2–3)

Hebrews 1:1–4 (5–12)

Long ago God spoke to our ancestors in many and various
ways by the prophets, but in these last days he has spoken to
us by a Son, whom he appointed heir of all things, through
whom he also created the worlds. He is the reflection of God's
glory and the exact imprint of God's very being, and he
sustains all things by his powerful word. (vv. 1–3)

John 1:1–14

And the Word became flesh and lived among
us, and we have seen his glory, the glory as of a father's
only son, full of grace and truth. (v. 14)

Isaiah 52:7–10

REFLECTION

We are, even on Christmas morning, still a people of the now and the not yet. Christmas morning is not a period in the story of Christianity, but a semicolon. Often, it seems that Christmas Eve or Christmas Day is the culmination of something, and the church then goes into a holding pattern until Ash Wednesday or even Easter. This text from Isaiah reminds us that the best is yet to come. This baby will not remain docile and quiet in that manger. He will rise and grow, then preach, teach, heal, and show us the way to live lives in the kingdom.   BETH LANEEL TANNER

Isaiah begins his vision marveling at the beauty of the runner's feet—beautiful because of the glorious news the runner brings—but it might be helpful to expand for just a moment on the length of the run, the weariness of such a runner, and the rough terrain he must penetrate to carry his joyful message through. Think of a marathon runner whose goal is not just to finish but to carry critical news. Now we can feel the excitement of one who has come as fast as he can from a great distance, bringing the astonishing good news of the return of the Lord to Zion. The parallels with our Christmas celebration are clear, but in our day how many of us are in touch with the intense excitement that this snippet of Isaiah evokes? Imagine the runner's beating heart. Imagine his being so out of breath that he can barely pant out the news he carries. Imagine challenging our Christian community to carry the good news of God's gift to us with that kind of intensity, and that kind of exultation!

LINDA LEE CLADER

Psalm 98

REFLECTION

On Christmas Day, amid the exhaustion of getting and spending, come to the quiet for a few moments and listen:

perhaps far off you might hear the angels singing. And as you tune into the meaning of the day, into the events commemorated, perhaps too something even more amazing might begin to be heard: the lands have lifted up their voices, and harps and trumpets and horns blow a song of praise from every corner of God's creation, while the seas and its creatures make their strange noise of praise, to the clapping of the rivers and the ringing of the hills. All this, because the Lord comes— to judge the world, but as an act of love and redemption.

ANDREW PURVES

On the festival of Christmas, a simple translation of the psalmist's insight would be that we have received not what we deserved but a justice beyond our wildest imagination!

GAIL A. RICCIUTI

God's greatest gift to us, Jesus Christ, is the source of our joyful noise at Christmas. "How can we keep from singing?" When we hear the night sounds of frogs and crickets, the morning sounds of birds' songs, and the evening sound of dogs barking, the whole of creation is "making a joyful noise." All of nature praises God as the moon waxes and wanes, as the sun rises and drops below the horizon, as the stars twinkle and frost silvers the earth. Psalm 98 reminds us that praise is given to God not only by humanity, but by all of nature and all the creatures! "How can we keep from singing?"   TRISHA LYONS SENTERFITT

Hebrews 1:1–4 (5–12)

REFLECTION

Both the OT and NT emphasize that although God is a potter who molds the clay, God is more than the fashioner or architect of the worlds. More centrally, God's actions are often "speech-events," his words causing events to occur and orbs to come into being. In creation "God said . . ." (Gen. 1). In redemption "the Word" (John 1) came in the flesh. God's doings result from

the pronouncements of God's voice. Word/words become the
media.   DONALD W. MUSSER

On Christmas Day we celebrate the astonishing news that, in
the person of Jesus Christ, we come to know this exalted being
as one who lives among us—who becomes, indeed, one of
us. The Son through whom God created the world was born
as a human baby, thus entering into the fragile fellowship of
creatures who suffer and die. Indeed, because he shared our lot
and suffered as all humans suffer, Jesus is able to sympathize
with us in our weakness (Heb. 4:15). The birth narratives of
Matthew and Luke help us to see Jesus' humanity and humility:
he was born under the most modest of circumstances, a babe
wrapped in swaddling clothes. The author of Hebrews helps us
to see the Christ also in his breathtaking majesty: he is the one
who is above all, and through whom all things exist.

                                         SUSAN R. GARRETT

Because God's self-revelation came through a person,
Christmas worshipers know that God is personal. In Christ,
we have living proof of how far God will go to create an
intimate, fulfilling relationship with each one of us. God loves
us unconditionally, cares for and about us, and wants what is
best for us. Through Jesus Christ, the faithful, regardless of the
situation in which they find themselves, are sustained.

                                         CATHY F. YOUNG

John 1:1–14

REFLECTION

The humanity of Jesus Christ is no mere costume. It is not a
temporary condition or thirty-three-year experiment on the
part of God. The real Word really became real flesh. This is the
content of the gospel. This is the miracle of Christmas. It is
through entering into our flesh that Jesus reveals to us who God
actually is, has been, and will be. It is through plunging deeply

into the sinful, ignorant realities of our existence in this world that Jesus restores us to that for which he created us. It is in this unlikely way that he is our true light.   CYNTHIA L. RIGBY

If we are paying attention, we recognize too that God is in the ordinary moments of our life—in the making of lunches and the folding of laundry, in daily kisses good-bye, in the moment when we look into the eyes of one whom the world considers unlovely at best and unworthy of notice at worst. It is why we aim to live the Christian life by not only talking about it or thinking about it, but by doing it—why our prayers are not only those of the heart, but those of the hands and the feet.

KIMBERLY BRACKEN LONG

The light that will come into the world full of grace and truth will not be the privileged gift of a select segment of the population, or even reserved for humankind alone. All of creation—fields, floods, rocks, hills, and plains—are overcome with glee! Awed by the Word of God, voices are raised in unison across the globe. Angels join the chorus and "repeat the sounding joy" as "heaven and nature sing"!

ASHLEY COOK CLEERE

RESPONSE

On this holy and joyful day, take extra time to sit quietly, to breathe in the peace of Christ, to revel in the amazing gift of God that we celebrate on Christmas Day.

PRAYER

Glory to you, O God, in the highest heaven; and on earth, peace among all those with whom you are pleased! May that, one day, be the entire world. Amen.

🌺 *First Sunday after* 🌿 *Christmas Day*

Isaiah 61:10–62:3

I will greatly rejoice in the LORD,
  my whole being shall exult in my God;
for he has clothed me with the garments of salvation,
  he has covered me with the robe of righteousness,
as a bridegroom decks himself with a garland,
  and as a bride adorns herself with her jewels. (61:10)

Psalm 148

Let them praise the name of the LORD,
  for he commanded and they were created.
He established them forever and ever;
  he fixed their bounds, which cannot be passed. (vv. 5–6)

Galatians 4:4–7

So you are no longer a slave but a child, and
if a child then also an heir, through God. (v. 7)

Luke 2:22–40

Guided by the Spirit, Simeon came into the temple; and
when the parents brought in the child Jesus, to do for him
what was customary under the law, Simeon took him in his
arms and praised God, saying, "Master, now you are dismissing
your servant in peace, according to your word; for my eyes
have seen your salvation, which you have prepared in the
presence of all peoples." (vv. 27–31)

⤳ MONDAY ⤶

Isaiah 61:10–62:3

REFLECTION

The nuptial imagery so common in Scripture is used here, as well, to connote the fulfillment of promise and to portray the renewed beauty of Israel. No longer a slave, she greets the Lord "as a bridegroom decks himself with a garland, and as a bride adorns herself with her jewels" (61:10 NRSV). This is not only a joyful reunion, but since the marital love between God and God's people is always creative, there is an expectation that the homecoming will be fruitful as well. The nuptial imagery is less about the separation of the past than it is about the promise of the future.

KATHERINE C. CALORE

Not everyone is happy at a wedding. Indeed, it is deemed one of the most stressful times in a life. People must be kept happy and involved. Traditions must be satisfied or explained away. Old rivalries and unfinished business give way to the ceremony. And out of it all, the history of the world is changed as lives embrace, for the first time, some deep and timeless thing.

G. MALCOLM SINCLAIR

RESPONSE

What is your one particular hope for the future?

PRAYER

I trust my future to your care, O God, and I do so with great hope. Amen.

↠ TUESDAY ↞

Psalm 148

REFLECTION

Praise as the fundamental expression of worship is not solely an acknowledgment of dependent creatureliness. It is an expression of astonished gratitude. It is a confession that existence is a mysterious, miraculous gift.

DWIGHT M. LUNDGREN

The very practice of praise as an expression of gratitude is, therefore, also the recognition of the dignity of one's life and the acceptance of a calling within the panoply of the creation. Praise and gratitude as confession and testimony lead to invitation and encouragement of others.

DWIGHT M. LUNDGREN

This is the purpose of creation, and the purpose of every creaturely being: to offer praise and glory to God.

KIMBERLY L. CLAYTON

RESPONSE

Think about the times when you are most prone to praising God. Is your praise dependent on your current circumstances?

PRAYER

I add my voice to the whole of creation that praises your name! Amen.

✦ WEDNESDAY ✦

Psalm 148

REFLECTION

What happens when we ourselves are too sad or too weak
to offer praise of God? This psalm exclaims the hopeful,
comforting message that we are not isolated or alone in our
vocation of praise. From start to finish, Psalm 148 places
us within a vast, diverse universe where continual praise is
being offered to God: Angels and stars, fire and frost, wild
and domesticated animals, men and women, young and old,
wealthy and poor . . . join in a terrestrial/celestial symphony of
praise. So, when our own song or spirit is silenced, praise still
fills the space all around us. In a time of personal darkness, we
may stand in the midst of the congregation or with one other
person, we may sit in a field or float on the water, we may listen
to the birds of the air or sit with the family pet and let this
creation, these creatures, these companions praise God for us
until we find our voice again.   KIMBERLY L. CLAYTON

RESPONSE

Who has prayed for you when you could not pray for yourself?

PRAYER

Thank you for all the prayers that have ever been offered on my
behalf, including those of the Holy Spirit. Amen.

✧ THURSDAY ✦

Galatians 4:4–7

REFLECTION

While our churches sing and rejoice in the days leading up to Christmas, is it possible that, like a new parent, God's rejoicing begins the first days after Christmas? Is Christmas a signal of renewed commitment on God's behalf to watch over us, to nurture our potential? Does God listen with a parent's anxious anticipation for our first, babbling attempts to say, "Abba"? Over time a newborn child will learn to recognize and respond to a parent's voice. Over time, a person emerging on the other side of Christmas may awaken to the change of spiritual environment both inside and out. This awakening to the voice of the Spirit takes time. God's love overflows, but we must learn to navigate its waters. Whether a person is conscious of a dramatic conversion or new birth in Christ takes a lifetime, our awareness is secondary to God's primary act of love. We are being made new because God has declared us heirs. Our status has changed, after Christmas.   JAMES W. MCTYRE

RESPONSE

How does your experience of this most recent Christmas live on in your spirit?

PRAYER

Let our hope in Christ's birth continue to be born in us this day. Amen.

Luke 2:22–40

REFLECTION

At the birth of every child, there is a wider company of persons who have hopes and fears for the future. Some will remain silent and watch from afar. Others, like Simeon, will step forward and be devoted enough and courageous enough to tell parents what lies deep in their hearts. The parents of Jesus "were amazed" at what was being said to them. They heard the good news! But, Simeon was also honest and caring enough to tell them the painful news as well. No parent wants to hear a painful prospect for his or her child. But every parent, in order to fulfill the responsibilities of parenthood, needs to have someone prepare them for the difficulties that are likely to lie ahead. It was the good fortune of Mary and Joseph to have such a person come to them early in their parental life.

WILLIAM V. ARNOLD

Because of this child, Simeon can die calmly, confidently. He can be as hospitable to his impending death as he has been to the child Mary brought to the temple, embracing it, blessing God for it.

JAMES C. HOWELL

RESPONSE

In what ways does the church permit you to fulfill the baptismal vows of loving, encouraging, and supporting one another?

PRAYER

Let me love with the love of Mary, even when my heart is broken. Amen.

✢ SATURDAY ✢

Luke 2:22–40

REFLECTION

We live in a society where it is hard to understand the blessings in poverty. Mary and Joseph, like many poor parents in our midst today, were trying to be faithful, but the journey was not easy. In the context of the capitalism of our generation, it is hard to accept the idea of being blessed but not prosperous. The challenge for us to wrestle with is the injustice that many poor people of faith face. They are blessed. They hold new life and future possibilities in their arms. They possess faith, and yet they must find a way to afford the social expectations of church life. For many of the poor but faithful in our time, this is still a painful reality.
SHELLEY D. B. COPELAND

RESPONSE

Describe an occasion when you felt blessed in a time of great need.

PRAYER

Your blessing is the most precious of gifts; with your grace, I am rich! Amen.

☀ SUNDAY ☀

Isaiah 61:10–62:3

REFLECTION

Like the carols that linger on this first Sunday of Christmas, this passage from Isaiah celebrates God's desire to be with God's people in a new way. The promise of reconciliation gives Israel hope. The promise of God's steadfast love gives Israel reason to sing again. From age to age, our congregations repeat the sounding joy: "I will greatly rejoice in the Lord, my whole being shall exult in my God" (v. 10).   ANDREW NAGY-BENSON

Psalm 148

REFLECTION

The psalmist includes in our praise realities that fill us with wonder: sun, moon and shining stars, the heavens and the waters above the heavens, the sea monsters in the deep. Perhaps we have grown so used to our surroundings that we have forgotten wonder. Amid the city lights we cannot see the stars. But there is wonder aplenty for those with eyes to see and ears to hear.   STEPHEN FARRIS

Galatians 4:4–7

REFLECTION

God is the parent who leaves a rich inheritance to all of the children. God is the liberator who sees human captivity and sends a Son to free slaves and give them a share in the Spirit's freedom. God has created in that Son's cross a way to widen the divine reach and welcome all peoples, Jew and Gentile alike, into the company of God's family.   ALLEN R. HILTON

As the prayers of Jesus are formed in us they form us, shape our faith and faithfulness. When we pray the prayer of Jesus

and profess the faith of Jesus, we begin to do the works of Jesus.
And should we die the death of Jesus, or any faithful death, we
will be raised to the life of Jesus, and all of this as God's once
and abiding Christmas present to the world.

THOMAS R. STEAGALD

Luke 2:22–40

REFLECTION

Just a child—but hardly safe and harmless. "This child is
destined for the falling and the rising of many." This child
provokes a crisis, a decision, for Simeon, for Anna, for all
people of every generation. How we respond to this one person
decides everything. The stakes are not trivial. It is not that, if
we go with Jesus, our lives are 17 percent better, our happiness
14 percent higher, our marriages 16 percent healthier. It's all or
nothing. You fall. Or you rise. JAMES C. HOWELL

RESPONSE

Imagine being this seasoned person of faith, who had the
chance to witness a poor teen mom and a dad with the
Anointed One in their care. Imagine knowing they had a child
with tremendous promise and possibility for an entire people.
If you were in such a position, would you do something more
for this family than offer a blessing? SHELLEY D. B. COPELAND

PRAYER

No matter what each day brings, no matter where this next
year leads, let the whole world praise your holy and wonderful
name! Amen.

Second Sunday after Christmas Day

Jeremiah 31:7–14

With weeping they shall come,
and with consolations I will lead them back,
I will let them walk by brooks of water,
in a straight path in which they shall not stumble. (v. 9)

Psalm 147:12–20

He sends out his command to the earth;
his word runs swiftly. (v. 15)

Ephesians 1:3–14

In Christ we have also obtained an inheritance,
having been destined according to the purpose of him who
accomplishes all things according to his counsel and will,
so that we, who were the first to set our hope on Christ,
might live for the praise of his glory. (vv. 11–12)

John 1:(1–9) 10–18

The true light, which enlightens everyone,
was coming into the world. (v. 9)

✥ MONDAY ✥

Jeremiah 31:7–14

REFLECTION

Jeremiah is offering God's people a promise of love, redemption, and renewal. He sees what is going to happen—defeat and exile—but he also sees that God will not abandon his people. Their punishment will not go on forever, and God will save them both from their enemies and from themselves. It is a pattern that is repeated in every aspect of the life of faith, from Jesus' crucifixion leading to the new life of resurrection, to the periods of decline and apathy that precede a people's vibrant renewal, to the dark and dry periods that precede spiritual consolations for individual believers.   KATHERINE C. CALORE

These verses in Jeremiah depict a restored life of wholeness (shalom) in which the entire creation, from fields to flocks to humankind, rejoices in right relationships and therefore flourishes. If sin is wrong relationship to God and to God's creation, then its absence is not a void but a joyful and harmonious dance.   CHRISTOPHER B. HAYS

RESPONSE

What is the difference between "peace" and "shalom"?

PRAYER

You never abandon us, O God, but I am still afraid. Divest me of my reluctance to believe in your love that never fails. Amen.

✦ TUESDAY ✦

Psalm 147:12–20

REFLECTION

To fear God is not about fearing judgment or avoiding punishment. It is about appreciating the blessings and dreading the violation of God's pleasure in the community that reflects the character of this creating, sustaining, and redeeming love. It is to rely on a care and mercy, to live hopefully from it and toward it.   DWIGHT M. LUNDGREN

Psalm 147:12–20 helps us to see this alternative view of ourselves not as givers but as "getters," and to see that this "season of giving" is instead the season of receiving. Psalm 147:12–20 brings us empty-handed into Jerusalem, into God's presence, to receive all that God has done and gives. The action in this psalm, the power at work in the world, belongs to God, not to us. God is both subject and verb throughout these verses.
                                      KIMBERLY L. CLAYTON

At Christmas, Christians claim that God has spoken the divine word anew. This time, however, the word is not indistinctly heard in the blowing of wind, nor is it to be found only in the cadences of the law. Rather, it comes to us as the Word, enfleshed and in a manger, and now at work in the world in a powerful new way.   PAUL K. HOOKER

RESPONSE

Do you fear God's displeasure? How does that motivate or inhibit you?

PRAYER

In this season of giving, I give my heart and soul to you. Amen.

✤ WEDNESDAY ✤

Ephesians 1:3–14

REFLECTION

Completing thank-you notes and putting ornaments in their attic boxes is not the signal for the Christ child to go into hibernation until next year. A second Sunday is an admonition that, just as the liturgical calendar won't let Christmas end, neither should we. Like the echoes of bells pealing, what we have learned of God must ring forth throughout all the earth—from the first to set their hope on Christ to the last, until all from the very greatest to the very least have heard and experienced the good news of God's great plan.

JAMES W. MCTYRE

Indeed, the passage is musical and lyrical, a kind of overture to the theme of salvation that will occupy the first half of Ephesians. For Paul (and his followers), "salvation" means nothing more or less than being a part of God's chosen people. To be a part of God's people—and we are!—is also to be a part of God's plan for the fullness of time and in fact to be a part of the agency for bringing that plan to pass.   THOMAS R. STEAGALD

RESPONSE

The good news of Christ's birth rings throughout the earth. Christ is born! Amen.

PRAYER

Artist, author, creator of all the world: even though the words alone are not enough, I say, "Thank you." Thank you! Amen.

✣ THURSDAY ✣

Ephesians 1:3–14

REFLECTION

In sum, the author proclaims that out of the love, power, and initiative of God we (meaning those who hope in Christ) have been chosen for relationship with God. This relationship is not bound by temporal, ethnic, or linguistic concerns. Indeed, it was forged in eternity and intended for all people everywhere, giving us the manifold blessing of being at once friends with God and friends with each other. This same grace enables us to befriend our enemies, for we know that they will not be our enemies forever.   THOMAS R. STEAGALD

RESPONSE

Befriend our enemies? How is that possible? How can we do that in pure sincerity?

PRAYER

I have been chosen by you, but others have been chosen too. That makes it necessary for each of us to trust you to the fullest. Help me to do so! Amen.

⁕ FRIDAY ⁕

John 1:(1–9) 10–18

REFLECTION

We often think of the incarnation as an emptying: Christ, "though he was in the form of God . . . emptied himself, taking the form of a slave" (Phil. 2:6–7). But this Word made flesh isn't a hollow vessel, an empty shell. The humanity of Jesus is full, it is Fullness itself. The emptying is not an emptying of grace. The Word made flesh is grace. The flesh is God's glory. Jesus was not pretending to be human; he really did enter into our flesh of weakness, mortality, pain. There is no other God, no other secret truth about God. We do not apologize for the suffering as an aberration from the glorious nature of God. God's glorious nature is the suffering. The Word made flesh is very full of grace and truth.

JAMES C. HOWELL

To decide to live as people in the light often means stirring up controversy. It means calling attention to things that others may not want to see. This is why we need the support of other believers. We need people of like mind and faith who will stand together as people of the light. It is not easy to live in the light. It means standing out as one on the hot seat, when many of us prefer life in the coolness of noncommitment.

SHELLEY D. B. COPELAND

RESPONSE

How are you good company for God?

PRAYER

I am in good company, for I am in the company of others who believe in you. Let me be good company to you, and to my brothers and sisters in Christ. Amen.

✦ SATURDAY ✦

John 1:(1–9) 10–18

REFLECTION

The world we live in is full of darkness. Wherever Jesus shows up, light enters the atmosphere. Without a doubt light always makes a difference in darkness and changes the atmosphere. That is an absolute truth to hold on to.

SHELLEY D. B. COPELAND

We live in a culture that cares little for truth. Everything is about what works, what sells, what seems true. Yet truth matters. Truth is our best defense against evil. Truth is the ground of peace. Truth is simpler than we might imagine. John the Baptist provides the clue: he simply pointed to Jesus, who is Truth.

JAMES C. HOWELL

The major forces that dominated the social world of empire and rule are dismissed. What counts is God's authority to enable all people to become children of God. This is the empowerment brought by the logos, and it is a direct challenge to the violence, privilege, power, and oppressive rule found in John's world.

WILLIAM R. HERZOG II

RESPONSE

If truth is simpler than we might imagine, why is it often so hard to be completely honest?

PRAYER

The truth will set us free, as long as it is your truth. Amen.

✦ SUNDAY ✦

Jeremiah 31:7–14

REFLECTION

We build something beautiful in our minds or with our hands, and we hope our work endures. Then the tide comes in and rolls over us. And yet, hurricane season after hurricane season, trial after trial, setback after setback, we rebuild. It is what we do. It is also what God does.   ANDREW NAGY-BENSON

This text presents what is going on behind the Christmas tableau. It shows what happens before the shepherds arrive and after the magi depart. This text may well speak to us more readily than the famous Christmas stories we have just heard. It offers a clean and undecorated tale of a caring God who does not forget who or where we are. This God accepts us in our disarray and gathers up every aspect of our lives. Gifts deepen to a sense of a gift of belonging. Greetings take the form of a personal touch and a guided walk toward something deeply homelike. This text carries the promise uncluttered by the cultural Christmas we have just known. It speaks to the unguarded part of us and gathers up the longings that the Christmas season cannot fulfill. Grief, regret, anger, neglect, and chances come and gone are somehow reclaimed and dealt with in this generous and all-inclusive vision. Beneath our church smiles and Christmas glee, we long to know such richness of soul.   G. MALCOLM SINCLAIR

Psalm 147:12–20

REFLECTION

The psalmist calls on God's people to respond to God's power and bounty with praise! To sing songs, make music, worship the

Lord with thanksgiving. Why? Because God works not only in the vastness of creation, but also in the specific life of a people.

KIMBERLY L. CLAYTON

Ephesians 1:3–14

REFLECTION

Churches have been both victims and victimizers of the power systems and spiritual captivities that racism, sexism, classism, heterosexism, religious prejudice, and other forms of systemic domination and exclusion have generated in societies and their institutions. The presence and praxis of God's Spirit empowers and leads sectors in the churches to keep the memory and work faithfully for "kin-dom" communities that God envisions and the gospel promises.

LUIS R. RIVERA

John 1:(1–9) 10–18

REFLECTION

Disbelief grows out of any number of things: fear that daring to hope will result only in further disappointment; recognition that acceptance of good news brings responsibility; numbness that makes new reality difficult to comprehend. Our calling, reflective of Jesus' purpose in the world, is not to assure acceptance. Rather, we come to introduce good news, a new reality, into a previously uncomprehending context.

WILLIAM V. ARNOLD

RESPONSE

God works in both the vastness of life and the specifics. Can you speak of this from your own experience?

PRAYER

In Christ we have inherited the fullness of God's kingdom. Let me be a worthy and joyful heir! Amen.

❧ *Epiphany of the Lord* ❧

(These reflections are to be used when the Epiphany falls on a Sunday. When it falls on a weekday, use these reflections for Epiphany day and follow the reflections for the week of the Baptism of the Lord.)

Isaiah 60:1–6

Arise, shine; for your light has come,
   and the glory of the LORD has risen upon you. (v. 1)

Psalm 72:1–7, 10–14

May he live while the sun endures,
   and as long as the moon, throughout all generations.
May he be like rain that falls on the mown grass,
   like showers that water the earth. (vv. 5–6)

Ephesians 3:1–12

Of this gospel I have become a servant
according to the gift of God's grace that was given
me by the working of his power. (v. 7)

Matthew 2:1–12

"And you, Bethlehem, in the land of Judah,
   are by no means least among the rulers of Judah;
for from you shall come a ruler
   who is to shepherd my people Israel." (v. 6)

⤝ MONDAY ⤞

Isaiah 60:1–6

REFLECTION

The light of the glory of the Lord is akin to the kingdom of heaven: it is already breaking into reality around us, but we often fail to see it. Insofar as the light is also identified with Christ, one might also reflect on Matthew 25's description of Jesus as present all around us in the hungry, sick, and imprisoned, but recognized in none of these forms. During the holiday season, rather than being too downcast to lift our eyes, we may instead be too busy and distracted, and may thus miss the true light of the world.   CHRISTOPHER B. HAYS

These revelations of increasing light, in Jerusalem and in the Christ, draw us closer to the nature of God and allow us to see ourselves more clearly. Indeed, we might ask ourselves: How do I respond to God's initiative of grace? What gift do I bring to the Christ and to this congregation gathered in his name? How is the global church drawn together in adoration of the Christ? What do the "outsiders" in the passages from Isaiah and Matthew's Gospel teach us about who we are and who Jesus is?

ANDREW NAGY-BENSON

RESPONSE

What gift do you bring to Christ through participation in a specific congregation?

PRAYER

Make me worthy to be a reflection of your light in the world. Amen.

✧ TUESDAY ✧

Psalm 72:1–7, 10–14

REFLECTION

So the story of the magi begins the public story of Jesus, the Messiah, by referring to what for the psalmist and the prophets is the end of the story. It is taking place now. Here are the foreign visitors seeking the new king. They have come for a magnificent exchange. They have come to present their gifts; they hope to return with the gifts of the awaited reign of peace. Their search, the journey that is more than geographical in nature, becomes part of the evangel process.

DWIGHT M. LUNDGREN

The true church is where the word is rightly preached and the sacraments rightly administered, to quote one ancient formulation, but too often our sermons are dull and our sacraments perfunctory. Yet tedium or liturgical sloppiness is scarcely the worst charge one could bring against the church! Even if we are not in open conflict with one another, as is often the case, in far too many churches, the reality of our life together does not show forth the loving presence of the Prince of Peace.

STEPHEN FARRIS

RESPONSE

What do you consider to be the marks of a true church?

PRAYER

May I show forth your loving presence to friends and strangers alike. Amen.

✣ WEDNESDAY ✣

Ephesians 3:1–12

REFLECTION

Perhaps the greatest mystery of faith is why Christ would choose to make us his servants in the first place, we who would be in the last place when compared to greater saints, we who are sinners, we who consistently break the laws of God. The mystery of faith is not a case to be solved, nor a problem seeking solution, nor a contest of wills. Paul's mystery reaches its pinnacle at the precise moment we understand there is no game. The contest is already won. Epiphany.

JAMES W. MCTYRE

The comprehension of Christ's entry into our lives is a moment of purest epiphany. We become wise men and women, not when we find the baby Jesus, but when we realize the crucified Jesus has found us.

JAMES W. MCTYRE

RESPONSE

How do you fit the job descriptions of sinner and saint?

PRAYER

Find me, Christ, in the hidden places of my heart. Amen.

✦ THURSDAY ✦

Ephesians 3:1–12

REFLECTION

God neither answers all our questions nor solves all our problems. But God loves. God loves with a love that stretches from creation to our next breath, to our final breath, and beyond.

Instead of anxiety and restlessness, God through the Spirit of Christ brings us the boldness and confidence to confess our faith, to turn ourselves in, to be free at last.   JAMES W. MCTYRE

Though we are recipients of this gospel, we have no hold on God or wisdom. Epiphany reminds us that our best wisdom is foolishness and that God's plans, though in the vanity of our thoughts we might deem them impossibly foolish, are wisdom and light indeed.   THOMAS R. STEAGALD

The church of Jesus Christ finds its identity and mission in proclaiming to the world the gospel of peace.   LUIS R. RIVERA

RESPONSE

Do you often feel anxious? How does the Spirit bring calm into your life?

PRAYER

I long to be bold and confident in my faith. Let it be so! Amen.

Matthew 2:1–12

REFLECTION

If Jesus is king, there is something upside down and just plain unkingly about his royal bearing. Poor fishermen stood as his court, his standard was a cross, his boast was not iron-fisted dominance but tender love. Little wonder King Herod was "troubled." All who cling to power, all who lust for dominance, are in for a headlong tumble before this Christ child.

JAMES C. HOWELL

One must also be attentive to what is going on in the immediate world—local and national, cultural and familial, earthly and heavenly. WILLIAM V. ARNOLD

RESPONSE

Which of the gifts of the magi represent most accurately the kind of gift you offer to the Christ child?

PRAYER

Let my faith in you be evident in the way that I live my life. Amen.

✣ SATURDAY ✢

Matthew 2:1–12

REFLECTION

As we travel—by foot, by camel, by auto, or in our mind—it is very important to seek guidance along the way. No one of us, not even any small group of us, can know it all. There are others who are seeking, and there are others who have a stake in what we are seeking—for good or for ill. WILLIAM V. ARNOLD

An epiphany is not something to be hidden. It is something to be shared. In fact, if one is inclined to hide an epiphany, as if it were some private possession to be protected, then there is reason to question whether it is a genuine epiphany at all. Spiritual maturity inspires one to be generous, rather than fearful or stingy. It triggers eagerness to share, rather than protectiveness and hoarding. WILLIAM V. ARNOLD

The star of Bethlehem was not necessarily an extraordinary celestial event, but an ordinary star seen through the extraordinary eyes of the magi. WILLIAM R. HERZOG II

RESPONSE

Who or what has served as markers on your road map of faith?

PRAYER

Help me not to be stingy with the gift of myself. Amen.

✢ SUNDAY ✢

Isaiah 60:1–6

REFLECTION

The images of this ingathering hearken back to God's call to Abraham to be a blessing upon all the families of the earth. Abraham's homeland will be the gathering place for all God's children, who will come bringing their finest treasures as an offering to God and for the benefit of God's people. For the Christian, these images hearken forward to the redemption of all creation in Jesus Christ—the One who on the cross opens his arms wide to draw all people to himself. However, here in the between times, readers are shown a people willing to be inspired by and work hard for a vision that is, as yet, out of their reach. The proclamation of this passage is one of hope, of something that is promised, but for which we are still waiting in faith.

KATHERINE C. CALORE

Psalm 72:1–7, 10–14

REFLECTION

The search for grace is prompted and sustained by grace. Psalm 72 prays for a king who is animated and guided by God's own goodness. But the vision and hope that gives birth to the prayer is the work of grace. The little drama that is played out between Herod and the magi is a drama that is replicated in every human. If we continue to desire to rule ourselves, we continue as oppressors of ourselves, and perhaps of others.

DWIGHT M. LUNDGREN

Ephesians 3:1–12

REFLECTION

But what if a church has no group epiphany to share? How does a congregation touch the untouchables? The church and Paul have always held conjoined the paradox of mystery and the gift of sacrament. Like an epiphany, a sacrament is the slightly open window through which we slide a finger toward relief. The Lord's Supper is a prime example of an activity in which we neither act nor accomplish, but through which we mysteriously draw closer to each other and find access to Christ. In the sacraments we stop solving mysteries and, for a marvelous epiphanic moment, allow the mysteries to solve us.

JAMES W. MCTYRE

Matthew 2:1–12

REFLECTION

The magi did not come to study Jesus. They came to worship a newborn king by following a special star. Sacrificing time and comfort, they brought gifts to a baby who demonstrated no outward signs of prophetic confirmation. They held no assurance of how the story would end. All they had was prophetic knowledge of a star and a coming messiah. Reflected in their eyes was an economically limited toddler, in modest surroundings, lying in a teen mother's arms. To the intellectually perceptive, this scene was not a scholar's formula for future success. Yet, by grace, the magi had the faith to experience unbridled joy. They beheld the substance of things hoped for and humbled themselves to worship the gift of God. Jesus was the promise of salvation for the world and the gift of joy that sent the wise home by another way.

SHELLEY D. B. COPELAND

RESPONSE

What are your thoughts when receiving Communion?

PRAYER

May I be a worthy servant of Christ's grace. Amen.

❧ *Baptism of the Lord* ❦

(First Sunday after the Epiphany)

Genesis 1:1–5

In the beginning when God created the heavens
and the earth, the earth was a formless void and darkness
covered the face of the deep, while a wind from God swept
over the face of the waters. Then God said, "Let there
be light"; and there was light. (vv. 1–3)

Psalm 29

The voice of the LORD is over the waters;
    the God of glory thunders,
    the LORD, over mighty waters.
The voice of the LORD is powerful;
    the voice of the LORD is full of majesty. (vv. 3–4)

Acts 19:1–7

He said to them, "Did you receive the Holy Spirit
when you became believers?" They replied, "No, we have
not even heard that there is a Holy Spirit." (v. 2)

Mark 1:4–11

[John] proclaimed, "The one who is more powerful than
I is coming after me; I am not worthy to stoop down and untie
the thong of his sandals. I have baptized you with water;
but he will baptize you with the Holy Spirit." (vv. 7–8)

✢ MONDAY ✣

Genesis 1:1–5

REFLECTION

"In the beginning God." That is the whole story in a nutshell. Then comes the verb: "created." Then comes the object of the verb: "the heavens and the earth." The first thing that happened to the formless earth, which was void and darkness, but which had a "deep" face, is this: the Spirit of God moved upon the face of the waters.

DONNA SCHAPER

Light is the palate for further creation. Yet light itself renders more than the possible perception of shapes and colors. Light is the basis of life and order, and light itself is judged by God as being good (v. 4), thus exhibiting its moral quality. Because of its sublime quality and ordering character, light subsequently serves as a profound symbol for the incarnation of God in Christ and for the fullness of life itself (John 8:12; 9:5).

JOSEPH L. PRICE

RESPONSE

What kinds of light do you use in your home? How would your life be different if you had no electricity to bring you light?

PRAYER

My life is filled with artificial light; let my life also be filled with your light. Amen.

⤖ TUESDAY ⤖

Genesis 1:1–5

REFLECTION

One might have thought that reverence was just a religious value. It is not! Reverence is the virtue that keeps us from acting like gods.   DONNA SCHAPER

This creation story is a way of holding onto hope when all signs of order in our lives have been destroyed and we must look out for signs of the creative work of God beyond our control. If God is still creating order out of chaos in the succession of day and night, maybe God will one day create order once more out of chaos in the lives of God's people. Hold on, and do not lose hope.   RICHARD BOYCE

RESPONSE

How do we restore the reverence we have for creation and allow it be a part of our daily living?   DONNA SCHAPER

PRAYER

Although I don't often think about it, my reverence for you is beyond my imagining. Amen.

✧ WEDNESDAY ✦

Psalm 29

REFLECTION

If contemporary Christians tend to emphasize God's grace
expressed in the self-sacrificial love of Jesus Christ, this passage
forcefully reasserts God's irresistible might and glorious power.
If contemporary Protestant Christians tend to emphasize
Scripture as the sole source of knowledge about God and God's
way, this psalm reminds us that God also reveals Godself to all
creatures through the general patterns and events of natural
world.   TIMOTHY A. BEACH-VERHEY

There is no clue in this psalm why God's people need "strength"
and "peace." Their predicament could be a natural disaster
(flood, famine, drought, etc.)—or it could just as easily be
political oppression, war, or exile. The point is, it does not
matter what the predicament might be. At any time, under any
circumstances when "storm clouds" roll, God's sovereign power
is available to bless and deliver God's people, to give them peace
even in the midst of storms. The same God who rules over the
universe, whose "voice" sends forth the thunderstorm, is the
God of Israel—the One in whom they can trust and to whom
their prayers ascend.   MARSHA M. WILFONG

RESPONSE

If God's voice came from the heavens and said something about
you, what might that be?

PRAYER

How can it be that you are the God who created the universe,
who sends forth the thunderstorms, yet who knows each of us
by name? Amen.

✦ THURSDAY ✦

Acts 19:1–7

REFLECTION

Baptism in the name of Jesus entails a divinely given reality, but this reality both empowers and disposes people to witness to God's deeds of power (Acts 2:11). The gift of the Spirit in baptism sweeps people up into the dynamic of the Spirit and its expansive Way. It drives believers to participate in the church's expansive mission. It empowers them to witness in word and in deed to a universally inclusive reality.   DOUGLAS F. OTTATI

This Holy Spirit inspires us to risk our very lives for the sake of the good news of Jesus Christ, and to trust that with God nothing is impossible. This Spirit is a powerful wind that breathes through our speaking and our acting to accomplish more than we can ask or imagine, even to the point of transforming the world, as the Spirit did through the first disciples.   RUTHANNA B. HOOKE

RESPONSE

Do you feel as though you've ever risked your life for the sake of the gospel?

PRAYER

You put your life on the line for me, dearest Christ; I thank you from my whole being. Amen.

✢ FRIDAY ✢

Mark 1:4–11

REFLECTION

John, the epitome of the prophets, also points forward to God's imminent intervention in human history to confer a new hope to humanity. Into the wilderness of our own broken lives and our own bleeding world erupts the promise of a baptism of new life.

LEE BARRETT

Jesus did not receive the Spirit in order to enjoy privately its spiritual benefits, but rather in order to pass it on.

LEE BARRETT

Here is a reminder that the gospel is down to earth, grounded in the real, tactile, sensual, fleshy world. In these few verses are references to river water, clothing from camels, diet from bugs, and tying shoes, a bird analogy, and an interesting weather phenomenon. Mark's earthiness gives us a hedge against faith and worship that are too ethereal, otherworldly, abstract.

ELTON W. BROWN

RESPONSE

Where is it that you most experience the presence of God?

PRAYER

I am not worthy to bend down and tie the sandal of my Savior; yet you have given your life for me. Unbelievable. Amen.

✣ SATURDAY ✣

Mark 1:4–11

REFLECTION

Spirit is the real substance of God acting in creation and redemption and final reconciliation. And yet Spirit is always tied to material—real water, real bread, inexpensive wine, beautiful baptismal dresses for our children, or soaking robes for our adults. Spirit fills us in church and then drives us from church (as it will drive Jesus from the Jordan to the wilderness). There, outside the walls, we wrestle with the beasts and pray for ministering angels . . . angels heavier than air.

ELTON W. BROWN

In this moment of Jesus' baptism, heaven and earth are transparent to one another. Jesus looks to the heavens in love, and the voice calls out in love. The Spirit, the love between the first and second persons of the Trinity, is manifest.

TED A. SMITH

RESPONSE

Have you ever felt that angels were ministering to you? When and why?

PRAYER

Let my spirit soar on wings of angels. Amen.

✢ SUNDAY ✢

Genesis 1:1–5

REFLECTION

Set in context literarily, historically, and liturgically, this story can only be heard as the first in a long series of stories about God creating order out of chaos: at the beginning of ordered time, through the waters of the Red Sea, in the muddy waters of the river Jordan, and down to the chaotic situations of God's people today. Now we can hear these verses as a prequel to a story whose sequel is still being spoken and enacted today.

RICHARD BOYCE

The universe in its immensity, with its spiral galaxies and nebulae, finds a small but final fulfillment in us.

LAWRENCE WOOD

Psalm 29

REFLECTION

The problem comes when believers do not expect anything to happen in worship. They approach worship casually, almost nonchalantly, hoping only to hear some practical piece of advice or to escape the problems of the world for an hour and lose themselves in an aesthetically satisfying experience. Worship is oriented horizontally toward the worshiper. The worship the psalmist describes is directed toward the living God who sits enthroned in the heavens. The worship going on here expresses awe to a transcendent and sovereign God, a God who is shrouded in mystery and power. DAVE BLAND

Acts 19:1–7

REFLECTION

Baptism in Acts is not a magical ritual that automatically brings down the Holy Spirit whenever it is performed. The baptism provides an optimal environment for the coming of the Holy Spirit in the narrative world of Acts, but it is also true that in the book of Acts the Holy Spirit has absolute freedom to come and work in whatever way the Spirit sees fit.

EUGENE EUNG-CHUN PARK

Mark 1:4–11

REFLECTION

Contemporary Christians trying to understand John the Baptist often have trouble getting beyond questions of style. Like a *Vanity Fair* report of a celebrity party, popular memories of John recall little beyond what he ate, what he wore, and some outrageous thing he said. Accessorized with camel's hair and a leather belt, dining on locusts and honey—and didn't he call someone a "brood of vipers"?—John has become an all-purpose container for any kind of radical content. And so everyone from John Brown to Mr. T has been called a "modern-day John the Baptist."

TED A. SMITH

The words spoken by the voice from the heavens identify Jesus as God's "beloved Son" (Mark 1:11). The rest of the Gospel describes how this beloved Son fulfills the mission given to him by God—a mission that will result in his execution. Christian baptism has transformed us into God's beloved children. Will we commit ourselves to completing Christ's work on earth despite the cost?

LESLIE J. HOPPE

RESPONSE

What do you remember about your baptism?

PRAYER

The people you call your beloved children are often those I would least expect—including me. Amen.

❧ *Second Sunday after* ❦ *the Epiphany*

1 Samuel 3:1–10 (11–20)

Now the LORD came and stood there, calling as before, "Samuel! Samuel!" And Samuel said, "Speak, for your servant is listening." Then the LORD said to Samuel, "See, I am about to do something in Israel that will make both ears of anyone who hears of it tingle." (vv. 10–11)

Psalm 139:1–6, 13–18

O LORD, you have searched me and known me.
    You know when I sit down and when I rise up;
        you discern my thoughts from far away.
You search out my path and my lying down,
    and are acquainted with all my ways. (vv. 1–3)

1 Corinthians 6:12–20

Or do you not know that your body is a temple of the Holy Spirit within you, which you have from God, and that you are not your own? For you were bought with a price; therefore glorify God in your body. (vv. 19–20)

John 1:43–51

Nathanael replied, "Rabbi, you are the Son of God! You are the King of Israel!" Jesus answered, "Do you believe because I told you that I saw you under the fig tree? You will see greater things than these." (vv. 49–50)

✦ MONDAY ✦

1 Samuel 3:1–10 (11–20)

REFLECTION

Imagine a world beyond gimmicks, with no gotchas, a world
that restores the dash between "noblesse" and "oblige," a world
where things are fair, where you are well, where those you love
are well, where swords have become art schools and weapons
have become warming centers for the elderly. . . .

Imagine a world of enchantment, where you look outside at a
child playing on a safe street, where good public transportation
pulls up to take you to a good job, where economic obsession
is gone and decent salaries replace it. Imagine a world where
health is insured and life is insured and you have decent choices
at the end to do what is right for you and your family. Imagine
hospitals as good as homes and hospices as good as hospitals.
Imagine good things and then believe that they are coming.
God has plans, already executed in Jesus, to do good things.
The way to tingle is to open both of your eyes and look around.
Look under the hassock, look back to the Scripture, look
forward in hope. Open both of your ears. Soon they will tingle.

DONNA SCHAPER

RESPONSE

In your life, do you feel summoned by God to a specific
vocation or course of action?

PRAYER

I am frequently blinded by the distractions of the world; clear
my inner vision, that I might see more clearly. Amen.

✣ TUESDAY ✣

Psalm 139:1–6, 13–18

REFLECTION

Speaking about God tends to tie theologians up in tense knots of contradiction. God is transcendent but also immanent, just but also gracious, omnipotent but also personal. The wonder of this cherished psalm is that it knits these complex threads of God's nature together into the single garment of divine providence.
TIMOTHY A. BEACH-VERHEY

Because God is at the farthest reaches of the universe and in the most secret depths of the human heart, God is the constant companion, who cannot be escaped, fooled, or ignored.
TIMOTHY A. BEACH-VERHEY

The conviction that human beings are autonomous, self-determining individuals is an illusion produced by pride. Human destiny is in the hands of a gracious God. Therefore genuine selfhood includes trusting dependence on God and grateful responsibility to God.
TIMOTHY A. BEACH-VERHEY

RESPONSE

How do you most often experience God—as the Creator of the universe, or the One who knows the inmost secrets of your heart?

PRAYER

Knit the threads of my life together with yours! Amen.

Psalm 139:1–6, 13–18

REFLECTION

Psalm 139 invites us to receive an identity rooted not in the things we say about ourselves or the labels others assign us, but in the One who knows us more deeply and more lovingly than we could ever know ourselves. . . . The value of our lives does not come from what we achieve or possess or what others may think of us. It comes from the God who knows and names us, from whose steadfast love nothing in all creation can ever separate us.   ALLEN C. MCSWEEN JR.

The difference between creator and creature, between God and human beings, is ultimately too great for us to fathom. Yet perhaps it is enough for us to know that God knows us— intimately and completely—and that we live our lives from beginning to end surrounded by God's discerning presence.

MARSHA M. WILFONG

RESPONSE

Does it frighten or comfort you to think about how deeply God knows everything about you?

PRAYER

O Lord, you have searched me and known me. You know when I sit down and when I rise up; you discern my thoughts from far away. You search out my path and my lying down, and are acquainted with all my ways (Ps. 139:1–3). Amen.

✦ THURSDAY ✦

1 Corinthians 6:12–20

REFLECTION

Our lives may be ordered by commitments to many different things: career, wealth, power, reputation, sex, nation, church, tribe, or ethnic group. But we are not meant only for these things. We are not fitted to live only for these things. These things, important as they are, need to be fitted into a broader context. They need to be put into their proper places. Indeed, when we are oriented toward these things alone, when our attitude and disposition is not adjusted by an appreciation for and loyalty to some greater and grander reality, we become skewed and enslaved. Then we do things that are neither beneficial nor helpful.   DOUGLAS F. OTTATI

Paul's teachings remind today's churches that the body and sex are good and that what we do with them matters. To be made as physical and sexual beings is to be given a powerful means of finding physical and spiritual union with other beings. However, this goodness and power also give us a profound responsibility to live in our bodies and express our sexuality in ways that glorify God and build up our communities. What might it mean for us to glorify God with our bodies, especially in the expression of our sexuality? What might it mean to think of our bodies as belonging to Christ and of sexual acts as done with Christ and to Christ?   RUTHANNA B. HOOKE

RESPONSE

Make a list of your weekly commitments. Is there anything on this list that doesn't really matter, that you can eliminate?

PRAYER

My life is filled with obligations, but none greater than serving you. Give me courage to let go of what I can. Amen.

✦ FRIDAY ✦

John 1:43–51

REFLECTION

Such vision required the unfolding of the full narrative of Jesus'
life, death, and resurrection. In the signs that follow in the
Gospel, particularly the pivotal sign of cross, the heavens are
indeed opened. The disciples will see the divine glory fully only
when the work of crucifixion and resurrection is completed.
The unveiling of the glory of God occurs in the history of Jesus,
in the mysterious conjunction of crucifixion and exaltation.

LEE BARRETT

This story begins with Jesus making a decision. It is comforting
to remember that even Jesus, though utterly Spirit-filled and
completely in tune with God's will, had to sort out his options
and make his own decisions. God thus honors the gift of
individual freedom. ELTON W. BROWN

RESPONSE

Which of the stories of the disciples most resonates with you?

PRAYER

It is time for me to make some decisions about how I plan to
live my life. Guide me, I pray! Amen.

✢ SATURDAY ✢

John 1:43–51

REFLECTION

Nathanael is excellent disciple material because he is without guile. Nathanael would make a terrible poker player but a wonderful friend. God thus honors the qualities of honesty, genuineness, integrity, and open-mindedness. This is not one of those cases where God takes a miserable sinner and turns him into a saint. This is one of those equally remarkable cases where God takes a person who is humanly praiseworthy in every way and makes of him something even more—a disciple.

ELTON W. BROWN

Our relationship with God is a two-way street, both parties talking and listening and reaching out to each other.

ELTON W. BROWN

RESPONSE

Do you call yourself a disciple? What qualifications for this calling are necessary, as far as you are concerned?

PRAYER

I do not always glorify you in my body, in the way I neglect my own health and spirit. May I be continually reminded of how important these things are. Amen.

1 Samuel 3:1–10 (11–20)

REFLECTION

To be called by God is an act of spiritual intimacy and divine
urgency. To be called by God means that God knows one's
name and, in knowing one's name, exercises a powerful
influence on the person. To be called by God also indicates a
need for immediate response because the Almighty has indeed
summoned one to a specific vocation or course of action.

JOSEPH L. PRICE

Psalm 139:1–6, 13–18

REFLECTION

God did not send Jesus in order to know what it was like to be
human. Rather, because God already knew what it was like to
be human, God sent Jesus. . . . God has always known what it
was like to be human. God's incarnation is primarily for our
benefit, not God's.   DAVE BLAND

1 Corinthians 6:12–20

REFLECTION

Our culture has an ambivalent relationship to the body. On one
hand we glorify the body, and much energy goes into tending
and beautifying it. This very energy, however, suggests that
on a deeper level there is shame of the body, since it has to
be constantly improved and worked on. Likewise the church,
perhaps inheriting some of the body-spirit dualism held by
the Corinthians, is at best squeamish or embarrassed about
the body. Regarding sex, both culture and church are lacking
in insight. Cultural forces tend to sexualize all aspects of our
lives, while at the same time inculcating a certain prudishness
regarding sex. The churches struggle to find a theologically and

pastorally coherent way of addressing this cultural situation, and tend either to avoid altogether teaching about sexual morality, or to make rigid rules that are not beneficial to Christians. These rules oversimplify the complexity of human sexuality and thus do not help Christians discern how to exercise morality in this domain of their personhood. Rather than offering slogans, the church needs to provide rigorous theological reflection to Christians seeking to live faithfully as sexual beings.   RUTHANNA B. HOOKE

John 1:43–51

REFLECTION

Jesus' opponents never accept Jesus, because they are unwilling to see beyond appearances. This is the great tragedy of the Fourth Gospel: "He came to what was his own, and his own people did not accept him" (John 1:11). The disciples were able to accept Jesus as the Messiah because Jesus chose them "out of the world" (John 15:19).   LESLIE J. HOPPE

Discipleship is first of all a willingness to walk with Jesus. It is not obedience to an abstract set of codes, but consent to a costly, joyful relationship. In walking with Jesus, we learn who he is. As we learn who he is, we learn what it means to follow him.   TED A. SMITH

RESPONSE

Using the words from 1 Samuel, insert your own name, then use this as a prayer.

PRAYER

Lord, you call to me, "(insert your name here)!" May my answer be, "Speak, for your servant is listening." Amen.

THE WEEK LEADING UP TO THE

❧ *Third Sunday after* ❦
the Epiphany

Jonah 3:1–5, 10

When God saw what they did, how they turned from their evil
ways, God changed his mind about the calamity that he had said
he would bring upon them; and he did not do it. (v. 10)

Psalm 62:5–12

For God alone my soul waits in silence,
  for my hope is from him.
He alone is my rock and my salvation,
  my fortress; I shall not be shaken. (vv. 5–6)

1 Corinthians 7:29–31

I mean, brothers and sisters, the appointed time has grown short;
from now on, let even those who have wives be as though they had
none, and those who mourn as though they were not mourning,
and those who rejoice as though they were not rejoicing, and those
who buy as though they had no possessions, and those who deal
with the world as though they had no dealings with it. For the
present form of this world is passing away. (vv. 29–31)

Mark 1:14–20

As Jesus passed along the Sea of Galilee, he saw Simon
and his brother Andrew casting a net into the sea—for they
were fishermen. And Jesus said to them, "Follow me and
I will make you fish for people." And immediately they
left their nets and followed him. (vv. 16–18)

✦ MONDAY ✦

Jonah 3:1–5, 10

REFLECTION

The story of Jonah affirms the character of God as persevering, responsive, and merciful to all who repent.   JOSEPH L. PRICE

It is very different to be poor or about to be deported than it is to be well-off and comfortable. The well-off and comfortable do not know what urgency is! Luckily we have prophets like Jonah to remind us that someone is about to be deported, someone is about to be laid off. If we cannot manage our own obsession with the self, then we can use a well-polished prophetic trick. Imagine yourself in the place of someone who is oppressed, or poor, or in trouble. That will focus our attention.

DONNA SCHAPER

Maybe the main joke and gospel in this strange book of Jonah is the sense that not even the Lord knows how far divine mercy and compassion can go, especially when it comes to sticking with this particular people God has chosen.   RICHARD BOYCE

RESPONSE

What have been the "Ninevehs" in your life—the places where you did not want to go?

PRAYER

Instead of judging the worth of others, I repent for the ways in which I have failed to see my need for you. Amen.

✦ TUESDAY ✦

Psalm 62:5–12

REFLECTION

Faith is not simply a set of beliefs, a function of the mind.
Fundamentally, it is a condition of trust or confidence located
in the heart or soul that orients one in the world through
certain persistent dispositions and affections.

TIMOTHY A. BEACH-VERHEY

Every pastor knows how easily such an assurance can sound
like merely wishful thinking to ones who feel assaulted by forces
beyond their control. That is why it is so important to make
clear that the psalmist's trust in God does not come from a
naive refusal to look reality in the face. There is nothing escapist
in the trust of the psalmist. There are indeed enemies among
us who assail and batter their victims, both the vulnerable
(symbolized by a "leaning wall . . . tottering fence") and the
seemingly strong and prominent. At one time or another, that
includes all of us. We are often the most vulnerable when we
think of ourselves as the most secure.   ALLEN C. MCSWEEN JR.

RESPONSE

Do you believe that those who do not repent can be forgiven?

PRAYER

For God alone my soul waits in silence, for my hope is
from God. God alone is my rock and my salvation, my fortress;
I shall not be shaken (Ps. 62:5–6). Amen.

✣ WEDNESDAY ✣

Psalm 62:5–12

REFLECTION

Faith does not shut its eyes to the assaults that beset us. It does not place its trust in those who seem to be the "winners" in the game of life. Faith clings to and relies on the living God alone. Authentic trust is not engendered by our own efforts at self-assurance. It comes from God's own self-revelation and clings to the assurance that "power belongs to God, and steadfast love belongs to you, O Lord. For you repay to all according to their work." That is the "good news of judgment" which enables people of faith to "wait in the Lord," not in passive resignation to the powers that be, but in eager expectation of every fresh epiphany of the "kingdom, power, and glory" of the vulnerable One who alone is our "rock and salvation."

ALLEN C. MCSWEEN JR.

The one who trusts in God will receive a blessing of inner peace and strength. We gain confidence knowing that in whatever the circumstances we find ourselves—whether in want or plenty, whether in life or death—God is present and we are richly blessed.

DAVE BLAND

RESPONSE

What burdens and griefs does God bear for you?

PRAYER

On God rests my deliverance and my honor; my mighty rock, my refuge is in God (Ps. 62:7). Amen.

✦ THURSDAY ✦

1 Corinthians 7:29–31

REFLECTION

The time has grown short for us to do that to which we were called, which is to proclaim Jesus Christ, and him crucified, and to devote our lives to Christian love, agape. This urgency can give us a healthy dissatisfaction with those structures of the world that hinder God's coming reign, and spur us to devote ourselves wholeheartedly to changing those structures as part of our participation in God's work in the world.

RUTHANNA B. HOOKE

Few Christians today are sitting up nights trying to decide if they really should marry their fiancées because Jesus might return before they can cut the wedding cake. "The impending crisis" (v. 26), at least the one Paul meant, is simply not on our minds. If it is coming at all, it is still pending.   CLYDE FANT

RESPONSE

Is Paul wrong, or is it not ever true today, as it was then, that the present form of this world is passing away?   CLYDE FANT

PRAYER

Give me renewed zest in proclaiming the good news of Jesus Christ! Amen.

✦ FRIDAY ✦

Mark 1:14–20

REFLECTION

Like those disciples who misunderstood and failed Jesus at every turn, we too are sinners in need of forgiveness for our multiple betrayals. Like them, we sinners, despite our failings, are slowly being transmuted into followers of Christ. Like them we are called not to the enjoyment of a private salvation but to a public vocation. Like them, and like Abraham, we are summoned by God to leave our parents' house, abandoning self-interest, security, and social approbation. Like them, we can find our inadequate attempts at ministry transformed by grace into extensions of Jesus' proclamatory activity. Just as it did for the disciples, the command "Follow me" points to the way of the cross for us. Just as it did for the disciples, the ominous reference to the arrest of John the Baptist warns that we too are called to a life of risk, insecurity, and self-abnegation.

LEE BARRETT

In calling the Galilean fishermen to discipleship, Jesus does not just ask them to add one more task to their busy lives. He calls them into new ways of being. TED A. SMITH

RESPONSE

Is discipleship for you a new way of life or one more task to check off the list of things to do someday?

PRAYER

My life belongs to you, O God. Amen.

✦ SATURDAY ✦

Mark 1:14–20

REFLECTION

The kingdom of God that Jesus proclaimed was not bolstered by the construction of monumental buildings and great cities. God's kingdom is manifest in the human embrace of God's rule through repentance and faith. LESLIE J. HOPPE

We do not repent in order to usher in the time of redemption, but because that time is already at hand. We do not become fishers in order to meet the quota that will summon up the reign of God, but because that reign has already come near. And we do not follow Jesus with the hopes that one day we might find him, but because he has already come to us and called us. TED A. SMITH

RESPONSE

What is your response to this quote: "Becoming a faithful Christian disciple takes both a moment and a lifetime"?

ELTON W. BROWN

PRAYER

You have given me life, all the time; may I give you my life, for all time. Amen.

✢ SUNDAY ✢

Jonah 3:1–5, 10

REFLECTION

God is a God of deliverance, even toward his rebellious
children.   RICHARD BOYCE

Apparently God's purposes can be accomplished with a
minimum of faithfulness; and such faithfulness turns out to be
a matter of not merely what one feels, but what one does.
                                                   LAWRENCE WOOD

If God really intends salvation for all the peoples, then in all
seriousness, we must at least talk to our enemies.
                                                   LAWRENCE WOOD

Psalm 62:5–12

REFLECTION

God is the only source of hope and peace for mortals. If life
has any significance, it will be found in God. If our families,
communities, nations, and churches have any worth, it will be
located in God.   TIMOTHY A. BEACH-VERHEY

God is the one on whom and in whom we can depend; God is
most worthy of our trust. God practices steadfast love toward
us (v. 12). God bears our burdens, shares our grief, forgives our
sins, and endures our unfaithfulness. God's sharing, forgiving,
and enduring qualities are most poignantly demonstrated in the
suffering of Christ on the cross. Experience and history and the
cross teach us that we can trust God.   DAVE BLAND

1 Corinthians 7:29–31

REFLECTION

Although we may not expect the return of Christ to happen in
our lifetimes, as Paul did, as Christians we nonetheless do not

simply resign ourselves to the givenness of the world, for we have planted within us a great hope that God's kingdom will come on earth as in heaven. This means that we are a people who look to the future in trust and hope, confident that God is working God's purposes out and that God's realm is even now breaking into our world.   RUTHANNA B. HOOKE

Mark 1:14–20

REFLECTION

Fishing involves more than the act of casting nets and pulling in the haul. There are also the preparations, the mending of nets, repairing the tools that are bound to be damaged and worn in the rough-and-tumble between the hunter and the hunted and the everchanging environment in which the drama is played out. You can't always be fishing, even if that's your favorite part.

ELTON W. BROWN

If we can take Jesus at his word—that if the disciples follow him, he will make them fishers—then the story of the disciples shows what fishers' lives look like. They find themselves astounded at Jesus' teaching. They witness the rebuking of unclean spirits, the healing of sick people, and the cleansing of lepers. They lose track of Jesus and must search for him again. They know that their lives unfold in the shadow of the arrest and execution of John. And this is only chapter 1.   TED A. SMITH

RESPONSE

What tools do you need as a disciple, or "fisher-person"? Do you give enough of your time to tending the tools of your trade?

PRAYER

Christ, you beckon us to come, and follow you. May each step be one on that journey. Amen.

Fourth Sunday after the Epiphany

Deuteronomy 18:15–20

Then the LORD replied to me: "They are right in what they have said. I will raise up for them a prophet like you from among their own people; I will put my words in the mouth of the prophet, who shall speak to them everything that I command." (vv. 17–18)

Psalm 111

Praise the LORD!
I will give thanks to the LORD with my whole heart,
   in the company of the upright, in the congregation.
Great are the works of the LORD,
   studied by all who delight in them.
. . . .
The fear of the LORD is the beginning of wisdom;
   all those who practice it have a good understanding. (vv. 1–2, 10a)

1 Corinthians 8:1–13

Indeed, even though there may be so-called gods in heaven or on earth—as in fact there are many gods and many lords—yet for us there is one God, the Father, from whom are all things and for whom we exist, and one Lord, Jesus Christ, through whom are all things and through whom we exist. (vv. 5–6)

Mark 1:21–28

They were all amazed, and they kept on asking one another, "What is this? A new teaching—with authority! He commands even the unclean spirits, and they obey him." At once his fame began to spread throughout the surrounding region of Galilee. (vv. 27–28)

❖ MONDAY ❖

Deuteronomy 18:15–20

REFLECTION

The question of the people in exile is not how to survive a confrontation with the power of their God. Rather, the question is where to find the presence of that God who seems absent—where and who is the God who let this happen to us? The answer of this text is that God is to be found in the word uttered by the prophet.   RICHARD A. PUCKETT

One of the greatest honors a pastor has is to hold the hand of someone who is dying and pray that person into heaven. Pastors are like ushers at the performance hall where a grand opera is about to be performed. Ushers are not the point; the great spectacle on the stage that is about to happen is the point. So also, pastors are ushering people into the presence of the Almighty, not only when they are dying, but when they come to worship. Preachers are not the point; Christ is. Our job is to get out of the way and allow the glory of God to shine through. The same is true for laity who witness on behalf of God in the world. Don't worry about what you are going to say. Open yourself to the Scripture, and allow God to speak through you to those who need to hear God's word.   WILLIAM J. CARL III

RESPONSE

Which do you do better: listen or speak? How do you achieve a balance between the two?

PRAYER

Give me ears to listen when I need to listen, and lips to speak when I need to speak. Amen.

✦ TUESDAY ✦

Psalm 111

REFLECTION

We human creatures seem to be born to wonder, to love, and to praise. We are born for other things as well, of course. We work, we speak, we create, and we make and keep covenants together. All these things are found in all human communities we know about, and they take central place in our lives as well. But wonder, love, and praise seem different somehow. They are expressions of our deepest being and deepest longing. No matter what happens to us or what we achieve, they point us to something greater, something better that surrounds our lives and makes us glad. THOMAS D. PARKER

If we ask, "Why should we praise God?" the answer is surely because it is the door to a life of mature spiritual wisdom. The eternal God, the Source of all, does not need our praise, as some divine figures need to be fed human goods or flattery. To gain a healthy spiritual self-understanding, we need to remember that our lives are set in the midst of an unimaginable greatness and goodness. THOMAS D. PARKER

RESPONSE

When have you uttered the phrase, "My God, look at that!" and meant it as an exclamation of praise?

PRAYER

I will give thanks to the LORD with my whole heart, in the company of the upright, in the congregation (Ps. 111:1). Amen.

❧ WEDNESDAY ❧

Psalm 111

REFLECTION

The beginning of wisdom begins with fear of the Lord—not fear in the sense of outright paralyzing terror closing in from all sides, but fear in the sense of reverence. Fear in the sense of awe for the Lord's amazing deeds.   ANNE H. K. APPLE

"Fear of the LORD" is a way of life, a posture in the world that acknowledges God's sovereignty and the place of humanity (our capacities and limitations) before God and creation.

CHRISTINE ROY YODER

The church is called to be the visible and witnessing community of the gospel of Jesus Christ. The essential structure of God's gathered people is to be an unfolding narrative, rather than a rigid institutional system.   ANNE H. K. APPLE

RESPONSE

Do you fear God with a sense of terror, or awe? Or neither?

PRAYER

Full of honor and majesty is your work, and your righteousness endures forever (Ps. 111:3). Amen.

✣ THURSDAY ✣

1 Corinthians 8:1–13

REFLECTION

Can a person know God through God the Creator, namely, through one's perception of order and beauty in God's creation (general revelation)? Or must one have knowledge through Christ, namely, through an unexpected "gospel" message (special revelation)? Paul's answer is carefully balanced. A person knows God, and is known by God, through knowing "both" God the Creator and Jesus Christ the "agent" of God's power in creation and the "agent" through whom we exist (v. 6). Neither one alone is sufficient, since both God and Christ are intimately related to creation, and we are created beings.

VERNON K. ROBBINS

At the heart of Paul's message is a peculiar understanding of Christian freedom. Freedom is not the right to choose to do as one wishes. It is not simply a lack of restrictions or a negation of the Law or of other requirements. Christian freedom is grounded in love, God's love for us in Jesus Christ. If love is a matter of knowledge, it is God's knowing of us.

V. BRUCE RIGDON

RESPONSE

How does creation teach you about Christ?

PRAYER

In the beauty of the earth, and in the places of my heart, I seek to understand you. Amen.

✣ FRIDAY ✣

Mark 1:21–28

REFLECTION

In the synagogue, the religious space, the kingdom is embodied in Jesus' communication skills—word and much more—and power over spirits. "They entered into Capernaum" (1:21). They have left the bank of the sea that is a fishing and calling place of the messengers of the kingdom, and they come to the space of security and tradition, where the old religious teachings are transmitted. There Jesus is, in the synagogue, and in that space of the synagogue he deploys a new power. He takes advantage of the Sabbath, the day the faithful ones meet, to teach them, as a trustworthy Jew who has a word for the people. Jesus' communication skill creates vitality: "he taught them as one having authority, and not as the scribes." OFELIA ORTEGA

Miracle stories are more often about the story told than the miracle itself. MIKE GRAVES

RESPONSE

Are you more comfortable worshiping God in a public place or in the privacy of your own home?

PRAYER

Heal the wounded places of my soul, that I may offer your praise. Amen.

✣ SATURDAY ✣

Mark 1:21–28

REFLECTION

Careful readers of Mark's Gospel are put on notice from chapter 1 that the boundary-breaking, demon-dashing, law-transcending Son of God has arrived in the person of Jesus, and he expects of his followers far more than "amazement."

GARY W. CHARLES

We are struck by Jesus' word in response to the forces of evil that dominate the impure one—"Be silent" (v. 25). The verb literally demands an action like putting on a muzzle.

OFELIA ORTEGA

The authority here in Mark is not power, a different Greek word altogether, but a willingness or right that has everything to do with seeing justice served. This is what Jesus' ministry is about.

MIKE GRAVES

RESPONSE

Who are you in this week's reading from Mark?

PRAYER

You are an amazing God! Let me never forget that. Amen.

⇥ SUNDAY ⇤

Deuteronomy 18:15–20

REFLECTION

The meaning of the Hebrew root for prophet is uncertain but is most likely "one who is called" or "one who calls." The combination of "called" and "calls," though, is helpful in understanding the prophet's twofold role. First, the prophet is the moral and ethical agent who summons the people to repentance; second, the prophet anticipates what YHWH will do in the covenant.   DAVID FORNEY

The prophet Moses conveyed God's wisdom and love through more than proclamations and sermons. He organized the nomadic community in the wilderness. He established God's laws and judged disputes. He even fed the people and pastored their insecurities and concerns. What are the ways in which deeds are as prophetic as words? Where have all the prophets gone? Perhaps they are in the streets and soup kitchens, in the halls of justice and government. Perhaps they labor unrecognized by a world they are changing every day.

VERITY A. JONES

Psalm 111

REFLECTION

To live as if there were no God is to live in a space too small for our souls to grow and flourish. Praise the Lord then, for the works of God are great, and there is great delight in studying them in the company of the faithful (v. 2).   THOMAS D. PARKER

Faith in Christ means letting our lives be shaped by taking God's love to heart. We receive love by becoming loving, just as we receive grace by becoming gracious.   THOMAS D. PARKER

The psalmist sings praise that rises from the inner seat of courage and passion, of appetites and emotions, praise uttered deep from her heart. Praising with clarity and brilliance, like that of a full moon's reflection on a still evening lake, abundant joy resounds.   ANNE H. K. APPLE

1 Corinthians 8:1–13

REFLECTION

Paul's point is that when we hurt others, we hurt Christ himself because we cause pain in his body, the church. To hurt those for whom Christ died is to commit sin. Above all else, we are called to show reconciling love in the church, and that has a direct bearing on what we do and how we do it.   V. BRUCE RIGDON

Mark 1:21–28

REFLECTION

So what is one in our time to make of these ancient accounts of Jesus' healing the afflicted, sick, deranged? First of all, one must note with seriousness the prominence of healing in Jesus' ministry. Mark, more than any other Gospel writer, emphasizes Jesus' miraculous power to heal and to exorcise. Of the eighteen miracles recorded in Mark, thirteen have to do with healing, and four of the thirteen are exorcisms. If nothing else, the early introduction of Jesus' healing power and the dominance of healing among the miracle stories suggest again what the Scriptures had been hinting all along; that is, the intractable relation between religion and health.   P.C. ENNISS

RESPONSE

Do you consider yourself to be a prophet, one who speaks on behalf of God?

PRAYER

Give me the words to speak of your majesty, even if I am the only one who hears. Amen.

THE WEEK LEADING UP TO THE

❧ *Fifth Sunday after* ☙ *the Epiphany*

Isaiah 40:21–31

Have you not known? Have you not heard?
The LORD is the everlasting God,
   the Creator of the ends of the earth.
He does not faint or grow weary;
   his understanding is unsearchable.
. . . .
those who wait for the LORD shall renew their strength,
   they shall mount up with wings like eagles,
they shall run and not be weary,
   they shall walk and not faint. (vv. 28, 31)

Psalm 147:1–11, 20c

Praise the LORD!
How good it is to sing praises to our God;
   for he is gracious, and a song of praise is fitting. (v. 1)

1 Corinthians 9:16–23

If I proclaim the gospel, this gives me no ground
for boasting, for an obligation is laid on me, and woe
   to me if I do not proclaim the gospel! (v. 16)

Mark 1:29–39

Now Simon's mother-in-law was in bed with a fever, and
they told [Jesus] about her at once. He came and took her by
the hand and lifted her up. Then the fever left her, and she
began to serve them. That evening, at sundown, they brought
to him all who were sick or possessed with demons. And the
whole city was gathered around the door. (vv. 30–33)

❖ MONDAY ❖

Isaiah 40:21–31

REFLECTION

God's transcendence and immanence are, at the end of the
poem, the word of hope for all who believe their plight to be
hidden and disregarded (v. 27). In Isaiah's contemplation of
God in relation to humanity, we see a tapestry of good news
that shows the way the exhausted, faint, powerless, and weary
renew their strength, mount up with wings like eagles, run
without growing weary, walk without fainting (v. 31). The way,
the poet says, is to wait (v. 31) for the Creator who gathers the
lambs and does not faint or grow weary in doing so.

DAVID FORNEY

We come to know how God works in the world through
years of living with God and God's people. Years of exploring,
seeking, reflecting, and acting with God. Over time, through
Bible study, worship, practices of faith like hospitality and
forgiveness, stewardship and service, we come to a place of
knowing God's ways, even if we cannot sufficiently put words
to it.   VERITY A. JONES

RESPONSE

How do we live in a world where we have to live by the rules
of the authorities and yet, at the same time, claim Christ as our
only authority?

PRAYER

You do not faint or grow weary; your understanding is
unsearchable. You give power to the faint, and you strengthen
the powerless. Amen.

✦ TUESDAY ✦

Isaiah 40:21–31

REFLECTION

The faint and the powerless will receive new strength and power. Times are so difficult and the challenges so severe that even the young will faint and grow weary. Hope may be hard to sustain, but if they depend on God and wait and trust in their own story, they will receive the ability to meet the challenges and, indeed, to rise above them.   RICHARD A. PUCKETT

Three things come to mind as we look at this text: (1) we are theological amnesiacs; (2) the psalmist reminds us that God really is in charge; and (3) only when we feel weak and helpless, whether young or old, are we vulnerable enough to experience the power and grace of a God who "raises us up on eagle's wings." So, this text is about us, about God and what God does with us when all we seem to be is down.   WILLIAM J. CARL III

RESPONSE

Is there someone close to you who feels lost and alone? How can these words from Isaiah be a comfort and strength?

PRAYER

As we wait for you, renew our strength, so that we may mount up with wings like eagles, run and not be weary, walk and not faint. Amen.

→ WEDNESDAY ←

Psalm 147:1–11, 20c

REFLECTION

Christians should never forget that there is nothing ungracious about nature or unnatural about grace. "Praise the LORD! How good it is to sing praises to our God; for [God] is gracious, and a song of praise is fitting" (v. 1).   THOMAS D. PARKER

Captivated with our own creativity and control, we frequently become oblivious to our capacity to become agents of God's grace and peace in this world. Consumed with our own creativity and control, we forget that it was God who after crafting, perused the created order and said, "It is good." In our own foolishness, we rush to the front of the line to take a turn at playing God.   ANNE H. K. APPLE

RESPONSE

There are so many competitive events in our society. How can we compete, but avoid the sense of always having to be a "winner" in the eyes of the world?

PRAYER

How good it is to sing praises to our God; for God is gracious, and a song of praise is fitting (Ps. 147:1). Amen.

❧ THURSDAY ❧

Psalm 147:1–11, 20c

REFLECTION

Each day, human understanding dresses up in what is measurable. We plan worship with a measurable time, which ultimately limits praise offered through song, prayer, and proclamation of the word. It's likely that if we were to stand in Abram's sandals, we'd want a measurable accounting and report of the names of the stars. Our sinful nature is to bundle God's mysteries into neatly wrapped packages tied tightly with rigid doctrine and time constraints.   ANNE H. K. APPLE

When we stop and think about how the words we speak and the actions we will perform will affect one another and the Lord's ongoing creation, we glorify God. When we direct all of our words and deeds in the spirit of God's peace, faithfulness, and steadfast love . . . the Lord delights. Praise the Lord!

ANNE H. K. APPLE

RESPONSE

Is there a sense of gratitude in your worship service? Where is it missing? How can that be changed—and should it be?

PRAYER

Great are you, our Lord, and abundant in power; your understanding is beyond measure! Amen.

✢ FRIDAY ✢

1 Corinthians 9:16–23

REFLECTION

For Paul, how the community orders its life and how members
relate to each other are part and parcel of the proclamation of
God's reconciliation of the world. The church is a community
that God calls into existence to incarnate, live out, and proclaim
this new reality. But this requires that in Christ people find the
radical freedom to identify fully with others, to become as they
are, and thus to experience a genuine transformation of the self.

V. BRUCE RIGDON

Paul clearly does not expect everyone to agree. Instead, he asks
something of both groups (the strong and the weak), which
he hopes will make it possible for all of them to move forward
together. What he asks is that those on each side identify with
those on the other side, in order to become as if they were the
ones with whom they disagreed. This will not involve a change
in conviction, at least not at first, but it means that they are to
recognize what it would mean to act in behalf of those to whom
they are opposed.

V. BRUCE RIGDON

RESPONSE

How do we agree to disagree without holding grudges, or
pronouncing judgment?

PRAYER

Keep me open minded; to know when to learn from an
opposing viewpoint, and when to stand firm in what I think
and believe. Amen.

✦ SATURDAY ✦

Mark 1:29–39

REFLECTION

Simon's mother-in-law interprets the gift that she has received; her service cannot be understood as a woman's menial work under the domination of lazy males, but as a true messianic ministry, creator of Jesus' new family. For that reason, this woman is Jesus' first servant and joins him in the radical announcement, in action, of the kingdom of God, his first deacon.   OFELIA ORTEGA

After Simon's mother-in-law is restored to health, she serves. This is how Jesus himself will live and what all of his followers will be called to do (10:45). By way of contrast, Simon, who stands for all of the disciples, does nothing in this text other than to request, or perhaps compel, Jesus to come back from his time of praying so that more healing may take place.

MIKE GRAVES

God knew the human need for nearness. Jesus is the incarnation of God's love, which makes it all the more demanding (if frightening) to realize that for some people, we are the only Jesus they will ever meet.   P. C. ENNISS

RESPONSE

Do you consider the so-called menial work you do to be a ministry offered in the name of Christ?

PRAYER

Take away my sense of grudging when it comes to ongoing tasks that bring little reward. Amen.

✣ SUNDAY ✣

Isaiah 40:21–31

REFLECTION

God created all of these wondrous things we cannot even begin
to fathom fully, but we ought to be thankful that this God, who
exists beyond our imagining, still cares for each one, "calling
them all by name" (v. 26).   VERITY A. JONES

When the poet bids us to lift up our eyes on high, we see that
the One who is Wholly Other is also the One who numbers and
names us all because, in sovereignty, not one thing in creation is
missing or lost.   DAVID FORNEY

Psalm 147:1–11, 20c

REFLECTION

God's work in the realm of nature and God's work the realm
of human history are not two but one. The world is made for
the gifts of grace bestowed in it, while the grace of God in the
history of human salvation fulfills the purpose of God for all
creation.   THOMAS D. PARKER

The ultimate fruit of the spirit that comes from such connection
is that of hope. This is not hope in the sense of a shallow
confidence that everything will work out as we expect, or even
well. It is the deep hope born out of a confidence in God's care
for each one of us and throughout the created order.
                                  ELIZABETH C. KNOWLTON

1 Corinthians 9:16–23

REFLECTION

In a world as conflicted and violent as ours, if the church were
to be a place where Christians learned to identify with their

opponents and to experience God's power to bring about transformation, the church would realize its calling to be a sign of hope and a witness to God's offer of life to the world.

V. BRUCE RIGDON

While Paul fully understands that salvation is God's gift and that he cannot achieve it through his own effort, he also knows that those who fail to live out the pattern of Christ's death can forfeit the blessings of salvation. Thus he "becomes all things," not to gain salvation for himself, but as a means of embodying the release of self for the well-being of the other. In this way, he becomes a fellow sharer in the gospel. STEVEN J. KRAFTCHICK

Mark 1:29–39

REFLECTION

Jesus doesn't want to be locked into a sacred structure. Here he is, for this he has come: "Let us go on to the neighboring towns" (1:38). The missionary work is extended; the disciples are those on the road, the outpost of the kingdom of love and justice.

OFELIA ORTEGA

This description of Jesus at prayer does not seem to be a "precious moments" image, suitable for framing. Rather, the disciples seem to have discovered Jesus in a time of his own searching, even as the disciples inform him, "Everyone is searching for you" (v. 37). MIKE GRAVES

RESPONSE

Who taught you how to pray? What do you remember about the way you learned to pray as a child?

PRAYER

I thank you, Lord, with the heart of a child. Amen.

❧ *Sixth Sunday after* ❧ *the Epiphany*

2 Kings 5:1–14

[Naaman] turned and went away in a rage. But his servants
approached and said to him, "Father, if the prophet had
commanded you to do something difficult, would you not
have done it? How much more, when all he said to you was,
'Wash, and be clean'?" (vv. 12b–13)

Psalm 30

Sing praises to the LORD, O you his faithful ones,
    and give thanks to his holy name.
For his anger is but for a moment;
    his favor is for a lifetime.
Weeping may linger for the night,
    but joy comes with the morning. (vv. 4–5)

1 Corinthians 9:24–27

Do you not know that in a race the runners all compete, but only
one receives the prize? Run in such a way that you may win it.
Athletes exercise self-control in all things; they do it to receive a
perishable wreath, but we an imperishable one. (vv. 24–25)

Mark 1:40–45

A leper came to him begging him, and kneeling he said
to him, "If you choose, you can make me clean." Moved with
pity, Jesus stretched out his hand and touched him, and said
to him, "I do choose. Be made clean!" Immediately the
leprosy left him, and he was made clean. After sternly
warning him he sent him away at once. (vv. 40–43)

✢ MONDAY ✢

2 Kings 5:1–14

REFLECTION

Humanity's struggle with suffering is grueling. It taxes us when we learn of pain and suffering in the world, it exhausts us to witness the suffering of another, and it is acute when we suffer personally. And when we suffer over an extended period of time, relief becomes our sole desire. Understandably, when we experience continual suffering, we will try every possible remedy that might bring comfort. Ideally, we would like to control when and in what ways relief comes, yet true healing lies in God's providence and not in our schemes.

DAVID FORNEY

Sometimes God asks you to do something too, especially to help bring about your salvation and cleansing. Do not worry; this is not salvation by works. God is still the one doing the saving and the cleaning. But we still have to step forward and admit we need it; in other words, we still have to repent.

WILLIAM J. CARL III

We are called to meet God, if not halfway, somewhere along the way. No wonder Paul says in Philippians 2:12, "Work out your own salvation with fear and trembling." WILLIAM J. CARL III

RESPONSE

Do you believe in miracles? How would you define a miracle?

PRAYER

I am willing to meet you somewhere along the way; keep nudging me closer to you. Amen.

✣ TUESDAY ✣

Psalm 30

REFLECTION

Any of us may be asking the question, "Is that all there is?" without being aware of it. Interrupted by pain, however, the question bursts forth powerfully and, with the question, the possibility of a faithful answer. Many things can suddenly break open protective shells of self-sufficiency. Psalm 30 mentions two of them: foes and ills. Foes threaten the peace anyone needs to attend to the daily business of living. Ills threaten the prosperity and health anyone needs to have resources and energy to work and to love gladly. THOMAS D. PARKER

When we've wept through the night, unable to breathe through our noses or see through swollen eyes, with a piercing glimpse of the Divine, we long for the joy that comes in the morning. As God's people we resist worldly ways through prayer, listening for the small voice that first cried out from the poverty of a manger. ANNE H. K. APPLE

RESPONSE

Do the words of Psalm 30 bring you comfort? Would you offer them as words of comfort to someone who is grieving?

PRAYER

For those who are weeping this night, may joy come with the morning. Amen.

✦ WEDNESDAY ✦

Psalm 30

REFLECTION

At Sunday lunches and meals for the homeless hosted in fellowship halls, despair can hover under a veil of shallowness. "Hi!" "How are you?" "Fine." Despair can even paralyze one's ability to cry to the Lord. The Lord alone, who crafted us in our mothers' womb, knows the language of repeated cries but also the nature of humanity to live numbly, afraid to cry. In despair, we are empowered by the psalmist to cry, "O Lord, be my helper!" (v. 10). The church is called by God and empowered by the Holy Spirit to make a way for God's people to dare and cry to the Lord, "What profit is there in my death? . . . Will the dust praise you?" (v. 9).   ANNE H. K. APPLE

The secret of faith is placing the negations of life within the bigger picture of God's creative goodwill.   THOMAS D. PARKER

RESPONSE

Do you often greet people with the words, "How are you?" Can you think of another way to greet someone without asking a question that is so overused?

PRAYER

When the sorrows of life seem greater than I can handle, keep my sight focused on a larger picture, the story of your grace unending. Amen.

✣ THURSDAY ✣

1 Corinthians 9:24–27

REFLECTION

If God became flesh and dwelt among us, perhaps serious thought about living in the flesh with self-control and carefully organized discipline can be a theologically serious way of living in the context of the great game of life God has invited us to play.

VERNON K. ROBBINS

Christianity is not a series of ideas to be held in the mind, analyzed in the classroom, or defended in the marketplace. Christianity is, above all else, a life to be lived.

V. BRUCE RIGDON

[Paul's] preaching of the Christ event must be applied to himself as well as to others. Otherwise, even if others respond to the message, it will have been worthless to Paul himself.

STEVEN J. KRAFTCHICK

RESPONSE

Recall a sermon that meant a great deal to you, and think about why it did.

PRAYER

Let my life be a living sermon of gratitude and praise. Amen.

✦ FRIDAY ✦

Mark 1:40–45

REFLECTION

It is as if Jesus himself had to learn: he has started a movement of the kingdom, and he has to wait for the reactions.

OFELIA ORTEGA

The centuries since Jesus' days on earth do seem to have produced some consensus on which most modern, as well as ancient, minds agree. For example, there exists a real, though not yet fully understood, relationship between mind and body— belief and health, the spiritual and the physical. The old dichotomies between body and spirit are questioned, if not challenged.

P. C. ENNISS

While Jesus surely was moved by pity for the leper, it is perfectly human that his act of healing was also motivated partially by anger at a social system that demonized and excluded an entire group of human beings guilty of nothing more than being "different."

P. C. ENNISS

RESPONSE

When is anger the proper response to a situation?

PRAYER

Life is too short to be forever angry; but let me know the times when it is the right response. Amen.

✢ SATURDAY ✢

Mark 1:40–45

REFLECTION

As a result of Jesus' radical invitation to the kingdom, and the manifestation of his disruptive, but liberative power, the leper is the first of the evangelists, that is to say, the first of those who devote their lives to the service of the new liberating action of Jesus.   OFELIA ORTEGA

Instead of Jesus being "moved with pity" (v. 41), some manuscripts read "moved with anger." Arguing that the so-called harder reading is usually preferred, and noting the stern warning Jesus issues in verse 43, some prefer the latter translation. Questions most definitely arise in the light of this possibility: Is Jesus angry with the man? With being interrupted once again? Angry with the disease itself, which separates people from society? Angry with the interpretation of the law that requires a statement of cleanness?   MIKE GRAVES

RESPONSE

Why do you think the leper disobeyed Christ's command to keep silent? Do you think the leper's was the proper response?

PRAYER

When it comes to offering you praise, let me never be silent! Amen.

2 Kings 5:1–14

REFLECTION

We all want to be cured by the wave of a wand over the spot of affliction. We all want to be able to cure like this. Both caregivers and care receivers in congregations would prefer this kind of healing, no doubt. But the long road to healing is neither quick nor glamorous; it can be as tedious as bathing in the Jordan seven times.

VERITY A. JONES

Some human beings respond to God's grace with thankfulness and praise; others demonstrate the ability of human beings to pervert and use God's grace for selfish goals. Regardless of the human response, YHWH's will ultimately has its way in human affairs.

RICHARD A. PUCKETT

Psalm 30

REFLECTION

One issue that often arises during illness or suffering is the unveiling of previously unconscious theologies. Intellectually one may believe that illness is random and not related to a particular person's worth or goodness. We might feel our faith is broad enough to tolerate the randomness of the created order. However, when pain and suffering strikes in unanticipated ways, we can find ourselves outraged that this suffering has come to us or to those we love. Following that initial reaction, we can then become consumed with guilt over our own lack of faith and confidence.

ELIZABETH C. KNOWLTON

Psalm 30 celebrates the saving action of God in the present. Even though we still await the hoped-for fulfillment, the present is not empty.

THOMAS D. PARKER

1 Corinthians 9:24–27

REFLECTION

The games known to Paul (Olympian and Isthmian) were all individual competitions. One can imagine what Paul might have done with this metaphor, had he known about the special challenges and demands of team sports.　　V. BRUCE RIGDON

Because the church is itself part and parcel of the good news, it matters very much how Christians live the Christian life with one another.　　V. BRUCE RIGDON

Mark 1:40–45

REFLECTION

In a perilous act of solidarity, instead of confirming the man's exclusion by shunning him, Jesus reaches out and symbolically draws him in. He shatters the traditional boundaries of purity and in the process rewrites the book on the nature of God's beloved community.　　GARY W. CHARLES

In disobeying Jesus' command, the leper has obeyed the truth and thus opens a way of hope in the process of oppression of our world.　　OFELIA ORTEGA

RESPONSE

When was the last time you reached out, unafraid, to someone who was considered "unclean" by today's standards?

PRAYER

Give me a spirit that is tireless in running toward the goal of a righteous life. Amen.

❧ *Seventh Sunday after* ✤ *the Epiphany*

Isaiah 43:18–25

Do not remember the former things,
    or consider the things of old.
I am about to do a new thing;
    now it springs forth, do you not perceive it? (v. 18)

Psalm 41

Happy are those who consider the poor;
    the LORD delivers them in the day of trouble.
The LORD protects them and keeps them alive;
    they are called happy in the land.
    You do not give them up to the will of their enemies.
The LORD sustains them on their sickbed;
    in their illness you heal all their infirmities. (vv. 1–3)

2 Corinthians 1:18–22

As surely as God is faithful, our word to you has not been "Yes and No." For the Son of God, Jesus Christ, whom we proclaimed among you . . . was not "Yes and No"; but in him it is always "Yes." For in him every one of God's promises is a "Yes." (vv. 18–20)

Mark 2:1–12

"Which is easier, to say to the paralytic, 'Your sins are forgiven,' or to say, 'Stand up and take your mat and walk'? But so that you may know that the Son of Man has authority on earth to forgive sins"—he said to the paralytic—"I say to you, stand up, take your mat and go to your home." (vv. 9–11).

✦ MONDAY ✦

Isaiah 43:18–25

REFLECTION

Our rituals and spatial configurations are so rigid that we rarely discover the faith afresh, renewed. Faith—and as a regrettable byproduct, faith communities—become more about stability, about that which is familiar, common and certain. God invites the community to see anew God's creation and redemption.

CARLOS F. CARDOZA-ORLANDI

Our most joyous memories may also be our most painful ones. The recollection of lost loved ones can bring fresh loneliness and grief. The memory of past success, contrasted with present failure, can drive us to despair. The point, for the prophet, is that the community must not cling to its past, either in resignation or in nostalgia, but must instead turn toward God's future. The Lord is "about to do a new thing" (43:19).

STEVEN S. TUELL

RESPONSE

Ponder a memory that was both joyous and painful. Which emotion is the overriding one for you at this moment?

PRAYER

Life can be such a mixture of sorrow and joy; and both can give meaning to life. May I be able to embrace both sides of the coin. Amen.

✣ TUESDAY ✣

Psalm 41

REFLECTION

Only those who consider the poor can be truly happy. It is not Israel's deliverance from the sorrow and plight of the poor that causes happiness, but rather the deliverance of the poor in their "day of trouble" (v. 1). Only this can be the cause of Israel's joy. There is no complex analysis here, no weighing of cost or benefits for acting on behalf of the poor, but rather a simple proclamation of what must be done and the joy that comes with having done it.   JOSEPH MONTI

This is not a prayer of a saint or someone we assume even to be very spiritually mature. This is a prayer of a sinner, a person in pain, one who is ready to try any port in a storm. This bargaining with God, so common in the psalms and the entire Hebrew Bible, has the air of the comedic amid the tragic. But that is precisely the point. The psalmist prays for a return to goodness—however flawed—not perfection.   JOSEPH MONTI

RESPONSE

Is it possible to do good deeds without any sense of self-satisfaction—and is it necessary to feel so?

PRAYER

Happy are those who consider the poor; the LORD delivers them in the day of trouble (Ps. 41:1). Amen.

Psalm 41

REFLECTION

Despite the unloveliness of the disheveled, the frequent ingratitude of the poor, the incorrigible circumstances of the lowly, the church will always be drawn to them (vv. 1–3). This is not because of our churning guilt or genteel discomfiture at their state, wanting to "fix" it. It is because we are but one step removed from being the lowly ourselves. More important, it is because our fate is tied up with theirs. Psalm 41 reminds us that we are all in "this" together, the gift of life, which God gives.

DALE ROSENBERGER

As we connect across our chasms in fortune, aside from the caprice of our estate in this world, we enter into a God-intended state of blessedness and favor. We can look to one another as the seasons of life shift and our fortunes with them, finding a steady center that buffers the extremes of individual circumstance. In this we experience that God does not abandon us, because God's own have shown up when it matters most, demonstrating spiritual solidarity through the kind of God-connectedness that makes a transforming impression upon people.

DALE ROSENBERGER

RESPONSE

What qualifications do you consider when choosing how to use your resources for the charity of those in need?

PRAYER

I cannot solve all of the world's problems, nor help everyone who asks me for help; but grant me wisdom to do what I can, when I can, for the right reasons. Amen.

✢ THURSDAY ✢

2 Corinthians 1:18–22

REFLECTION

How extraordinary! If our very words and deeds are the gospel of Jesus Christ (cf. 1 Cor. 2:2), we can be God's very voice spoken to others.   JOHN W. RIGGS

In this simple correlation between a God who is utterly trustworthy and the human self that trusts wholeheartedly, lies the foundation of Christian life.   JOHN W. RIGGS

Paul starts with the claim that the gospel that preaches the true God is always a matter of Yes, not No, and certainly not Maybe. The good news is good because it always declares God's unswerving affirmation of God's creation and of God's people.

DAVID L. BARTLETT

RESPONSE

In this past week, have you served as God's mouthpiece?

PRAYER

May the words of my heart, and the resulting actions, speak volumes about my love for you, O God. Amen.

✦ FRIDAY ✦

Mark 2:1–12

REFLECTION

Ironically, the scribes may have been more aware than we are
of the profound interplay between the individual human body
and the societal norms in which it makes its way. Is the Galilean
paralytic a sinner, an individual who has chosen to forsake
his God–given capacity to work the land, or is he a reflection
of a social system that offers him nothing but misery for his
labor? Is the young American woman with an eating disorder
a sinner, an individual who simply chooses to abuse her God-
given body, or is she the reflection of a society that celebrates
a distorted female image and spends billions in trying to
achieve it? Whether in the first century or the twenty-first, the
interconnected relationships between sin and sickness, the
individual and society, and religion and politics are complex.

JERRY IRISH

The Spirit is present in the margins of society, including among
stigmatized and rejected sinners. The Spirit works for holistic
healing in and among our communities through those who
follow the lead of the Spirit.   EUNJOO MARY KIM

RESPONSE

How is your church prepared to meet the needs of those who
are physically or mentally disabled?

PRAYER

I pray for a heart that lives by walking in the shoes of others.
Amen.

✦ SATURDAY ✦

Mark 2:1–12

REFLECTION

The story invites us to ponder the relationship between sin and sickness or disability. Some behaviors, such as drug abuse or promiscuity, directly lead to illnesses, but sometimes sources of illness are beyond our control. In declaring forgiveness, Jesus first restores the paralytic's relationship with God, thus disputing the common belief that sin caused the paralysis. The passage emphasizes the connection among faith, forgiveness, and healing.   AL MASTERS

If we, as members of the mainline Christian church or as a privileged group of believers, limit our understanding and experience of God's revelation to our fragmented knowledge and imperfect language, with pride for being experts in knowing God, we may overlook God's amazing redeeming acts of reconciliation and healing among the people in the communities that we do not belong to.   EUNJOO MARY KIM

RESPONSE

How can we open ourselves to God's forgiveness and to forgiving others?   AL MASTERS

PRAYER

You are amazing, God! How is it that I often fail to see this? Amen.

✧ SUNDAY ✧

Isaiah 43:18–25

REFLECTION

Repentance is the gospel call not only for individuals but also for nations. It is a personal and national ethic marked by a willingness to turn in another direction, to reorder both policies and patterns of living. Repentance is an interior conversion that finds expression in social justice.

ROSS MACKENZIE

God promises forgiveness "for my own sake." We are forgiven, not because of who we are, but because of who God is. Our repentance is always a response to what God has done. God's word of acceptance and forgiveness comes first. STEVEN S. TUELL

Psalm 41

REFLECTION

Tellingly, before describing sins against him in the form of hateful mistreatment and persecution by those who seek his demise, the psalmist confesses his own sinfulness before God (v. 4).We never go wrong in this instinct: knowing ourselves as sinners before examining the sins of others. . . . Awareness of our own sinfulness—leading with our confession despite how badly we have been wronged—is the fountainhead in living and showing forth forgiveness.

DALE ROSENBERGER

2 Corinthians 1:18–22

REFLECTION

The Christian gospel ultimately speaks not a "Yes and No," but simply a divine "Yes."We learn to trust God, not because of what we might avoid and what we might receive, but simply because our faith has known a God so unequivocally good to

us that we, out of sheer thanksgiving for such goodness, want
to love God back by loving and caring for all whom God also
loves, our neighbors, here and everywhere.   JOHN W. RIGGS

So of course Yes must be made flesh, or it morphs into No.
After all, the primal Word did not just stay on the page or
ringing in the air. The Word did become flesh and dwells
among us even to this day. And so if God's word in Christ is
Yes, then helping that Yes get fleshed out in the lives of those in
pain, need, or trouble is the job description for every follower
of the Yes-sayer.   MARTHA STERNE

Mark 2:1–12

REFLECTION

When readers expect Jesus to say something about his disease,
Jesus tells the man that his sins are forgiven. It is not that his
sins will be forgiven only after he visits the religious authorities
and completes a rite of purification; they are forgiven now.
Jesus does not draw the conclusion that this man was ill and
therefore had sinned, though such a conclusion would not have
been uncommon. Mark draws the reader's eye, not to the nature
of sin, but to the authority of Jesus to forgive it.

                                            GARY W. CHARLES

Can we trust healing and cure when they happen
simultaneously? Jesus did not ask which is easier to do, but
which is easier to say. Both forgiveness and healing are easy to
say, but both are also hard to do.   AL MASTERS

RESPONSE

Would you rather be forgiven or healed?

PRAYER

May my spirit be willing ground in which you can cultivate the
new things you desire to bring about. Amen.

❧ *Eighth Sunday after* ❦ *the Epiphany*

Hosea 2:14–20

I will make for you a covenant on that day with the
wild animals, the birds of the air, and the creeping things of the
ground; and I will abolish the bow, the sword, and war from the
land; and I will make you lie down in safety. And I will take
you for my wife forever. (vv. 18–19a)

Psalm 103:1–13, 22

Bless the LORD, O my soul,
 and all that is within me,
  bless his holy name.
Bless the LORD, O my soul,
 and do not forget all his benefit. (vv. 1–2)

2 Corinthians 3:1–6

You yourselves are our letter, written on our hearts,
to be known and read by all; and you show that you are a
letter of Christ, prepared by us, written not with ink but with
the Spirit of the living God, not on tablets of stone but on
tablets of human hearts. (vv. 2–3)

Mark 2:13–22

When the scribes of the Pharisees saw that he was eating
with sinners and tax collectors, they said to his disciples, "Why
does he eat with tax collectors and sinners?" When Jesus heard
this, he said to them, "Those who are well have no need of a
physician, but those who are sick; I have come to call not the
righteous but sinners." (vv. 16–17)

→ MONDAY ←

Hosea 2:14–20

REFLECTION

This steadfastness of God is at the heart of covenant. This is the case because when a covenant is made between God and God's people, the mutually binding agreement is made between parties who are not equals. The lack of parity between the parties pushes us to remember that redemption flows from God's grace and not from human effort. In the context of covenant, humans must never confuse faithfulness in fulfilling covenantal obligations with winning favor with God or manipulating God's love for humanity. God is the maker of the covenant, and God's covenant is inclusive and not limited to humanity.
MARCIA Y. RIGGS

The commitment of the Christian, therefore, is to face the class, sexual, and economic issues that separate people in society and to seek ways of providing for a community of mutual service and support along democratic lines.
ROSS MACKENZIE

RESPONSE

What is the difference between a covenant and a promise?

PRAYER

Let my love for you and my love for neighbor be inseparable. Amen.

✧ TUESDAY ✦

Psalm 103:1–13, 22

REFLECTION

This psalm is a study in the transformative power of praise within Christian community and how praise invariably strengthens and edifies all parties involved. Praise—whether of God or each other—is discouragingly rare in our world. What blessing that it is so firmly lodged at the center of who we are and what we do as the church. For just as someone will rightfully glow when praised at a job well done, a whole people will radiate light as the goodness of God is lifted up!

DALE ROSENBERGER

The psalmist's longing is full of wonder at how a Lord so elevated and mighty could also deign to be the same God who is personal and accessible. The psalmist cannot quite get over that, his incredulity further fueling his wonder. In this regard, the psalm anticipates a Messiah at once fully human, fully divine. The human desire to experience God, even more than knowing about God, points us toward the gift of the suffering-victorious Messiah whom the church affirms.

DALE ROSENBERGER

RESPONSE

Begin and end this day in praise; and let that become a habit!

PRAYER

Bless the Lord, O my soul, and all that is within me, bless God's holy name (Ps. 103:1). Amen.

❖ WEDNESDAY ❖

Psalm 103:1–13, 22

REFLECTION

"Benefits" are our due, and that is precisely what the psalmist most definitely wants to say is not the case, is not the manner in which God gives to us. We are *not* given what is due us; we do *not* receive what we have earned; we get much better than that!

PATRICK J. WILLSON

The psalmist understands our separation from God in terms of forgetting. Forgetting God's bounty, we may assume an accusing and angry God bent on exacting full compensation for every sin, every slight, every failure, every stupid thing we ever did. As if aware of that dreadful characterization of the OT God as angry, vengeful, and accusing, the psalmist engages in a profound remembering: You remember the law you have broken? Remember also the character of the Lord who gave it: gracious and merciful, slow to anger. Remember God's bounty and do not forget.

PATRICK J. WILLSON

RESPONSE

How does feeling that the world owes you something affect the way you approach life?

PRAYER

Lord, you give me so much more than I would ever ask for myself! Thank you. Amen.

✢ THURSDAY ✢

2 Corinthians 3:1–6

REFLECTION

Simply put, the inner, subjective experience of the Spirit forms a conversation partner with the outer, objective testimony of the Word, both authorities authorized by God. Between these two poles we must hammer out an adequate theology for our context.
JOHN W. RIGGS

Every human being, from the moment the umbilical cord is cut, is trying to find a way to attach and belong, while also being a separate person. One might dare to say the seekers of the day are exactly whom Jesus had in mind when he invited people to leave their mothers and fathers and journey with him in faith. Instead of church leaders moaning about the fluidity and fickleness of seekers in our day, would it be possible for us rather to imagine them as especially open to new paths of healing and forgiveness and a new heaven, new earth, new faith, just as Jesus prayed we all would over and over again?
MARTHA STERNE

RESPONSE

Write a letter of introduction about yourself.

PRAYER

Use me as a letter of introduction to my Savior, Jesus Christ. Amen.

⇢ FRIDAY ⇠

2 Corinthians 3:1–6

REFLECTION

The new covenant is written in flesh and blood by the Spirit of the living God. Here is an invitation to break free of arguing about this little point and that little point, and to remember the ways that people have seen this new covenant in Christ, in the lives of those around them, and in the grace God gives each of us, if we will but accept it. God making us competent is through the power of the Spirit, and not the letter.   MARTHA STERNE

Is the competence of those who minister responsible for the effective establishment of a new covenant in human hearts? "No," Paul says. Only the competence of God to bring about a new order of creation makes anyone sufficient for a ministry of service. God's sufficiency honors weakness as a source of life. How can highly competitive, driven people grasp the plausibility of this claim?   MARY LIN HUDSON

RESPONSE

Are there ways in which your weaknesses actually make you stronger as a person of faith?

PRAYER

Use my weaknesses and my strengths to serve you. Amen.

✢ SATURDAY ✤

Mark 2:13–22

REFLECTION

If Jesus is our Epiphany, our revelation of God, then his table
fellowship reveals a God who welcomes all of us without
reference to our social status. Where we were born, who our
parents are, our physical appearance, how many degrees we
hold, how much money we make, what we have accomplished
in life, how old or healthy we are—these are not criteria for
receiving God's interest and compassion. All of us are welcome
at God's table. And so is everyone else.   JERRY IRISH

New life in Christ is reorientation of mind, heart, and lifestyle.
Surrender and lordship do not come easily for us. We tend to
follow Christ at a safe distance, maintain control, and integrate
our faith into older, established patterns of thinking and
behavior. But the church that is not culturally bound finds new
wineskins in every generation. The essence of Christianity does
not change, but the cultural wrappings are always changing.

                                                    AL MASTERS

RESPONSE

When you sit at the table of Christ, do you think you will be
surprised by those who are gathered at the table with you?
Whom do you hope to see there by your side?

PRAYER

Is there someone I need to forgive, Lord? What is holding
me back? Amen.

✦ SUNDAY ✦

Hosea 2:14–20

REFLECTION

So far as we know, Hosea was the first to apply this image to Israel and YHWH. The marriage metaphor can be used negatively (see Ezek. 16 and 23) or positively (see Rev. 21:9–27). However, it must never be forgotten that it is a metaphor! In no sense does the tormented, topsy-turvy relationship described in Hosea 1–3 represent a picture of what marriage is or ought to be. Rather, through the window of the stormiest of human passions, the text strives to give us a means to understand ourselves and our God.   STEVEN S. TUELL

Psalm 103:1–13, 22

REFLECTION

The overall message of the psalm, then, is that human weakness and disobedience cannot permanently destroy the family bond between God and Israel. The bond remains, waiting to be enjoyed by a future faithful community. God remains faithful and steadfast, even if a particular Israelite community does not.
                    ROBERT R. WILSON

This great psalm of praise ends where it began. The Lord is to be blessed in all of the Lord's works, and everything—all in all—is a work of the Lord. All places are the Lord's dominion (v. 22). No other divine power is necessary than the *hesed* (steadfast love) of God's presence—God-with-us as the compassionate Other, like us and not like us at the same time.   JOSEPH MONTI

2 Corinthians 3:1–6

REFLECTION

No matter what our favorite biblical fight or passage, Paul invites all of us to look for the spirit of Christ in the ways we understand Scripture and, more important, in the way we live our lives.   MARTHA STERNE

As human hearts are made alive by the Spirit of Christ, people themselves stand as living witnesses to the glory of God and commend the ones who provided the ministry of service for them to enter into this new creation. Letters no longer have power to confer favor when God's favor is alive in human hearts. Even now, we are the public letters of commendation toward God's great sufficiency, written by the crucified and resurrected Christ by the Spirit.   MARY LIN HUDSON

Mark 2:13–22

REFLECTION

For Jesus, there are no boundaries between insiders and outsiders, because God's grace and mercy are not limited to insiders who are righteous, but rather are extended to outsiders marginalized as sinners in society. By freely crossing boundaries between the community and the rest of the world, Jesus reveals the presence and work of God's Spirit, who makes the human community a whole.   EUNJOO MARY KIM

RESPONSE

Who are the tax collectors and sinners of today? Do you consider yourself to be among their number?

PRAYER

Christ, erase the boundaries that separate your people from one another, that we may truly be one in you. Amen.

THE WEEK LEADING UP TO THE

❧ *Ninth Sunday after* ❦
the Epiphany

Deuteronomy 5:12–15

Observe the sabbath day and keep it holy,
as the Lord your God commanded you. Six days
you shall labor and do all your work. But the seventh
day is a sabbath to the Lord your God. (vv. 12–14a)

Psalm 81:1–10

I am the Lord your God,
  who brought you up out of the land of Egypt.
  Open your mouth wide and I will fill it. (v. 10)

2 Corinthians 4:5–12

For we do not proclaim ourselves; we proclaim Jesus Christ as
Lord and ourselves as your slaves for Jesus' sake. For it is the God
who said, "Let light shine out of darkness," who has shone in our
hearts to give the light of the knowledge of the glory of God in the
face of Jesus Christ. But we have this treasure in clay jars, so that it
may be made clear that this extraordinary power belongs to God
and does not come from us. (vv. 5–7)

Mark 2:23–3:6

Then he said to them, "The sabbath was made for
humankind, and not humankind for the sabbath; so the
Son of Man is lord even of the sabbath." (2:27–28)

⁜ MONDAY ⁜

Deuteronomy 5:12–15

REFLECTION

Rest is not simply the cessation of work; rest as a practice of
faithfulness requires that the doing of work is replaced by the
worshiping of God. A community at rest keeping the Sabbath
holy is a community that is worshiping God for the purpose of
thanking God for deliverance and redemption. A practice that
embodies this meaning of rest is worship—worship marked by
thanksgiving and rituals that evoke historical memory of the
ways that God has delivered and redeemed us.

MARCIA Y. RIGGS

A community at rest keeping the Sabbath holy is a community
that respects interpersonal and interspecies relationships. A
practice that embodies this meaning of rest is hospitality, and
hospitality will be manifest through acts of care, service, and
justice toward those from whose labors we reap benefits or
over whom we have power. For if hospitality as described is
practiced over time, then hospitality that is in effect justice
making will become part of the character and actions of the
community all of the time. MARCIA Y. RIGGS

RESPONSE

If verse 12 demands that the Sabbath be observed and kept
holy, does that mean that all we do during the other six days is
unholy? CARLOS F. CARDOZA-ORLANDI

PRAYER

May my home and my heart be a place of hospitality for you,
and for others. Amen.

→ TUESDAY ←

Deuteronomy 5:12–15

REFLECTION

The discernment of the Holy in our vocation, of the relationship between the six days and the Sabbath in our daily life experiences, demands a time for rest, a time to be renewed. Sabbath is irrelevant without transcendence and meaning in our daily work!

CARLOS F. CARDOZA-ORLANDI

It is amazing: God demands time and space for us to deliberately rest. Focusing our attention and self on God prevents us from burnout and exploitation of others. While some may think that the Sabbath is a day for God, the Sabbath is commanded for our sake: to liberate us from being trapped in a loop of overanalysis and overwork in our vocation and, consequently, protect those who are intertwined with our vocation.

CARLOS F. CARDOZA-ORLANDI

RESPONSE

How do you keep the Sabbath holy on a regular basis?

PRAYER

You commanded us to keep the Sabbath holy. Thank you for making this a necessary part of our lives. Amen.

✣ WEDNESDAY ✣

Psalm 81:1–10

REFLECTION

How are we to live as inhabitants with others—those within our own community and, most especially, with travelers, strangers, and immigrants? The theology of dwelling raises profound questions of identity and character. Character is always intertwined with how we abide, interact, and dwell with others.

JOSEPH MONTI

Practically speaking, the church's faithful response has to do less with individual devotions at home than with pointed litanies prominent within our worship at the watershed moments in the church year, such as at the Sunday after our national Thanksgiving, the busiest shopping days of the year. No one will thank us for doing this—no one other than God.

DALE ROSENBERGER

By grounding the call to celebration in God's direct command, the psalmist suggests that worship and liturgy are not simply human activities. Rather, they are of divine origin. God mandates worship, provides an order for it, and in the Psalms even provides the words that are to be used in the process.

ROBERT R. WILSON

RESPONSE

How do you keep the Sabbath in the presence of the community of believers, and outside of this community?

PRAYER

Fill me as a mother bird fills her hungry babies, and let my mouth be open to receive your grace. Amen.

✦ THURSDAY ✦

2 Corinthians 4:5–12

REFLECTION

Paul wrote to the Corinthians that the power of the gospel, which constituted authentic Christian ministry centered on Jesus (cf. 2 Cor. 11:4), cannot be found in extraordinary human feats. Rather, the power belongs to a great God, and we, in contrast, bear this power in frail, earthen vessels. Unlike glass containers, which the ancients could melt and recast, earthen vessels were fragile and, once broken, were gone.

JOHN W. RIGGS

Christian life and discipleship are frequently confused with good citizenship, appropriate decorum, and following socially acceptable norms and lifestyle. Doing good seems to be a part of doing well.

MARTHA STERNE

This passage doesn't imply that the pain of suffering should not be a part of people's faith experience. It reveals that the resurrection life of Christ that is already at work in us continues even as we suffer.

MARY LIN HUDSON

RESPONSE

What kind of vessel are you? Glass? Ceramic? Wood?

PRAYER

May I empty myself so that I have more room for your Spirit to fill me to overflowing. Amen.

✥ FRIDAY ✥

2 Corinthians 4:5–12

REFLECTION

If you are looking at Jesus and passionate about the well-being of others, many things in your universe shift. You no longer worry so much about your own competence, for the "extraordinary" power comes from God, not from you. You may be tried and afflicted, but you are not crushed. You may be puzzled and perplexed at some turn of events or some strangeness or meanness in yourself or others, but you are not driven to despair. You may be persecuted, but you are not alone. You may be struck down, but you will not be destroyed.

MARTHA STERNE

Clay jars are concrete objects, which can be transposed onto the canvas of the listener's imagination through sensory language within the sermon. Clay jars are crafted by careful hands of a potter from a lump of cool, thick earth into something useful that can serve the needs of people. Once formed, shaped, fired, and cooled, the malleable substance becomes hard and brittle. Jars of clay are fragile, easily broken, dispensable. So are human bodies: useful, but full of vulnerability, susceptible to injury and even death. In every nation, bodies mangled and crushed by violence testify to the fragility of physical existence. Clay jars break easily.

MARY LIN HUDSON

RESPONSE

Have you ever felt complete despair? What got you through?

PRAYER

Let there be light—your light—in all the earth. Amen.

✦ SATURDAY ✦

Mark 2:23 – 3:6

REFLECTION

Keeping the Sabbath may deepen our awareness of God and thus heighten our awareness of human need and our own role in meeting that need. . . . On the other hand, keeping the Sabbath in a legalistic manner may inhibit that very divine-human interaction. As with any religious practice, what was meant to enhance our relation with God and neighbor can become idolatrous and inhumane.   JERRY IRISH

Jesus' anger at the Pharisees' hardness of heart is not a quick emotional reaction, but rather rises in depth from a feeling of tremendous sadness over how closed their hearts are against the will of God.   EUNJOO MARY KIM

RESPONSE

"We do not keep Sabbath; Sabbath keeps us!" How does that thought strike you?

PRAYER

Have I been too busy to notice the ways you bless my life? Then I shall strive to be less busy and more aware. Amen.

✢ SUNDAY ✢

Deuteronomy 5:12–15

REFLECTION

The Sabbath is also commanded to protect those abused and exploited by our misguided vocation and by those who do not have a vocation but have an income-oriented task totally submitted to the insatiable but mistaken values of wealth and prosperity typical of the global economy.

CARLOS F. CARDOZA-ORLANDI

Should empathy prove insufficient, the installation of Sabbath is made a divine commandment. No one is to be deprived of the God-given right to rest.   STEVEN S. TUELL

Sunday for Christians is a day to hear the God of creation calling them to celebrate the new creation. When the first Christians chose Sunday as their principal day of worship, commemorating Christ's resurrection, they laid aside the notion of enforced rest on the seventh day and stressed instead, on each first day of the week, the coming of a new age.

ROSS MACKENZIE

Psalm 81:1–10

REFLECTION

When worshipers gather on Sunday morning, is it in expectation that God speaks in this celebrative drama? Do they hope for a word from the One who pleads, "if you would but listen to me!" or are their hopes confined to more ordinary hopes, that the sermon will be interesting and not too long?

PATRICK J. WILLSON

2 Corinthians 4:5–12

REFLECTION

One way, then, that our mortal lives bear treasure is that they inwardly contain, in and to all our living moments, a divine revelation that is not ours to possess, any more than an earthen vessel can possess fresh water. We do not possess God. Yet our very lives, anywhere and at any moment, cannot fail to be the object of divine love.   JOHN W. RIGGS

The first words of the first creation—"let there be light"—are now echoed in the word God speaks to and through Paul: "Let light shine out of darkness!" And because the light shines in Paul's own heart, Paul can bring the light of the gospel to those who hear him.   DAVID L. BARTLETT

Mark 2:23–3:6

REFLECTION

Even the most ambitious career climber has moments of regret at the loss of relationships sacrificed for the job, the promotion, and the power they bring. Perhaps fear is also an underlying motif. We do not know how to be fluid, nimble, open to the transforming power of the Holy Spirit. We each find our own way to create control, erect boundaries and prejudices. We decide to whom we will minister and when and how and to what degree.   AL MASTERS

RESPONSE

Celebrate! Celebrate the joy that God has planted in the depths of your soul.

PRAYER

I celebrate the gift of who you are, O God, and who I am as your child. Amen.

❧ *Last Sunday after* ❦ *the Epiphany*

(Transfiguration Sunday)

2 Kings 2:1–12

Now when the LORD was about to take Elijah up to heaven by a whirlwind, Elijah and Elisha were on their way from Gilgal. Elijah said to Elisha, "Stay here; for the LORD has sent me as far as Bethel." But Elisha said, "As the LORD lives, and as you yourself live, I will not leave you." (vv. 1–2)

Psalm 50:1–6

The mighty one, God the LORD,
 speaks and summons the earth
 from the rising of the sun to its setting.
Out of Zion, the perfection of beauty,
 God shines forth. (vv. 1–2)

2 Corinthians 4:3–6

For it is the God who said, "Let light shine out of darkness," who has shone in our hearts to give the light of the knowledge of the glory of God in the face of Jesus Christ. (v. 6)

Mark 9:2–9

[Peter] did not know what to say, for they were terrified. Then a cloud overshadowed them, and from the cloud there came a voice, "This is my Son, the Beloved; listen to him!" Suddenly when they looked around, they saw no one with them anymore, but only Jesus. (vv. 6–8)

2 Kings 2:1–12

REFLECTION

Too many good-intentioned Christians seem willing to make do, to go without, to give without ceasing, while refusing the balm that they need. Whether driven by a culture of rugged individualism, an unhealthy self-denial, or a theology of scarcity, we are both convicted and inspired by Elisha's determination to follow Elijah through river and town until he receives what he knows he will need for his own ministry. Elisha's faithfulness to the process allows for his transformation. How too might we be transfigured by such faithful perseverance in our journeys with God and one another?

MARYANN MCKIBBEN DANA

Elisha is rewarded by the revelation of God bridging the boundaries between time and timelessness, endings and endlessness. Soon he finds that God's spirit remains and rests on him (2 Kgs. 2:14).We worry the spirit will leave us. The truth is that the spirit stays; it is we who must go. WM. LOYD ALLEN

RESPONSE

Are you as determined as Elijah to get what you need to be a more faithful follower of the One who leads you?

PRAYER

I am eternally grateful that your Spirit rests upon me. Amen.

✦ TUESDAY ✦

Psalm 50:1–6

REFLECTION

Many psalms represent the speech of the worshiping community, whether in lament, praise, or thanksgiving. This psalm, by contrast, is one that represents the speech of God alone. Sometimes it is necessary for us simply to remain silent before God. How else will we be or become and remain God's faithful, merciful ones (v. 5)? It is as if God is begging and demanding of us that we stop—now, at this very moment. Stop. Pray. Listen. Reflect. Listen, again. Perhaps now we will be empowered to hear and know at some deeper level how God wills for us to respond—and to do it.   CHARLES QUAINTANCE

A cringing response to judgment or the threat of judgment is our attempt to avoid bad feelings or other consequences of our behavior. The alternative for people of faith is to trust in the love of God and the promise that God's desire is that we should know salvation and live. As we trust God for life, we can face anything, including the consequences of our own behavior. We can mark well God's judgment, renew our commitment to following Jesus as the way of life, and see the promised salvation of God.   GEOFFREY M. ST. J. HOARE

RESPONSE

What brings you awe? Music? Art? Nature? Give a few examples.

PRAYER

The mighty one, God the LORD, speaks and summons the earth from the rising of the sun to its setting (Ps. 50:1). Amen.

→ WEDNESDAY ←

Psalm 50:1–6

REFLECTION

Faith is more than a matter of heart alone. The unique position of Transfiguration Sunday and its beautiful theophanies declares that the mountain is never the end of the journey. God does not gather us together just for a divine fireworks display, God always has something to say, usually something to ask.

BRIAN ERICKSON

There is room for both those whose eyes have been burned with the brightness of God's glory and those whose hearts have been burned by God's absence. Faith inspires both silence and song, and awe requires patience as much as proclamation.

BRIAN ERICKSON

The issue is not whether we believe the psalmist literally intended for us to hear the transfigured, risen Christ speaking in Psalm 50. Rather, the issue is whether we listen to God and change our lives, whether we become more Christ-like.

CHARLES QUAINTANCE

RESPONSE

What is God asking of you?

PRAYER

Inspire me in both silence and in song, in the name of the One who created all. Amen.

☩ THURSDAY ☩

2 Corinthians 4:3–6

REFLECTION

What illuminates Paul and shines through his words is the light
of the knowledge of the glory of God in the face of Jesus Christ.
This light does not demand that our reasoning be sound or
our lives be perfect or our faith be immovable. This light is not
something that shines on us but through us. This light reveals,
not so much who we are, but whose we are, and has the power
to transform us. This light is the glory of God, the glory of
Christ.   SHAWNTHEA MONROE-MUELLER

The gospel isn't about us. It is about Jesus the Christ, "who is
the image of God" (v. 4). . . . Note how in the story of Jesus'
transfiguration all eyes and ears are left on him. Glory belongs
there and not on our pulpits, our politics, or our current church
projects. Paul preaches Jesus Christ, not Paul.

G. OLIVER WAGNER

RESPONSE

How is the image of God found in you?

PRAYER

Your glory gives me reason to live my life to the fullest. Amen.

☩ FRIDAY ☩

Mark 9:2–9

REFLECTION

The necessity of the passion remains, in this Gospel, a mystery hidden in the mind of God. But if the reason is hidden, its inevitability should be obvious from the perspective of history. Jesus' devotion to the reign of God on earth inevitably provoked "the powers"—the fear, hatred, greed, falsehood, violence, and despair that pervade and distort everything human—to make their oppressive, murderous response, even if this response also, ironically, made possible the disclosure of the triumphant power of God's nonviolent love in their very midst.

The transfiguration is therefore also a powerful word to us to take up our cross and follow Christ, to walk in his way that in one way or another will provoke the powers against us, but that ultimately discloses the eternal truth and trustworthiness of God's nonviolent love and justice in the midst of evil.

RODNEY J. HUNTER

We all want to travel to the mountaintop and experience the transfiguration with Jesus. Yet the text eventually moves us back down the mountain into the normal routine of life. Even if we have a mountaintop experience, we often do not know how to share it with the faith community. At the same time, the faith community may not know how to receive an experience with God on the mountaintop.   DONALD BOOZ

RESPONSE

Have you taken up the cross, or are you still hesitating?

PRAYER

I am afraid of taking up my cross; but I am willing. Amen.

✦ SATURDAY ✦

Mark 9:2–9

REFLECTION

It is important, however, when speaking of the way of the cross, to be clear about what it does not mean. It does not mean that we should seek or regard suffering as a spiritual good in itself or as inherently saving and redemptive—as centuries of misguided Christian theology and piety have often maintained. Jesus did not die because his suffering as such could purge the world of sin and evil. He died because the powers of evil sought to destroy his witness to nonviolent love, justice, and truth. His passion revealed, not only the "evilness of evil"—its intrinsic, deadly violence—but the transforming power of divine love, a powerful, assertive love that does not dominate and defeat evil so much as challenge, expose, and seek to transform it. Such love alone ultimately carries the day; it alone is truly redemptive and saving.

RODNEY J. HUNTER

Only after Jesus is crucified and raised can the disciples comprehend that a new world is coming into being, where the threat of death no longer dominates human imagination and where God's Son liberates those who follow his path to the cross.

STANLEY P. SAUNDERS

RESPONSE

We are not asked to carry the cross alone. Who makes it possible for you to bear the weight of the cross upon your shoulders?

PRAYER

I love you, God of my whole life. Even when I am afraid, I am willing to trust in you. Amen.

❖ SUNDAY ❖

2 Kings 2:1–12

REFLECTION

The text suggests at least two faithful responses to the crises of the in-between times: persistence and silent watchfulness.

WM. LOYD ALLEN

It is unclear what Elisha expected to receive from Elijah in terms of the double portion. What he does receive is the awareness that whatever Elijah has taught him up to now will have to be enough; he must go on alone. What he receives is grief.

MARYANN MCKIBBEN DANA

Having crossed the river, Elisha entreated Elijah to grant him a double portion of the prophet's spirit (v. 9). Double portion was the share of inheritance the elder son and legitimate successor received from his father in the patriarchal structure of ancient Israel (cf. Deut. 21:17). Elisha was making a bold claim, and Elijah assured him that it would be granted if he would be courageous enough to witness Elijah's departure. Here we see a final test of his courage. Would he be able to withstand an encounter with the Divine?

DIANNE BERGANT

Psalm 50:1–6

REFLECTION

We neither pray nor worship in order to create some kind of religious experience. Prayer and worship are responses to God by which we orient ourselves toward that which is of ultimate worth. In worship we open ourselves to being shaped in conformity with what truly matters for life, and shaped by the ground and source of our being. . . . The place to seek the effects of our prayer is not in the prayer itself but in our lives. We do not worship in order to "get something out of it," but in order that our lives may be more fully in accord with the purposes and intention of God, more fully in accord with the deepest desires of our hearts, and more fully a manifestation of the person we were created to be. GEOFFREY M. ST. J. HOARE

2 Corinthians 4:3–6

REFLECTION

God is discontent with the fractiousness of the present age and ever offers the world opportunities to become a greater sphere of blessing. Even if conditions do not immediately improve, communities are empowered to resist exploitation and brutality, and to call for a world of community, justice, abundance, peace, love, and life. RONALD J. ALLEN

Mark 9:2–9

REFLECTION

Functionally speaking, Jesus self-identifies as the Messiah who will be rejected and killed by the establishment, who will rise on the third day and return in glory. And Jesus identifies his disciples as the ones who take up their cross, who love Jesus more than our lives, who are not ashamed to confess Jesus publicly, the ones whom Jesus will acknowledge before the Father upon his glorious return (8:34–38). . . . What Mark's Gospel works to drive home is how—for Jesus' first disciples— resurrection glory proved more of a scandal than crucifixion.
MARILYN MCCORD ADAMS

RESPONSE

How do you explain the resurrection to someone who does not believe?

PRAYER

Your light is brilliant as the sun, and gentle as the starlit sky. Shine upon your world, now and forevermore. Amen.

THE WEEK LEADING UP TO THE
❧ *First Sunday in Lent* ❧

Genesis 9:8–17

God said, "This is the sign of the covenant that I make between
me and you and every living creature that is with you, for all future
generations: I have set my bow in the clouds, and it shall be a sign
of the covenant between me and the earth." (vv. 12–13)

Psalm 25:1–10

To you, O Lord, I lift up my soul.
O my God, in you I trust;
    do not let me be put to shame;
    do not let my enemies exult over me.
Do not let those who wait for you be
    put to shame. (vv. 1–3)

1 Peter 3:18–22

And baptism, which this prefigured, now saves you—not
as a removal of dirt from the body, but as an appeal to God for a
good conscience, through the resurrection of Jesus Christ, who
has gone into heaven and is at the right hand of God, with angels,
authorities, and powers made subject to him. (vv. 21–22)

Mark 1:9–15

In those days Jesus came from Nazareth of Galilee
and was baptized by John in the Jordan. And just as he was
coming up out of the water, he saw the heavens torn apart and
the Spirit descending like a dove on him. And a voice came
from heaven, "You are my Son, the Beloved; with you I
am well pleased." (vv. 9–11)

✢ MONDAY ✢

Genesis 9:8–17

REFLECTION

The biblical flood narrative is not merely a story of the return to primordial chaos; it also contains a story of deliverance and of relationship with God. God directed Noah, the only one who found favor with the Lord, to build an ark so that he and his family and some of the animals might escape the punishing waters of the flood. From this small community God then fashioned a new human family and established a covenant with that family and with the world as a whole. This is a story of deliverance and new beginnings.   DIANNE BERGANT

RESPONSE

Where and with whom is God's covenant making needed today?

PRAYER

God of Creation, as I move more deeply into each day of Lent, remind me of my own experiences of deliverance and the new beginnings you always provide. Amen.

✦ TUESDAY ✦

Genesis 9:8–17

REFLECTION

Think about it. In the scene depicted in today's reading, God binds God's own self to humanity, and indeed to all the world, in a new and different way. God is no longer only the creator; God is now also the protector, committed to refrain from punishing humanity or destroying the world. This is the import of God's choosing to hang his "bow" in the heavens as a sign of this covenant. Ancients, including the Israelites from whom we inherit these Scriptures, conceived of lightning as God's arrows (Ps. 7:12–13) fired from a mighty bow. Thus the rainbow serves as a reminder not simply of the beauty of the earth after a rainstorm but of God's refusal ever again to take up the divine bow against humanity or the world. Further, by binding God's self to the fate of humanity, God becomes inherently invested in the fate of humanity and in this way keenly vulnerable, even exposed. God cannot simply sit back oblivious to the fate of humanity, much as the Greek or Roman gods might. Rather, God's fortunes are now bound up with those of humanity, as God is not simply committed but deeply invested in the fate of God's creation.

DAVID J. LOSE

RESPONSE

In what ways do this text and reflection expand your understanding of God's immanence with creation?

PRAYER

God who creates and protects, whenever I see your bow in the sky, I will remember your promises to all creation. Amen.

❧ Ash Wednesday ❧

Joel 2:1–2, 12–17

Yet even now, says the LORD,
    return to me with all your heart,
with fasting, with weeping, and with mourning;
    rend your hearts and not your clothing.
Return to the LORD, your God,
    for he is gracious and merciful,
slow to anger, and abounding in steadfast love,
    and relents from punishing. (vv. 12–13)

Psalm 51:1–17

Have mercy on me, O God,
    according to your steadfast love;
according to your abundant mercy
    blot out my transgressions.
Wash me thoroughly from my iniquity,
    and cleanse me from my sin. (vv. 1–2)

2 Corinthians 5:20b–6:10

We entreat you on behalf of Christ, be reconciled to God.
For our sake he made him to be sin who knew no sin, so that in
him we might become the righteousness of God. (5:20b)

Matthew 6:1–6, 16–21

"Beware of practicing your piety before others in order
to be seen by them; for then you have no reward from your
Father in heaven. . . . Do not store up for yourselves treasures
on earth, where moth and rust consume and where thieves
break in and steal; but store up for yourselves treasures in
heaven, where neither moth nor rust consumes and where
thieves do not break in and steal. For where your treasure is,
there your heart will be also." (vv. 1, 19–20)

Joel 2:1–2, 12–17

REFLECTION

The global context for the twenty-first-century congregation is complex, fraught with conflict. The threat of global warming with its ecological and economic consequences looms large. The First World is warring with the Third World over non-renewable energy resources. Terrorism is the preferred strategy of competing religious and political ideologies. Poverty with its accompanying issues of hunger and homelessness continues to grow across the globe, as the gap between rich and poor grows ever wider. In this global context we are invited to hear the prophet's words from a vantage point beyond the cleansing of our individual souls. The Christian community is challenged by the ancient words of the prophet to consider its communal soul as well. It is all too apparent that in the web of life on this earth we are connected globally, economically, politically, and spiritually. We are dependent on one another for our survival. Here the global context connects with the liturgical context. In the intonation of "ashes to ashes and dust to dust," we are reminded that all creation comes from the hand of the same Creator and from the same particles of energy. The universe is truly one and connected within all its parts.   JANE ANNE FERGUSON

Psalm 51:1–17

REFLECTION

Psalm 51 holds a permanent place in today's readings, and for good reason. While it shows up again in the lections, this is its natural habitat—with the cross-smeared foreheads and raw holiness of Ash Wednesday. Of all the penitential psalms, this is the one that most passionately witnesses to the pain of sin and the hunger for salvation. This psalm is not for reading; it is meant to be wailed. It outlines the paradox of the Lenten journey: our liberation will come through our suffering, not in spite of it.

A young woman came up to me following a Bible study on the campus where I pastor. She introduced herself, told me a little about her relatively new Christian faith, and then thanked me for leading the Ash Wednesday service. It was the middle of October at the time, and I assumed she had her novice liturgical wires crossed. But sure enough, she was talking about Ash Wednesday, almost seven months after the fact. Explaining herself, she said, "A friend made me go—I had never been to an Ash Wednesday service before. My church back home never did anything like that, with the ashes and all, and at first I was pretty freaked out about it. I was surprised at how ashamed and embarrassed those ashes made me feel. I found myself avoiding public places—I almost did not go to class the rest of the day.

"But that whole day was so powerful for me, walking around with that big black mark on my forehead. The more I thought about it, and still think about it, I began to feel so . . . hopeful. I know that sounds strange, but that service felt so honest. I am not the person I want to be, and deep down I know that, but most church services just feel like strung-out apologies. But since that day, I just feel like God can change me. That God wants to change me. And that feels hopeful." BRIAN ERICKSON

2 Corinthians 5:20b–6:10

REFLECTION

Preachers who take up this text will look beyond their own understandings of salvation, which Paul uses variously to describe something that has already happened (Rom. 8:24), something that is in the process of happening (2 Cor. 2:15), and something that will happen very soon (1 Cor. 5:5). The far reach of these verb tenses offers preachers an opening to speak of salvation as something that happens in time and transcends it, even as the Ash Wednesday liturgy happens in time and transcends it. BARBARA BROWN TAYLOR

Matthew 6:1–6, 16–21

REFLECTION

Ash Wednesday is the day Christians attend their own funerals.
Whether or not worshipers receive ashes on their foreheads
in the sign of the cross, the liturgy reminds them of their own
demise: "Remember that you are dust, and to dust you shall
return." Even in traditions where ashes are not imposed, the
name of the day remains. Everything else that is said or done in
the service happens in the presence of ashes, which offers the
preacher a rare opportunity to speak of death before death, to
listeners who are not preoccupied with mourning the loss of a
particular friend or family member.   BARBARA BROWN TAYLOR

RESPONSE

What pains of sin have you witnessed this year? Name them out
loud.

PRAYER

I return to you again, O God, with a sign of ashes on my
forehead. Bathe me in your love and mercy and wash away
my sin. Amen.

✣ THURSDAY ✣

1 Peter 3:18–22

REFLECTION

A third provocative theological theme in this passage is
its multilayered picture of baptism in verses 20–21. At one
level, baptism is an ark through which God saves. Amid the
floodlike conditions of suffering, baptism communicates to
believers the sense of their belonging to God and thereby
of making their ways safely through the floods ravaging the
present age. At another level, baptism is performed by means
of immersion in water. Floods, of course, are water in the mode
of destruction. The power of God is so awesome that God
transforms the flood water into the means of salvation. From
this perspective, 1 Peter's attitude toward baptism is similar to
that of the Reformers: Baptism is a sign from God to assure the
congregation of God's continuing providence, even amid the
suffering that comes from faithfulness.   RONALD J. ALLEN

RESPONSE

What has been your most recent experience of ravaging waters?
Where was God present in this experience?

PRAYER

Creator God, when dams break and raging waters drown all
life, I remember a font and the gentle water washing over me,
with the promise of your abiding love and providence that
surround all creation. Amen.

✦ FRIDAY ✦

Mark 1:9–15

REFLECTION

And as in so many other transformative religious experiences, "Spirit" is shown here to be at once gentle and dovelike, yet acting with awesome, disruptive effect—descending without warning from a heaven "torn apart," reorienting one's self and world, and setting one on a new and revolutionary spiritual path. In time, such a recipient of "Spirit," such a religious revolutionary, is bound to confront the world with his or her own special vision and claim—the urgency of the inbreaking reign of God for Jesus in Mark's Gospel—and to encounter the world's resistance and rejection. Such is the transforming power of Spirit in the Bible. When Spirit comes, one is changed and, in Mark's theology, set on the road of discipleship to a cross and beyond.   RODNEY J. HUNTER

RESPONSE

How is God's Spirit disrupting your life? In what ways has she reoriented your world?

PRAYER

Your Spirit's presence, O God, challenges, renews, and reorients my life of faith. Amen.

✣ SATURDAY ✣

Mark 1:9–15

REFLECTION

As often as Christians use phrases such as "kingdom of God,"
"repentance," and "good news," few compare notes on what
they mean by those words. Could that be because no one has
ever asked them? Like many other words central to Christian
faith, these words are entirely abstract. They have no weight,
no smell, no shape, no temperature—no direct reference to
lived experience. . . . Of all the words that come out of Jesus'
mouth this Sunday, "good news" may be the one most in need
of refreshment at the beginning of Lent. What is the good news
for this particular congregation at this particular time in this
particular world? Can the preacher forget what the phrase is
supposed to mean long enough to uncover the meaning that
listeners are dying to hear? BARBARA BROWN TAYLOR

RESPONSE

Take some time this day to reflect on the ways you have
experienced the meaning of these phrases: "kingdom of God,"
"repentance," and "good news."

PRAYER

Refresh my understanding of the good news that is needed in
my community of faith this week. Amen.

✦ SUNDAY ✦

Genesis 9:8–17

REFLECTION

What does the body of Christ look like in the light of the rainbow? What would it mean for a Christian community to put God's "rainbow in their house"? God's bow in the heavens is the sign of the first covenant that God makes with humankind and with all creation. It is a sign that God is a changed (and changing) God. . . . Taken seriously and intentionally, it would profoundly change a faith community. Not into a utopia, but into a place where people were willing to let their hearts be remade in the image of God's heart; a place where people would let their hearts be broken open, with grief over their own hard-heartedness and the hard-heartedness of the world and its chaos. And when their hearts were broken open the people would be moved to partner with their Creator through patient, forgiving, loving, and prophetic action for the renewal of all creation.

JANE ANNE FERGUSON

Psalm 25:1–10

REFLECTION

To read of the psalmist's troubles is helpful to the contemporary church. The psalmist sought to learn of God's ways, not in a time of comfort, but in the midst of difficulties. The poet's depiction of God as a God of salvation (v. 5) is a reminder of the roots of that concept in the OT. The word originally had a concrete, this-worldly connotation of God's intervention in danger and distress. That emphasis enables the contemporary Christian to understand God as active in life now.

CHARLES L. AARON JR.

1 Peter 3:18–22

REFLECTION

Our text reminds us that our Lord suffered terribly before he died on the cross. Yet his suffering was not caused by God; rather, it was the result of Christ's faithfulness to his mission of reconciling us to God. . . . Hispanic theologians like Roberto Goizueta describe the work of Jesus Christ as "accompaniment." Through his life, suffering, death, and resurrection, Jesus has become the one who walks with us. SHAWNTHEA MONROE-MUELLER

Mark 1:9–15

REFLECTION

Jesus' baptism marks for him the end of the old world and the beginning of a new one, as is made clear as soon as he arises from the Jordan and sees the heavens themselves being torn apart. The image is both violent and hope-filled. The only other place Mark uses this word for ripping and tearing is in the description of the events that take place at the moment Jesus dies on the cross, when the veil of the temple is torn in two, from top to bottom. In both cases, God is doing the ripping. . . . As the heavens are being torn apart, Jesus also sees the Spirit coming down from heaven, like a dove, not just upon him, but into him. This is the same Spirit of God that moved over the face of the waters of the deep at the creation of the world. The descent of the Spirit signals that God is now remaking the broken, sin-filled creation. STANLEY P. SAUNDERS

RESPONSE

What images are evoked for you in your reading of these texts and reflections? Meditate on them.

PRAYER

God, you accompany me in all the days of my life. In you I place my trust. Amen.

❧ *Second Sunday in Lent* ❦

Genesis 17:1–7, 15–16

When Abram was ninety-nine years old, the LORD appeared to Abram, and said to him, "I am God Almighty; walk before me, and be blameless. And I will make my covenant between me and you, and will make you exceedingly numerous." (vv. 1–2)

Psalm 22:23–31

All the ends of the earth shall remember
    and turn to the LORD;
and all the families of the nations
    shall worship before him.
For dominion belongs to the LORD,
    and he rules over the nations.
To him, indeed, shall all who sleep in the earth bow down;
    before him shall bow all who go down to the dust,
    and I shall live for him. (vv. 27–29)

Romans 4:13–25

For the promise that he would inherit the world did not come to Abraham or to his descendants through the law but through the righteousness of faith. (v. 13)

Mark 8:31–38

He called the crowd with his disciples, and said to them, "If any want to become my followers, let them deny themselves and take up their cross and follow me. For those who want to save their life will lose it, and those who lose their life for my sake, and for the sake of the gospel, will save it." (vv. 34–35)

✣ MONDAY ✣

Genesis 17:1–7, 15–16

REFLECTION

The pastoral gift of Genesis 17 is its reminder that at the center of our being rest blessing and promise, naming and covenant. We are followers of the One who established a never-ending covenant with Abraham and brought that covenant to fullness in Jesus Christ. In our baptism we have been given a new name, "disciple of Jesus," that tells us everything we need to know about ourselves and everything we need to know about God. Through the extravagant grace of God, the life of the church, and the waters of baptism, the covenant established with Abraham and Sarah has been opened to us. Even in the darkness of Lent and under the shadow of the cross, the promise that God made to Abraham remains. God is our God, and we are God's people. This is a covenant that cannot be broken, even as we follow the one named Emmanuel, whose destiny is our destiny: the cross, the grave, the skies.

CRAIG KOCHER

RESPONSE

What is at the center of your being?

PRAYER

Write your covenant on my heart again and again, loving God. I need to remember it! Amen.

✦ TUESDAY ✦

Genesis 17:1–7, 15–16

REFLECTION

On the Second Sunday in Lent, this point merits attention. We do not head straight to Easter from the spa or the shopping mall. Instead, we are invited to spend forty days examining the nature of our own covenant with God. Upon what does that relationship depend? What do we trust to give us life? What concrete practices allow us to become bodily involved with God? If we were to ask God for a new name, what might that name be? What new purpose might that name signify? While Lent focuses naturally on the example of Jesus, Jesus focused just as naturally on the example of Abraham (Matt. 8:11). Like his forebear in faith, Jesus walked toward God's promise with steady trust, leading God to give him a new name too: "You are my Son, the Beloved; with you I am well pleased."

BARBARA BROWN TAYLOR

RESPONSE

What Lenten practice will you take up this year? What is your hope for how it will involve you with God's presence in your life?

PRAYER

God of my Lenten journey, bless me, name me, mark me as your own. Amen.

✢ WEDNESDAY ✦

Psalm 22:23–31

REFLECTION

God's providential care is put into the context of the expansion
of the rule of God. The psalmist enlarges the rule of God
geographically from the people of Israel to the whole earth,
and temporally from those who are now living to future
generations.   CHARLES A. WILEY

RESPONSE

How will you remember God this day? In what ways have you
experienced God's deliverance?

PRAYER

You give me sleep to renew my life. As I close this day, I
remember you and offer you my life. Amen.

✣ THURSDAY ✣

Romans 4:13–25

REFLECTION

On the other hand, we Christian folks may believe our
sinfulness is somehow beyond forgiveness. We despair that
our sin has cut us off from God, and there is no healing the
relationship. Again, Paul would beg to differ. He might say
something along the lines of, "Don't be silly. Remember how
God has chosen to break into history in Jesus Christ. Your right
relationship with God cannot be earned through obedience to
the law, or faith would be useless and Christ would have died
in vain. No. A right relationship with God is built on trust in
Jesus Christ who died 'for our trespasses and was raised for
our justification' [v. 25]. So quit rehearsing your failures and
whining about your sins. Live in confident trust that you are
forgiven and you are given yet another chance to try to be
obedient."

JEFF PASCHAL

RESPONSE

Whom do you know who needs to be reminded of God's
forgiveness?

PRAYER

God, you broke into history with your Son Jesus Christ, and
this day I recall his acts that broke open new ways of seeing and
believing. Amen.

✢ FRIDAY ✢

Mark 8:31–38

REFLECTION

As long as self reigns, we will forever be seeking painless shortcuts to the kingdom. We will try and try again to substitute another way for the way of the cross. But only when we deny self and take up the cross can we follow Jesus. All of our attempts to save our lives are futile (vv. 35–38). All our efforts to make another way are a denial of the one who showed us the way, the way of the cross. This is true discipleship. In the end, true messiahship and true discipleship are inextricably connected. When we are finally willing to accept Jesus for who he is, the suffering one who lays down his life for others, then we can understand who we are to be, and denying self, we can take up the cross and follow him. W. HULITT GLOER

RESPONSE

What evidence of discipleship have you witnessed this week?

PRAYER

God of my life, may the way I live and act this day reflect true discipleship. Amen.

✦ SATURDAY ✦

Mark 8:31–38

REFLECTION

The church that rightly lifts high the cross of Christ all too often neglects the narrative of faith articulated in Jesus' teaching here: that discipleship involves giving up our own lives through sacrificial love, leading to the surprising and ultimately saving discovery that in giving we have received. We know this, of course. We preach it on occasion, and sometimes even live it out, too. Frequently the final words of worship—our benedictions to the congregation—are exhortations to go forth to love and serve God. But the absence of permanent symbols of Jesus' call to take up our own crosses, to be his disciples by taking full responsibility for going ourselves on the sacrificial journey that Jesus pioneered, perhaps helps to explain why churches become preoccupied with membership and not with discipleship. Perhaps what we need is a multitude of crosses, one for each of us, at the back door of our sanctuaries, to be taken up as we return to the world of home and family, work and commerce, service and play—symbols of the call to discipleship that we have heard and accept anew.

PAUL C. SHUPE

RESPONSE

How have you received love through giving? How have you received love through receiving?

PRAYER

Place the cross of your Son in front of me each day, so I remember my call as your disciple. Amen.

✣ SUNDAY ✣

Genesis 17:1–7, 15–16

REFLECTION

The second week of Lent is not only a slow week; it is a hard week. The journey to the cross has just begun, the drama of Holy Week is a long way off, and the glory of Easter morning is not even a shadow in the distance. During Lent, the church in its wisdom calls us to reflect on our sin and brokenness, on all the ways we have fallen short of the high calling of following Jesus. Repentance is a painful process. Lenten self-reflection can be a dizzying undertaking and, when done well, frequently sends us reeling with the hurts, public and secret, that disfigure our lives and with all we have done and left undone that has led to the undoing of the kingdom. CRAIG KOCHER

Psalm 22:23–31

REFLECTION

God's praise and the saving effects of the works of God on our behalf extend even to "all who sleep in the earth . . . all who go down to the dust" (v. 29). The physically, emotionally, and spiritually lifeless are summoned to join the community in giving praise and thanks (in spite of Psalm 6, which asserts the dead can no longer praise God; there it seems an urgent nudge for the living to get on with our primary task and privilege). For the Christian community on another annual Lenten journey and for new baptismal candidates alike, sin's death dealing or an all-too-customary way of life can give way to a renewed season of praise. MARK E. STANGER

Romans 4:13–25

REFLECTION

Only God can create faith, but the church can cultivate religious faith in hearts where mistrust has predominated.

Contemporary culture is marked by overwhelming suspicion. Vietnam, Watergate, political corruption, our growing awareness of sexual harassment and abuse, and church scandals put us at odds with potential relationships of trust. Faith of all kinds, including Christian faith, can grow only if cycles of mistrust are broken. This requires leaps of faith: having faith in people who do not yet have faith in God or in the church. It requires balancing our faith in others with our willingness for others to have faith in us, so that we may become equal partners of faith in God.   ADAM E. ECKHART

Mark 8:31–38

REFLECTION

The truth about who God is contradicts what we expect on the basis of our own feelings about divinity. The truth is that God's mercy is given to sinners, not reserved for the righteous; God's strength is exposed in weakness, not displayed in power; God's wisdom is veiled in parable and paradox, not set out in self-help maxims; God's life is disclosed in death. Thus it is that Jesus says those who want to save their life (*theologia gloriae*) will lose it, while those who lose their life for the sake of the gospel (*theologia crucis*) will save it. God is not conformed to human expectations or desires, for God is found in uncertainty, danger, and suffering . . . precisely where human wisdom perceives God's absence.   JOSEPH D. SMALL

RESPONSE

How have you fallen short? What leap of faith is required of you?

PRAYER

God of promise, I want to follow you. Be with me and those I love in times of certainty and in times of suffering and doubt. Amen.

❧ *Third Sunday in Lent* ❦

Exodus 20:1–17

Then God spoke all these words:
I am the LORD your God, who brought you out
of the land of Egypt, out of the house of slavery;
you shall have no other gods before me. (vv. 1–3)

Psalm 19

The law of the LORD is perfect,
   reviving the soul;
the decrees of the LORD are sure,
   making wise the simple;
the precepts of the LORD are right,
   rejoicing the heart;
the commandment of the LORD is clear,
   enlightening the eyes. (vv. 7–8)

1 Corinthians 1:18–25

For God's foolishness is wiser than human wisdom, and
God's weakness is stronger than human strength. (v. 25)

John 2:13–22

Jesus answered them, "Destroy this temple, and in three days I
will raise it up." . . . But he was speaking of the temple of his body.
After he was raised from the dead, his disciples remembered that
he had said this; and they believed the scripture and the word
that Jesus had spoken. (vv. 19, 21–22)

❧ MONDAY ❧

Exodus 20:1–17

REFLECTION

Since the giving of Torah on Sinai is celebrated during the Jewish festival of Shavuot, a wealth of story and tradition surrounds the first hearing of the commandments. One midrash says that the people had little choice but to accept Torah from God, since God plucked up Sinai and held it over their heads, threatening to drop the mountain on them if they did not receive the commandments. In happy counterpoint to this legend, more and more religious Jews observe the first night of Shavuot by staying up all night to study Torah, Talmud, and other sacred writings together. They offer this annual all-night gathering, known as a *tikkun*, for the mending of the world.

BARBARA BROWN TAYLOR

RESPONSE

How can the world be mended by living in response to Torah?

PRAYER

Help me find ways to join with sisters and brothers of all faith traditions in acts of *tikkun olam*. Amen.

✣ TUESDAY ✣

Exodus 20:1–17

REFLECTION

If nothing else, stories and traditions like these remind
Christian interpreters of the Ten Teachings that these teachings
have been around a long time. They are never our possession,
any more than the God who uttered them is. Instead, we stand
among a people counted as God's peculiar possession, set apart
by holy speech and practice for the mending of God's holy
world.   BARBARA BROWN TAYLOR

RESPONSE

Who are the people with whom you live and breathe, people
counted as God's peculiar possession? Pray for them this day.

PRAYER

O God, it is easy to recite these ten teachings, for I know them
by heart. Walk with me as I try to practice them. That is harder
to do! Amen.

⤞ WEDNESDAY ⤝

Psalm 19

REFLECTION

What marks the way of the cross now? What and who are the Christ-bearers, suffering the pain of sin in our town? Perhaps the answer is found in the women's shelter, the fire station, the emergency room—or in creation itself. Animals and birds are homeless; oceans are dying; humans multiply at rates beyond global food supply. Yet the ironic hope is that deep in our own destruction, were we to prevent one another and other creatures from honoring God's longing for companionship, nonetheless, in the brilliant sun, racing across the heaven, making day and night—with neither chirp nor hum nor growl nor speech— God's glory would still be proclaimed, and God's word would still be imparted to the end of the world.

SUSAN MARIE SMITH

RESPONSE

How do you know God? Where do you see marks of God's presence in your life, in your community?

PRAYER

O God, open my eyes and my ears to all of your creation. Amen.

✣ THURSDAY ✣

1 Corinthians 1:18–25

REFLECTION

The message is paradoxical. God's definitive disclosure of what God is like is in powerlessness. . . . The Creator of the universe, whom we understandably associate with power (after all, the universe is a big entity to create), reveals God's true nature by becoming weak and vulnerable. It is difficult for anyone to understand; so it is not surprising that Paul's Jewish and Greek contemporaries both find it puzzling. It is not simply the message that is paradoxical, but also the community in which the message is birthed. The church is not made up of the powerful, the wise, and the aristocratic, but the weak, the foolish, and the poor. God wants a countercultural community to witness to a paradoxical gospel. In an echo of the Gospels, those least esteemed become the most important in the church.

IAN S. MARKHAM

RESPONSE

Where is the power of God at work in your church and community?

PRAYER

Surprising God, you shatter all expectations in revealing your power through weakness and vulnerability. Remind me to look and see and notice those whom you love. Amen.

John 2:13–22

REFLECTION

Last Sunday's text focused on the Lenten question "What does it mean to be a disciple of Jesus?" Today's text focuses on the question "What does it mean to be the church of Jesus?" As our text begins, Passover is near. Hearts and minds are focused on the exodus event and expectations of deliverance. A faithful Jew, Jesus comes to the temple, sacred space, the dwelling place of God on the earth. It was a magnificent place. . . . The message to John's readers is clear. You cannot understand Jesus until you have the whole story. During Lent we are reminded that the story of Jesus culminates at the cross but does not end there. Taking only parts of the story will lead us to an incomplete and inadequate understanding of Jesus. And that might leave us in a temple of our own construction that is dedicated to the purposes of God but actually stands in opposition to them.

W. HULITT GLOER

RESPONSE

What does it mean to be the church of Jesus today in your dwelling place?

PRAYER

I know that your story continues, God of my life. It continues through the witness of faithful disciples. Strengthen me for my role in this story. Amen.

✦ SATURDAY ✦

John 2:13–22

REFLECTION

It is important for us to tolerate and explore through prayer,
preparation, and preaching the queasy anxiety of seeing Jesus
with the whip of cords in his hands and hearing him with the
righteous judgments of God on his lips—knowing that he
speaks for us, yes, and with us, but also to us and even against
us. . . . It is a scary proposition to dive into the murky waters
that may hide unseen monsters capable of threatening our
institutions if we speak too prophetically. Though no one has
ever seen these deep sea monsters, we fear them anyway and
are driven to be quiet, accommodating ourselves to the evils
around us. Only by facing our fears forthrightly can their power
over us and over our communities be broken, so that we can at
last, however haltingly and imperfectly, embody the prophetic
impulse.   PAUL C. SHUPE

RESPONSE

What judgments would Jesus make in your community? What
sins would he name?

PRAYER

Help me face any fears I may have as I struggle with what it
means to be a prophetic leader. Amen.

✦ SUNDAY ✦

Exodus 20:1–17

REFLECTION

The Commandments play an indispensable, positive role in Christian life. They are, as the Bible tells us, a "lamp unto our feet." They guide us as we journey in our life before God and our life with our neighbors. They do not show us what we must do or how we must live in order to receive God's covenantal grace. They light our way and show us how we should live as people who have already been freely given God's grace in Jesus Christ.
GEORGE W. STROUP

Psalm 19

REFLECTION

Torah revives the soul, makes wise the simple, makes the heart to rejoice, and enlightens the eyes. Heaven and earth disclose God, but Torah ministers to the human person. The law's work is salvific—it is the specific work of this God in the gift of the law that nourishes the human person. This law is so wonderful that it is to be desired more than riches, tasting sweeter than any food.
CHARLES A. WILEY

1 Corinthians 1:18–25

REFLECTION

God challenges us during Lent to confront the world's fatalistic wisdom, to recognize its tempting power and its insufficiency. The old hypothesis of perishing is not as much wrong as it is incomplete. Before there was evolution and survival of the fittest, there was God's creating word; and while there is still death, in the end there shall be new life in Christ, bestowed and breathed upon us by the Holy Spirit. The message of the cross, God's weak and foolish new hypothesis, absorbs the old hypothesis into the wholeness of the resurrection.

ADAM E. ECKHART

John 2:13–22

REFLECTION

The phrase "the Jews" is used in a distinctive way in this Gospel. It does not refer to the Jewish people per se, but to those who reject Jesus or have inadequate faith (see, e.g., 5:16; 6:41; 9:22). Because of this, "the Jews" often refers, as here, to the Jewish authorities, who consistently show hostility to Jesus (cf. Mark 11:18).

JOUETTE M. BASSLER

RESPONSE

In this third week of Lent, what wisdom of the world needs to be challenged?

PRAYER

Torah revives my soul, and I give thanks to you for a heart that rejoices. Amen.

❧ *Fourth Sunday in Lent* ❧

Numbers 21:4–9

The people came to Moses and said, "We have sinned by speaking against the Lord and against you; pray to the Lord to take away the serpents from us." So Moses prayed for the people. And the Lord said to Moses, "Make a poisonous serpent, and set it on a pole; and everyone who is bitten shall look at it and live." So Moses made a serpent of bronze, and put it upon a pole; and whenever a serpent bit someone, that person would look at the serpent of bronze and live. (vv. 7–9)

Psalm 107:1–3, 17–22

O give thanks to the Lord, for he is good;
for his steadfast love endures forever. (v. 1)

Ephesians 2:1–10

For by grace you have been saved through faith,
and this is not your own doing; it is the gift of God. (v. 8)

John 3:14–21

For God so loved the world that he gave his only Son,
so that everyone who believes in him may not perish
but may have eternal life. (v. 16)

✦ MONDAY ✦

Numbers 21:4–9

REFLECTION

What concrete things do we focus on that epitomize our fear? In what sense do these things become idols that keep our fear in place? What is God capable of doing with those idols, once they have been plucked out from under our feet and set up on a pole where we can see them clearly? How does God respond to our fear, both in the wilderness and at the foot of the cross?

BARBARA BROWN TAYLOR

RESPONSE

What do you fear the most? What fears do you hear expressed by others?

PRAYER

I offer my fears to you, merciful God, placing them on a pole in plain view. Amen.

→ TUESDAY ←

Psalm 107:1–3, 17–22

REFLECTION

The season of Lent calls the community to repent not only of personal wrongdoing but also of corporate and systemic evil that diminish human lives and the Creator's gift of the natural environment. The cultivation of the human spirit and body, of healthy relationships and culture, of just civilizations, and of the earth's resources belong to God's people as a sacred calling.

MARK E. STANGER

RESPONSE

Name those things that you repent of this week of Lent.

PRAYER

I pause and name the evils—personal, corporate, systemic—and give thanks for your love and deliverance. Amen.

✦ WEDNESDAY ✦

Ephesians 2:1–10

REFLECTION

A redemptive ethic calls the church to begin the actual process of critiquing and transforming the powers. As Christ's body, we seek to continue Christ's work of rising from trespasses and sins and being made alive together again. This work begins within the church.
ADAM E. ECKHART

RESPONSE

In what ways are you and your church involved in God's redemptive ethic?

PRAYER

Saved through faith, I offer my life to you for all that I may be and do in this world. Amen.

✦ THURSDAY ✦

Ephesians 2:1–10

REFLECTION

The church's best bet is to enlist the least and weakest of its membership in redemptive ministry. How can children be prophets to congregations concerning powers? How can teenagers become conscious of their participation in powers before they are tempted to define themselves by the powers? As the powers of media and commerce exert greater and earlier influence on children, offering young people the alternative vision of common weakness in Christ becomes more urgent.

ADAM E. ECKHART

RESPONSE

In what ways can the gifts of children and youth in your congregation be called forth for prophetic ministry?

PRAYER

Prepare me for my role in mentoring children and youth, sharing your grace in kindness and love. Amen.

☘ FRIDAY ☘

John 3:14–21

REFLECTION

Even in our own day, when established powers have sought to limit God's love by the exclusion of others from full participation in the community, divine compassion for the oppressed and divine passion for justice have called forth prophets to declare that God's love includes all, regardless of age or race, nationality or creed, gender or sexual orientation. The cumulative weight of the biblical record and the multifaceted experience of salvation within the contemporary church seem clear: God so loves the world. PAUL C. SHUPE

RESPONSE

What limits on God's love do you notice this week?

PRAYER

God of all life, whom do you love that I don't even see, that I overlook? Open my eyes. Amen.

John 3:14–21

REFLECTION

What if, instead of signing on to a program that would limit God's love to the insiders, to the believers who walk in the light, a prophetic voice were raised instead to imagine a world in which God's love is at work yet again among the oppressed, the outsiders?
PAUL C. SHUPE

RESPONSE

Who are the insiders? Who are the outsiders who need God's love?

PRAYER

Show me the ways my prophetic voice is needed in your world. Amen.

✦ SUNDAY ✦

Numbers 21:4–9

REFLECTION

"Faith" in the Bible is regularly understood as "trust" rather than "belief." Moses did not challenge the people to "believe" in some doctrine about God. The aim of Moses was for the people to move forward trusting that God would keep the divine commitment to lead the people to a new land.

W. EUGENE MARCH

Psalm 107:1–3, 17–22

REFLECTION

Lent is a time of honest self-examination, of correcting course, of forgiving self and others. There are natural consequences to the failure to receive the fullness of God's love and to live into its demands.

SUSAN MARIE SMITH

It is no accident that the words of this opening section of Psalm 107 have been appropriated in Christian tradition for celebration around the Lord's Table where we receive food and drink for the soul. The opening invitation to the Table often echoes the words of Psalm 107, where the redeemed come "from the east and from the west and from the north and from the south" to sit at table with the Lord. For Christians, the people of God are redeemed because of the steadfast love of the Lord who satisfies the thirsty and gives the hungry good things to eat through the body and blood of our Lord Jesus Christ.

CHARLES A. WILEY

Ephesians 2:1–10

REFLECTION

We are recipients of a remarkable gift from God—the gift of absolutely everything. The goal is a transformed life (one created for "good works," v. 10), which God has created in Christ Jesus. We are playing a privileged role in God's plan (v. 10).   IAN S. MARKHAM

John 3:14–21

REFLECTION

John's Gospel plays the themes of belief, judgment, and eternal life over and over, each time in a different key. This passage contributes its own powerful message to John's complex symphony: God's extraordinary love for the world; God's desire to save the entire world; human responsibility for the outcome; and a connection between believing and moral actions and God.   JOUETTE M. BASSLER

The relationship between grace and faith may best be characterized as a mystery. This does not mean it is a mystifying conundrum, however. A theological "mystery" refuses to ignore difficulties in understanding and resolves to plumb the depths of theological tensions in order to probe more deeply into the riches of the gospel. Mystery is not an excuse for a lack of understanding, but a journey into understanding that leads ever deeper into the fullness of comprehension and appreciation. With mystery, the more we know, the more we realize that there is more to be known.   JOSEPH D. SMALL

RESPONSE

In this fourth week of Lent, what corrections in your life course need to be made?

PRAYER

I place my trust in you, God of love, God of my life. Amen.

THE WEEK LEADING UP TO THE

Fifth Sunday in Lent

Jeremiah 31:31–34

But this is the covenant that I will make with the house of
Israel after those days, says the LORD: I will put my law within
them, and I will write it on their hearts; and I will be their
God, and they shall be my people. (v. 33)

Psalm 119:9–16

With my whole heart I seek you;
  do not let me stray from your commandments.
I treasure your word in my heart,
  so that I may not sin against you. (vv. 10–11)

Hebrews 5:5–10

Although he was a Son, he learned obedience through what he
suffered; and having been made perfect, he became the source of
eternal salvation for all who obey him. (vv. 8–9)

John 12:20–33

"Now my soul is troubled. And what should I say—'Father, save
me from this hour'? No, it is for this reason that I have come to this
hour. Father, glorify your name." Then a voice came from heaven,
"I have glorified it, and I will glorify it again." (vv. 27–28)

✣ MONDAY ✤

Jeremiah 31:31–34

REFLECTION

Presumably this text invites us to confess and repent boldly, because of the already-and-not-yet promise that God remembers our sins no more. Perhaps it also invites us to confess that the covenantal calculus, our quid-pro-quo approach to God, does not always hold. This deep into Lent, the shadow of the cross falls over everything—a reminder that, even for God's most faithful one, there is no path around the darkness. Yet there lingers also the hope, the already-and-not-yet promise, that the days are surely coming when even the cross gives way to life.

RICHARD FLOYD

RESPONSE

What is God writing on your heart?

PRAYER

My sin is before you, forgiving God. As you forgive me, help me remember to forgive others. Amen.

✦ TUESDAY ✦

Psalm 119:9–16

REFLECTION

The identity of God's people, then, is grounded not in names or church buildings or even in right doctrine, but in relationship with God for all those who seek God with their whole heart.

AUDREY WEST

RESPONSE

Consider your identity. What is most formative? What do you seek? What have you found?

PRAYER

With the psalmist, I promise never to forget your word. Amen.

✦ WEDNESDAY ✦

Psalm 119:9–16

REFLECTION

During this season of Lent, as the Christian community focuses its eyes on the cross and tastes the bread and wine with its lips, it is useful to be reminded that no part of our selves is left behind on this journey we travel with God. The way of the Lord is not simply a matter of right belief or proper speech, but it involves the totality of one's being, including the flesh and blood of our earthly bodies. Lenten disciplines related to food (what one will eat or not eat) and to prayer (particularly, to prayer at structured times) can serve as memory cues designed to remind us of this fact and to connect us in a real way to the God incarnate in Christ Jesus. AUDREY WEST

RESPONSE

How have you traveled with God this Lenten season? What practices feed you on this journey?

PRAYER

Slow me down, O Lord. Feed me in ways I cannot even imagine. Amen.

✥ THURSDAY ✥

Hebrews 5:5–10

REFLECTION

Jesus' baptism is linked to our own by this liturgical season: the early church's Lenten practice of discipling culminated at baptism during the Easter vigil, now less than a fortnight away. So the high priesthood of Jesus begins where all our journeys begin: in the visceral experience of the unconditional love of God poured out in water and in Spirit, sealing the new covenant in each heart (cf. Jer. 31).   RICHARD E. SPALDING

RESPONSE

Recall what you know of your own baptism.

PRAYER

God of water, thank you for your loving presence in my life as I live in response to the waters of my baptism. Amen.

✢ FRIDAY ✢

John 12:20–33

REFLECTION

"The world" (*kosmos*) here is not synonymous with
God's creation, but is rather the fallen realm that exists in
estrangement from God and is organized in opposition to God's
purposes. (My interpretation of *kosmos* and my treatment of
the "myth of redemptive violence" are taken from Walter Wink,
*Engaging the Powers: Discernment and Resistance in a World of
Domination* [Minneapolis: Fortress Press, 1992], 13–31, 51–59.)
The "world" is a superhuman reality, concretely embodied in
structures and institutions, that aggressively shapes human life
and seeks to hold human beings captive to its ways. *Kosmos*
is probably best translated as "the System." And this System is
driven by a spirit or force ("the ruler of the world"), whose ways
are domination, violence, and death. Indeed, in this text the
crucifixion is interpreted as an exorcism, in which the System is
judged and its driving force ("ruler") is "cast out" by means of
the cross. . . . What are the primary aspects of the System that
hold us captive and take us down the path of death rather than
life? Consumerism is one option. How many of us consume
and consume, even though we know such consumption is not
giving us life, and we know it is killing others in sweatshops
throughout the System? Domination might be another focus.
We live in a System shaped by hierarchies of winners and
losers, and often we do not seem to be able to think with other
categories or metaphors.   CHARLES L. CAMPBELL

RESPONSE

What other evils of the System need to be named?

PRAYER

Help me confront the forces that deny life and love. Amen.

⁂ SATURDAY ⁂

John 12:20–33

REFLECTION

Another aspect of the System that is particularly important in our contemporary context is violence. Walter Wink has suggested that the "myth of redemptive violence" is the primary myth of the System. According to this myth, the way to bring order out of chaos is through violently defeating "the other." And the way to deal with threats from enemies is by violently eliminating them—as the System seeks to do to Jesus. . . . Many of us have trouble even imagining alternatives to this myth—a grim signal of our captivity to it.

Throughout his jorney to the cross, Jesus enacts his freedom from this myth, refusing to respond in the System's own violent terms. Indeed, in his trial before Pilate, Jesus suggests that violence, which he rejects, is central to the System. In response to Pilate's questioning, Jesus replies, "My kingdom is not from [this System]. If my kingdom were from [this System], my followers would be *fighting* to keep me from being handed over to the Jews. But as it is, my kingdom is not from here" (John 18:36). Jesus' rejection of violence is precisely what distinguishes his way from the way of the System.

CHARLES L. CAMPBELL

RESPONSE

Where do you struggle with the "myth of redemptive violence"?

PRAYER

I wish to see Jesus. I hope to see him this week in the faces and hands of those who reject violence. Amen.

⤳ SUNDAY ⤝

Jeremiah 31:31–34

REFLECTION

What would it be like if God wrote the law on our hearts so
that we would live within the creation, not above it, so that
we would cherish our neighbors, the birds, animals, and fish?
What would this creation look like if we lived with restraint and
humility, living for the whole creation, not just for our singular,
insular selves and our own narrow corner of creation?

WOODY BARTLETT

Psalm 119:9–16

REFLECTION

The writer understands that our deepest yearnings are not
found just in intellectual pursuits. Rather, our deepest longings
are longings of the heart, the longings to know what really
matters, to know how to live, to know who and what to trust,
and to know how to love. These are things that we cannot
discern with our minds alone. It takes our hearts; indeed it
takes our whole beings—our lips (v. 13), our mouths (v. 13), our
eyes (v. 15), our emotions (v. 16: "I will delight . . . "), as well as
our minds (v. 16: "I will not forget . . . "). In short, the purpose
of the word of God is not simply to dispel ignorance. It is to
transform, and transformation comes when Scripture becomes
conversant with both tradition and the world in which we find
ourselves living today. God's activity is not found only in a static
past, nor is it confined within the territory of our minds. God
presents a living, dynamic word that opens the future to those
who are open to such dynamism.   STEPHEN R. MONTGOMERY

Hebrews 5:5–10

REFLECTION

The promise of this passage is that because God in Christ
endured sufferings, the way to eternal salvation has been

opened up to us. Meditation on this might provoke an attitude of wonder and gratitude for Christ's work, even as we also continue to shudder at the horror of Christ's crucifixion, and all the crucifixions we continue to witness in our world today.

MARTHA L. MOORE-KEISH

John 12:20–33

REFLECTION

Martin Luther King Jr.'s nonviolent campaigns illustrate Jesus' work. When the white "powers-that-be" turned the hoses and dogs on the marchers— and the images were splashed across television—the reality of white racism was graphically and publicly exposed for all to see. And King knew exactly what he was doing: "Let them get their dogs," he shouted, "and let them get the hose, and we will leave them standing before their God and the world spattered with the blood and reeking with the stench of their Negro brothers." It is necessary, he continued, "to bring these issues to the surface, to bring them out into the open where everybody can see them" (Richard Lischer, *The Preacher King: Martin Luther King, Jr. and the Word that Moved America* [New York: Oxford University Press, 1995], 157). And King was to some degree successful. Once exposed, the spirit of racism began to lose some of its power over many people.

This is what happens on the cross. Jesus exposes the System, and by exposing it he judges it and casts out its ruler.

CHARLES L. CAMPBELL

RESPONSE

In this fifth week of Lent, consider the ways these four texts are conversation partners with your social location.

PRAYER

I do treasure the word you have placed in my heart, in front of my eyes, on my lips, and in my hands. Amen.

THE WEEK LEADING UP TO

❧ *Palm/Passion Sunday* ❧

Psalm 118:1–2, 19–29

O give thanks to the LORD, for he is good;
his steadfast love endures forever! (v. 1)

Mark 11:1–11

Those who went ahead and those who
followed were shouting, "Hosanna! Blessed is the one
who comes in the name of the Lord!" (v. 9)

Isaiah 50:4–9a

The Lord GOD helps me;
  therefore I have not been disgraced;
therefore I have set my face like flint,
  and I know that I shall not be put to shame. (v. 7)

Psalm 31:9–16

But I trust in you, O LORD;
  I say, "You are my God."
My times are in your hand;
    deliver me from the hand of my enemies
      and persecutors. (vv. 14–15)

Philippians 2:5–11

[Christ Jesus] emptied himself,
  taking the form of a slave,
  being born in human likeness.
And being found in human form,
he humbled himself
  and became obedient to the point of death—
  even death on a cross. (vv. 7–8)

Mark 14:1–15:47

Then Jesus gave a loud cry and breathed his last.
And the curtain of the temple was torn in two, from top
to bottom. Now when the centurion, who stood facing him,
saw that in this way he breathed his last, he said, "Truly
this man was God's Son!" (15:37–39)

❖ MONDAY ❖

Psalm 118:1–2, 19–29

REFLECTION

There was once a very faithful, active, urban church that opened its doors to those on the margins of society, including those who were homeless. One day a mentally deranged man made his way into the church office and threw a brick at the receptionist, hitting her in the face. After she was admitted to the hospital, the entire church staff gathered around the communion table, held hands, and offered prayers on behalf of their sister, friend, and colleague.

The pastor recounted that he began with a very Presbyterian prayer, full of the right words, asking that God's will be done, praying for strength, and even praying for the poor, mentally ill perpetrator. Then the janitor began to pray. The prayer began with gratitude, "for waking me up in the morning, for the sun that is shining, for the food I was able to eat at breakfast." But then the prayer moved from praise to petition. Not the "nice" petitions in the pastor's prayer, but hard-core demands on God. "God, we expect you to heal our sister! Make her well. Bring her back to full health." On and on the janitor went, beseeching God to deliver his friend, expecting God to be God. It was then and only then that his praise went from what God had done to what God would do. His prayer, like this psalm, did not look simply to the past, but to the future as well.

STEPHEN R. MONTGOMERY

RESPONSE

Who has helped you remember that God's love endures forever?

PRAYER

I give thanks, O God, for the enduring presence of your steadfast love in my life. Amen.

✣ TUESDAY ✣

Mark 11:1–11

REFLECTION

Palm Sunday shows us how often we misinterpret God's love, as well as our love for God. The true measure of our love must comprise the capacity to extend ourselves in real acts of compassion toward the afflicted, forcing us to come out of ourselves. So Jesus gets on a jackass and parades among palms toward Jerusalem. This act requires the greatest love. A great Christian mystic, Simone Weil, writes: "Those who are unhappy have no need for anything in this world but people capable of giving them their attention. The capacity to give one's attention is a very rare and difficult thing; it is almost a miracle; it *is* a miracle." Jesus entering Jerusalem, riding humbly on a donkey, is the miracle of God's complete attention. In Jesus, the world recognizes how different its kind of love is from God's kind of love, and in this recognition—in Jesus—we are transformed from fighting God tooth and nail into creatures who actually love God.   MICHAEL BATTLE

RESPONSE

We live in times of constant partial attention. We always have our eyes on our phones, our e-mail, text messages. In what ways does this text call for your complete attention? What new thing emerges for you as you contemplate it?

PRAYER

Blessed are you, O God. Hosanna is my song. Amen.

✦ WEDNESDAY ✦

Isaiah 50:4–9a

REFLECTION

As we engage this text in our context, we must recognize that the Servant's mission has not been exhausted by the people of Israel or by Jesus. There have been other servants, people who have allowed themselves to be emptied, people who have sustained the weary and endured the persecutions of the powerful in obedience to God. And wherever you find one of these servants, the world changes. A soft-spoken man named Mohandas Gandhi overthrows the British Empire in India without firing a shot. A prisoner named Nelson Mandela is set free and overturns the powers of apartheid in South Africa. An unassuming woman named Rosa Parks refuses to move to the back of the bus, and a system of segregation begins to collapse. A black Baptist preacher named Martin Luther King Jr. dreams of a day when his children will have the freedoms and opportunities promised to every child, and his inspiration and courage change hearts and laws in the United States. These and countless other servants of God, in large and small ways, relied on soft power—not the power of coercion, but the power of suffering love. They saw a world no one else could see; they saw the world God intended to be.   RICHARD FLOYD

RESPONSE

As you pause with this text and this reflection, what does your ear need most to hear? What in this text does God most want you to hear and to teach?

PRAYER

I must admit, O God, that sometimes I am weary with sustaining others. Sometimes my ears are weary with listening, and I wonder what words there are left to speak. Renew me, sustain me, refresh me. Amen.

✢ THURSDAY ✢

Isaiah 50:4–9a

REFLECTION

Jesus, Gandhi, Mandela, Parks, King—these faithful ones can be as intimidating as they are inspiring. But we too have been called to be servants. We too are invited to make ourselves available, to allow ourselves to be used, to be God's response to a broken and suffering world, a response not of destructive power but of suffering love.

It is important to recognize that the path of suffering love is *chosen* by the Servant, or at least *willingly* endured. This text is not a call to remain in situations of suffering or abuse because one thinks abuse is somehow part of God's "purpose." God's way leads always toward healing and wholeness. We tread a dangerous road when we acknowledge that—*sometimes*—vicarious suffering willingly endured can be redemptive, while simultaneously fighting to liberate people from unwilling suffering. We must proceed cautiously.

Notice the personal feel of this Servant Song. The name of God is used four times in six verses, suggesting a deep intimacy. It is an invitation to each of us to open ourselves to divine intimacy, to make ourselves available to be God's response to a broken world—and to choose as that response, not the path of hard power, violence, or destruction, but the path of soft power, nonviolence, listening, teaching—suffering love.

RICHARD FLOYD

RESPONSE

Recall those with whom you have been in conversation, those for whom you have been praying in this season of Lent.

PRAYER

Sustain me with a word so that I may be your presence in this world, healing, working for peace, listening, teaching. Amen.

✧ FRIDAY ✧

Philippians 2:5–11

REFLECTION

The "mind" Paul hopes to evoke is a communal consciousness,
a faith held in trust together. It is the faith that he has seen in
them all along, the faith that has inscribed them on his heart,
the faith that prompts him, even in prison and facing possible
execution, to express in this letter what Ron James has called
"a joy wider than the world." Yes, there are tensions within
the community, interpersonal and institutional distractions
from life in Christ. Paul the pastor knows them well. But he is
speaking to his beloved church at a level deeper than all their
contentions. To them—and to us—he says, *you have more than
enough of everything you need.* For underneath the struggles
of the moment, and beyond the threats of the times, Paul says,
there *is* encouragement in Christ, there *is* consolation in love,
there *is* sharing in the Spirit. This is a text about abundance—in
a letter about abundance.   RICHARD E. SPALDING

RESPONSE

As you prepare to move out of this last week of Lent into the
Holy Week journey, take a few moments to sit with the text and
the simplicity of Paul's synthesis of the story. And think about
this text in light of your congregation. What is your abundance?

PRAYER

Abundant God, sometimes I fail to remember that living in
your steadfast love, I have more than enough of everything I
need. I am indeed thankful. Amen.

✦ SATURDAY ✦

Philippians 2:5–11

REFLECTION

For a church of power and privilege, even one that is waning in public influence, the call to kenosis may in fact be liberating. Rather than grasping after (or mourning the loss of) worldly power, the church might hear in these words a call to give up trying to be "like God" and instead willingly assume the role of servant. This means identifying completely with human suffering and marginalization—even to the point of death. The church as church is not called to be "like God," if that means having power over the world. Rather, the church is called to be like Christ Jesus, who gave up power and privilege to be in the midst of the suffering world. We can respond to this kenotic call, trusting that in Christ, we will also be exalted—but only on the far side of death. The promise of exaltation, then, comes as a gift of utter grace at the hand of God. For any church struggling with its own survival today, this invitation to the life of kenosis may be good news indeed. MARTHA L. MOORE-KEISH

RESPONSE

What power and privilege are you being called to relinquish?

PRAYER

Remind me of my confession, O Lord. Remind me that bending down on my knees is an act of giving up my own needs and emptying myself to you. Amen.

✦ PALM/PASSION SUNDAY ✦

Psalm 118:1–2, 19–29

REFLECTION

By its testimony about God's salvation, manifested in a steadfast love that will not let go of God's people, the psalm stands as a sign of hope for all whose lives are caught up in fear and danger.

AUDREY WEST

Mark 11:1–11

REFLECTION

Just as we do not adequately understand the suffering of Jesus Christ unless we see it as it reaches down through centuries to the suffering of individuals and groups today, so we do not adequately understand the humiliations of Jesus, and the truth of dignity within indignity, unless we see them in the lives of those who are otherwise judged among the humiliated today. We know them well—those upon whom we impose humiliation because we find them "different" from ourselves; those on whom we turn our suspicious stares, our demeaning glances; those who are shamed in the name of order in society, pushed to the "outside" so that we may stand tall and pure; those we abandon and no longer want to see and those we stigmatize with our self-righteous judgments.

MARGARET A. FARLEY

Isaiah 50:4–9a

REFLECTION

Good teaching allows others to persist in the face of life's struggles, finding new energy to continue on the path that God would have people follow. A servant's teaching is an empowering act.

JON L. BERQUIST

Psalm 31:9–16

REFLECTION

From the perspective of the passion, we know that suffering ends in death, but death is not the end. The psalmist's prayer—Christ's prayer—becomes the prayer of all the faithful. Jesus' suffering and his appeal to God declare in letters writ large that the Messiah understands the very worst of human suffering. There is no pain that the Christ has not endured.   AUDREY WEST

Philippians 2:5–11

REFLECTION

The "emptying" encouraged here is not a servile spirit that exploits or crushes human dignity, but a free, generous, and life-giving act of love that represents the most noble qualities of human life and commitment.   DONALD SENIOR

Mark 14:1–15:47

REFLECTION

Disciples have always had a hard time staying awake with Jesus. Most of us approach Jesus' reality like the coal miners who used to take a canary down in the mines with them to test the air. When the canary started to die, it was time for the miners to surface and think things over. This kind of testing for self-interest is usually what drives our relationship to Jesus, but Jesus' passion continually surprises us—inviting us into a deeper life of transformation.   MICHAEL BATTLE

RESPONSE

Follow Jesus' path to Jerusalem this week. Try to look, using his eyes. Whom do you see, whom do you meet?

PRAYER

Jesus, following you is never easy, often exhausting, sometimes discouraging. But I walk on, with palms in my hand. Amen.

❧ *Holy Week* ❧

✦ MONDAY OF HOLY WEEK ✦

Isaiah 42:1–9

I am the LORD, I have called you in righteousness,
   I have taken you by the hand and kept you;
I have given you as a covenant to the people,
   a light to the nations,
   to open the eyes that are blind,
to bring out the prisoners from the dungeon,
   from the prison those who sit in darkness. (vv. 6–7)

REFLECTION

People who are committed to justice never give up. They do
not succumb to what some have called "compassion fatigue."
Because the cause of justice is ultimately God's cause, one can
be steadfast, knowing that even failures can be the prelude to
new possibilities. God can take our little efforts, including our
failures, and turn them to a greater good beyond our imagining.
We are reminded in verse 5 that God is ultimately in charge of
everything.   J. PHILIP WOGAMAN

RESPONSE

What acts of justice define your life of faith?

PRAYER

Thank you, God, for giving me a breath of hope when I most
need it. Amen.

⤇ TUESDAY OF HOLY WEEK ⤆

Isaiah 49:1–7

"Kings shall see and stand up,
    princes, and they shall prostrate themselves,
because of the LORD, who is faithful,
    the Holy One of Israel, who has chosen you." (v. 7)

REFLECTION

In the twenty-first century CE, the idea of salvation extending
to the end of the earth remains captivating. If consistent with
Isaiah 49, such deliverance will be based on a principle of
justice and involve political, and not just spiritual, realities.

DAVID L. PETERSEN

RESPONSE

In this week called holy, how are you involved in justice and
political realities of salvation?

PRAYER

O Lord, my God, I live my life, listening for the ways you call
me, knowing you have chosen me, you have loved me. Amen.

✦ WEDNESDAY OF HOLY WEEK ✦

Psalm 70

But I am poor and needy;
hasten to me, O God!
You are my help and my deliverer;
O Lord, do not delay! (v. 5)

REFLECTION

The world is a painful and treacherous place. Its needs are urgent and overwhelming. Yet God has not given us Psalm 70 so that we can adopt it hastily and force deliverance from our own trials. We have it to remember the trials and the vindication of the One broken for us. We pray Psalm 70 rightly as participants in Christ's sacrificial body and blood. When our own humiliations and sufferings find their place in his atoning death, when we are willing to acknowledge that we might be among the very enemies we are praying against, when we seek him in his beatific poverty and are glad in his great victory, and when our most urgent request is that he come quickly to judge the living and the dead, then we are its true psalmists.

TELFORD WORK

RESPONSE

Read this psalm out loud. How does Jesus' brokenness speak to your life?

PRAYER

I am poor and needy; hasten to me, O God! You are my help and my deliverer; O Lord, do not delay! Amen.

✦ MAUNDY THURSDAY ✦

Psalm 116:1–2, 12–19

I love the LORD, because he has heard
　my voice and my supplications.
Because he inclined his ear to me,
　therefore I will call on him as long as I live. (vv. 1–2)

REFLECTION

As profoundly personal as this psalm is, it is thoroughly
communal. It does not isolate or set the individual apart from
the life of the community in the way that suffering and despair
often do. A mark of testimony is that it connects those who
hear it and draws them into the flow of praise and thanksgiving.
Testimony exemplifies the deepest convictions of a community
and reconvenes the community around its reason for being. The
congregation provides the acoustical context for transforming
personal experience into public testimony. Too often the
mainline church is embarrassed by such public displays of
devotion. The church is often much better at preserving privacy
than it is at tutoring testimony. Testimony of the kind embodied
in this psalm, while no doubt residual in the lives of individuals
in every congregation, more often than not remains unspoken
and unheard.   MARGARET ANN FOHL

RESPONSE

What is your testimony this Maundy Thursday?

PRAYER

You hear my voice, my requests, and I love you, my God. Each
day I am grateful because you listen closely when I call on you.
Amen.

✣ GOOD FRIDAY ✣

Isaiah 52:13–53:12

Surely he has borne our infirmities
    and carried our diseases;
yet we accounted him stricken,
    struck down by God, and afflicted.
But he was wounded for our transgressions,
    crushed for our iniquities;
upon him was the punishment that made us whole,
    and by his bruises we are healed. (53:4–5)

REFLECTION

Isaiah's vision of the Suffering Servant and its historical origins
leads us to ask both, who are today's sacrificial victims? and
how shall we live out our suffering servanthood? Scapegoating
may be virtually obsolete as a religious practice, but it is alive
and well nearly everywhere else. Immigrants, refugees, various
minorities, the young, the elderly, the poor, and the infirm
all get burdened with the reluctance of others to shoulder
responsibility for the problems that afflict us all. Many millions
die each year owing to the willingness of some to allow others
to suffer so they can maintain relatively affluent styles of living.
Affluent cultures send their poor to prison to avoid questions of
cultural injustice or to war to fight and die on their behalf.

GREGORY LEDBETTER

RESPONSE

Who are today's sacrificial victims? Whom do you despise,
reject? How shall we live out our suffering servanthood?

PRAYER

Tend our wounds, hear our prayers, heal us, loving God. Amen.

✢ HOLY SATURDAY ✢

Job 14:1–14

If mortals die, will they live again?
   All the days of my service I would wait
   until my release should come. (v. 14)

REFLECTION

"Remember me," Job reminds God just a breath after he has
pleaded with God to leave him alone. Someone kindles the
fire of the Easter Vigil, and the disciples are comforted in the
warmth of each other's arms. Having paused the appropriate
number of days, Mary Magdalene and the other sleepless
women meet. While it is still dark, they prepare all they will
need to anoint and wrap the lifeless body of Jesus. They prepare
to visit the tomb where he is buried. Job's question echoes as
they step into the night. "If mortals die, can they live again?"
If Jesus died, can he live again? If Jesus died, can we live again?
And if we can, what will our lives become?

CHRISTINA BRAUDAWAY-BAUMAN

RESPONSE

What will your life become in light of Jesus' birth, death,
resurrection?

PRAYER

I am never far from your presence, O God. Remember me!
Amen.

THE RESURRECTION OF
THE LORD
(EASTER DAY)

Isaiah 25:6–9

It will be said on that day,
Lo, this is our God; we have waited for him,
so that he might save us.
This is the LORD for whom we have waited;
let us be glad and rejoice in his salvation. (v. 9)

Psalm 118:1–2, 14–24

This is the day that the LORD has made;
let us rejoice and be glad in it. (v. 24)

Acts 10:34–43

They put him to death by hanging him on a tree; but God raised him on the third day and allowed him to appear, not to all the people but to us who were chosen by God as witnesses, and who ate and drank with him after he rose from the dead. He commanded us to preach to the people and to testify that he is the one ordained by God as judge of the living and the dead. (vv. 40–42)

John 20:1–18

Jesus said to her, "Woman, why are you weeping? Whom are you looking for?" Supposing him to be the gardener, she said to him, "Sir, if you have carried him away, tell me where you have laid him, and I will take him away." Jesus said to her, "Mary!" She turned and said to him in Hebrew, "Rabbouni!" (which means Teacher). (vv. 15–16)

Isaiah 25:6–9

REFLECTION

In speaking about God, language is always "borrowed," as the hymn attributed to Bernard of Clairvaux says: "What language shall I borrow to thank thee, dearest friend, For this thy dying sorrow, thy pity without end?"Whether we are seeking to express the mystery of creation or redemption, the power of the cross or (as this week) the glory of the resurrection, the most we can do is reach for image and metaphor, poetry and song, because what we are trying to express extends so far beyond the reach of ordinary language.   CYNTHIA M. CAMPBELL

Psalm 118:1–2, 14–24

REFLECTION

The spirit of the message of the psalm and the communal and public context in which it took place can be seen in Protestant Latino congregations when they enact a procession in the streets during Holy Week, stopping along the way to give public testimony of the steadfast love of God in their lives. These are accounts of deliverance from difficult situations, like the ones in the psalm. "This is the day that the Lord has made" is sung in different languages throughout the global Christian community. We are an Easter people.   ELIZABETH CONDE-FRAZIER

Acts 10:34–43

REFLECTION

In a day when the church is confronted with various causes of divisions—ethnic splits, abortion, gender questions, gun control laws, the war in the Middle East, immigration, to name only a few—it is essential to hear on Easter, that Jesus' resurrection from the dead is not only the guarantee of a future life, but the declaration of the end of ancient strife and the hope of a new day. Gentiles belong in the church alongside Jews. The work of the Spirit in the lives of these Gentile people confirms that the resurrection throws open the doors to all who trust in God. CHARLES B. COUSAR

John 20:1–18

REFLECTION

We do not go to church simply to remind our conscious minds that God lives and we are called to follow Christ. We need to show up so that our bodies can be reminded of him too, and so the unconscious recesses of our psyches can be moved anew, our dispositions toward grace rejuvenated, our anxieties quelled as the world shifts once again into place and Easter comes, and comes, and comes again. In this yearly event we enter into the ripe, cinematic fullness of our embodied, uniquely personal lives—this is the shared space where Jesus meets us, calling our name, receiving our touch, calming our anxious worries, and reminding us again and again that grace is not an object to be known but a gift to be lived. SERENE JONES

RESPONSE

How are you meeting Jesus this Easter day? From whom did you receive his touch? How did you receive the gift of God's grace this day?

PRAYER

This is the day that the LORD has made. I will rejoice and be glad in it (Ps. 118:24). Alleluia! Christ has risen. Christ has risen indeed! Amen.

✲ *Second Sunday of Easter* ✲

Acts 4:32–35

There was not a needy person among them, for as
many as owned lands or houses sold them and brought the
proceeds of what was sold. They laid it at the apostles' feet, and
it was distributed to each as any had need. (vv. 34–35)

Psalm 133

How very good and pleasant it is
    when kindred live together in unity!
It is like the precious oil on the head,
    running down upon the beard,
on the beard of Aaron,
    running down over the collar of his robes. (vv. 1–2)

1 John 1:1–2:2

If we say that we have no sin, we deceive ourselves,
and the truth is not in us. If we confess our sins, he who is
faithful and just will forgive us our sins and cleanse us from all
unrighteousness. If we say that we have not sinned, we
make him a liar, and his word is not in us. (1:8–10)

John 20:19–31

Then [Jesus] said to Thomas, "Put your finger here and
see my hands. Reach out your hand and put it in my side.
Do not doubt but believe." Thomas answered him, "My Lord
and my God!" Jesus said to him, "Have you believed because
you have seen me? Blessed are those who have not seen
and yet have come to believe." (vv. 27–29)

✦ MONDAY ✦

Acts 4:32–35

REFLECTION

The image of a community so at one in heart and mind that not even physical possessions would be spared in face of need, shows the contemporary world an absurd picture of a people whom many would accuse of naiveté, communism, or plain stupidity and poor judgment. But that is how resurrection words and lives, in radically caring community, will always look to a world that lives in fear, isolation, and individualism.

ANDRÉ RESNER JR.

RESPONSE

What would it mean if your church really believed and acted as "one heart and soul"?

PRAYER

Remind me of your renewing Spirit alive within a radically caring community. Amen.

✦ TUESDAY ✦

Acts 4:32–35

REFLECTION

Biblical Christianity stands in stark contrast with the values of our consumer society. "Greed is good" may go down well at Wall Street, but not in the pages of Scripture. Proclaiming this truth in our churches today may be the most prophetic ministry we can have in the pulpit. ALAN G. PADGETT

RESPONSE

Read /listen to the news today alongside this text. Which truths are harder to hear?

PRAYER

In your world, loving God, there is enough for all, enough food, enough water, enough land. Help me as I struggle with what is enough. Amen.

✢ WEDNESDAY ✢

Psalm 133

REFLECTION

The fact that the psalmist is honest about the challenges of unity does nothing to negate its importance. "A house divided against itself cannot stand." In the summer of 1858, his nation on the verge of schism, Abraham Lincoln spoke of the dangers of disunity. The blessings of unity thus have a shadow reflection in the deep dangers of disunity. Is the work and unpredictability and messiness worth it? Ask Bishop Tutu. Or better yet, ask the children of Seeds of Peace. Since 1993, this organization has been forging unity, doing the hard work of reconciliation among the youth of the world. Starting with Palestinians and Israelis and now building unity in South Asia, Cyprus, and the Balkans, Seeds of Peace helps young people experience both the possibilities and challenges of unity as they develop relationships with those they have been taught to see as enemies. In working for peace, they work for the very survival of their families and societies.   MICHAEL D. KIRBY

RESPONSE

What seeds of peace need to be planted in your community?

PRAYER

God of peace, bless our efforts as we continue to learn how to live together as one. Amen.

✧ THURSDAY ✧

1 John 1:1–2:2

REFLECTION

Christians who live in communion with God need not deny that they are sinners, or pretend that shadows do not continue to fall across their journey toward the light. They should not despair when in the days and weeks that follow Easter the longed-for perfection of life does not appear, because in the communion they have with God they have an advocate, Jesus the Son, who is righteous, even when they are not, and it is his truthfulness, his atoning sacrifice, that calls them out of the shadows and enables them, with confidence and not in terror, to confess their sins and to walk toward the light.

GEORGE W. STROUP

RESPONSE

In confidence of God's atoning work, confess your sins of this day.

PRAYER

When shadows are near and darkness slowly creeps in, send the light of your Spirit to surround me so that I may walk in the light of your love. Amen.

✣ FRIDAY ✣

John 20:19–31

REFLECTION

John's story names the disciples' fears, and in the face of those fears, Jesus' grace increases. Allow these stories to speak for themselves—the disciples do not need to become object lessons, because Jesus did not make them into object lessons. He never lectured the disciples for hiding behind closed doors even after they had received the Spirit, nor did he censure Thomas for wanting a tactile experience of the risen Lord. The stories are parables of grace. The centrality of grace—even for "those who have not seen and yet have come to believe"—shapes the proclamation of this lesson. 	GAIL R. O'DAY

RESPONSE

Where do you see yourself in this resurrection story? Tell your own story of meeting Jesus.

PRAYER

I confess my doubts, my questions, my need to see in order to believe. Thank you for the assurance that believing leads to life in the name of Jesus, the risen Christ. Amen.

✦ SATURDAY ✦

John 20:19–31

REFLECTION

Despite what he has declared earlier, that he must both see
and touch Jesus with his own hands, Thomas does not touch,
but responds instead with the simple greeting, "My Lord and
my God!" Mary Magdalene and the disciples have earlier
recognized Jesus as Lord, but it is only Thomas who declares, in
the words of the prologue, that this is the Word that was God
(1:1). Verse 29 concludes the scene by turning Thomas's faith
outward; his faith in what he can see will be replicated by those
who do not see. BEVERLY ROBERTS GAVENTA

RESPONSE

What is required for your belief?

PRAYER

The signs of your presence are all around me. Give me eyes to
see them as I open my heart to the touch of your love. Amen.

✦ SUNDAY ✦

Acts 4:32–35

REFLECTION

Does the resurrection of Jesus still have power to transform?
What are the signs that we who have been baptized into Christ
share not only in his death but also in his victory over death?
The season after Easter was the time when those who had
just been baptized were led into deeper understanding of the
"mysteries" (the sacraments) and what their new life in Christ
meant. In the contemporary post-Easter season, perhaps
our efforts should be directed to helping people see concrete
glimpses into the power of God's transforming presence in this
world.
CYNTHIA M. CAMPBELL

Psalm 133

REFLECTION

Hospitality as recognition involves respecting the image of God
in others and seeing their potential contributions as being of
equal value to ours. Valuing is of the utmost importance, for
when persons are not valued, they become socially invisible,
and their needs and concerns are not acknowledged. Therein
lies the root of social injustice and suffering. When we resist
devaluing others, we witness to the importance of transcending
sociocultural boundaries that are exclusive. This practice also
helps us to resist the temptation of doing mission work from a
distance.
ELIZABETH CONDE-FRAZIER

1 John 1:1–2:2

REFLECTION

The writer invokes three theological themes: the koinonia
Christians have in Christ with God and with one another; the

reality and deceptive power of sin; and the atoning sacrifice
of Jesus Christ. It is these three themes, taken together, that
provide Christians hope as we continue to struggle with sin as
one Easter turns into another and "the longed-for perfection of
life does not appear."   GEORGE W. STROUP

John 20:19–31

REFLECTION

How are we to know when God arrives if, in our doubt, our
capacity for seeing God is sure to fail? John gives an answer to
this question that brings us to the heart of faith's peculiar form
of knowing. Jesus offers Thomas two clues to his identity. He
speaks the simple words, "Peace be with you," and then asks his
doubtful friend to put his doubtful fingers into the wounds that
he, Jesus, bears from the nails and swords that destroyed his
body only days before. What does this tell us about faith? When
God comes, we will recognize God's presence in those moments
when peace is offered, in those moments when life's most brutal
violence is honestly acknowledged, and when, in the midst of
this bracing honesty, we realize that we are not alone but have,
in fact, been always, already found.   SERENE JONES

RESPONSE

Where is God's transforming presence needed this day? Where
have you seen God this week? Where has God found you?

PRAYER

I pray that I will recognize you, O God, in simple acts of
kindness, mercy, justice, and love. Amen.

❦ *Third Sunday of Easter* ❦

Acts 3:12–19

"And now, friends, I know that you acted in ignorance,
as did also your rulers. In this way God fulfilled what he had
foretold through all the prophets, that his Messiah would
suffer. Repent therefore, and turn to God so that your
sins may be wiped out." (vv. 17–19)

Psalm 4

I will both lie down and sleep in peace;
   for you alone, O LORD, make me lie down in safety. (v. 8)

1 John 3:1–7

Beloved, we are God's children now; what we
will be has not yet been revealed. What we do know
is this: when he is revealed, we will be like him, for we
will see him as he is. And all who have this hope in him
purify themselves, just as he is pure. (vv. 2–3)

Luke 24:36b–48

And he said to them, "Thus it is written, that the
Messiah is to suffer and to rise from the dead on the third day,
and that repentance and forgiveness of sins is to be proclaimed in
his name to all nations, beginning from Jerusalem. You
are witnesses of these things." (vv. 46–48)

✧ MONDAY ✧

Acts 3:12–19

REFLECTION

Christ's church may have been born in a graveyard, but that baby grew quickly, beyond anyone's imagination. Given all that has happened since then—the grievous abuses of Messiah's gifts as well as the healing applications of them—what have we learned about what it means to be Easter people? How did Peter's sermon work on our forebears, and how is it still working on us today?   BARBARA BROWN TAYLOR

RESPONSE

What does it mean to you to be an Easter people? How is Peter's sermon working on you?

PRAYER

Open my heart and dwell deeply within me as I struggle with the meaning of new life. Amen.

→ TUESDAY ←

Psalm 4

REFLECTION

Psalm 4 confirms some of the things we assert about God.

> God answers prayer.
> God gives (breathing) room in human suffering.
> God is gracious.
> God is the source of our safety.

As God's rest on the Sabbath was an act of love— an example for us who are made in the divine image and likeness to emulate—human rest is an act of divine trust. The psalmist declares that "you have put gladness in my heart"—gladness beyond trouble, beyond the darkness of night, beyond the pain of broken relationships.   GARY V. SIMPSON

RESPONSE

Which of these affirmations about God from the psalmist do you most need to hear and remember?

PRAYER

God of my life, when pain is great and there are no words, you make room for me. When my suffering offers only tears, you hear my prayers. I sleep in the peace and safety of your loving arms. Amen.

✣ WEDNESDAY ✣

1 John 3:1–7

REFLECTION

In a culture of individualism, we belong to a community, the body of Christ. In an age that seeks security through violence, we seek solidarity, forgiveness, and peace. In a society that finds personal identity through social networking, we find our true name in baptism and in following Christ. We are odd, and we smooth over our oddities at our peril. When we feel right at home here, we should wonder whether we have traded the joy of divine love for the comfort of social acceptance. The source of our oddness is the love of God that makes us into God's children. RONALD COLE-TURNER

RESPONSE

How do you smooth over the oddities of your calling as a Christian?

PRAYER

Disturb my comfort. Remind me of my baptism as your own child. Amen.

→ THURSDAY ←

1 John 3:1–7

REFLECTION

Like most moderns, we trust experience more than we trust God. We believe the sorry facts of our broken lives more than we trust the saving promises of Scripture. God's truth is more true than ours because it is a deeper truth, a final truth, a truth not of what is, but of what shall be. It is the truth of grace that is greater than our sin. "Not me" may be experientially true, but even now it is theologically false. When we look into our hearts and ask, "Am I a child of God?" we have to learn to stop saying, "Not me," and instead learn to utter the deeper truth: "Not yet complete, but Yes! By grace I am God's own." Not yet appearing, but already claimed. Not yet complete, but already begun.

RONALD COLE-TURNER

RESPONSE

Look into your heart, see what God sees.

PRAYER

I am, I confess, not yet complete as your child, O God. I am indeed a work in progress, yet already claimed and named by you. Amen.

✣ FRIDAY ✣

Luke 24:36b–48

REFLECTION

The power of the resurrection is the power to plant the seeds
of transformation. The hope of the resurrection is grounded
in the experience of those first followers. Closed minds can be
opened. The potential is for a release in a prophetic way. The
word of God calls us to peace rather than security.

NANCY R. BLAKELY

RESPONSE

What is most frightening about following Jesus? What doubts
do you have?

PRAYER

Sometimes I long for security, not for change that comes in
planting seeds of transformation. Ground me in hope, and give
me an open mind. Amen.

→ SATURDAY ←

Luke 24:36b–48

REFLECTION

Jesus suddenly appeared in the midst of his early followers. He brought change to their lives as they moved from (1) fright and alarm to (2) joy mixed with disbelief and puzzlement to (3) open and understanding minds and hearts. That marked shift in the core of their beings led them forth to take great risks, witnessing to the risen Christ. Jesus did not bring them security. Rather, they risked all in following his call. For they had come to understand that Jesus had conquered the ultimate threat, death itself, and their fears were groundless. Jesus' words "Peace be with you!" came to fruition in their hearts.

NANCY R. BLAKELY

RESPONSE

The disciples experienced a triadic movement in response to meeting the resurrected Jesus. What risks are you willing to take as testimony to the risen Christ?

PRAYER

I am a witness to the risen Christ! Let my testimony be revealed in the actions of my life. Amen.

⊹ SUNDAY ⊹

Acts 3:12–19

REFLECTION

In this pericope, one notes the piling up of christological terms. In spite of human ignorance and malfeasance, God again visited his people through God's servant, the Holy and Righteous One, the Author of life. The crucified man from Galilee was indeed God's Messiah, raised from the dead and alive in the healing power of the disciples. In words that echo Israel's prophets, Peter implores his hearers to "repent" (*metanoia*)—literally "to change their minds" about Jesus of Nazareth. These Jerusalem Israelites are challenged to "turn around" (*epistrephō*) in their thinking about Jesus, so that they, like the prodigal son, might return to a joyfully waiting God.   PAUL W. WALASKAY

Psalm 4

REFLECTION

"You gave me room when I was in distress." The writer has reason to expect God's attention because she has already received blessing and release in times past. God has given her "room." In the King James we find, "thou hast enlarged me." Often, the Hebrew (*rahab*) has a sense of increasing territorial or agricultural room (as in Gen. 26:22, Exod. 34:24, Deut 12:20, 19:8). It is used frequently in the Psalms as metaphor, indicating an enlargement of heart (Pss. 25:17, 119:32), mouth (Pss. 35:21, 81:10), and steps (Ps. 18:36). The psalmist is indicating that God has provided space, perspective, openness where once there was constriction and the feeling of being hemmed in. This remembrance offers confidence to approach God once more.

                    KENT M. FRENCH

1 John 3:1–7

REFLECTION

The most difficult part of this passage is working to open minds
to a central kind of relationship that does not define itself by
difference. In this text, cooperation is the goal; difference in
name and culture and place is a distraction to the goal of right
relationship. . . . Think, then, of your children or of your own
childhood. Remember group play. Try to imagine yourself
working very hard at being understood. Try to think of the
importance of being heard clearly. Remember the power of
discovery as children participate in a world they create. Think
of how important it was to include everyone, to make a place
for those standing outside of the circle. Think of the hard work
of children. This text is about beginnings. We are called to start
fresh, with one another and under the guardianship of the most
powerful Caretaker. CLAUDIA HIGHBAUGH

Luke 24:36b–48

REFLECTION

Just when we thought the story is over, God had something
to say. It has always been about God and continues to be so.
Jesus did not launch into explanations about the mechanics of
resurrection, nor did he provide an itinerary of his whereabouts
since Friday. Instead, Jesus taught and commissioned: his whole
life, death, and rising were about what God is doing in the
world—reconciling the world to God's self. BARBARA J. ESSEX

RESPONSE

Meditate on these words to connect you with the texts: "repent,
turn around, room, beginnings." What images are evoked?

PRAYER

God, you continue to invite me into your old story, which is
ever new. Help me bring wholeness to your creation. Amen.

❧ *Fourth Sunday of Easter* ☙

Acts 4:5–12

"There is salvation in no one else, for there
is no other name under heaven given among mortals
by which we must be saved." (v. 12)

Psalm 23

The LORD is my shepherd, I shall not want.

. . . .

Surely goodness and mercy shall follow me
   all the days of my life,
and I shall dwell in the house of the LORD
   my whole life long. (vv. 1, 6)

1 John 3:16–24

Little children, let us love, not in word or
speech, but in truth and action. (v. 18)

John 10:11–18

"I am the good shepherd. The good shepherd
lays down his life for the sheep." (v. 11)

✤ MONDAY ✤

Acts 4:5–12

REFLECTION

A key issue in Acts is this: is the institution responsive to the Spirit, or is it curved in on itself? Whenever political or religious authorities set themselves up as the only legitimate broker of what people need and defend that authority, inevitably the Holy Spirit breaks down those structures. There was a time when the Roman Empire forbade the marriage of slaves, but the Christian church, in tune with the Spirit, upset the structures by encouraging and honoring such marriages. There was a time when Jim Crow laws excluded African Americans from full participation in public life, but the Spirit summoned civil rights leaders who challenged such strictures. Yet the temple authorities were not interested in the Spirit; they were interested in temple authority for its own sake. "By what power do you do these things?" they wanted to know, implying that if the disciples wanted to do religious business in Jerusalem, then they needed to get a license from the temple power brokers. "By the power of the name of Jesus," countered Peter and John.   THOMAS G. LONG

RESPONSE

In what ways is your church responsive to the Spirit? What powers and authorities would Jesus challenge today?

PRAYER

May your Spirit move deeply within my soul. May your Spirit be alive and well, challenging and sustaining your power and authority in my church and the world. Amen.

⟶ TUESDAY ⟵

Psalm 23

REFLECTION

The goodness of God is in every place before we ever arrive at any particular place. The good things that happen to us along life's journey do not happen because we have arrived. God's goodness has already been where we are planning to go. The goodness of God is so present that every direction that we turn to look, wherever we are, we bump into goodness again. It is perhaps egocentric and arrogant to think that goodness follows us. The goodness of God goes ahead of us, clearing out new ground, pulling us to new terrain, lighting a pathway in the dark places of new possibility, opening doors that no one can shut.

But mercy—that is another consideration altogether. Mercy is made necessary and nonnegotiable soon after the human is created.   GARY V. SIMPSON

RESPONSE

Where have you bumped into God's goodness today? Where has God's mercy met you?

PRAYER

Merciful God, your goodness surrounds my life. I will live in your house all of my life. Amen.

✢ WEDNESDAY ✢

Psalm 23

REFLECTION

We need mercy behind us, sweeping up the refuse we have inadvertently left in our wake; we need mercy to erase even the memory of our sins as God casts our sins as far as the east is from the west. Shutting doors that no one can open. This is the reality that gives the writer certainty at the psalm's ending: "Surely!" Thank God we live between these two shielding and protecting provisions of God, sandwiched between the goodness of God in front and the mercy of God behind—no matter which way we turn.   GARY V. SIMPSON

RESPONSE

Meditate on this familiar psalm heard from a new translation.

PRAYER

You protect me, O God, my whole life long. I am blessed as I live in the middle of your goodness and mercy. Amen.

✣ THURSDAY ✣

1 John 3:16–24

REFLECTION

The Spirit is the gift promised by Jesus to the Johannine community for the time after his resurrection and his return to the Father. The Spirit is the guide that strengthens the community and undoubtedly the guide who inspires the elder to write the words he writes. There is a multiple meaning in the Greek of 1 John 3:24 that the NRSV probably cannot capture with any single translation. "And by this we know that he abides in us," the NRSV reads—and then the Greek preposition is *ek,* "from"—"by the Spirit that he has given us." The sentence means two things. Believers know that Christ abides in them because they perceive that they have the Spirit. Believers know that Christ abides in them because through the Spirit God testifies to the presence of God's Son.   DAVID L. BARTLETT

RESPONSE

In what ways has the Spirit been a gift in your life? In what ways has the Spirit been a guide in the life of your faith community?

PRAYER

Thank you for the many ways, realized and yet to be seen, that your Spirit has gifted and guided my life. Amen.

✦ FRIDAY ✦

1 John 3:16–24

REFLECTION

Perhaps the portion of this text that is worth investigating is "let us love, not in word or speech, but in truth and action." . . . In the justice movement of the sixties a small black girl in New Orleans, Ruby Bridges, went to school and sat alone in a classroom for one year to integrate a public school. Responding to the needs of the community, her action of love was obedience to the court system and the sacrifice of her own comfort and security to make a better learning environment for other children. Ruby was respectful and responsible. Her source of "goods" was simply the patience of a small child to take the time necessary to make a difference for her young brothers and sisters. CLAUDIA HIGHBAUGH

RESPONSE

How has your love been expressed in truth and in action?

PRAYER

Abiding God, remind me of the saints who have gone before me, mentors of love in action. Amen.

✦ SATURDAY ✦

John 10:11–18

REFLECTION

Today's text speaks of intimacy and security. The shepherd is
sufficient for the care of the flock—the shepherd and sheep
know each other. We all long and hunger to know and to be
known—we create "virtual" communities on the Internet and
in chat rooms. Forming authentic and holistic community is
hard work—we dole out parts of ourselves in stingy bits and
pieces, avoid being vulnerable with each other, hold back our
feelings and thoughts, are afraid to confront each other, judge
each other without mercy, hold grudges, set impossibly high
standards for ourselves and each other. Our good intentions
are misunderstood and rejected, and we avoid commitments
because we do not want to risk exploitation or abuse. We have a
difficult time trusting each other. How can we form community
that is real and life giving? . . .

As you consider your preaching context, what kinds
of dangers threaten your community? Against what does
your community struggle? In what ways does a life of faith
address those dangers? What stifles rather than promotes
connectedness and community? How does the church provide a
place where people feel they belong?   BARBARA J. ESSEX

RESPONSE

Consider the questions raised in this reflection. What is your
hunger? How is the hunger for community and intimacy being
expressed in your congregation?

PRAYER

God you created us to live in community. As we struggle with
our own individual wants and needs, remind us of the blessings
of connectedness. Shepherd us, O God, as your beloved flock.
Amen.

✣ SUNDAY ✣

Acts 4:5–12

REFLECTION

The final verse of today's text, "There is salvation in no one else [but Jesus]," is often used to divide people into two camps: those who are for Jesus and those who are not for Jesus. While the author of Acts certainly believes that God has acted decisively and uniquely in Jesus Christ, the function of this text is the opposite of division. The purpose of this passage, instead, is to announce that no human being or human authority can erect a religious tent—a temple or a church or a movement—and say, "Unless you come into my tent, you cannot have God." God has acted on behalf of the whole of humanity in Jesus Christ, and there is "no other name," no human channel, that can make exclusive claim to religious power—no denomination, no one theology, no sect, no franchise on the power of the Spirit.

THOMAS G. LONG

Psalm 23

REFLECTION

Finally, in verse 6, the psalmist is convinced of God's protection. She is home, certain that God's goodness and steadfast love (*hesed*) will follow, even pursue her on the path. In 1 Kings, "the house of YHWH" refers to Solomon's temple (1 Kgs. 7:12, 40–51), correlating to the exodus notion of the ultimate abode of God's chosen people. The faithful will remain in this house for all the length of days. God's leading and protection will be fulfilled.

KENT M. FRENCH

1 John 3:16–24

REFLECTION

Believing and loving come from a single grace and result in a single act of obedience. The commandment cannot be split apart, because Jesus Christ is the concrete embodiment of God's love. We cannot believe in Jesus without believing in love, and we cannot have love without action. John gives us no room to negotiate.   RONALD COLE-TURNER

John 10:11–18

REFLECTION

The voice of Christ calls out to all the others just as it calls out to us; thus now is the time to examine our attitudes, practices, and behaviors that keep us safe from the concerns and needs of Christ's other sheep. To the extent that we decline to enter into the world of these other sheep due to discomfort or limited perceptions of our advantage, it is we who are refusing the voice that insists "one flock" is a correlate of the principle "one shepherd."   STEPHEN A. COOPER

RESPONSE

What attitudes, practices, and behaviors keep you safe from the concerns and needs of others in your world?

PRAYER

I struggle to be your child, knowing that believing and loving do emanate from a single grace. Amen.

❧ *Fifth Sunday of Easter* ❧

Acts 8:26–40

As they were going along the road, they came to some
water; and the eunuch said, "Look, here is water! What is
to prevent me from being baptized?" He commanded the chariot
to stop, and both of them, Philip and the eunuch, went down
into the water, and Philip baptized him. (vv. 36–38)

Psalm 22:25–31

All the ends of the earth shall remember
    and turn to the LORD;
and all the families of the nations
    shall worship before him. (v. 27)

1 John 4:7–21

Beloved, let us love one another, because love is from God;
everyone who loves is born of God and knows God. Whoever
does not love does not know God, for God is love. (vv. 7–8)

John 15:1–8

"Abide in me as I abide in you. Just as the branch cannot bear fruit
by itself unless it abides in the vine, neither can you unless you
abide in me. I am the vine, you are the branches. Those who abide
in me and I in them bear much fruit, because apart from me you
can do nothing. Whoever does not abide in me is thrown away like
a branch and withers; such branches are gathered, thrown into the
fire, and burned. If you abide in me, and my words abide in you,
ask for whatever you wish, and it will be done for you." (vv. 4–7)

✦ MONDAY ✦

Acts 8:26–40

REFLECTION

This story is thick with the presence of the Holy Spirit, which raises interesting questions about how that Spirit works. If God is the Law-maker, then God is also the Law-bender, or at least the Law-transcender, who both places limits on the faithful and inspires them to challenge those limits when right relationships with God and neighbor are at stake. This dynamic shows up in both testaments, not just one. When Philip follows the Spirit's leading to go to the Ethiopian eunuch, he follows in the footsteps of his ancestor Elijah, who was led by the Lord to a widow of Zarephath (1 Kgs. 17:9). When Philip comes up with nothing that might prevent the Ethiopian from being baptized, he acts on the eschatological prophecy of Isaiah 56:4–5.

BARBARA BROWN TAYLOR

RESPONSE

What relationships with neighbors is the Spirit inspiring you to challenge?

PRAYER

Your Spirit is both a comforting and challenging gift. Help me to be open to her leading in my life. Amen.

✦ TUESDAY ✦

Psalm 22:25–31

REFLECTION

This psalm also gives us the opportunity to see the practical definition of deliverance in action, and to see the role of the congregation in that experience. Here deliverance is simply defined as moving through pain to praise. Here the congregation functions powerfully as an agent of deliverance, as it provides "space" for the authentic deliverance of this one in pain to take place. The congregation is truly "sanctuary," a safe space for people who are brought together by pains, hoping for—yearning for—praise. The congregation of God keeps calling us to gather together through all of life's experiences—including adversity, death, illness, and the troubling times in the world.

GARY V. SIMPSON

RESPONSE

How does this psalm speak to your own recent experiences of adversity, death, illness, or troubling times in the world?

PRAYER

When I and those I love weep, you are there. When I and those I love rejoice, you are there. I live surrounded by your abiding presence. I am grateful, O God. Amen.

✦ WEDNESDAY ✦

Psalm 22:25–31

REFLECTION

The gathered community is an authentic acknowledgment of present laments. Too often gathered communities are not honest about the degree to which we suffer hurt as individuals, as communities of faith, as a nation, as a world of disconnected connectivity. Life hurts, and too often worship is used to mask pain and not to serve as a deliverance station. True deliverance comes about because our pains are not totally ignored by God. God cares. God knows pain too. The gathered community is a space for thanksgiving, even when we give thanks for the "not yet."

GARY V. SIMPSON

RESPONSE

In what ways has liturgy helped you connect with suffering and pain of others?

PRAYER

God, you have created humankind for community. I give thanks for my church, where songs of lament and songs of praise are heard. Amen.

✦ THURSDAY ✦

1 John 4:7–21

REFLECTION

With stunning brevity, John tells us what God is and what God is not. John might have said that God is power or order or goodness. In our insecurity and longing for protection, we often yearn for a God who can control nature and prevent sickness or violence, a God who will protect us from all harm. In a world of moral confusion, we wish for a God who lays down the law with complete clarity and holds everyone accountable, catching the cheaters and rewarding the faithful. In our hunger to possess, we might even imagine a God of prosperity, one who promises to make us rich if we obey a few principles.

Whatever may be true about God's power or moral order or generosity, John avoids all these descriptions in favor of the simple word *agape* or love.   RONALD COLE-TURNER

RESPONSE

Do you know someone who is searching for God, seeking to understand who God is in relation to the meaning of their life? How might this text help them?

PRAYER

It is so simple, yet so complex, this thing called love. You loved us first, and so you expect us to love our neighbor. Amen.

✦ FRIDAY ✦

John 15:1–8

REFLECTION

Jesus tells the disciples to abide in him, as he abides in them. In his translation *The Message: The Bible in Contemporary Language*, Eugene H. Peterson uses the words, "Live in me. Make your home in me just as I do in you." The notion of making a home, of finding the heart's true home in Jesus, brings a settled peace to the turmoil that often characterizes our lives.

NANCY R. BLAKELY

RESPONSE

What room do you make in your home for Jesus' abiding presence?

PRAYER

My heart is at rest as I make my home with you, God of my life. Amen.

⇥ SATURDAY ⇤

John 15:1–8

REFLECTION

When someone is having a difficult time, we casually give the advice to "hang in there." Those are not very helpful words for one who desperately wonders how to do just that. Jesus offers so much more than hanging in there. Yes, hard times will invariably come, but living, abiding, finding our home in Jesus the vine and God the grower sustains us, promoting even greater well-being. Recall the Hebrew notion of shalom, which speaks of wholeness, completeness, and health. Recovering that sense of shalom addresses the deep yearnings of our lives. Shalom enters into all the cuts and hurts we endure day to day. It even enables us to speak of healing when there is no hope for a cure. Hope for relief from suffering does remain—a hope that God's miracles of growth bring to fruition.

NANCY R. BLAKELY

RESPONSE

What connections do you make between the concept of abiding and the Hebrew notion of shalom?

PRAYER

I abide in you, knowing that your presence in my life gives me hope. Amen.

✛ SUNDAY ✛

Acts 8:26–40

REFLECTION

But Philip heard the voice of the Holy Spirit speak a different
answer to the man's question. "What is to prevent me from
being baptized?" asked the eunuch. "Absolutely nothing,"
whispered the Spirit. "Absolutely nothing." So the eunuch
commanded the chariot to stop, and he was baptized right on
the spot. Walls of prejudice and prohibition that had stood for
generations came tumbling, blown down by the breath of God's
Holy Spirit, and another man who felt lost and humiliated was
found and restored in the wideness of God's grace in Jesus
Christ.   THOMAS G. LONG

Psalm 22:25–31

REFLECTION

Psalm 22 is such a sweeping passage from darkness to light,
from despair to hope, that it is a shame to divide it up in the
lectionary. Today's selection provides the blessing of the psalm's
conclusion without the hard theological and spiritual struggle
that has gotten us there. It is triumph without the trial. . . .
These seven verses from Psalm 22 show the hopeful exultation
of one who has suffered, has despaired, and is now ready to
rejoin the communion of the faithful. They show a joyful,
almost giddy, excitement about the reign of the Lord, in the
past, present, and future. The psalmist, however, has arrived
at this celebratory state only through the hard-fought struggle
against her enemies, both internal and external. Worship
leaders preparing this passage would do well to read the psalm
in its entirety, to understand the cumulative significance of the
triumphant promise in these final verses.   KENT M. FRENCH

1 John 4:7–21

REFLECTION

We know God in the fullest and most authentic sense only when the love of God flows through us. God is love; only the one who loves can know this love that is God. Love is not a concept, known abstractly. It is an action, lived concretely. It is not enough to remember Jesus' self-sacrifice, to think about it, or even to be moved by it. We must live it. To know the God of love is to live the love of God. God's love is perfect, while ours is always flawed. Even so, we should not fear or be held back by our inadequacies, John tells us. Act lovingly, even if imperfectly. The love and the perfection come from God, whose perfect love casts out fear. We can honestly admit that we are not yet perfect in love, for it is God's love that makes us loving, and it is God's perfection that is making us ever more holy.   RONALD COLE-TURNER

John 15:1–8

REFLECTION

The notion of "abiding" comes into play when we think of the vineyard. The Greek root for "abide" (*menō*) carries a range of meanings—"staying in place," "enduring," "holding out"—that imply the steadfastness and reliability of God's presence in and for God's community. God's care is constant, and whatever pain or suffering results from God's pruning and cleansing is redemptive rather than arbitrary.   BARBARA J. ESSEX

RESPONSE

What phrases in these four reflections most speak to the affirmations and contradictions in your life of faith?

PRAYER

Your abiding presence in my life does not go unnoticed. The breath of your Spirit and the sacrifice of your Son sustain my life of faith and enable me to live your love. Amen.

✣ *Sixth Sunday of Easter* ✣

Acts 10:44–48

While Peter was still speaking, the Holy Spirit fell upon all who heard the word. The circumcised believers who had come with Peter were astounded that the gift of the Holy Spirit had been poured out even on the Gentiles, for they heard them speaking in tongues and extolling God. Then Peter said, "Can anyone withhold the water for baptizing these people who have received the Holy Spirit just as we have?" So he ordered them to be baptized in the name of Jesus Christ. Then they invited him to stay for several days. (vv. 44–48)

Psalm 98

Make a joyful noise to the LORD, all the earth;
    break forth into joyous song and sing praises.
Sing praises to the LORD with the lyre,
    with the lyre and the sound of melody.
With trumpets and the sound of the horn
    make a joyful noise before the King, the LORD. (vv. 4–6)

1 John 5:1–6

Everyone who believes that Jesus is the Christ has been born of God, and everyone who loves the parent loves the child. By this we know that we love the children of God, when we love God and obey his commandments. (vv. 1–2)

John 15:9–17

"This is my commandment, that you love one another as I have loved you." (v. 12)

✦ MONDAY ✦

Acts 10:44–48

REFLECTION

Ours is a world full of boundaries. No-trespassing signs warn
the uninvited to stay out. A floating rope separates the shallow
and deep sections of a swimming pool. Lines painted on a
gym floor delineate the playing area from "out of bounds."
Railroad tracks divide one part of town from "the other side of
the tracks." Mighty rivers, mountain ranges, or even carefully
negotiated invisible borders partition the land into nations.
From fenced yards to fenced borders, our boundaries seek to
keep the insiders in and the outsiders out. Whether visible or
invisible, boundaries not only segregate but also function to
reinforce our identities. We learn and know who we are by both
our identification with "our people" and our differentiation
from those who are not. Families, groups of friends, cliques
at school, departments at work, denominations and religions,
nations and alliances, and countless other groupings and
associations depend on various boundaries to create and
sustain themselves.   JEFFREY D. PETERSON-DAVIS

RESPONSE

Consider this reflection in light of Peter's question, "Can
anyone withhold the water for baptizing these people who have
received the Holy Spirit just as we have?"

PRAYER

Spirit of the living God, reveal to me the needless boundaries I
set up. Amen.

✦ TUESDAY ✦

Acts 10:44–48

REFLECTION

The Holy Spirit was working a powerful transformation among the early Christians. Their perspective of who was "in" and who was "out" was being changed not by their own doing, but by the intervention of the Holy Spirit. The boundaries of the "inner circle" kept widening to the point that the assumed boundaries were no longer legitimate. Peter's own utterance that God shows no partiality is a radical departure from his own definitions of what or who is clean and unclean. In this brief text we find exemplified the extravagance of the Holy Spirit and the wideness of God's grace. This story demonstrates that the Spirit is not bound by the limitations that even faithful believers have. The Spirit is not only poured out on the Gentiles; it is given to the Jewish Christians, enabling them to see with new eyes and capture a new vision of the kingdom of God. This is an important text for the church today. Not only do the wounds of exclusion run deep in our culture and in the church; the realities of uncrossed boundaries still exist. Neither society nor the church has overcome racism, sexism, classism, ageism, nationalism, heterosexism, and other prejudices. We continue to propagate segregation in many forms as we hold firm to the visible and invisible boundaries between "us" and "them."

JEFFREY D. PETERSON-DAVIS

RESPONSE

Meditate today on your own experience of the wideness of God's grace.

PRAYER

Spirit of the living God, in your extravagant presence, empower your church to see beyond the safety of exclusivism to the welcoming waters of baptism. Amen.

✦ WEDNESDAY ✦

Psalm 98

REFLECTION

We are invited to sing anew the old songs—songs that recall all that God has done and the promise that God is alive and active in our own time. We too are in bondage to many things. We are overwhelmed and saddened by the messiness of the world and our contribution to the chaos that surrounds us. We are mired in greed, addictions, and estrangement from God, each other, and our own selves. Our communities are no longer neighborhoods of cooperation and camaraderie. Instead of block parties and potluck suppers, we are held captive by our computers that promise "virtual" community in chat rooms and blogs.

BARBARA J. ESSEX

RESPONSE

What new song is God inviting you to sing?

PRAYER

I join with all creation in singing a new song to celebrate your presence in this world, Creator God. Amen.

✤ THURSDAY ✦

1 John 5:1–6

REFLECTION

So how exactly is fulfilling God's commandments not burdensome or exploitative? The first verse of this passage states the answer in plain terms: "everyone who believes Jesus is the Christ" is welcomed into the community—indeed is "born" into the family (v. 4)—where love flows freely. The love we give is simply the love we have first received, as children receive life from and give life to parents. Love is a birthright of faith. Faith "conquers" the dross and drag of this world. When love arrives under the most mundane circumstances and in the dire social times of the 1960s and today, it comes as gift and grace. Genuine love is invited, not forced, motivated by faithfulness rather than fear, counts not as "loss" but gain in some deeper way, and leads to more just and loving relationships.

BONNIE J. MILLER-MCLEMORE

RESPONSE

In what ways have you experienced the gift of God's love this week? In what ways have you given God's love to someone else?

PRAYER

I pray that my faith is strengthened to meet the challenges of this world. Amen.

✧ FRIDAY ✧

John 15:9–17

REFLECTION

Which are some of the implications of these biblical and theological dimensions for contemporary preaching? For more than thirty years I have been a missionary in Latin America and the Caribbean in three different countries. In the 1970s and '80s a contextual pastoral theology coming out of the pastoral praxis of Catholic and Protestant communities of faith was born: *Pastoral de Acompañamiento* (Pastoral of Accompaniment) integrates the spiritual, emotional, psychological, anthropological, sociopolitical, and economic dimensions in the journey in faith for so many Christians in situations of brokenness, alienation, injustices, and exclusion. The faithful have learned to trust in a liberating gospel that promises hope in the midst of oppression. They experience God's presence in their deepest need.

CARMELO ÁLVAREZ

RESPONSE

With whom is your abiding presence needed this week?

PRAYER

God who accompanies me in my journey of faith, strengthen and support me as I accompany others in need of your love and care. Amen.

✦ SATURDAY ✦

John 15:9–17

REFLECTION

Today this Pastoral of Accompaniment can become relevant in communities of faith in the United States as preachers commit themselves to address concrete situations, keeping in mind the situations confronting their parishioners and offering new insights and new alternatives. The tasks confronting these parishioners include strengthening communities of solidarity, affirming diversity, promoting healthy relationships in families and communities, embracing strangers, and promoting intercultural and interreligious dialogues. A community of celebration that affirms life and offers hope in joyous moments of remembrance and commitment to God's reign is a good place to start.   CARMELO ÁLVAREZ

RESPONSE

Which of the tasks mentioned above are most important for your congregation?

PRAYER

Thank you for your abiding presence in my life and the life of my congregation. Show us the tasks we must face as we continue grow as a community of faith. Amen.

Acts 10:44–48

REFLECTION

We should be careful preaching these stories in the church. Those who are hearing the voice of God, the young who have visions and the old who dream dreams (Acts 2:17; Joel 2:28), might just be empowered to speak truth, share their visions, tell of their dreams. Or perhaps if we do preach these words, we should be prepared to be led to the threshold to cross a boundary.

JEFFREY D. PETERSON-DAVIS

Psalm 98

REFLECTION

God's new, unexpected, and marvelous acts do not just sustain order but point toward the creation of new possibilities of life beyond all human expectations. A new song thus becomes imperative, so that all creation praises and celebrates these unexpected, unique, and marvelous deeds of the Lord. We can sing new songs of praise because we have witness of how the Lord is in control and that nothing will stand against or defeat God's liberating purpose. We can sing new songs of praise because God too is constantly doing new things among us— new things to renew nature and history as well.

ISMAEL GARCÍA

1 John 5:1–6

REFLECTION

Kinship with God, faith in God—apart from the daily down-to-earth discipline of treating folks "like family" (and of discerning what that entails when conflicts and quandaries arise)—these theological notions remain abstractions. But rules and regulations, strategies and action plans—apart from a deep awareness of the mystical union we have with God in Christ and with all those whom God calls children—by themselves reduce ethical responsibility to merely mechanical methods.

DAVID J. SCHLAFER

John 15:9–17

REFLECTION

The love that structures the inner life of God gives us a sense of the proper pattern for Christian love. Far from a mere feeling of euphoria, it is a disciplined habit of care and concern that, like all the virtues, can be perfected only over a lifetime. As Jesus observes, this love should be so deeply woven into our lives that we might even find ourselves called to die for it.

DAVID S. CUNNINGHAM

RESPONSE

What new thing is God doing? How are you being renewed in faith?

PRAYER

God, you weave the strands of love so deeply in our lives. Help me extend those strands to others so that a blanket of faith surrounds them. Amen.

THE WEEK OF THE
❧ *Ascension of the Lord* ❧

Acts 1:1–11

When he had said this, as they were watching, he was lifted up, and a cloud took him out of their sight. While he was going and they were gazing up toward heaven, suddenly two men in white robes stood by them. They said, "Men of Galilee, why do you stand looking up toward heaven? This Jesus, who has been taken up from you into heaven, will come in the same way as you saw him go into heaven." (vv. 9–11)

Psalm 47

Clap your hands, all you peoples;
   shout to God with loud songs of joy.
For the LORD, the Most High, is awesome,
   a great king over all the earth.
He subdued peoples under us,
   and nations under our feet. (vv. 1–3)

Ephesians 1:15–23

God put this power to work in Christ when he raised him from the dead and seated him at his right hand in the heavenly places, far above all rule and authority and power and dominion, and above every name that is named, not only in this age but also in the age to come. (vv. 20–21)

Luke 24:44–53

Then he led them out as far as Bethany, and, lifting up his hands, he blessed them. While he was blessing them, he withdrew from them and was carried up into heaven. (vv. 50–51)

✦ MONDAY ✦

Acts 1:1–11

REFLECTION

Artists who have portrayed this story in paintings and woodcuts have not only pictured Jesus' feet disappearing into the clouds. Many of them have also shown us something else. If you look closely at these paintings and woodcuts—not up in the clouds, but down on the ground—you will see footprints on the earth. Some artists have painted indentations in the rock. Others have etched black-and-white footprints on the ground not far from where the disciples are standing with their mouths open. Perhaps the artists simply have been imagining details that are not in the text. Or, perhaps, they keep pressing us with the question asked long ago: "Why do you stand looking up toward heaven?"

BARBARA K. LUNDBLAD

RESPONSE

Use colored pencils, crayons, or makers and connect to this text with your own images or drawings. How would you depict this scene?

PRAYER

I confess that sometimes I do stand looking, waiting. Help me to remember the power of the witness of life sustained by your Spirit. Amen.

⇥ TUESDAY ⇤

Psalm 47

REFLECTION

To read Psalm 47 is not to applaud the United States—rather, it is to reclaim the church's subversive posture in the world. Israel struggled for a place on the world stage by seeking to be like other nations. Israel saw its world crash and burn—land lost, city sacked, temple destroyed, palace raided, dynasty thwarted, and priesthood desecrated. Israel needed to regroup and remember who and whose they were and why they were chosen in the first place. They remembered and praised the One who gave them life and held them in their bleakest days of despair, depression, and devastation. They remembered and praised the One who still had a word of life for them.   BARBARA J. ESSEX

RESPONSE

As you prepare for Ascension Day, what does this psalm invite you to remember, to praise?

PRAYER

God of my life, I remember your presence in my life, and I join with choirs through the ages in singing your praise. Amen.

✣ WEDNESDAY ✣

Psalm 47

REFLECTION

Rather than a psalm of imperialist, death-dealing power, Psalm 47 is one of hope and imagination. If we believe that God is the Most High, is awesome, and is a great ruler, then we can trust this God to be refuge and strength whenever and wherever we gather and acknowledge God. . . . By reciting Psalm 47 on Ascension Day, we are reminded that Moses requested that Pharaoh let God's people go, not so they could grab power and rule oppressively, but so they could worship God (see Exod. 5:3). And so, despite all the structures with which we must contend—social, political, economic, ideological—we must never forget who is really in charge. God reigns and we are assured that all will be good—not only for us, but for all peoples, all nations, and all of creation.   BARBARA J. ESSEX

RESPONSE

Reflect on this psalm and the places where it invites you to hope and imagine new possibilities.

PRAYER

God, you are in charge, not me. Amen.

✢ ASCENSION DAY ✦

Ephesians 1:15–23

REFLECTION

In the last verse, the author suggests a final pastoral angle on hope gained from the perspective of Christ's ascension: Salvation is a corporate affair, known through the church as it grows into the "fullness" of Christ's body. This is not personal salvation or new-age spirituality. Christ saves through tangible, corporeal, committed community. One does not remember many sermons over a lifetime. But I remember one on the feeding of the five thousand. The Episcopal priest simply noted that when Jesus provides, there is plenty to go around and some left over. Contrary to all our grabbing and grasping after more—more time, more money, more status, more beauty—we already have enough. In Christ's promise of salvation, we have enough. We have the "fullness of him who fills all in all" (v. 23). For this, we have much to celebrate.

BONNIE J. MILLER-MCLEMORE

RESPONSE

In what ways have you experienced the saving grace of Christ through your experiences within the faith community?

PRAYER

For the body of believers who surround me, I give you thanks. Amen.

⤜ FRIDAY ⤛

Luke 24:44–53

REFLECTION

Ascension Day is not so much about the physical act of
ascension, or even about the reuniting of the incarnate Word
with the unbegotten Source. Rather, it is concerned with the
divine act of making space so that the mission of the church
can begin. So long as God was in the world in human form,
all eyes and hearts were fixed there. Jesus' ascension makes
space for the disciples to turn their gaze upon the world, where
"repentance and forgiveness of sins is to be proclaimed in [the
Messiah's] name to all nations, beginning from Jerusalem"
(24:47).   DAVID S. CUNNINGHAM

RESPONSE

As you meditate on Jesus' ascension, what new space for
ministry is opened up?

PRAYER

Slow me down, remind me to make space to see your world and
its needs in new ways. Amen.

✦ SATURDAY ✦

Luke 24:44–53

REFLECTION

The Gospel of Luke does not end in tears or a final embrace or
a conclusive good-bye. It ends in blessing: "Then he led them
out as far as Bethany, and, lifting up his hands, he blessed them.
While he was blessing them, he withdrew from them and was
carried up into heaven" (Luke 24:50–51). That was the disciples'
last wondrous glimpse of their friend, their teacher, their Lord.
They saw his raised hands and heard his voice as he withdrew.
Christ was in the act of blessing them as he left. Their last
memory was not that he had blessed them and then stopped.
Not that he had finished and they all said, "Amen." Not that
they wrote down the words of blessing and used it ever after
as a part of their prayer life. But, rather, the process of blessing
was continuing as he left them. I wonder how many times the
disciples must have retold the story. We human beings treasure
our last memories of those who were dear to us and are now
gone.   THOMAS H. TROEGER

RESPONSE

How have you experienced Jesus' blessing in your life and
ministry?

PRAYER

Jesus, you left in the act of blessing your disciples. And even
today, your blessings continue. Amen.

✣ SUNDAY ✣

Acts 1:1–11

REFLECTION

In Luke's Gospel, Jesus' footprints are all over the pages of the text. The Holy Spirit is not left to our imagination but takes shape in the life of Jesus. His inaugural sermon in Luke 4 outlined the Spirit's work: to bring good news to the poor, release to the captives, recovery of sight to the blind, and freedom to those who are oppressed. At the end of Luke, Jesus promised the gift of that same Spirit to his disciples. Picking up the image of the footprints, the preacher can help people see where the Spirit is moving in our time. Walk to the community lunch program where a hundred fifty people are sitting down to eat. Walk to the detention center where asylum seekers are encouraged by visitors from the local congregation. Walk to the women's shelter where women and children find freedom from violence and oppression. Perhaps some will say, "What are these small efforts in the face of enormous problems?" Jesus reminds us that we cannot know when God will fulfill all things—*but*—that little word always brings us down to earth again.   BARBARA K. LUNDBLAD

Psalm 47

REFLECTION

Let your sacred imagination dream the scene. Like children, all peoples, foreigners and Israelites, are summoned by God to the divine throne room. The invitations command that all must bring their weapons for inspection and presentation. Sheepishly, the huge warriors comply, from both sides of the conflict, and one by one pass in front of the Lord of heaven and earth. Facing each soldier, and inspecting each shield, God says, "That's mine. Hand it over." Soon there is a huge pile of shields, and no one can tell any more which shields are Israelite or which are Korean or American or Iraqi. Suddenly, the sound of clapping is heard, started by a Chinese soldier who is joined by an Indian, then a Pakistani, then an Afghani. Finally all are clapping, and the sound drowns out hatred and contempt and fear. Because after all, the sovereign, the Most High, is enthroned in awe over all. JOHN C. HOLBERT

Ephesians 1:15–23

REFLECTION

The heart of Easter is not simply that (all reasonable expectations to the contrary) Jesus came back to life from death; that in so doing Jesus (by whatever theory of atonement) "saves us from sin"; that because Jesus lives, death is not the final word for those who believe in him. Resurrection, ultimately, as the author of Ephesians says, means being raised—uplifted to a place from which Jesus is able (as the author of John's Gospel says) to draw all people (or, as some ancient texts say, "all things") to himself (John 12:32). DAVID J. SCHLAFER

Luke 24:44–53

REFLECTION

—Are people more comfortable with meditation and prayer, or with action? . . .

—Does your church or congregation engage in a balance of spiritual disciplines and active outreach? The Benedictine principle of *ora et labora* ("pray and work") is a very helpful model. . . .

—Does the gospel call people simply to believe, or to act on their beliefs? CARMELO ÁLVAREZ

RESPONSE

What new ideas for Ascension Day are evoked for you?

PRAYER

Help me, O God, to be open to see the ways that your Spirit is moving in these days. Amen.

❧ *Seventh Sunday of Easter* ❦

Acts 1:15–17, 21–26

Then they prayed and said, "Lord, you know
everyone's heart. Show us which one of these two you
have chosen to take the place in this ministry and apostleship
from which Judas turned aside to go to his own place." And
they cast lots for them, and the lot fell on Matthias; and
he was added to the eleven apostles. (vv. 24–26)

Psalm 1

Happy are those
    who do not follow the advice of the wicked,
or take the path that sinners tread,
    or sit in the seat of scoffers;
but their delight is in the law of the LORD,
    and on his law they meditate day and night. (vv. 1–2)

1 John 5:9–13

Those who believe in the Son of God have the testimony
in their hearts. Those who do not believe in God have made
him a liar by not believing in the testimony that God has given
concerning his Son. And this is the testimony: God gave
us eternal life, and this life is in his Son. (vv. 10–11)

John 17:6–19

"They do not belong to the world, just as I do not
belong to the world. Sanctify them in the truth; your word
is truth. As you have sent me into the world, so I have
sent them into the world." (vv. 16–18)

⤏ MONDAY ⤎

Acts 1:15–17, 21–26

REFLECTION

This story of the selection of Matthias pushes us to ask questions about how we discern the will of God and the confidence we place in systems we employ. While casting lots seems primitive and out of step with reason, could we trust that God might reveal the divine will in such a simple and definitive way? To what extent do the methods we employ in discernment get tangled up in our own need to control circumstances and outcomes? How do we see the community of the early followers of Jesus engaging in discernment? How does prayer influence our decision making?   JEFFREY D. PETERSON-DAVIS

RESPONSE

Where in the church might a discernment model for decision making be most effective?

PRAYER

I want to be your faithful disciple, O God, a living witness for you. Amen.

✦ TUESDAY ✦

Psalm 1

REFLECTION

One cannot skim a chapter of the Bible a day, offer up a
mumbled prayer, without pondering and meditating and
musing over a lifetime, and expect to gain a happy blessedness.
What may result instead is a pernicious wickedness, fueled
by selective reading, by brief musing, by little delight. So
much of the use of the Bible in our century smacks of these
three mockeries of the psalmist's call for rich reading, lengthy
pondering, and genuine joy. Rather than stout trees, such Torah
misuse breeds chaff, driven away by the next false wind of
hatred, bigotry, or triumphalist nationalism.   JOHN C. HOLBERT

RESPONSE

What time do you make in your life for the joy of rich reading
and lengthy pondering of the Word of God?

PRAYER

Water my soul, O God, so that I may continue to grow in love
and faith. Amen.

✦ WEDNESDAY ✦

Psalm 1

REFLECTION

What Psalm 1 affirms is that all we need to know
about God and ourselves can be found in Torah, in a
deep and rich appropriation and meditation on its surprises.
The psalmist believed that only if one is steeped in Torah can
one hope to survive the risks, the dangers, the ever-new horrors
that the world continues to present. However grayer the world
of the preacher is now, she will want to proclaim as clearly
as did the psalmist, that in Torah may still be discovered the
resources needed to steer our boats past the shoals of the raging
river and toward the still waters promised by the God who gave
Torah to us all.   JOHN C. HOLBERT

RESPONSE

In what ways does this psalm comfort you and/or
challenge you?

PRAYER

Your still waters surround me, God of my life. Amen.

✣ THURSDAY ✣

1 John 5:9–13

REFLECTION

God testifies. For some, this is an astounding claim that touches the intricate tapestry of divine disclosure and condescension found throughout the Scriptures. God speaks in word and deed, through individuals, and in forming a hearing community. God "bore witness" in Israel and through Israel. That history of witness culminates in testimony to the Son. All along the way, God places the divine witness alongside human witness. God's willingness to be humbled and made lowly in this way is one of the most profoundly disturbing realities of the divine testimony. God's witness lives in the same space and time as human witness. It drinks the same dirty water, walks the same dusty roads, and sleeps in the same fragile tents as human witness. That witness is very often indistinguishable from other human witnesses. We see in Scripture God's testimony mingled with human testimony, and God wills this to be the case.

WILLIE JAMES JENNINGS

RESPONSE

Reflect this day on God's witness in your life. Reflect on the witness of the lives of people you know.

PRAYER

May my life, my words, and my acts be a testimony to you. Amen.

⇥ FRIDAY ⇤

John 17:6–19

REFLECTION

The wisdom of John's sermon, delivered as the instruction of Christ, is this: it provides an alternative to retreat from world without giving into the pressures of the world. Again and again we read that Jesus and his disciples "do not belong to the world," that is to say, the world's claims do not shape their essential identify, faith, and values. But at the same time Christ is crystal clear that there is no escape from the reality of the world. He says, "I speak these things in the world so that they may have my joy made complete in themselves" (v. 13). Christ speaks to them in the same world where they live and where they will find joy "in themselves" or, to provide another equally valid translation, "among themselves." Yes, they can be a community, and yes, they can find joy in that community, but no, the community is not to abandon the world.

THOMAS H. TROEGER

RESPONSE

What joy do you find in the world?

PRAYER

Even as I sit alone before you, O God, I know that I am not alone, that there is joy and hope abounding in the community of faith that surrounds me. Amen.

✦ SATURDAY ✦

John 17:6–19

REFLECTION

How can the church be more faithful to Jesus' radical demands? How should we confront corruption in local, state, and federal governmental agencies? How can we exercise a vigilant attitude about corruption in the church and church institutions? How does the church become more accountable to its own structures and the public realm?   CARMELO ÁLVAREZ

RESPONSE

How is God sending you and your church into the world?

PRAYER

Open my eyes and ears to the radical demands of your Son. Amen.

✦ SUNDAY ✦

Acts 1:15–17, 21–26

REFLECTION

It is widely agreed and accepted by scholars and students alike of the Scriptures that the first chapter of the Acts is about transition and change in leadership of the church. According to the first fourteen verses Jesus took forty days in which he taught the disciples the mysteries of the kingdom of God as he prepared them for a change in leadership. Jesus would leave, ascend to God, and the apostles would assume leadership for the church. Preparation for leadership in the church included the gift of the Holy Spirit. They would receive Spirit power that would guide them and make them aware of the exigencies that were sure to confront them in their role as leaders of the church. They would come to learn through the agency and presence of the Holy Spirit that Jesus their teacher and Lord would always be with them. NOEL LEO ERSKINE

Psalm 1

REFLECTION

Psalm 1 provides the blueprint for moral living under the law of the God of Israel. We call the psalm a "torah psalm" because it is legalistic in nature. As Wisdom literature it is instructive and offers guidance to all those who will enter the gates into the Psalter. The lessons offered therein are more than a word to the wise. The psalm is a word to be wise in action, in choices, in character, and in our lived ethos in relationship to the God of Israel. Thus, it is not merely a directive parable encouraging the selection of the road less traveled; it is an edict against traveling the wrong road. It is also a warning not to step outside the appropriate boundaries of the Creator and God's created paradigm. SAKENA YOUNG-SCAGGS

1 John 5:9–13

REFLECTION

The Son brought to us eternal life. This is his testimony, and it is also the testimony of God. The Son overcame death from within the space and time that death claimed as its own, our space and our time. All who believe in the Son have the testimony of God at work in their lives. Indeed, our testimonies to Jesus Christ participate in this living testimony of God in his Son. This joining of testimonies is a gift brought to us by the incarnate life of God. This joining of testimonies also creates a powerful reality of inclusion. Our witness, joined to the witness of the Son, becomes a word of eternal life.

WILLIE JAMES JENNINGS

John 17:6–19

REFLECTION

In preaching on the truth of the gospel, there are some challenging ethical questions that might be considered. First, when the Gospel stresses "live by the truth" (3:21 NIV), it means to accept the ethical demand that leads to the doing of the truth in concrete actions. Second, it requires faithful people to "tell the truth" (Dietrich Bonhoeffer), as a consequence of a conduct and testimony (15:26) that witnesses to that truth. Third, it calls to a discipleship in solidarity and the promotion of true reconciliation. Today, more than ever, reclaiming the centrality of the truth of the gospel and living the gospel in truth are daring tasks.

CARMELO ÁLVAREZ

RESPONSE

What truths of the gospel are revealed to you this day?

PRAYER

Reveal to me the ways that my testimony is joined with that of your Son, Jesus. Amen.

❧ *Pentecost* ❦

Acts 2:1–21

When the day of Pentecost had come, they were
all together in one place. And suddenly from heaven there
came a sound like the rush of a violent wind, and it filled the
entire house where they were sitting. Divided tongues, as of fire,
appeared among them, and a tongue rested on each of them. All
of them were filled with the Holy Spirit and began to speak in
other languages, as the Spirit gave them ability. (vv. 1–4)

Psalm 104:24–34, 35b

I will sing to the LORD as long as I live;
I will sing praise to my God while I have being. (v. 33)

Romans 8:22–27

Now hope that is seen is not hope. For who hopes for
what is seen? But if we hope for what we do not see, we wait for
it with patience. Likewise the Spirit helps us in our weakness;
for we do not know how to pray as we ought, but that very Spirit
intercedes with sighs too deep for words. (vv. 24–26)

John 15:26–27; 16:4b–15

"I still have many things to say to you, but you cannot bear them
now. When the Spirit of truth comes, he will guide you into all the
truth; for he will not speak on his own, but will speak whatever he
hears, and he will declare to you the things that are to come. He
will glorify me, because he will take what is mine and declare it to
you. All that the Father has is mine. For this reason I said that he
will take what is mine and declare it to you." (16:12–15)

✢ MONDAY ✢

Acts 2:1–21

REFLECTION

Peter's association of the Pentecost event with the outpouring of the Spirit foretold by Joel means that there is now a new community of women and men where the one Spirit bestows many gifts—on all people, regardless of who they are. As Jürgen Moltmann put it, "In the kingdom of the Spirit, everyone will experience his and her own endowment and all will experience the new fellowship together" (Jürgen Moltmann, *The Spirit of Life: A Universal Affirmation,* trans. Margaret Kohl [Minneapolis: Fortress Press, 1993], 239). The church is the place where this new fellowship begins to take shape as it recognizes the gifts of the Spirit in and for all people. To realize that "all flesh," all people, receive the Spirit, enables us to watch and participate in God's work in this world with a wide-open vision. We live in eager anticipation of the Spirit's work in our midst as we join with all others to accomplish the Spirit's purposes.

DONALD K. MCKIM

RESPONSE

In what ways is God's Spirit working in the life of your congregation? What new thing is God's Spirit calling forth?

PRAYER

Pour out your Spirit on me this day. Amen.

✣ TUESDAY ✣

Acts 2:1–21

REFLECTION

Finally, Pentecost has something to say to individuals who do not feel that belonging to the body of Christ is necessary for personal Christian discipleship. It also speaks to those who feel discouraged, disillusioned, or excluded by the church. From the very beginning, Christ calls individuals into community as the church. Pentecost allows us to speak boldly to the church as we are and about the church Christ would have us be. The many dimensions of the church's identity—global, local, and personal—are interrelated and essential. None can exist apart from Christ or from the others.   KRISTIN EMERY SALDINE

RESPONSE

In what ways might this text be heard by those who do not think they need to belong to a faith community?

PRAYER

Everyone who calls on the name of the Lord shall be saved. Amen.

✦ WEDNESDAY ✦

Psalm 104:24–34, 35b

REFLECTION

It is a central aspect of biblical anthropology that we cannot understand ourselves or the nature of reality apart from the Spirit. Anthropology is rooted in theology. All of life, including human life, is grounded in and sustained by God. This does not mean that we become one with God or a part of God. Unlike pantheism or certain kinds of mysticism, in biblical thinking there is real differentiation between God and human beings. We are not gods. We remain creatures—often rebellious, ungrateful and even unaware of our true origins— and, as is made clear in this very psalm, God allows us the space and creates the conditions in which our distinctive forms of creatureliness can flourish or fester. But the fact remains that we are utterly dependent on God for our existence. This is why it is impossible for the human race to be truly godless. We may deny God with our lips, but the very breath we employ to do so is granted us by the Creator. The breath of the Spirit leaves its traces deep within.

IWAN RUSSELL-JONES

RESPONSE

As you begin this week of Pentecost, notice your breath. Breathe in, breathe out. Listen, wait, hear the sound of your life, a gift of God. What traces of the breath of the Spirit lie within you?

PRAYER

This week, try a simple breath prayer each day, either one that is here or one that you think of yourself. A breath prayer is something you can pray in one breath. Bless the LORD, O my soul (Ps. 103:1). Amen.

✣ THURSDAY ✣

Psalm 104:24–34, 35b

REFLECTION

Given the vicissitudes of life, even for faithful people and communities, it would be hard to assert that this psalm would stand up to serious scrutiny of the details of its poetic theology of creation, providence, and the dependence of the creation on the One who made it all. We do not always feel so cared for by God, nor do we recognize God's hand so clearly and closely in our doings, nor do we appreciate it every time we do. Bad things happen to us and to the world. Those we love and trust betray us. We are heedless of the good or resent our dependency. Communally, the most faithful congregations may be the ones struggling the most to live in difficult situations and circumstances. Fidelity to God is no guarantee of closeness or gratitude, and if that same God rules the universe with power, it makes things all the more confusing. Someone will no doubt hear this psalm and ask: Where is that loving Creator? Why do I feel distant? Such questions leave us in the dark. Perhaps they can be answered only with a hymnic assertion of trust such as this, and a life that is lived against the seeming grain.

MARK MILLER-MCLEMORE

RESPONSE

When have you experienced God's immanence recently? And conversely, when have you felt most distant from God's life-giving breath?

PRAYER

Another breath prayer: I will sing to the LORD as long as I live (Ps. 104:33). Amen.

✦ FRIDAY ✦

Romans 8:22–27

REFLECTION

As pastors listen and walk with their flocks through the darkest valleys, they boldly claim in faith, hope, and love that the "Spirit helps us in our weakness" (v. 26). This strong assurance comes to the faithful even when "we do not know how to pray as we ought" (v. 26). When we cannot find words, the Spirit, according to Paul, is one with us in our "sighs." The presence of the Spirit in the time of the present suffering is an ever-present reminder that God is present with the faithful always. Paul anticipates fully the work of the Trinity: God searches the heart, loves us in Jesus Christ, and knows the mind of the Spirit. Finally, in our weakness God is present with us in the one "who died, yes, who was raised, who is at the right hand of God, who indeed intercedes for us" (v. 34).   J. BARNEY HAWKINS IV

RESPONSE

What weakness is the Spirit helping you with this day?

PRAYER

And a breath prayer from the text: For in hope we were saved (Rom. 8:24). Amen.

→ SATURDAY ←

John 15:26–27; 16:4b–15

REFLECTION

The individual who strives to discover what is deepest in the human soul in order to find God in the midst of life finds the answer to the struggle for meaning in Jesus, who is the way, the truth, and the life (John 14:6). Jesus is not with us now; but while he is with the Father, he has left with us his presence in the person of the Paraclete, the Spirit of truth. It is the Spirit of truth who guides each generation along that way to uncover the grace and beauty in life. It is the Spirit of truth who teaches us to find God in the midst of life, to see life as Jesus taught us to see. It is the Spirit of truth who speaks in our hearts the presence of Jesus. And with that Presence we can indeed glorify God.   JUDITH M. MCDANIEL

RESPONSE

What evidence of the work of the Spirit of truth do you see in your life, in the life of your congregation?

PRAYER

May the Spirit of truth guide me into all the truth. Amen.

✢ SUNDAY ✢

Acts 2:1–21

REFLECTION

Peter is speaking as a brother of the Jewish family to beloved
family members. He notes that Jews and Gentiles alike rejected
Jesus (v. 23). He pleads his case not for the condemnation
of Israel but for her own salvation. With respect to faithfully
hearing and responding to its own revelation, the Christians
today are in a similar position to the Jews gathered in
Jerusalem. We need not look beyond ourselves to find scoffers
and sincere disbelievers, much less to cast blame upon others
for our own inability to hear the good news. Peter proclaims
that "everyone who calls on the name of the Lord shall be
saved" (v. 21). It is a proclamation spoken not in judgment but
in love to all.   G. LEE RAMSEY JR.

Psalm 104:24–34, 35b

REFLECTION

Finally, to call on the spirit of God is to call on a spirit that
desires order, that has provided places and times for all created
things and that delights in them in their times and places. We
may imagine the spirit of Pentecost as powerful and explosive—
as powerful as an earthquake, as explosive as a volcano (v. 32);
Acts describes it as wind and fire (as the psalmist describes
God, riding the wind with fire as his ministers, vv. 3–4); but we
do God's spirit wrong if we imagine it as wild. God's spirit may
be as exuberant as the psalm itself, but it is not out of control.

RICHARD S. DIETRICH

Romans 8:22–27

REFLECTION

Hope thus requires a willingness to risk trusting in that which is
not empirically verifiable (God's promise), even when physical

evidence suggests that doing so is foolish. One who hopes considers the unseen world of God's promises to be more real (and dependable) than the material world.

MATTHEW S. RINDGE

John 15:26–27; 16:4b–15

REFLECTION

A summons to a way of life that allows the Spirit of truth to penetrate our very being is a call to a continuous process of *alētheia*, the Greek name for truth. *Alētheia* means unconcealing, uncovering such as is done in theological reflection, an art that one could argue is 5 percent our effort and 95 percent the guidance of the Paraclete. Such an effort on our part requires openness to learning the truth and personal engagement with the mystery of grace, an attitude of receptivity and a sense of awe. The trouble is, we live in a culture that offers us little assistance in the art of seeking truth and grace in life.

Some would contend that in this country there is very little schooling that is education in its primary sense of leading or drawing out. . . .

A revelatory view of art, on the other hand—whether that art be painting or music, creative writing or theological reflection—sees these arts as shafts of light cast on the reality that is God. The revelatory approach to life looks on these modes of unconcealing as forms of truth and sees them not as just affirmative and pretty, not as commercially viable, but as visions of reality so deep as to reflect some aspects of God.

JUDITH M. MCDANIEL

RESPONSE

As you have listened to your breath each day this week, how have you heard or experienced the presence of God's Spirit?

PRAYER

Spirit of the living God, breathe with me. Amen.

❧ *Trinity Sunday* ❧

Isaiah 6:1–8

Then I heard the voice of the Lord saying,
"Whom shall I send, and who will go for us?"
And I said, "Here am I; send me!" (v. 8)

Psalm 29

The LORD sits enthroned over the flood;
the LORD sits enthroned as king forever.
May the LORD give strength to his people!
May the LORD bless his people with peace! (vv. 10–11)

Romans 8:12–17

For all who are led by the Spirit of God are
children of God. For you did not receive a spirit of
slavery to fall back into fear, but you have received
a spirit of adoption. (vv. 14–15)

John 3:1–17

Nicodemus said to him, "How can anyone be born after having
grown old? Can one enter a second time into the mother's womb
and be born?" Jesus answered, "Very truly, I tell you, no one can
enter the kingdom of God without being born of water and Spirit.
What is born of the flesh is flesh, and what is born of the Spirit is
spirit. Do not be astonished that I said to you, 'You must be born
from above.' The wind blows where it chooses, and you hear the
sound of it, but you do not know where it comes from or where it
goes. So it is with everyone who is born of the Spirit." (vv. 4–8)

Isaiah 6:1–8

REFLECTION

These first eight verses of chapter 6 describe one of the best known of Isaiah's prophetic visions. Summoned to the throne of God and surrounded by the awe and terror of the Lord, Isaiah is struck with the realization of his own unworthiness and that of his people. He is not worthy to stand before the Lord, yet here he is in the presence of the Lord. He knows he is unworthy to serve, yet what other option does he have here at the throne of God? This is not the time to say no; it is the time, in Isaiah's words, to say woe. "Woe is me! I am lost." There is a deep mystery at work here, and it profoundly upsets Isaiah's equilibrium. But in the upsetting, Isaiah is able to confess his sin, be cleansed of his guilt, and receive a clean heart. Only then can he hear God's call with clarity.

Isaiah's vision is intended for earthly readers just like us, and the narrative accentuates at least three characteristics of God's relationship with us: God encounters us in our historical context, God's word is revealed in our worship, and God calls us to serve.   KRISTIN EMERY SALDINE

RESPONSE

As you consider your own life of faith and response to God's call in your life, how do you see God's deep mystery at work?

PRAYER

I confess, O God, that sometimes like Isaiah, I feel lost, unprepared for your vision for my life. Continue to reveal your abiding presence to me where I live. Amen.

✣ TUESDAY ✣

Psalm 29

REFLECTION

We likely have no final or even satisfying answer to the big questions or to the personal ones. There is a complex relationship between created and Creator around benevolence and evil that has never been settled, within the canon (Job) or outside (Voltaire's *Candide*, among many). The NRSV concludes this psalm with a hopeful petition in verse 11: "May the LORD bless his people with peace." Other translations (KJV, NIV) conclude the psalm on a more assertive note and offer the assurance, "The LORD will bless (or "blesses") his people with peace." This is the reading I prefer, for it offers within the text itself a sense that, despite the ambiguity, God stands with God's people, even in time of trial. This is a psalm to be read aloud and treasured, as it pronounces God's power, as it raises hard questions, and as it assures us of God's grace, strength, and peace.

MARK MILLER-MCLEMORE

RESPONSE

How have you experienced the blessing of God's peace in the last week?

PRAYER

Even in the midst of my questions and my doubts, the strength of your love, O God, surrounds me and provides me with peace. Amen.

✦ WEDNESDAY ✦

Romans 8:12–17

REFLECTION

Daily living, however, often collides with theological truths.
What does it mean to live daily as a "joint heir" with Christ?
Many of the people with whom we share ministry are not
simply slaves to the flesh, nor do they know themselves to be
heirs with Christ. It would be easy to feel defeated by Paul's
stark contrast between the flesh and the Spirit, the body and the
mind; this world—even now—and the next—the end of history
and the reign of God. Does Paul's either/or solution leave room
for the inevitable conflict that most people have with living in
this world and following Jesus Christ? Paul presents pastoral
challenges but also offers pastoral hope.   J. BARNEY HAWKINS IV

RESPONSE

In what ways does this text challenge your life of faith? In what
ways does this text offer you hope?

PRAYER

It is not easy to follow Jesus. It is hard, but then, O God, you
have always known that. Expect more of me, and walk with me.
Amen.

☀ THURSDAY ☀

Romans 8:12–17

REFLECTION

Whether we belong to a street gang or a country club, we drape our flesh in symbols of those groups that provide us a sense of belonging. Paul identifies a more certain identity. It has nothing to do with what we wear or how we decorate or mutilate our flesh. In fact, when we are in the Spirit, things of the flesh—whether fashion or food, self-expression or sex—are put into perspective. The basic things of life—food, clothing, relationships— are needed and enjoyed by all people. But they should not define or consume us. Christian identity is found in relationship to God. The intimate relationship of faith is richer than others because it is established by the Spirit of God and will not fail. And even if it leads us into threatening or challenging circumstances as we share in Christ's suffering, we have the assurance of God's parental love, the Spirit's power, and presence of our brother Christ.   CLAYTON J. SCHMIT

RESPONSE

What symbols are illustrative of the groups that provide you with a sense of belonging? What symbols are illustrative of your Christian identity?

PRAYER

God of my life, drape me in your love. Show me how to live as Christ would have me live. Sustain all that I do surrounded by the power of your Spirit. Amen.

✣ FRIDAY ✣

John 3:1–17

REFLECTION

God searches for us to complete the revelation of God's being. God searches for us to participate in God's life. God's seeking is not brought about by our circumstance, our worthiness, our sufficient understanding. Rather, that seeking derives from the anguish of God, God's longing for the work of God's hands. God did not send the Son into the world to condemn the world, but in order that the world God created might be saved. So how might we live in that kingdom where life is reborn?

JUDITH M. MCDANIEL

RESPONSE

In what ways are you participating in God's life, in the work of God's hands?

PRAYER

Thank you for so loving this world and for loving me. Amen.

❖ SATURDAY ❖

John 3:1–17

REFLECTION

In the rain forest of Olympic National Park in Washington State stand groves of towering trees, the source of whose life is not visible, yet is apparent. The roots of these trees fan out like ribs of an umbrella, seemingly embracing the air for support, for these trees were given birth by nurse logs. Nurse logs are fallen trees, left to lie on the earth until they crumble into dust. But before they disintegrate, something else transpires: A seed falls on the downed log, draws nourishment from the log even as that log decays, and creates roots that ultimately surround an empty space through which the wind blows. The snapshot of a tree with ribbed umbrella roots above ground embracing only the wind takes us behind such a picture to contemplate origins and interpret reality with new eyes, eyes that expect the unexpected, look to new truths, and come to understand the world in new ways. Such contemplation suggests the offer of a kingdom of communion whose realm we can realize only if we accept it, trust in a relationship between death and life beyond our imagination, new life bestowed by the giving of life, a Giver as real as the wind. Living with faith in this God's reality, we have and will have life eternal.
JUDITH M. MCDANIEL

RESPONSE

"How can these things be?" was Nicodemus's question. What is your question?

PRAYER

Giver of life, giver of breath, I live and breathe in response to this gift. Amen.

Isaiah 6:1–8

REFLECTION

Prophets are often called to speak the word of the Lord to those who have forgotten the distinction between holy and human. The sudden shift from the historical reference to Uzziah to the heavenly throne of God is meant to set us on edge: God is holy; we are not. This is the sad realization that hits Isaiah with such overwhelming force. We are sinners, we dwell among sinners, and we live in sin-filled times. Too often we do not recognize this until it is forced upon us, and there is nothing like an encounter with the divine to shatter our self-centeredness and bring us to our knees in lament. Yet it is this realization that opens Isaiah to the possibility of forgiveness. He is touched by divine intervention and made clean. Isaiah is now free to answer when God calls.

KRISTIN EMERY SALDINE

Psalm 29

REFLECTION

The term takes us right back to Genesis 1. In the beginning God said, "Let there be!" and there was. A word is spoken and things spring into being. When God speaks, God acts. To exist, to be, is to obey the command of creation. . . .

Psalm 29 bears witness to a God who speaks—creatively, articulately, and meaningfully—and who draws human beings into the conversation. It points to the Trinitarian God who is transcendent and immanent, revealed in the earthquake and the still, small voice, present at Sinai and Bethlehem, Lord of heaven and earth.

IWAN RUSSELL-JONES

Romans 8:12–17

REFLECTION

Everyone needs to know where they belong. Jesus, who knew no permanent home, surrounded himself with people he felt at home with. He even assigned them nicknames (James and John were the Sons of Thunder) and spoke of intimate things with them. He drew them into his most intimate relationship, the one he had with Abba, to whom he frequently prayed. Paul is also drawing on this relationship. It belongs, he says, to everyone who follows Christ. He even uses the same intimate term that Jesus used. It was such a fitting way to speak about the parental nature of God that the earliest followers of Jesus used it too and refrained from translating it from Aramaic into Greek. When Paul speaks of the family of God here, he says that by the Spirit, we also "cry, 'Abba!'" When we do this, "it is the Spirit himself bearing witness with our spirit that we are children of God" (8:15, my translation).   CLAYTON J. SCHMIT

John 3:1–17

REFLECTION

Today's Gospel story presents Nicodemus as one who is trying to make up his mind about Jesus. The great Roman Catholic NT scholar of blessed memory, Raymond Brown, suggests that Nicodemus represents secret disciples of Jesus (he does come "by night"). We do know that he appears twice more in this Gospel. He defends Jesus, asking that he be given a hearing (7:50–51), and he joins with Joseph of Arimathea, a disciple of Jesus, to bury Jesus (19:38–40). In John, Nicodemus comes to Jesus near the beginning of his ministry, defends him in the middle, and is with him at the end. Is this not what a disciple would do?   PAUL L. HAMMER

RESPONSE

From your reading of these texts, what conversation is God inviting you to join?

PRAYER

I am your disciple, show me what to do. Amen.

❦ *Proper 3* ❦

Hosea 2:14–20

I will make for you a covenant on that day with the wild animals, the birds of the air, and the creeping things of the ground; and I will abolish the bow, the sword, and war from the land; and I will make you lie down in safety. (v. 18)

Psalm 103:1–13, 22

Bless the LORD, O my soul,
  and do not forget all his benefits. (v. 2)

2 Corinthians 3:1–6

Such is the confidence that we have through Christ toward God. Not that we are competent of ourselves to claim anything as coming from us; our competence is from God, who has made us competent to be ministers of a new covenant, not of letter but of spirit; for the letter kills, but the Spirit gives life. (vv. 4–6)

Mark 2:13–22

"No one sews a piece of unshrunk cloth on an old cloak; otherwise, the patch pulls away from it, the new from the old, and a worse tear is made. And no one puts new wine into old wineskins; otherwise, the wine will burst the skins, and t he wine is lost, and so are the skins; but one puts new wine into fresh wineskins." (vv. 21–22)

✣ MONDAY ✣

Hosea 2:14–20

REFLECTION

Hosea 2:14–20 speaks about what it means to be a people claimed by God's love, a people who stumble and fail and yet are redeemed by God's great faithfulness. The word of grace prevails over the word of judgment. All of this is conveyed through the language of God's covenant, especially in the references to the exodus, wilderness, sin, repentance, forgiveness, and divine promise of salvation. This covenantal language is also the language of baptism, and it would be appropriate to include the sacrament of baptism or a liturgy for the renewal of baptism for this Lord's Day service. Baptismal liturgies often include an extended prayer that recounts salvation history from creation to Christ, an account that includes the flood, the exodus, and the witness of the prophets. This is the great and continuing story of how God calls us, loves us, and still seeks us, even when we have turned away.

KRISTIN EMERY SALDINE

RESPONSE

Today, recall the story of how God calls and claims God's people throughout history. Consider God's role in your life. Recall an experience when you turned away. How did God find you?

PRAYER

I come to you as I am, with my sin and with my repentance, knowing that your forgiving love is an everlasting covenant. Amen.

✦ TUESDAY ✦

Psalm 103:1–13, 22

REFLECTION

God is, first and foremost, a God of mercy who forgives sins. It may be that the poet connects the power of God's forgiveness to the healing of diseases and to deliverance from death. As we experience the compassion and mercy of the Lord, our bodies are made well and our lives are allowed to flourish (see Ps. 32:1–5). To live in our sins is to be sick and finally to die (to go to "the Pit"), but to live in God's forgiveness is to have a life bejeweled with love and mercy. To live under the weight of sin is to have a life that is drained of vitality, but to live under God's forgiveness is to have wind under our wings so that we sail like an eagle. Those who know God's mercy and steadfast love are forever young in the Lord.   ROBERT WARDEN PRIM

RESPONSE

How have you experienced the forgiving love of God? In what ways has your life been "bejeweled with love and mercy"?

PRAYER

The wind of your forgiveness, O God, is a blessing for my soul. Amen.

✦ WEDNESDAY ✦

Psalm 103:1–13, 22

REFLECTION

Those who fear God and are part of the people of God may
know such moments of joy in community as well, even though
our often individualistic and competitive culture may make
them harder to apprehend. . . . These moments of communal
exhilaration, satisfaction, and joy are powerful and entirely real,
even if they may be more rare in our experience and harder
for most listeners to call to mind. They are the blessings that
come to those communities who "fear God" daily by knowing
and practicing a life together centered around the Source of
life—in holy covenant, in wisdom sought and found, in mission
discerned, in lives dedicated in commitment and service to
others, in accomplishment and completion in Christ's name,
in grateful praise and worship that connects. Much of human
life is troubled by misunderstanding or overestimating or
forgetting our place and our powers. Many communities are
marked by practical idolatry, by sins of seeking after power or
prestige. This reading joyously reminds us of the personal and
communal blessings we realize when "God's in his heaven and
all's right with our world." For these special times, how else can
we respond but with thankfulness?   MARK MILLER-MCLEMORE

RESPONSE

Recall moments around tables of deliberation where you have
been present recently. In what ways has God's presence been
discerned in the deliberations and actions that were taken?

PRAYER

With all my soul, with all that is in me, I bless the Lord. Amen.

✦ THURSDAY ✦

2 Corinthians 3:1–6

REFLECTION

A final word of grace is found in this passage. Paul says that the ministry for which we are enabled is a ministry of the new covenant. We do not serve in order to satisfy the old covenant, that is, the law. We serve in ministry because we are part of something new, something that the Holy Spirit is involved in. To serve by the law is to serve futilely, for "the letter kills" (3:6). In other words, fulfilling legal obligations will earn no reward and achieve nothing in the kingdom of God. But engaging in new covenant ministry means that we are empowered by the Spirit of God to do what is required and to be filled with life in the process: "the Spirit gives life," and does not deplete it.

CLAYTON J. SCHMIT

RESPONSE

What new thing is the Spirit empowering in your life and the life of the congregation of which you are a part? How does the Spirit give life?

PRAYER

I offer my heart to you, loving God. Use it as a living letter of your mercy, justice, and kindness. Amen.

✤ FRIDAY ✤

Mark 2:13–22

REFLECTION

Jesus is speaking of the incompatibility of the old ways with the new, signaling by his actions the presence of a new reality. He eats with the confused majority, the people of the land. Those in this crowd are poor in many ways: Some of their debts or sins are the result of ignorance of Jewish law. Some are too financially impoverished to adhere to the strict codes of purity demanded by temple authorities. Eating with this impure rabble violates pharisaic practices of table fellowship whereby withholding food from the stranger is equivalent to murder, but sitting with the stranger at table is forbidden. Jesus reinterprets these codes, embracing everyone in a new creation based on the coming kingdom. JUDITH M. MCDANIEL

RESPONSE

Take a few minutes and recall those with whom you have shared a meal or a cup of coffee or tea this week. In what ways are they poor? In what ways are they rich? In what ways is your presence with them offering them the presence of Jesus?

PRAYER

As I break bread with friends, families, and strangers this week, remind me of the new creation that is at work among us. Amen.

✦ SATURDAY ✦

Mark 2:13–22

REFLECTION

So there really is something new and different about Jesus'
religious movement. It is made up of ritually unclean and
socially disregarded people who recognize their need for help
and healing and so begin to follow him. His presence with them
is an occasion for joy and gladness. It is a time of healing and
salvation. Unlike the "old cloth," this is new and cannot simply
be sewn onto the old. Like new wine it is likely to burst old
wineskins, because as the new wine ferments, the gases that
come forth will be more than the inelastic old wineskins can
bear. When we attempt to graft new attitudes, behaviors, and
ideas onto the old, the results are often disastrous. Much more
radical action is required. New, flexible structures are needed.
New thoughts, attitudes, and behaviors need the creation of
new lifestyles and new structures capable of containing and
promoting them. The old structures simply cannot cope with
the power of the new. Sometimes the most caring thing we can
engage in is the formation of new and different structures able
to contain and sustain the new.   EMMANUEL Y. LARTEY

RESPONSE

What old ideas and behaviors need to die? What new ideas and
behaviors is God calling forth in you, in the congregation of
which you are a part?

PRAYER

I confess that sometimes the breaking in of the new stretches
me in ways that I am not yet ready to handle. Hold me, loving
God, as I learn how to live into this new life. Amen.

⚹ SUNDAY ⚹

Hosea 2:14–20

REFLECTION

The terms here are tremendously rich: righteousness, justice, steadfast love (Heb. *hesed*), mercy, and faithfulness. These are marks of the way Israel is to relate to God; but even more, they are what God promises to be and do for the people. This new way of living, grounded in the covenant and introduced by hope, is an act of God's great and unexpected grace. God overcomes faithlessness and restores the people with the promise that they shall "know the LORD" (v. 20). This embraces the whole response of the people so their total life is grounded in what God has revealed and done. To "know the LORD" is the great goal of life, in this age and the age to come. . . . God's deep covenant loyalty opens redemption and salvation. God gives the people of Israel a vision of new life, marked by the most profound ways the reconciled people should relate to each other and to God.

DONALD K. MCKIM

Psalm 103:1–13, 22

REFLECTION

So who is this God whom the soul is called upon to bless? Here we venture ever deeper into strange and unfamiliar territory. This is YHWH, whose name is known only because YHWH has revealed it. This is the God of the covenant with Israel, the relationship with a people who once were not, but now are, God's people. This is not a God who is the product of the imagination or social construction or philosophical word games or ideological power play. The soul stands before a God whom it did not invent. This is a truth that theologians and preachers and disciples need to discover and rediscover afresh every day. We are always the servants, never the masters, of the Word. YHWH, the Lord, is revealed through self-revelation in history: "He made known his ways to Moses, his acts to the people of Israel" (v. 7). And what are these ways? This God forgives, heals, redeems, crowns, satisfies, vindicates, works justice for the oppressed (vv. 3–6). These are acts of costly, covenantal love, of blessing.   IWAN RUSSELL-JONES

2 Corinthians 3:1–6

REFLECTION

Paul shows us we have to read Scripture in another way. He says that God has made us competent to be ministers of a new covenant, not in a written code but in the Spirit (v. 6). We read the Bible in this way and not in another because the Bible is the signpost to Jesus Christ. And when we read it in this way, then we are—in spite of our weaknesses and doubts—in fact a letter of Christ, for the welfare and salvation of many of our contemporaries.   EBERHARD BUSCH

Mark 2:13–22

REFLECTION

Our text moves from dinner party, to fasting, to cloth and wineskins. These parts all conclude positively: a barrier-breaking dinner party, a fast-concluding wedding, unshrunken new cloth and bursting new wine. What for Mark lies at the heart of all this celebrating? What provides the framework for telling this story? Is it not Jesus' resurrection?   PAUL L. HAMMER

RESPONSE

In what ways are you a servant of God's Word?

PRAYER

Spirit of the living God, you dwell in my heart and in my life. May the words that you write on my heart be visible in my life and actions in the world. Amen.

❧ *Proper 4* ❦

1 Samuel 3:1–10 (11–20)

Now the LORD came and stood there, calling
as before, "Samuel! Samuel!" And Samuel said, "Speak, for
your servant is listening." Then the LORD said to Samuel, "See,
I am about to do something in Israel that will make both
ears of anyone who hears of it tingle." (vv. 10–11)

Psalm 139:1–6, 13–18

O LORD, you have searched me and known me.
You know when I sit down and when I rise up;
    you discern my thoughts from far away.
. . . .
I praise you, for I am fearfully and wonderfully made.
    Wonderful are your works;
that I know very well. (vv. 1–2, 14)

2 Corinthians 4:5–12

But we have this treasure in clay jars, so that it
may be made clear that this extraordinary power belongs
to God and does not come from us. (v. 7)

Mark 2:23–3:6

Then he said to them, "Is it lawful to do good or to do
harm on the sabbath, to save life or to kill?" But they were
silent. He looked around at them with anger; he was grieved at
their hardness of heart and said to the man, "Stretch out your
hand." He stretched it out, and his hand was restored. (3:4–5)

✦ MONDAY ✦

1 Samuel 3:1–10 (11–20)

REFLECTION

How do we hear God's call? How do we discern the meaning of the call? What should be our response? Some, like Jonah, pack up and run the other way, and some of us have tried to emulate his response down through the centuries. Others struggle for years, even lifetimes, to figure out just what God is calling them to do. Still others seem to hear God's call with absolute clarity; they know right away exactly what it is they are to do, and they set out to accomplish it. In the church we speak of a "sense of call" among both clergy and laity. Many churches emphasize that all are called to be in ministry in some way or another, and that there is a multitude of avenues for serving the gospel. Certainly, most clergy feel called to their vocation. Many church members also feel called to be in ministry in a variety of ways. The prophetic call narratives in Scripture perhaps provide a model by which we think of ourselves as called by God, although most of our personal call narratives are not nearly as dramatic as Samuel's. But they are nevertheless every bit as unshakable and every bit as real to us.   BERT MARSHALL

RESPONSE

How did God call you to your own particular ministry? How is God calling you today in this time and place?

PRAYER

Sometimes I think I hear your voice calling me, O God. Sometimes it's clear, sometimes a bit fuzzy. Sometimes the clarity of it scares me. Sometimes I know I need to wait and listen. Wake me up, slow me down, O God. Amen.

✦ TUESDAY ✦

1 Samuel 3:1–10 (11–20)

REFLECTION

Our text is framed by family tragedy (Eli and his sons) and
a disastrous war in which the Israelites are defeated by the
Philistines and, in the process, lose the ark of the covenant.
Into this crucible of harsh judgment, war, and loss comes the
word of God, rare in these times as we have been told. And God
speaks not to the learned, nor to the religious leaders, nor to
the powerful, but to an unsuspecting boy who thus far knows
nothing of such things. As always, God does the unexpected,
and one thinks immediately of the boy Jeremiah, and Amos
the farmer, Sarah and Ruth, the young Mary, fishermen and
tax collectors and sinners, and many others. Here God raises
up a prophet in the midst of trouble. Here God prepares once
again to speak the divine Word into a world still bent on
ignoring it. Down through the ages, God has raised up prophets
in desperate times—men and women who seem to suddenly
appear out of nowhere, yet who seem to have been called for a
particular time and place. We know some of them by name, and
others carry out their missions in obscurity and anonymity.

BERT MARSHALL

RESPONSE

What Word is speaking today? In what ways is it being ignored?
In what ways is it being heard?

PRAYER

There are prophets around me, O God. Help me recognize their
prophetic work in the actions of their lives. Amen.

✦ WEDNESDAY ✦

Psalm 139:1–6, 13–18

REFLECTION

In acknowledging that God has "searched me and known me," I may become aware of ways in which I need to know myself or God more deeply. A preacher who is a pastor has unique license to encourage Sabbath keeping, self-examination, and disciplines of prayer or meditation to the flock at any time; here is a beautiful meditation, ready-made, on the creativity and omnipresence of God. Taking the time to listen like Samuel for God's call in the Sabbath quiet helps to strengthen us for the path ahead. Even in our fear-filled times, these intimate truths hold the promise of healing and peace.

The lectionary offers this psalm for our consideration in early summer, in those years when Easter falls on or before April 2. Education and Christian formation programs often take hiatus about this time; families travel on holiday as the school year ends; opportunities to gather the community of faith tend to be fewer than in the busy seasons of the fall or Lent. Psalm 139 insists that wherever we go, God is there; nothing we do goes unnoticed by God. Because we belong to God, nothing—not even death—can "separate us from the love of God in Christ Jesus our Lord" (Rom. 8:39). We belong.

MARY DOUGLAS TURNER

RESPONSE

Where are you traveling this summer? Be open to the places where you will see God.

PRAYER

God, you know my life, and in knowing my life you know me. Thank you for your abiding presence in my life. Amen.

✣ THURSDAY ✣

2 Corinthians 4:5–12

REFLECTION

Paul's argument in these verses juxtaposes the ecstatic and joyful visionary experience of members of the church with the relentless hardships they face. These sufferings are transformative for those who undergo them, just as the vision of the glory of the Lord transforms those who see (3:18). The extraordinary power of God in their midst is contained in weak clay jars, vulnerable to damage and destruction. Not only does the death (*nekrōsis*) of Jesus change those who carry it, but it becomes revelatory for those who see the paradoxical expression of weakness and power manifested in the ministry of Paul and those who share this apostolic work.

CYNTHIA BRIGGS KITTEREDGE

RESPONSE

What treasure is contained in your clay jar?

PRAYER

The life and ministry of your Son, Jesus, remind me of the ways that I am weak and the ways that I am strong. Thank you for the life I know in you. Amen.

✦ FRIDAY ✦

Mark 2:23–3:6

REFLECTION

We must always keep our eyes on this conflict and on the
fact that Jesus is provoking this conflict. What is he trying
to provoke? What is so dangerous about him? Feeding his
disciples? Healing a man? . . . He is proclaiming—in word
and deed—a new way of understanding who God is. Jesus
proclaims to his own generation—and to every generation,
including ours—that God is not confined to our rules about
God or to our way of perceiving God. Jesus is reconfiguring
our relationship to God, not just as individuals, but in the
structures of society as well. Such a reconfiguration is very
threatening. The difficult truth of the cross is that we would
rather kill Jesus than be transformed by his love. Our resistance
is great to his reconfiguring our relationship to God. It is one of
the continuing mysterious realities of life in the church, a reality
that is exposed in this passage: we prefer a dormant God who
is subject to our rites and rituals to the active, category-busting
God who is ever present in our lives. When God gets too close
to us, challenging us as Jesus challenged the religious order of
his day, we begin to construct our crosses and prepare a place
for God there too.   NIBS STROUPE

RESPONSE

There are a number of excellent questions raised in this
reflection. Select one or two for your meditation this day.

PRAYER

Help me to be open to the fields that Jesus is walking through in
my life, revealing that which needs to be plucked. Amen.

✦ SATURDAY ✦

Mark 2:23–3:6

REFLECTION

In calling us back to the original intent of the Sabbath
commandment, Jesus reminds us that our lives are meant for
God, not for getting and spending. In this sense, what Jesus
threatens is our love of money, money that defines us and
falsely promises us life. Lottery fever across the country is
dominated by this idea: "if only I could win the lottery, I
would . . ." In lifting up the Sabbath and how important it is
(and how misused it is), this passage asks us to hear the difficult
truth that we cannot imagine a life not dominated by money
and work and consumption. Yet, as always, there is powerful
good news here as well. At the same time that we are threatened
by Jesus, our hearts long for him. Who among us does not want
to be freed from our consumer lifestyle that is killing our souls
and polluting the earth? This text reminds us that the journey
to life goes through the cross, but that the resurrection awaits as
well. Jesus did not go to the cross to tell us how bad we are, but
to point us to new life. So may it be with our sermons on this
text—there is life available, greater and more abundant than we
ever imagined.

NIBS STROUPE

RESPONSE

What new life is Jesus pointing out to you? What Sabbath
practices nurture and sustain your life of faith?

PRAYER

Renew my life of faith with those practices that nourish my
soul. Help me eliminate those practices that pollute the earth
and provide no life-sustaining value. Amen.

✦ SUNDAY ✦

1 Samuel 3:1–10 (11–20)

REFLECTION

Notice that the boy Samuel, priest-in-training, dedicated to
the service of God by his grateful mother, is already a part
of the faithful, worshiping community when his special call
comes in the nighttime. Notice that he does not recognize God's
voice when it comes. God is sufficiently patient to call several
times, and even then it takes the special discernment of Eli,
Samuel's mentor, for him to recognize whose voice it is. The
emphasis in the story is clearly on listening—"deep listening,"
we might call it.   JOHN ROLLEFSON

Psalm 139:1–6, 13–18

REFLECTION

People who lived into the divine reality described in this psalm
would be transparent in offering all they are up to God for
completion or transformation. They would approach God
with perfect trust in their creator, and would be open to the
wonder of the world around and within them, responding with
awe and humility to the love of God present and incarnate
in themselves. . . . We cannot take the words of this psalm
seriously without being moved to awe, not only at the work of
God in ourselves, but also at God's handiwork in one another.

DEBORAH ANNE MEISTER

2 Corinthians 4:5–12

REFLECTION

After a tree falls into the water, a slow process of disintegration
begins. David James Duncan observes, "The fallen tree becomes
a naked log, the log begins to lead a kind of afterlife in the
river, and this afterlife is, in some ways, of greater benefit to the

river than was the original life of the tree." While a living tree provides shade on the river and shelter for animals, a tree that has snapped in two and has fallen into the water "creates a vast transfusion of nutrients . . . a river feast." As these immersed trees break apart they assume an appearance similar to rocks. Duncan remembers as a child he called them "river teeth" (David James Duncan. *River Teeth* [New York: Bantam, 1996], 1–2). As we seek to serve Jesus Christ we can often fall from the shore, break into two, and tumble into the flowing waters of ministry. Call us "river teeth." Or just call us "broken." . . . Yet, as Paul reminds us, it is often in our brokenness, within our submerged selves, that new life bursts forth. How? Paul believes the resurrected Christ actually resides in the apostles. We might say through the power of the resurrection Paul and the apostles are now Christ's own "river teeth."   MARK BARGER ELLIOTT

Mark 2:23–3:6

REFLECTION

Mark's Jesus should startle, if not unsettle, us. The opposition to him is coming from earnestly religious persons, not from outside skeptics. His surprising vision of God's intention for the Sabbath made for humanity may upset our own habitual religious ideas. Something deeper than religious ideology or juridical thinking is here. It is so easy to forget the spirit of religious institutions and practices in the attempt to apply regulations with absolute human certainty. Mark has opened his account of the "good news" with a serious challenge to those of us who wish to enforce on others a narrow version of God's rule and reign.   DON E. SALIERS

RESPONSE

What new ideas about this text are evoked for you?

PRAYER

Help me to listen deeply for your voice in my life. Amen.

❧ *Proper 5* ❦

Genesis 3:8–15

[T]he man and his wife hid themselves from the presence
of the Lord God among the trees of the garden. But the Lord
God called to the man, and said to him, "Where are you?" He said,
"I heard the sound of you in the garden, and I was afraid, because
I was naked; and I hid myself." (vv. 8b–10)

Psalm 130

O Israel, hope in the Lord!
  For with the Lord there is steadfast love,
    and with him is great power to redeem. (v. 7)

2 Corinthians 4:13–5:1

So we do not lose heart. Even though our outer nature is wasting
away, our inner nature is being renewed day by day. For this slight
momentary affliction is preparing us for an eternal weight of glory
beyond all measure, because we look not at what can be seen but at
what cannot be seen; for what can be seen is temporary, but what
cannot be seen is eternal. (4:16–18)

Mark 3:20–35

And he called them to him, and spoke to them in parables,
"How can Satan cast out Satan? If a kingdom is divided against
itself, that kingdom cannot stand. And if a house is divided against
itself, that house will not be able to stand. And if Satan has risen
up against himself and is divided, he cannot stand, but his
end has come." (vv. 23–26)

✦ MONDAY ✦

Genesis 3:8–15

REFLECTION

What might the Lord God walking in the garden sound like?
A rustling of leaves, the snapping of twigs, the swishing of tall
grass? Sandals touching the earth perhaps, or bare feet? Feet?
There is great possibility in imagining the sounds of God. The
God of the written word is silent—trapped on a page, read
silently in studies and offices, on desks and kitchen tables,
wherever the preacher prepares to preach. What, indeed, does
God sound like? How might your congregation respond to this
question? Sometimes when you ask, you will get answers: a
baby's cry, a voice in song (male and female!), thunder, the roar
of a lion, someone's grandmother, the ocean. In what ways do
we hear the sound of God in the world?   BERT MARSHALL

RESPONSE

Think about the questions asked in this meditation. Quietly
meditate on your own response to this one: When and where
do you hear the sound of God in the world?

PRAYER

As I walk through this day, open my ears to the sound of your
presence in this world. Amen.

✦ TUESDAY ✦

Genesis 3:8–15

REFLECTION

The broken "vertical" relationship of God and humanity spells the breaking of "horizontal" relations too, as shown by the triple-play blame game that follows, moving from Adam to Eve to the serpent. These "free will" responses to God, including the eloquent serpent's sudden silence, are lame, no-honor-among-thieves excuses, at the "gotcha, come-clean, tell it like it is" moment of reckoning. Protests of feminist and other theologies against the historical bias, injustice, and misogyny of blaming Eve (= woman in particular) are certainly apt. Adam not only sets the blame game in motion but turns it into a theodicy issue: blaming God. No creature is guileless. Deception and self-deception appear in paradise. Nor is God deceived about that point. This was already the case earlier on, when God's quasi-legal command was violated.

Thus theologians have had cause to inquire into features of sin and sinfulness far deeper and more multidimensional than "I didn't do what I was told to." In any case, considered theologically, the blame game itself is the telltale sign of broken relationship, alienation, estrangement—with God and with one another at the same time. JAMES O. DUKE

RESPONSE

With whom are you in a broken relationship? What set the blame game in motion? How can the relationship be repaired?

PRAYER

In brokenness and humility I come to you, O God. Heal the broken relationships in my life. Amen.

✦ WEDNESDAY ✦

Psalm 130

REFLECTION

Any fool can see evidence of sin in our world, but only through the eyes of faith can we begin to see signs of redemption. Psalm 130 plays within this space, standing in the black night of despair and scanning the horizon for the bare glow of hope. . . . Another challenge the text highlights is the contrast between the pace of the spiritual life and that of the modern world. The striking image in verse 6, that "my soul waits for the Lord more than those who watch for the morning, more than those who watch for the morning," implies the patience that is required in the gradual unfolding of the spiritual life. This can be hard to grasp for those who have grown accustomed to instantaneous communication through cell phones, text messaging, and information accessed through ever-faster Internet connections. Exploring this theme in terms of pastoral care (such as the patience of waiting by a hospital bed), in prayer (the slow disciplines of sanctification), and in the life of Christ (dealing with pig-headed disciples, or in the passion, whose Latin root links the ideas of patience and suffering) might provide real food for reflection to a twenty-first-century congregation.

DEBORAH ANNE MEISTER

RESPONSE

What signs of God's redeeming work do you see this day?

PRAYER

My soul waits for you, God, more than those who watch for the morning. Amen.

✣ THURSDAY ✣

2 Corinthians 4:13–5:1

REFLECTION

Paul thus sets the tone for Christians who for twenty centuries
have wondered when the end will come: very soon? in the
more distant future? not at all in the literal sense? Paul teaches
us how to live in a "between time," when the new age has been
inaugurated in Christ and renewal has begun, but the old
age persists. In many ways hope remains unfulfilled. And yet
the new has already begun. Paul's best explanation is that the
faithful have received the Spirit as an *arrabōn*, an earnest, a
down payment, a guarantee of what will be conferred in full at a
later time (2 Cor. 1:22; 5:5). Life in the presence of Christ is not
yet possessed. But the Spirit is a guarantee that all God's gifts
are to be possessed in the future (cf. Rom. 8:18–27).

EUGENE TESELLE

RESPONSE

In what ways is God's Spirit at work in you, using your gifts?

PRAYER

Thank you for your sustaining presence in my life and the life
of my family, so that whatever we face, we do not lose heart.
Amen.

✦ FRIDAY ✦

Mark 3:20–35

REFLECTION

Did Jesus believe that a personality named Satan actually existed? He likely did, and that makes this passage difficult to preach. Yet we should also look for the reality signified by the name "Satan." Satan does not necessarily mean a personality with horns and a red tail, but it does name a demonic power that is actively engaged against the compassionate and reconciling love of God. This is the reality that Jesus names here, and whether we believe in a person named "Satan" is not as important as hearing about our captivity to the powers of evil signified by "Satan," powers that continue to seek our allegiance. Stated in this way, the reality of Satan and Beelzebub become disturbingly clear. They name the forces and configurations of power that capture us and cause us to hurt ourselves, to hurt others, and to hurt God. To name a few of these, there is the power of race, which tells us to believe that one group is superior to another simply because of skin color or cultural heritage. There is the power of patriarchy, which tells us that men should dominate women. There is the power of materialism, which roars at us that money gives us life. And the power of militarism—the belief that weapons and war bring us peace and security—causes us to kill one another, often in the name of God.

NIBS STROUPE

RESPONSE

What powers of evil hurt you, others, and God? Name them now.

PRAYER

In naming the powers of evil in this world, Lord of my life, I commit to working to destroy them. Amen.

→ SATURDAY ←

Mark 3:20–35

REFLECTION

In these verses in Mark, Jesus indicates that the power of these categories must be recognized and confronted in our lives if we are to experience the gracious and stunning love of God. He uses the metaphor of tying up the strong man in order to plunder his property. In using this parable, he speaks of the need of the gospel to expose our captivity to the "strong men" of our lives. In so doing, he seeks to free up our imaginations, which have become the property of Satan. Our captivity to Satan must be exposed in order for us to begin to discover the glorious freedom of the children of God, as Paul puts it so powerfully in Romans 8:21.   NIBS STROUPE

RESPONSE

In what ways are you held captive by the powers of Satan?

PRAYER

Free up my imagination, God of my life, so that evil has no power in my life and I am freed to share your love in this world. Amen.

✣ SUNDAY ✣

Genesis 3:8–15

REFLECTION

To hear this story as a literal historical account is to trivialize it
beyond recognition, to deny it its depth, and power, and truth,
to confine it to the realm of silliness. God and serpent, man
and woman, garden and wilderness, blessing and curse—these
are the very elements of our existence and the objects of our
lifelong quest for understanding and enlightenment. For the
gathered congregation here is a story for the ages, theological
manna, and the sound of God walking in the primeval garden.

BERT MARSHALL

Psalm 130

REFLECTION

The God of steadfast love is thus a forgiving God toward all
who stand before God in sinfulness and shame. Indeed, the
worship of God arises from this unconditional acceptance by
God of those who are unacceptable in their own right (Tillich).
. . . But it can scarcely be otherwise with the God who is defined
by loyalty and love. To the extent that anyone feels shut off
from God by their sinfulness, mired in depths of self-loathing,
disappointment, or shame, Psalm 130 speaks the only word of
gospel that there is: "If you, O Lord, should mark iniquities,
Lord, who could stand? But there is forgiveness with you, so
that you may be revered" (vv. 3–4).   D. CAMERON MURCHISON

2 Corinthians 4:13–5:1

REFLECTION

Paul's point is that at some point we will all die—that in time
everything human will crumble and perish, whether it is a city,
a home, or even our own life. In the face of our death, and the

struggles of life and ministry, Paul then steers his readers to the hope found in "eternal" things.   MARK BARGER ELLIOTT

Mark 3:20–35

REFLECTION

When we think about who is near Jesus, it is not the morally perfect. It is just the diverse mess of humanity, with all of its moral, physical, spiritual beauty and imperfection. The only ones not in the picture, the ones not pressing in at the doors and windows, desperate and aching to be near Jesus, are the ones who think they know what religion and family life is supposed to look like. Jesus, infinitely patient with the crowd, blasts away at these people. Everyone will be forgiven, except people who blaspheme the Holy Spirit. The inability to tell the difference between the power of the Holy Spirit and the demonic is an *unforgivable sin*.

For most of us, this is pretty bad news. Like the Jews of the first century, we live in troubled times and try our best to figure out how to be faithful. . . . What if we make the wrong discernment? Perhaps if we pay attention to the theme of healing that runs through these stories, we might find a way to orient ourselves. It was the desire for healing that drew people to Jesus. Perhaps if we had compassion for our own wounds and the wounds of others, we might find ourselves in the crowd devoted to Jesus, instead of in the "legitimate" family that Jesus rejects.   WENDY FARLEY

RESPONSE

What "theological manna" do you find in these reflections? In what ways do they feed you?

PRAYER

Help me be attuned to the thin places in the world this Sabbath day. Amen.

❧ *Proper 6* ❦

Ezekiel 17:22–24

All the trees of the field shall know
    that I am the LORD.
I bring low the high tree,
    I make high the low tree;
I dry up the green tree
    and make the dry tree flourish.
I the LORD have spoken;
    I will accomplish it. (v. 24)

Psalm 92:1–4, 12–15

The righteous flourish like the palm tree,
and grow like a cedar in Lebanon. (v. 12)

2 Corinthians 5:6–10 (11–13), 14–17

So if anyone is in Christ, there is a new
creation: everything old has passed away; see,
everything has become new! (v. 17)

Mark 4:26–34

With many such parables he spoke the word to
them, as they were able to hear it; he did not speak to
them except in parables, but he explained everything
in private to his disciples. (vv. 33–34)

✦ MONDAY ✦

Ezekiel 17:22–24

REFLECTION

The preacher cannot in good conscience detach this beautiful little text from its context. God's tenderhearted response is addressed directly to the exiles. These words derive their depth and power precisely from the background of suffering and defeat. In a situation where the powers of the world seem to have prevailed with devastating fury and finality, the prophet comes along speaking a word that God will yet have the final say. All the great powers of the world throughout history, down to this day, ought to tremble inside at the speaking of this word. On the other hand, our congregations are not great empires bent on invasion and conquest. Our people live their lives in the crucible of the world's opportunity and violence, its good and evil, its beauty and brokenness. We can say with confidence that God plants the cedar sprig for us too, so that one day we shall all find shade under its branches.   BERT MARSHALL

RESPONSE

What is God accomplishing in your life?

PRAYER

I pray today for others in the congregation of which I am a part. Sustain them as they live in the midst of the world's beauty and brokenness, its evil and good, the violence and all the opportunities. Amen.

✢ TUESDAY ✢

Psalm 92:1–4, 12–15

REFLECTION

Psalm 92 makes a fundamental theological-ethical assertion. It claims that the moral life, exemplified in a commitment to justice and righteousness, is the key to genuine human flourishing. Such a life flourishes truly because it is rooted in the creative and redemptive work of a sovereign God. This theological ethical awareness in the psalm results in theological testimony that takes the form of doxology. Based on this theological conviction about who God is, the psalmist eloquently witnesses to an accompanying ethical conviction: that this power of steadfast love and faithfulness in creation and history extends into the moral lives and experience of God's people. Genuine human flourishing occurs as personal moral life is grounded in God's life, which is full of righteousness and justice. The image in which the assertion is made is one of deep contrast with the grasslike flourishing of the evildoers. Rather than exhibiting passing, effervescent growth, the righteous person is said to flourish like the palm tree or a cedar in Lebanon (v. 12).   D. CAMERON MURCHISON

RESPONSE

As you read this psalm and read this reflection, spend some moments journaling or drawing about your own testimony: Who is God?

PRAYER

Be my rock; help me flourish like the palm tree. Amen.

Psalm 92:1–4, 12–15

REFLECTION

Verses 12–15 pose more problems for the preacher with their claim that "the righteous shall flourish like the palm tree, and grow like a cedar in Lebanon" (v. 12). They evoke the obvious objection that sometimes the righteous do not appear to flourish; anyone who has ever seen good people trapped in grinding poverty or stricken with a horrendous illness will challenge these words as mere wishful thinking. One way to approach the issue would be to explore differing concepts of well-being: both Scripture and our culture depict material prosperity as one way to flourish, but Scripture includes other concepts as well, most notably in the Beatitudes, which subvert ordinary understandings of blessedness and confront them with a blessedness of spirit that does not rely upon external factors, but enables the individual or community to persevere in wholeness through whatever may be happening in his or her life. The comparison to a cedar might allow one to pick up on the idea of growth and to ask what experiences enable us to grow in faith; often, our times of greatest growth will not be our times of tranquility!

DEBORAH ANNE MEISTER

RESPONSE

What experiences in your life have been most important in your faith formation?

PRAYER

O Lord, when I see what your hands have created, I sing for joy. Amen.

✣ THURSDAY ✣

2 Corinthians 5:6–10 (11–13), 14–17

REFLECTION

What we have in Paul's letters is rich and multiform, and
many of them are fairly long. It is good, therefore, to read
them aloud in one sitting so that we have a sense of their
function as letters, of their rhetoric and practicality and real
relationships, and so that we are not so inclined to milk or mine
their individual verses without a sense of the human voice and
purpose involved. The perspective afforded by such light and
quick reading will help us see what is at stake, *who* it is who is
speaking and *why*. Without it, reading only in verses, chapters,
or pericopes, we may not only mishear the vital word; we may
also glut ourselves and our hearers with all the spiritual riches
that we can mine from each piece of the text—riches that
delight us but do not nourish the hungering soul.

JOHN K. STENDAHL

RESPONSE

As you have lived into your life of faith, being in Christ,
what old things are no more? What new things have been
created in you?

PRAYER

Nourish the hungers in my soul, God of my life. Amen.

→ FRIDAY ←

Mark 4:26–34

REFLECTION

This text closes with a mystery first noted in 4:11–12: "And he said to them: 'To you has been given the secret of the kingdom of God, but for those outside, everything comes in parables in order that "they may indeed look, but not perceive, and may indeed listen, but not understand, so that they may not turn again and be forgiven."'" Jesus uses these words to punctuate the parable of the sower, yet another farming story in an agrarian setting. In his closing words to that parable, Jesus seems to indicate that he uses parables to guard against too many people comprehending what he is saying. A likely interpretation is that he is looking for hungry hearts, those longing for the bread of life, those for whom the world's answers are not adequate. In all of these parables in Mark 4, the seed is an important image, and indeed it is important throughout the biblical story. Ezekiel uses it (17:22–24); John uses it (12:24); and Paul uses it (1 Cor. 15:35–38). It is an enduring symbol of life growing out of what seems not only small but dead. Out of the most insignificant beginnings, God creates a mighty wind that will blow throughout the entire world. In these parables, Jesus invites seekers in every age and every place to consider joining in this kind of journey.

NIBS STROUPE

RESPONSE

What questions of faith are most urgent for you today?

PRAYER

Plant seeds of faith in my life. Blow these seeds into the world, use my talents and gifts for healing of hungry hearts. Amen.

⇥ SATURDAY ⇤

Mark 4:26–34

REFLECTION

It is interesting to observe how frustrated Jesus gets in
these stories. He is trying to convey some fantastically good
news as clearly as possible, in healing, in parables, in private
explanations, in his (odd, even offensive) choice of companions.
But the disciples, the crowd, and 2,000 years of Christians
find whatever he is trying so hard to give us incredibly hard
to receive. Perhaps in working with these passages we
should avoid explaining them. Perhaps we should simply
let them vibrate in their strangeness so that our habituated
patterns of understanding and feeling begin to loosen enough
to allow something of Jesus' strange and wonderful news to
break into us.   WENDY FARLEY

RESPONSE

As the writer of this reflection suggests, hear these parables in
new ways. Let them vibrate, shaking up everything you know,
so that new feelings and understandings emerge.

PRAYER

Open my heart, O God, to the wonderful news of your love and
imaginative possibilities planted in my soul. Amen.

✢ SUNDAY ✦

Ezekiel 17:22–24

REFLECTION

The words of verses 22–24 were addressed to a group of
disenfranchised, desperate exiles whose future looked
extremely bleak. The promise that God would "make high
the low tree" and "make the dry tree flourish" is a message of
hope for the refugees of the sixth century BCE as well as the
oppressed people of the twenty-first century CE. Likewise, the
promise to "make low the high tree" and to "dry up the green
tree" serves as a warning to the rich and powerful of ancient
and modern times, that their wealth and power are fleeting. By
humbling the powerful and elevating the powerless, ultimately
all the people of the earth will come to acknowledge that the
destiny of the world lies in the hands of YHWH.

DAVID W. MCCREERY

Psalm 92:1–4, 12–15

REFLECTION

The images of stability and rootedness evoked by the palm
and cedar trees may offer comfort to one who needs shelter
and protection in one of life's storms: God's faithfulness is to
be declared by night, God's "steadfast love in the morning." In
short, God is trustworthy, and that is a truth worth sharing with
the world.   MARY DOUGLAS TURNER

2 Corinthians 5:6–10 (11–13), 14–17

REFLECTION

We dwell either "at home" or "away from home." Being away
from home was the situation of the sojourner in ancient
Israel and the Greek and Roman worlds. The metaphor of the
sojourner was a perfect one for gathering up many themes in

the Bible. All of us are born children of Cain, the founder of the earthly city (Gen. 4:17); but some are reborn as citizens of the heavenly Jerusalem (Gal. 4:26). Then we become sojourners in the earthly city. But that does not mean being indifferent to the earthly city.

EUGENE TESELLE

Mark 4:26–34

REFLECTION

To follow this teller of parables is to become alive to all the paradoxes and the tensions of his life and death: goodness appears in human form, and human powers are threatened; yet death leads to life. We struggle to understand while yet standing under the signs of God's offer of life. Jesus told so many parables he became one. He told so many because he is the very parable of God in human flesh. This is the extraordinary under the signs and words of the ordinary. So the hope is in the question: "What is God's kingdom like? To what shall we compare it?" No one answer will ever exhaust the meaning of this question, but the pulse of Jesus' words, deeds, death, and resurrection point to the secret hid from a distracted, hopeless world. This pulse is the heartbeat of God, whose rule and reign is coming with the terrible speed of mercy.

DON E. SALIERS

RESPONSE

As you read these lectionary texts and consider these reflections, what is revealed to you of the pulse of God's heartbeat?

PRAYER

As your faithful child, I do struggle to understand as I stand under the remarkable signs of the life you offer me. Amen.

❦ *Proper 7* ❦

Job 38:1–11

Then the LORD answered Job out of the whirlwind:
"Who is this that darkens counsel by
   words without knowledge?" (vv. 1–2)

Psalm 107:1–3, 23–32

Then they cried to the LORD in their trouble,
   and he brought them out from their distress;
he made the storm be still,
   and the waves of the sea were hushed.
. . . .
Let them thank the LORD for his steadfast love,
   for his wonderful works to humankind. (vv. 28–29, 31)

2 Corinthians 6:1–13

We are putting no obstacle in anyone's way, so that no fault may
be found with our ministry, but as servants of God we have
commended ourselves in every way: through great endurance, in
afflictions, hardships, calamities, beatings, imprisonments, riots,
labors, sleepless nights, hunger; by purity, knowledge, patience,
kindness, holiness of spirit, genuine love, truthful speech, and the
power of God; with the weapons of righteousness for the right
hand and for the left; in honor and dishonor, in ill repute and good
repute. We are treated as impostors, and yet are true. (vv. 3–8)

Mark 4:35–41

He said to them, "Why are you afraid? Have you still no faith?"
And they were filled with great awe and said to one another, "Who
then is this, that even the wind and the sea obey him?" (vv. 40–41)

✦ MONDAY ✦

Job 38:1–11

REFLECTION

Even the most skeptical of Christians will sometimes pray
for the supernatural when desperate circumstances leave few
other choices: prayers for healing when the doctors know the
cancer will stay the course, or prayers for peace in places where
violence has lived for a thousand years. But mystery, according
to Job, is located primarily not in what is exceptional, but in
what is natural, regular, and known—the morning stars, the sea,
the womb, the clouds. They invite Job, and us, to ponder the
breadth of the depth of this God with whom we must struggle.
In the world unfurled for us in the words of poetry, we find that
our questions lead not to answers but to an awareness of how
deep and fathomless are the mysteries of the God we struggle
to understand. The temptation of many churches, drenched
in the cherished theologies of our traditions, is to give our
people answers. But faith, by its very nature, is not the product
of right answers. The deepest places of our knowledge of God
are often those places that we cannot explain: experiences of
tranquility in the presence of fear, comfort known deeply near
death, the enigma of undeserved suffering visited on the life of
a child—these and many other moments experienced regularly
by people in the church.   ANDREW FOSTER CONNORS

RESPONSE

How comfortable are you with inviting people into the
mysteries of God? What deep places in your life have been
revelatory in revealing God?

PRAYER

Like Job, I would like some right answers. But I also know that
there is so much I learn about you, O God, in the intersection
of life and the experience of not knowing. Amen.

✦ TUESDAY ✦

Job 38:1–11

REFLECTION

These are the kinds of moments people of faith cherish, puzzle over, and pay attention to. These are the mysteries that the church cannot often explain. Most of the time people do not want an explanation. They want an experience of the presence of God, more unpredictable than they had originally hoped, more mysterious than they had first imagined, perhaps more real than the gods we all construct to our own specifications. These moments of mystery are the answers to the questions about God most of us do not know how to ask: comfort, challenge, joy, and hope, all wrapped up into moments that do come. Perhaps the church's vocation has less to do with explaining the root of that mystery and more to do with making space for that kind of mystery to be known and shared. In the hospital room, like every other room in our lives, not everything has its place, not everything is given a meaning that we can understand. Like Job, the people of God ask for explanation, for an accounting. More often than not, what we are given are moments of mystery. The church's role is to support people in the midst of this encounter, to teach them the interpretive tasks of recognizing God's work, not just in the exceptional moments of our lives, but in the regular moments of every human life, where God can be known but never finally explained.   ANDREW FOSTER CONNORS

RESPONSE

What time do you make in your life and in your ministry for the work of interpretation and translation?

PRAYER

As your child, help me to be an interpreter of your creative work in this world. Amen.

✣ WEDNESDAY ✣

Psalm 107:1–3, 23–32

REFLECTION

In bearing his own witness, the psalmist models how to do this. He is specific. He talks about real life events—things that readers then, as now, find in their own lives or the life of their community. Likewise Paul, writing to the Corinthians in the lectionary's Epistle reading, is specific as he lists the "affliction, hardships, and calamity" that have befallen him (2 Cor. 6:1–13). By being specific in naming the storms, we are also specific in naming the praise. "This you did, God. This is where your steadfast love was seen." . . .

God's love and care is for all, and it is to all God's beloved children that the psalmist's call goes out: "Let the redeemed of the Lord say so!" As each of us bears witness to what God has done in our lives, we proclaim God's faithfulness to all God's children. Each grace bestowed, each grace declared, confirms God's promises. Others can hear our story and find hope in the midst of their darkness. Others can hear our praise and find voice to speak their words of gratitude. Each voice strengthens the other in both the hard times and the good. Then indeed the glad hymns will rise from both land and sea.

NETA LINDSAY PRINGLE

RESPONSE

As a redeemed child of God, what can you testify to about God's work in your life?

PRAYER

I do give thanks to you for your steadfast love, which lasts forever. Amen.

✴ THURSDAY ✦

2 Corinthians 6:1–13

REFLECTION

Paul seeks to make of the Corinthian church a community
defined by mutual charity rather than by competition for
spiritual "knowledge," and he demonstrates a model of
authority based not upon superior personal wisdom, but rather
upon willingness to surrender comfort, safety, and personal
ego (no small challenge for Paul!) in service to the gospel. Paul,
however imperfectly, seeks to embody "servant leadership."
Servant leadership does not claim personal power, but rather
seeks to give itself away in Christian love for others. It does not
employ threats or manipulation, but only the proper tools of
charity: "patience, kindness, holiness of spirit, genuine love,
truthful speech, and the power of God" (v. 6). How does a
pastoral leader help to build a genuine Christian community,
fully reconciled with God and with one another? By loving that
community unconditionally ("There is no restriction in our
affections") with a love that will risk speaking the unpopular
truth that the community needs to hear ("We have spoken
frankly to you Corinthians," vv. 11–12). If Aquinas is correct
in saying that it is our destiny to be made friends with God,
we must practice being friends to others who also seek to be
made friends with God. For Christians there can be no such
friendships unless they are rooted in charity. JOHN T. MCFADDEN

RESPONSE

What parts of this model of servant leadership are hardest
for you?

PRAYER

In giving my life to you, O God, I am rich beyond belief. Help
me remember the riches that you desire, a life given to you.
Amen.

✦ FRIDAY ✦

Mark 4:35–41

REFLECTION

The particular word spoken by Jesus in this text is a word of peace and stillness. It is a word we need to hear every day of our lives. The preacher need not look far for individual and corporate "storms" that call for a word of peace. Like the disciples, we are challenged in the midst of those storms to rediscover our faith in the promise of God's powerful word. The question Jesus poses to the disciples is the question he continues to pose to us in our moments of despair: "Why are you afraid? Have you still no faith?" (v. 40). The disciples are rendered speechless in the face of Jesus' great work. They respond with awe and with a glimmer of understanding of the nature and power of Jesus.

A photograph taken shortly after Hurricane Katrina struck New Orleans in the fall of 2005 shows the devastation of a cemetery in the historic district of the city, with trees toppled, debris covering the ground, and several burial vaults broken and smashed. But in the middle of the devastation, untouched by the storm, stands a statue of the risen Christ, arms extended wide, offering a benediction of calm amid the chaos. Such is the image conveyed by this text: the image of Christ with his arms extended wide over the chaos of our lives and world, saying, "Peace! Be still!"

BEVERLY ZINK-SAWYER

RESPONSE

What storms are passing in your life? Of what are you most afraid? What peace do you seek?

PRAYER

I seek your peace in my life. Calm my fears; awaken me to the possibilities of life lived in your abiding love. Amen.

✦ SATURDAY ✦

Mark 4:35–41

REFLECTION

Although we often confuse them, saying, "there's nothing to be afraid of" is a very different thing from saying, "do not be afraid." The hard truth is that fearsome things are very real: isolation, pain, illness, meaninglessness, rejection, losing one's job, money problems, failure, illness, and death. As we grow in faith, we come to understand that even though such fearsome things are very real, they do not have the last word. They do not have ultimate power over us, because reigning over this world of fearsome things is a God who is mightier than they.

Time and again in Scripture the word is, "Do not be afraid." It is, you might say, the first and the last word of the gospel. It is the word the angels speak to the terrified shepherds and the word spoken at the tomb when the women discover it empty: "Do not be afraid." Not because there are no fearsome things on the sea of our days, not because there are no storms, fierce winds, or waves, but rather, because God is with us.

MICHAEL L. LINDVALL

RESPONSE

Consider an experience when you were as afraid as the disciples were. Where did you find strength and hope?

PRAYER

When winds arise and the howling is deafening and my hope is almost gone, throw me a lifeline; help me remember that you are with me and I need not be afraid. Amen.

⁂ SUNDAY ⁂

Job 38:1–11

REFLECTION

The reference to God as YHWH here in Job reminds us (and Job) of this reality. It forces an integration of philosophy and history, of faith and life. Creation and redemption are inextricably linked. The God who magnificently created the world, who is inherently sovereign and wise, is the same God who enters into covenant and in whom human beings can trust. The naming of God as YHWH also underlines a more subtle point evident in the divine speeches: there is a parallel between the natural order and the moral order. The suffering and injustices of the moral order have their counterpart in the forces of chaos (personified by Behemoth and Leviathan, 40:6–41:34) that threaten the created order. God is sovereign over both realms.   JO BAILEY WELLS

Psalm 107:1–3, 23–32

REFLECTION

The dramatic movement of *need, petition, rescue, and thanks* voices the epitome of Israel's faith. The sequence here is no doubt tightly stylized for liturgic use. That stylization, however, derives from the raw, lived experience of Israel. Israel inhabits a world of threat in which YHWH makes a decisive difference. Such a decisive difference evokes specific words and acts of generous gratitude in response.   WALTER BRUEGGEMANN

2 Corinthians 6:1–13

REFLECTION

Paul is speaking to the critical issues of how we create and sustain genuine Christian community and how authority is expressed responsibly within that community. Christian community is not formed or maintained through holding tastes and interests in common, and authority within Christian community is not to be confused with popularity.

JOHN T. MCFADDEN

Mark 4:35–41

REFLECTION

Here is the conundrum: Jesus has godlike authority over the primordial chaos; he is king of the created order. Yet the immediate response to this demonstration of kingly power is not joy, not praise, not acclaim, but fear. Theologically, the significance of this jarring reaction is the power of Jesus' demonstration of kingly power to show up in stark contrast our lack of faith. Mark's anthropology, always illustrated primarily in the personalities and actions of the disciples, is distinctly and uncomfortably thin on charity here. The reaction of the storm-tossed faithful in Psalm 107 is notable by contrast: They are glad, they are thankful, they extol (praise) God's exercise of power on their behalf. This is the response of faith. The disciples, for their part, are scarcely celebratory. Their reaction shows up a particular aspect of Mark's understanding of those yet to come to faith that may be seen in comparison with those who meet God's power with the response of faith—and, in its perfect expression, the absolute obedience of Jesus' faith, which from the ground of its obedience speaks fully the power of God in the created order.

MARK D. W. EDINGTON

RESPONSE

What threads connect these readings for this week? How do you experience God's immanence?

PRAYER

God, you are a mysterious presence in my life, one that continually is revealed in times and places that surprise me. Amen.

❦ *Proper 8* ❦

Wisdom of Solomon 1:13–15; 2:23–24

For God created us for incorruption,
    and made us in the image of his own eternity,
but through the devil's envy death entered the world,
    and those who belong to his company experience it. (2:23–24)

Psalm 30

Sing praises to the LORD, O you his faithful ones,
    and give thanks to his holy name.
For his anger is but for a moment;
    his favor is for a lifetime.
Weeping may linger for the night,
    but joy comes with the morning. (vv. 4–5)

2 Corinthians 8:7–15

As it is written, "The one who had much
did not have too much, and the one who had
little did not have too little." (v. 15)

Mark 5:21–43

He took her by the hand and said to her, "Talitha cum,"
which means, "Little girl, get up!" And immediately the girl
got up and began to walk about (she was twelve years of age).
At this they were overcome with amazement. (vv. 41–42)

✧ MONDAY ✧

Wisdom of Solomon 1:13–15; 2:23–24

REFLECTION

Christians often envision eternity or immortality as a perpetual state of being, like that evoked by the final stanza of the hymn "Amazing Grace": "When we've been there ten thousand years, bright shining as the sun, we've no less days to sing God's praise than when we'd first begun." The author of Wisdom has a rather different idea of immortality. Here, immortality is not so much about a state of being, with the soul continuing endlessly onward. Instead, immortality signifies a relationship, an enduring relationship with God. It was for this relationship that humans were created. Human dignity rests in our relationship to the divine. Even in the midst of pain and suffering, even surrounded by injustice, essential human nature does not change. We were created for good. We are meant for enduring relationship with God. This text urges the community of faith to take a long view of human life—a view that begins with the creation of the universe and extends to an ongoing relationship with God that is beyond time. Such a long-term view provides hope for human life rather than despair. It frees the faithful to do things that do not make any sense in the short term: Work for justice. Give to the poor. Care for widows and orphans. Build peaceful relationships. Delight in God's presence. This, says Wisdom, is what we are created for.   LEANNE PEARCE REED

RESPONSE

What does it mean to you that God made you in the image of God's own eternity?

PRAYER

I am created to do your work in this world now, to give to the poor, care for those in need, work for justice, and delight in your presence. Amen.

⁜ TUESDAY ⁜

Psalm 30

REFLECTION

This short psalm maps so many contours of our emotional landscape: the exaltation of knowing that we have been delivered from a hopeless situation, the wonder at how things that seem so sinister can turn to blessing, the chagrin of knowing we had been overcontent and haughty, and the bewilderment at seeing how things can turn on a dime; it includes a self-affirming, winking prayer for help, quick desperation, and utter joy dancing in praise— exaltation, wonder, embarrassment, astonishment, playfulness, anguish, and delight, all in twelve verses.

The psalm is less a map of our condition than it is a cubist painting, simultaneously showing side, front, and bottom views of our human face. The body of Christ is a community that has all those faces at once. This psalm reveals that complex reality, but with that complexity come pastoral challenges in expositing the psalm. . . . The psalmists complain to God with as much regularity as they praise God. Their intimacy with God allows them the expression of every facet of their inner being. Their trusting God's discerning eye on them means that they do not shy away from what is hidden within them but express it to the One they know has heard it all and can surely bear their cubist prayers.　　　　　　　　　　　CHANDLER BROWN STOKES

RESPONSE

In response to Psalm 30 and this reflection, write your own psalm that maps the contours of your spiritual landscape.

PRAYER

My soul praises you and will not be quiet. With the psalmists across the centuries, I give thanks to you, my Lord and my God. Amen.

✦ WEDNESDAY ✦

2 Corinthians 8:7–15

REFLECTION

How far might this passage be applied to the relationships
among Christians in the global society of the twenty-first
century? Is there a reciprocity between the once-missionized
saints of the global South, who are now recalling their
secularized brothers and sisters in the North to the gospel, and
the affluent Christians of the North, who are able to supply
the material needs of the church in the developing world?
Such a reciprocity of material and spiritual gifts is suggested
by Paul's discussion of the collection in Romans 15:27, but it
is unclear to what extent our 2 Corinthians passage is making
a similar point. Finally, Paul appeals to a scriptural example
of economic reciprocity by citing, nearly verbatim from the
Greek Old Testament, a passage about the bread from heaven
that the Israelites ate in the wilderness (Exod. 16:18): "Whoever
gathered much had nothing left over, and whoever gathered
little had no lack" (8:15). Here too the point seems to be not
a strictly quantitative equality but rather, as Calvin writes,
"such an equality that nobody starves and nobody hordes his
abundance at another's expense."   GARRETT GREEN

RESPONSE

What is your response to the question raised in this reflection:
How far might this passage be applied to the relationships
among Christians in the global society of the twenty-first
century?

PRAYER

Help me find the fair balance in my own life between the
abundance I have and the need of others. Amen.

✣ THURSDAY ✣

2 Corinthians 8:7–15

REFLECTION

For the pastoral leader, this text serves to remind that we are called to be agents of transformation, and in no arena is this more challenging than in that of financial stewardship. Measuring worth and success through personal wealth and material possessions is not a modern invention (although one might fairly claim that we have taken its excesses to new heights); members of the comparatively affluent Gentile churches struggled with the same temptation to "give a little something" to those in need without compromising their own lifestyles, and were prone to measure their giving against their peers ("Did we give more to the relief offering than the Galatians did? Did our church make the 'top five' list?"). The task of pastoral leadership is to lead our congregations, from the crippling fear that if we share our abundance with others there will not be enough left for us, into joyous trust in the God who provides for all our needs. Paul concludes his appeal by recalling how God distributed the manna in the wilderness: "The one who had much did not have too much, and the one who had little did not have too little" (v. 15). Replacing fear with trust is the most challenging, and most rewarding, transformation of all.   JOHN T. MCFADDEN

RESPONSE

What new ideas about being a steward of God's gifts emerge from your reading of this text and this reflection?

PRAYER

I confess: I do want to give a little something to others. I do want to keep something for myself. Help me reflect on what I have, what I need, what I have to give, as I am reminded of you, who provide all I need. Amen.

→ FRIDAY ←

Mark 5:21–43

REFLECTION

If we were to give this text a title, it might be something like "Jesus the Multi-tasker." In our fast-paced twenty-first-century world, this story within a story might not seem terribly odd. In the context of the slower pace of the first-century world, however, the story conveys a sense of urgency, frenetic energy, and even confusion—qualities, it appears from the Gospel stories, that were neither unknown nor frightening to Jesus. Jesus' attention to the desperate needs of both petitioners portrayed in this text becomes a reminder for us of the God who is never too busy to hear our prayers and respond to our pleas in amazing and unexpected ways.

BEVERLY ZINK-SAWYER

RESPONSE

As you read this text, hear it from the point of view of the hemorrhaging woman or the parent of the child. What new insights do you get from this perspective?

PRAYER

Touch me, healing God, so that I may hear and see those in my life in need of your healing presence. Amen.

✤ SATURDAY ✦

Mark 5:21–43

REFLECTION

For Mark's Christology, then, the implications of this pericope
are manifold. How is Jesus a king? Jesus is king of life and law.
He exercises godlike authority over life and death, health and
sickness, clean and unclean. His authority is exercised gently,
in direct relationship with those who come by faith. Priority is
accorded to the marginal, the outcast, the silent. And within
that faith—the faith of Jesus' absolute obedience, the imperfect
yet insistent faith of his followers in him—lies the source of his
kingly authority and its exercise on behalf of those who believe.

MARK D. W. EDINGTON

RESPONSE

As you consider this pericope and this reflection, recall those
whom you know who are marginal, outcast, or silent. How is
God inviting you to hospitality to them?

PRAYER

I admit, O God, that it is hard to respond to everyone around
me who is reaching out for comfort, for healing, for wholeness.
Sometimes it just feels overwhelming, and I don't know how to
respond. Fill my soul with faith, and remind me of Jesus' gentle
and firm authority. Amen.

Wisdom of Solomon 1:13–15; 2:23–24

REFLECTION

If the rich and powerful believe they have free license to run over the poor, the widows, the orphans, and those who raise questions about the ethic of carpe diem, it is because they wrongly believe that death is the end that awaits everyone. Not so, says Wisdom of Solomon. Only those who forsake a holy ethic will taste death. God's chosen will know immortality. Stay faithful, Wisdom of Solomon assures those in the real world of self-interest and domination, because life does not end the way the world presumes.   ANDREW FOSTER CONNORS

Psalm 30

REFLECTION

"Can I have a witness?" calls the voice of the preacher. "Yes, here is my witness," and the psalmist speaks: Weeping may linger for the night, but joy comes with the morning. Yes, it is hard. Sometimes almost more than we can bear, but this too will pass. Your joy will return. Here is my story, says the psalmist. I have moved from feeling that God is angry with me to believing that I have God's favor. I no longer see the moment, but am able to look at all my life. My weeping has been changed into joy. Whereas before I saw only the shadows of the night, now I live in the brightness of the morning. Mourning has become dancing; and rather than wear sackcloth, now I am dressed in joy. It takes maturity, hard-won maturity, to reach that point. Yet the thanks that come after such a time are far deeper, far richer, far more heartfelt. And it is such insight that will carry us through the next shadow, and the next—even through the shadow of death.   NETA LINDSAY PRINGLE

2 Corinthians 8:7–15

REFLECTION

He [Paul] says that the Corinthians need not go to the extent of becoming poor, as Christ did, so that the Jerusalem churches can become rich, but he is challenging the economic disparity between the Corinthians and the Jerusalem churches, and he is calling the Corinthians to correct this disparity. [Paul] is trying to get the Corinthians to think beyond their borders so that the needs of the poor can be met through the desire of the Corinthians to give out of their abundance.

STEPHEN P. AHEARNE-KROLL

Mark 5:21–43

REFLECTION

Every person of faith who suffers, such as the hemorrhaging woman and the desperate parents of the dying little girl, prays for—and usually believes in—the possibility of miraculous healing, but dramatic physical healing is rarely the response to those prayers. Here, then, is an opportunity to explore healing in its less obvious, less dramatic dimensions: healing as peace and acceptance in the face of disappointment, and as awareness of the continuing presence of God in our times of despair. A related question has to do with what role faith plays in our healing. . . . These examples challenge us to examine our own faith, asking how we find the strength to claim God's promises of healing and hope for ourselves, and how we empower others to do the same. BEVERLY ZINK-SAWYER

RESPONSE

What are the sources of your strength that provide healing and hope to others? How are you a witness?

PRAYER

Hear my prayers for health and wholeness and healing. Amen.

❧ *Proper 9* ❧

Ezekiel 2:1–5

He said to me, Mortal, I am sending you to the people
of Israel, to a nation of rebels who have rebelled against me;
they and their ancestors have transgressed against me to this
very day. The descendants are impudent and stubborn. I am
sending you to them, and you shall say to them, "Thus says
the Lord GOD." (vv. 3–4)

Psalm 123

Have mercy upon us, O LORD, have mercy upon us,
  for we have had more than enough of contempt.
Our soul has had more than its fill
  of the scorn of those who are at ease,
  of the contempt of the proud. (v. 3–4)

2 Corinthians 12:2–10

Therefore, to keep me from being too elated, a thorn was given me
in the flesh, a messenger of Satan to torment me, to keep me from
being too elated. Three times I appealed to the Lord about this,
that it would leave me, but he said to me, "My grace is sufficient
for you, for power is made perfect in weakness." So, I will boast all
the more gladly of my weaknesses, so that the power of Christ may
dwell in me. (vv. 7–9)

Mark 6:1–13

Then Jesus said to them, "Prophets are not
without honor, except in their hometown, and among
their own kin, and in their own house." (v. 4)

→ MONDAY ←

Ezekiel 2:1–5

REFLECTION

Ezekiel's testimony serves as a cautionary reminder that at the heart of the church's life is not a set of activities, but an encounter with the holy; an encounter that ought to knock us off our feet and leave us there until God gives us the strength to respond. Out of that encounter comes a call. Once again, God's choice of Ezekiel is rather baffling. Ezekiel is to go to the people of Israel—"a nation of rebels"— and say whatever God tells him to say (v. 3). The enormity of the task—sending one person to speak to a nation—stands in stark contrast to the limitations of Ezekiel, who we are reminded more than once is simply another one of us ("mortal"). As if the call itself were not intimidating enough, YHWH goes on to say that it is likely that the people will not receive this message favorably, since they are "impudent" and "stubborn" (v. 4).   ANDREW FOSTER CONNORS

RESPONSE

Think back over the last week and all the activities in which you were engaged. Now pause and reflect on Sunday, a Sabbath day where you see and experience the heart of a church's life and witness. Where did you encounter the holy yesterday?

PRAYER

When you ask me to stand before you and listen to your voice, I pray for the presence of your Spirit, helping me with my response. Amen.

⟡ TUESDAY ⟡

Ezekiel 2:1–5

REFLECTION

The church can stand in at least two places in this text: as proclaimer and as receiver of proclamation. Neither interpretive choice need be exclusive of the other. There are times when the church finds itself in both locations. As proclaimer, this text gives courage to a church already limping from its myriad wounds. God has chosen to send this church, sprawled out on the floor hardly able to move, to say to the nations, "Thus says the Lord GOD" (v. 4). According to Ezekiel, this is really all we need to know. The church often doubts this is so. On those occasions when the church does make a witness in the public square, the proclamations and the press releases rarely seem to make much of a difference. The church has lost the political weight it used to throw around. But while these observations may be correct, Ezekiel would call them irrelevant. The church is sent to say whatever God instructs it to say. "Whether they hear or refuse to hear" is beside the point (v. 5). The role of the proclaimer, according to Ezekiel, is measured not by results but by whether or not we deliver the message.

ANDREW FOSTER CONNORS

RESPONSE

As you look back over the first half of this year, where do you see your church involved in being a witness in the public square in your community?

PRAYER

Whether I am receiving a proclamation for you, or involved in proclaiming your Word, support me, O God, that I, like Ezekiel, may be a reliable prophetic witness. Amen.

✣ WEDNESDAY ✣

Psalm 123

REFLECTION

If we go back in U.S. history, we find more than enough examples of what it was to be a slave—and "slave" really is the word to use. It means dependence and obedience and deprivation and humiliation. If you are a slave, the quality of your life is defined by the kind of master who owns you. . . . Hear again the words of the psalmist who looks to God as a slave looks to her master. To this God who holds the power to make a life joyful or miserable the plea is made: "Have mercy upon us, O Lord, . . . we have had more than enough of contempt." While we may not understand what it was to live as a slave, being the object of scorn is something that we can understand. Scorn and contempt wear thin very quickly. Such attitudes wear people down, attack sense of self, and are not limited to the world of the ancients. People of faith have experienced such treatment in every age. To be faithful in today's secular world is to open oneself to that age-old experience.   NETA LINDSAY PRINGLE

RESPONSE

Whom does God see—someone who needs the support and ministry from your congregation? Look outside the doors of your church. Whom would a contemporary psalmist cry out on behalf of?

PRAYER

I too lift my eyes to you, merciful God. On this day I give thanks for the community of faith that surrounds me. Amen.

✣ THURSDAY ✣

2 Corinthians 12:2–10

REFLECTION

Paul boasts not of his experiences of transcendent wonder, but rather of his human weakness, his thorn. As is true in so many dimensions of faith, there is a paradox here: we express humility before God by boasting of our weakness because the love, power, and glory of God are made manifest through the good we are able to accomplish in spite of that weakness. "Whenever I am weak, I am strong" (v. 10). Through this rich text, pastoral leaders are reminded that cultivating an inner spiritual life is important in deepening our own walk with God, but it is generally wise to speak of that inner life cautiously, if at all. Rather, that inner life should form us in ways that make our public ministries more faithful. Rather then describe our personal encounter with the risen Christ in transcendent clouds of glory, our calling is to be the presence of Christ to others. But we can, and should, speak humbly and honestly of our weaknesses and limitations, bragging not of our own accomplishments, but of what God is able to accomplish through our lives, despite our weakness. JOHN T. MCFADDEN

RESPONSE

Here in this long season after Pentecost, what spiritual practices deepen your own walk with God? What new practice could you try?

PRAYER

Help me to be the presence of Christ with others. Sustain me for the witness of my life as I come to you in prayer and Sabbath practices. Amen.

✢ FRIDAY ✢

Mark 6:1–13

REFLECTION

The story of Jesus' own rejection at Nazareth sets up the mission of the twelve disciples. The reason for Mark's inclusion of Jesus' embarrassing experience at Nazareth at this particular point in the Gospel appears to be the preparation of the Twelve for what might be a mixed reception. The disciples are warned: "'If any place will not welcome you and they refuse to hear you, as you leave, shake off the dust that is on your feet as a testimony against them'" (v. 11).We cannot help but be reminded of Jesus' experience in Nazareth. Nevertheless, just as Jesus persists in his work by healing and curing even "a few sick people" amid the "unbelief" (vv. 5, 6) of the people of Nazareth, the disciples are commanded to persist in their own work in his name (v. 13). The word for us in this text is that we are not held responsible for the response to our ministries in Christ's name, but only for our own faithfulness. With such assurance, we can witness boldly and faithfully.   BEVERLY ZINK-SAWYER

RESPONSE

In what ministries in Christ's name have you been most involved this year?

PRAYER

God, help me to remember that in ministering in your name, I offer your peace, your mercy, your justice, and your love. In ministering in your name, I give thanks for my continued growth in my faith. Amen.

✢ SATURDAY ✢

Mark 6:1–13

REFLECTION

These verses encompass parallel stories about mission and the rejection, or at least the potential rejection, of Christian mission and missionaries. The first six verses tell of Jesus' preaching and healing mission to his hometown and the offense the people of Nazareth take at him. The second story, verses 6b–13, tells of the commissioning of the Twelve to go out "among the villages" in pairs to heal and preach, with instructions about how to respond to the rejection that they also will encounter. When they leave a place where they have been rejected, they are to "shake off the dust that is on your feet," a strong symbolic action recalling the tradition that Jews returning to Israel would shake off the defiling dust of the Gentile lands from whence they traveled.

Many Christian congregations have made sharp distinctions between "mission" and "evangelism"—between outreach in deeds and outreach in words—sometimes gravitating toward the former out of anxiety about doing the latter. In such a pastoral context, a pastor might explore the false "either/or" dichotomy between mission and evangelism. It is clear that both Jesus' ministry in Nazareth and that of the Twelve to "the villages" was unitary, encompassing both healing—"mission"— and proclamation—"evangelism."   MICHAEL L. LINDVALL

RESPONSE

Review a Sunday bulletin, your church newsletter, your Web site. What kind of ministries of evangelism and mission are available to people of all ages?

PRAYER

Help me discern those ministries to which you call me. Empower me with all wisdom as I seek to help others discern their gifts for ministries of mission and evangelism. Amen.

✦ SUNDAY ✦

Ezekiel 2:1–5

REFLECTION

Ezekiel's call to be a prophet underlines the way in which God communicates with humanity. It is language that is the vehicle for divine communication. This does not deny the possibility of other means of communication; rather it affirms that words have the greatest and fullest potential for understanding the mind of God. God's revelation is, normally, word based. It may involve action also—Ezekiel in particular among Old Testament prophets is renowned for "acting out" his message—but most essentially it takes the form of words. JO BAILEY WELLS

Psalm 123

REFLECTION

This psalm is one of the loveliest prayers in all of Scripture, simple and direct, trusting and confident, spoken out of need and in much hope. . . .

The prayer is the voice of one in the "servant class" who looks to an alternative "master." What a way to think of prayer, as a recharacterization of social relationships with the new character YHWH, God of mercy, as defining reference! The prayer presents the socially humiliated turning from the ones who "are at ease" to the one "enthroned in heaven," a turn that means a departure from contempt and an embrace of mercy. The God of mercy thus is presented as alternative and antidote to unbearable relationships and social inequity.

While the psalm does not say so, we imagine that "mercy" here is not only divine attribute and intention, but also a matter of practice by adherents of YHWH, who will not engage in scorn and contempt toward the needy. The prayer is an immense act of hope, a conviction that demeaning social relationships are not the norm and need not endure. The ground of such hope is in the one addressed, the God of all hope, who will, soon or late, turn the world to well-being, even for those whom the world holds in contempt.

WALTER BRUEGGEMANN

2 Corinthians 12:2–10

REFLECTION

Do we dismiss the validity of all claims of personal revelation? To do so would be to deny the witness of Scripture and the experience of many persons of deep and mature faith. Do we argue that such experiences are indeed possible, but that those claimed by the evangelist in question cannot possibly be authentic? There are no external standards by which any person's claims to personal revelation can be evaluated.

JOHN T. MCFADDEN

Mark 6:1–13

REFLECTION

In Mark's Gospel the person who acts beyond social norms through faith in God is rare. No socially constructed categories serve predictively: they may be rich and powerful (Jairus), poor and marginalized (the hemorrhaging woman), or acting selflessly on behalf of others (the paralytic's friends). Even the demons that afflict the Gerasene are quicker in their faith than Jesus' own neighbors.

MARK D. W. EDINGTON

RESPONSE

In what ways is God's mercy clearest to you this week in the words you have said and the actions you have taken? In what ways is God's mercy clearest to you in the words you have not said and the actions you have postponed?

PRAYER

God of mercy, open my eyes to see those I don't really see. God of mercy, open my ears to those whom I never really hear. Amen.

❧ *Proper 10* ❧

Amos 7:7–15

Then Amos answered Amaziah, "I am no prophet, nor a prophet's son; but I am a herdsman, and a dresser of sycamore trees, and the LORD took me from following the flock, and the LORD said to me, 'Go, prophesy to my people Israel.'" (vv. 14–15)

Psalm 85:8–13

Steadfast love and faithfulness will meet;
righteousness and peace will kiss each other. (v. 10)

Ephesians 1:3–14

Blessed be the God and Father of our Lord Jesus Christ, who has blessed us in Christ with every spiritual blessing in the heavenly places, just as he chose us in Christ before the foundation of the world to be holy and blameless before him in love. He destined us for adoption as his children through Jesus Christ, according to the good pleasure of his will. (vv. 3–5)

Mark 6:14–29

When his daughter Herodias came in and danced, she pleased Herod and his guests; and the king said to the girl, "Ask me for whatever you wish, and I will give it." And he solemnly swore to her, "Whatever you ask me, I will give you, even half of my kingdom." She went out and said to her mother, "What should I ask for?" She replied, "The head of John the baptizer." Immediately she rushed back to the king and requested, "I want you to give me at once the head of John the Baptist on a platter." (vv. 22–25)

✢ MONDAY ✢

Amos 7:7–15

REFLECTION

Amos responds to Amaziah's strong words with strong words
of his own. He refuses to be quantified as some professional
prophet, prophesying for his supper, as it were. He challenges
Amaziah's order to go from Bethel with God's order for him
to go to Bethel. As Amos stands before Amaziah and all of
his believed power and might, he can hear the echo of his
earlier words in his mind, "He is so small!" (v. 5). We are so
small. As much as we huff and puff ourselves up—especially
when we huff and puff ourselves up—we are so small. The
relative prosperity and prestige by which many of us are
surrounded can be crippling to our relationship with God. In
our beautifully adorned sanctuaries we can begin to believe
they are for us. In our lovely homes we can begin to believe that
it is we who have provided for ourselves. In the vast variety and
abundance of this world we can begin to believe that somehow
it belongs to us.   DOUGLAS T. KING

RESPONSE

Take a walk today around your neighborhood or around
the neighborhood of your church. Where might Amos set a
plumb line?

PRAYER

Gracious God, as I am surrounded by the bounty of my life,
may the words of your prophets continue to cause me to wrestle
with the places where plumb lines are needed. Amen.

✦ TUESDAY ✦

Amos 7:7–15

REFLECTION

But we are so small. When we deny our smallness, our place as created and not as creator, we risk being unable to hear the call of God's word upon our lives. When we accept human systems as possessors of ultimate authority, we are living a lie. When we believe our position gives us the ability to control the will and movement of God through the institution of the church or any institution, we are lost. It is we who must be receptive to how God chooses to be at work in the world, not God who must conform to our systems and structures. This text is an illustration of the idolatry of human power. When our sole focus is upon our own achievements and place in the world, we lose sight of where we are placed in this greater creation and who has placed us here. We pile up our resumes and our awards and our bank accounts and stand upon them, believing that they make us big. But what we stand upon is mere froth in front of God's measuring plumb line. We are small. What makes us inherently valuable is our identity as the children of God. When we remember this valuable truth, we are given the freedom of recognizing both how small we are and how cherished we are. From this location we have the wonderful opportunity to keep our eyes peeled to the surprising ways God may be at work in the world.   DOUGLAS T. KING

RESPONSE

Today take a walk in a part of town that may not be as familiar to you. In what ways is God working there?

PRAYER

Thank you, God, for calling me your child. Help me keep my eyes open to the many and surprising ways that you are at work in this world. Amen.

✦ WEDNESDAY ✦

Psalm 85:8–13

REFLECTION

"Let me hear what God the LORD will speak, for he will speak peace to his people." Someone among the people of God listens for a word of salvation. The historical circumstance may have been postexilic, when the grand dreams of restoration had fallen short of the prophetic visions articulated while still in exile. Whether the psalm refers to this historical situation or another, the circumstance fits many occasions for the people of God in every generation. The psalmist is listening for the word of shalom that God will speak to God's people. He or she anticipates a word of steadfast love and faithfulness, of righteousness and peace. In the midst of communal distress, someone remembers the promises of God and becomes the speaker of holy promises. Sometimes all we have from God is a promise. In the midst of injustice, Amos said, "Let justice roll down like waters" (Amos 5:24). In the face of violence, Micah imagined the day when "they shall beat their swords into plowshares" (Mic. 4:3). Trapped in exile, Isaiah prophesied, "Comfort" (Isa. 40:1). . . . To speak the promises of God in all their fullness requires speech to reach beyond that which we see and that which we know. To speak the fullness of God's promises is to speak the truth of the world as it is, as well as the truth of the world as the power of God's shalom will make it.   TOM ARE JR.

RESPONSE

What examples do you see today of places where steadfast love and faithfulness are meeting, where righteousness and peace are kissing each other?

PRAYER

Help me pause in silence and stillness in the midst of a busy day to listen for your voice and the words of shalom. Amen.

✣ THURSDAY ✣

Ephesians 1:3–14

REFLECTION

Ephesians reminds us of God's love for us, and the flowing words of our passage envelop us with that kind of love: excessive, tender, richly abundant. Yet the language of Ephesians is not individualistic. As beloved as we are, we are lifted up into something far greater than ourselves. We are blessed in Christ, we are chosen in Christ, we are destined for adoption through Christ. In Christ we have obtained our inheritance, and our hope is set on Christ. Moreover, the constant plural pronouns remind us that this gift is not an individual blessing but always for the community of Christ. This passage offers a counter to the world's understanding of "worth." It isn't merely that we are somehow special, but rather that we have been taken up into something extraordinary and offered this gift to receive as our own. Like a pauper invited to take the place of a prince or princess, we have been invited to share in the riches of God's grace. God has accomplished all this on our behalf through Christ, so we might live as God's own children.   KAREN CHAKOIAN

RESPONSE

What spiritual blessings are you most thankful for this day?

PRAYER

In and through Christ's saving grace, I am reminded of your excessive, tender, and richly abundant love encompassing me and all those whom God has created. Amen.

✦ FRIDAY ✦

Mark 6:14–29

REFLECTION

Mark's account, stark and spartan, is unique in its ability to hide what is plain and reveal what is hidden. Extreme and even grotesque characters will suddenly appear out of nowhere, revealing a reality that is mysteriously cloaked yet very real. Hidden in plain sight is a world that is demon infested, and evil coexists with normal day-to-day existence, inflicting pain and chaos. No one is immune from this power, especially the innocent and the weak. . . . Almost daily the media bring into our comfortable homes images of needless deaths and the slaughter of the innocents. Our congregations are filled with people, hidden in plain sight, who are dealing with their own texts of terror: deaths of loved ones, broken relationships, and abuse. The beheading of John shows us how to read our own tragic stories. Our worship services should, at times, open the windows and allow the stench of death to permeate the sanctuary. This passage lends itself to a service of stark visuals and calls for the congregation to tarry awhile in the darkness, inhabiting the pathos. CHERYL BRIDGES JOHNS

RESPONSE

What evils are hidden in plain sight in front of you this day? Name them.

PRAYER

May the powers that I have, abilities you have strengthened in me, O God, be used for good and justice, not for evil or corruption. Amen.

✦ SATURDAY ✦

Mark 6:14–29

REFLECTION

On these occasions the preacher is to pull back the curtain and
call forth what is hidden in plain sight, namely, the fragrance of
life found in margins of the text. In these moments the presence
of grace can be felt—waiting to be accepted or rejected. It is
a grace that does not gloss over pain or downplay the horror
of evil. This grace redeems the narrative. Like John's disciples,
the text comes to claim the body. It tenderly holds the broken
and scarred tissue of devastated lives and, with sighs too deep
for words, groans for the day of resurrection. When this grace,
this groaning and pathos embracing power, is accepted, the
fragrance of life fills the sanctuary, and worship fills the hearts
of the faithful. This worship is not naive in regard to suffering.
It is not escapist. It is worship that is eschatological in its
knowledge that all things will be made new.

CHERYL BRIDGES JOHNS

RESPONSE

What fragrances of life do you find in the margins of this text?

PRAYER

God of grace, you fill my life. Sustain me in the face of
brokenness, pain, and evil. When groans are all I have,
surround me with the fragrance of your sustaining love and
presence. Amen.

✦ SUNDAY ✦

Amos 7:7–15

REFLECTION

One cannot read more than a few lines of Amos without
sensing divine anger coursing through the book. God has lost
patience with God's people. The Lord's justice breaks forth in
Amos against the king and his minions and a people willingly
misled for their own gain and comfort. The Lord's justice
breaks out as divine fury against injustice. . . . The hypocrisies
of people who stand on their religion while neglecting
common humanity, who have moved the boundary markers of
compassion in their own hearts so they can trample the needy
and bring ruin to the poor, have inflamed the anger of the Lord.

MICHAEL JINKINS

Psalm 85:8–13

REFLECTION

Psalm 85 reminds us of the importance of memory. The
testimony of the people of God through the generations is that
God's salvation has been experienced. God's divine character
has been revealed as one of steadfast love and faithfulness.
God's dreams for creation include righteousness and shalom.
During times of testing or seasons of emptiness, the psalmist
calls on the people of God to remember all that God has done.

TOM ARE JR.

Ephesians 1:3–14

REFLECTION

Election or predestination is a joyous affirmation of the
sovereignty of God's grace, but it has also troubled many
Christians, including those in denominations that traditionally
have emphasized the doctrine. Does election mean a divine
determinism that turns God into a tyrant and human beings

into robots without any agency or freedom? Does election make faith moot and superfluous? Are some people the recipients of God's grace and others not? Why some and not others? That would seem to suggest God is capricious and perhaps cruel. Does election mean that the gospel is good news for some people and bad news for others? Or does election mean that all people are saved? If so, if salvation is universal, why do discipleship and mission matter? . . . Election is the good news that God's grace in Jesus Christ precedes us, surrounds us, and sustains us, or, in the words of 1 John 4:19, "We love because [God] first loved us."

GEORGE W. STROUP

Mark 6:14–29

REFLECTION

Daily life also presents a series of Herod-like personal and spiritual dilemmas for persons to negotiate. For a harried mother of a toddler, there is the question of how best to love and parent a child in the face of a defiant "No!" and a full-fledged temper tantrum in aisle 6 of the grocery store at the end of a long day. For a father of three, it is the struggle to explain the importance of rearranging travel plans for a work trip so he can attend a Little League playoff game. . . . Across the lifespan, persons question who they are and how they should act as life pushes and pulls them in conflicting directions. And as in the story of Herod's struggle, there are lives at stake as they decide which actions they will take.

KAREN MARIE YUST

RESPONSE

What photographs of God are revealed in the texts for this week? What memories do they evoke? What experiences of life are connected with them?

PRAYER

As I negotiate the next steps in my life of faith, I rejoice that you always remember me, sustaining me with each breath I take. Amen.

❧ *Proper 11* ❦

Jeremiah 23:1–6

The days are surely coming, says the LORD, when I will raise up
for David a righteous Branch, and he shall reign as king and deal
wisely, and shall execute justice and righteousness in the land. (v. 5)

Psalm 23

Even though I walk through the darkest valley,
    I fear no evil;
for you are with me;
    your rod and your staff—
    they comfort me.
You prepare a table before me
    in the presence of my enemies;
you anoint my head with oil;
    my cup overflows. (vv. 4–5)

Ephesians 2:11–22

But now in Christ Jesus you who once were far off have been
brought near by the blood of Christ. For he is our peace; in his
flesh he has made both groups into one and has broken down the
dividing wall, that is, the hostility between us. (vv. 13–14)

Mark 6:30–34, 53–56

And wherever he went, into villages or cities or
farms, they laid the sick in the marketplaces, and begged
him that they might touch even the fringe of his cloak;
and all who touched it were healed. (v. 56)

✦ MONDAY ✦

Jeremiah 23:1–6

REFLECTION

So how do we live in response to this hope we have been promised? The receipt of this powerful gift of hope comes with responsibility. Our knowledge of this gift changes the entire landscape of our reality. We are no longer bound to the fears of an uncertain future. We "shall not fear any longer, or be dismayed, nor shall any be missing, says the LORD" (v. 4). The first way we wisely use this power is by sharing it. The steadfast promise of God's deliverance is one to be shared. We are called to share our knowledge of this powerful promise by word and deed. If we believe that a shepherd is on the way who will lead us in the ways of justice and righteousness, we need to be preparing for their arrival. What better greeting would there be for this shepherd of righteousness than to be living in the ways of God's righteousness as best we can in this time and place? Sometimes when we receive the promise that God will bring deliverance, we mistakenly believe we are removed from the pursuit of improving our current condition. On the contrary, we need to be deeply engaged in the world, doing all we can to prepare for the arrival of the shepherd. But in the midst of our very best efforts we are to be ever mindful that it is the Lord who "will raise up for David a righteous Branch." . . . We stand strong in the promise of God's redeeming work as we seek to be faithful in the work we do for justice and peace for all God's children.

DOUGLAS T. KING

RESPONSE

What examples of deep engagement in the world do you see in the congregation of which you are a part?

PRAYER

Faithful Shepherd, help me to be a strong presence, active in your redeeming work in this world. Amen.

✦ TUESDAY ✦

Psalm 23

REFLECTION

The central claim of the psalmist is that God's care is like that of a faithful shepherd. If God is described through the metaphor of the shepherd, then we are the sheep. One does not need to know much about sheep to understand the image provided in the psalm. This is evidenced in the popularity of this psalm. Confirmation classes memorize it. No fewer than six arrangements of the psalm are found in the hymnal of the denomination in which I serve. It is requested for services bearing witness to the resurrection. And yet, many who have uttered these words as faithful confession have known nothing about shepherds, or even seen a real sheep. . . . They are herd animals. They are defenseless. They are vulnerable. Most commonly noted, sheep are unintelligent. But these are not the characteristics the psalmist has in mind when speaking of the shepherd and the sheep. The psalmist speaks of the sheep's dependence on the shepherd. Sheep cannot survive making their own way. Sheep are absolutely dependent upon the shepherd for life. Sheep can trust the shepherd. Knowing the dependence sheep have on the shepherd brings into focus the central testimony of the psalm: the shepherd is faithful.   TOM ARE JR.

RESPONSE

Read this psalm from a variety of translations or paraphrases, such as *The Message*, NRSV, Tanakh, or *The Common English Bible*. Read it three times in the style of *lectio divina*, listening for a word, an image, and finally the invitation that God is offering to you.

PRAYER

With each breath I breathe today, I give thanks for your sustaining, life-giving, life-directing presence in my life. Amen.

✣ WEDNESDAY ✣

Psalm 23

REFLECTION

When we bring our hearts to the edge of the grave, we know
we cannot make our own way through the season of grief.
When we face the end of our own days, our dependence upon
the shepherd stands before us with more clarity than perhaps
at other times. We are not the creator, but the created, and the
prevailing reality for the creature is our dependence upon God
for life. Perhaps this is why the community of faith finds Psalm
23 so comforting at the time of death. But the witness of the
psalmist is that the shepherd is faithful throughout the whole of
life. That which is confessed in the season of grief remains true
in every season. Sheeplike dependence would be paralyzing,
save for the knowledge that the one on whom we depend is the
good shepherd. This shepherd leads, restores, comforts, and
prepares. In the care of this shepherd, there is no want.

TOM ARE JR.

RESPONSE

As you continue your hearing and meditating on this beloved
psalm, consider this question: In what ways is God leading you,
restoring you, comforting you? For what is God, your shepherd,
preparing you?

PRAYER

Shepherd of my life, thank you for restoring my soul, for
providing signs along the way of my life so I do not get lost.
Amen.

✦ THURSDAY ✦

Ephesians 2:11–22

REFLECTION

But what is this peace to which all Christians are called in the one body of Christ? What is it that constitutes peace? Ephesians makes it clear that the peace to which all Christians are called is Jesus Christ himself. "For he is our peace; in his flesh he has made both groups into one and has broken down the dividing wall, that is, the hostility between us" (v. 14). Peace is not something apart from Christ, some program or policy independent of him. Christ himself, says Ephesians, Christ in his flesh, "is our peace." This means peace is not something Christians need discuss, debate, and construct. Christ himself is that peace. Christians do not apply some understanding of peace to Christ; rather, Christ himself and his reconciliation of all people to God is the true reality of peace.

GEORGE W. STROUP

RESPONSE

Look around you today. Where do you see evidence of the peace of Christ at work?

PRAYER

There are days when your peace is very near to me. On days when I feel far from you, grant me your peace. Amen.

☙ FRIDAY ❧

Ephesians 2:11–22

REFLECTION

Because Christ is our peace, we as Christians understand
peacemaking differently than do many other people. We
recognize that peace has already been made, even if the rest of
the world does not. Peace has already been made, even though
hostilities and bloodshed continue, in the same sense that death
is no more, even though people continue to die. The peace
Christians have in Christ enables us to engage boldly, perhaps
even foolishly, in what may appear to the rest of the world to be
hopeless situations. Christians know it is not our task to bring
peace to the world. God has already done that in the person
of Christ. Luke reports that as Jesus approached Jerusalem
and his passion, he wept and said, "If you, even you, had only
recognized on this day the things that make for peace! But
now they are hidden from your eyes" (Luke 19:42). For those
who are in Christ, the things that make for peace are no longer
hidden.   GEORGE W. STROUP

RESPONSE

To what places in your church, your life, your community is
God calling you to work as a peacemaker?

PRAYER

I confess that this work of living as a peacemaker is hard, never
easy. Sustain me for this call. Show me the things that make for
peace. Amen.

Mark 6: 30–34, 53–56

REFLECTION

The Gospel of Mark speaks of people rushing and begging for an opportunity to be made whole through an encounter with God. This is not how a contemporary congregation typically experiences the neediness of the world of which it is a part. Persons in search of healing are far more likely to seek out therapists, physicians, self-help books, and prescription drugs than to enter a church building. Perhaps this is because persons outside the church do not recognize Christ's healing presence within communities of faith. The people described in this passage recognize Jesus as a healer and respond accordingly. If the church today is unrecognizable as a place of healing, then we need to reflect on what our mission and purpose in the world are and how we communicate the good news of God's healing grace in this time and place. . . . Just as persons come to the church in need of God's grace, the faith community engages in ministry because it needs to live as Christ has commanded, as the body of Christ sent into the world to help God repair the brokenness caused by sin. By embracing its role as the fringe of Christ's cloak, the church can expect to have a healing effect on all who reach out to Christian communities with the desire to be made whole.   KAREN MARIE YUST

RESPONSE

In your moments of mediation today, recall the faces of those whom you saw this week. What kinds of healing do they need?

PRAYER

God, you are a healing presence in the life and the life of my congregation. Help me see all those who are need of healing. Help me see the healing power of the many hands and hearts of those in my community of faith. Amen.

✦ SUNDAY ✦

Jeremiah 23:1–6

REFLECTION

The messianic dimension of this prophecy stands as a promise and challenge to today's church. The prophecy itself is rooted in a challenge to corrupt and ineffectual government over the people of Israel—to the shepherds who have destroyed and scattered God's sheep. After pronouncing judgment on these evil shepherds, God promises to shepherd God's people Godself and then to raise up surrogate shepherds over them. In this promise we find a hope for peace, security, and prosperity—all of these rooted in the faithfulness of God as manifest in God's Messiah, the righteous Branch who will reign as king.

STEPHEN EDMONDSON

Psalm 23

REFLECTION

God's people are God's sheep—and they do not have to be more than that. . . . Sheep are, in fact, not the smartest animals. They are defenseless in nature, weak, timid, shy, and likely to go astray. Nonetheless, all God's people are asked to be is to be God's sheep. There is no pressure to be better, more inventive, productive, strong, or independent. All we are asked to do is to listen to the voice of the shepherd. EDWIN CHR. VAN DRIEL

Ephesians 2:11–22

REFLECTION

Human beings need boundaries both for self-protection and to prevent interference with their neighbor's life. "Do not kill, do not steal, do not commit adultery" all define boundaries. *This* is yours, and not *that*. To love one's neighbor is to honor their boundaries. Why would God, in the name of peace, abolish the law with its commandments and ordinances, the law that was created to protect people? Eliminating boundaries does not in itself create peace. Peace comes only by eliminating the hostility behind the dividing walls. God does not merely tear down walls, but unites people in the One who is our peace, creating one new humanity.

KAREN CHAKOIAN

Mark 6:30–34, 53–56

REFLECTION

Two fundamental questions emerge today from the welter of global religious striving: (1) How does your God view the world?—the basic theological question; and (2) How does your God ask you to view the world?—the basic ethical question. . . . This passage of Scripture contains, in its briefest and most contextually pertinent form, the answer that Christians give—or ought to give!—to this two-sided question. It is stated with extraordinary forthrightness in this one key verse: "he saw a great crowd; and he had compassion for them, because they were like sheep without a shepherd" (v. 34). The term "compassion" is explicitly used of Jesus' attitude toward human beings in at least eight Gospel references, and it is implicit in the entire witness to his life, including his healing ministry that is prominent also in this text. Since for Christians Jesus, supremely, is revelatory of God and indeed God's unique representative in history, compassion must be said to be of the essence of the One who created us and before whom all life is lived.

DOUGLAS JOHN HALL

RESPONSE

Where and with whom have you experienced God's grace this week? What have you heard or seen that gives you hope?

PRAYER

Compassionate God, having so greatly received, help me see those who will know you through acts of compassion. Amen.

❧ *Proper 12* ❧

2 Kings 4:42–44

A man came from Baal-shalishah, bringing food from the first fruits to the man of God: twenty loaves of barley and fresh ears of grain in his sack. Elisha said, "Give it to the people and let them eat." But his servant said, "How can I set this before a hundred people?" So he repeated, "Give it to the people and let them eat, for thus says the LORD, 'They shall eat and have some left.'" He set it before them, they ate, and had some left, according to the word of the LORD. (vv. 42–44)

Psalm 145:10–18

The LORD is just in all his ways,
  and kind in all his doings.
The LORD is near to all who call on him,
  to all who call on him in truth. (vv. 17–18)

Ephesians 3:14–21

I pray that you may have the power to comprehend, with all the saints, what is the breadth and length and height and depth, and to know the love of Christ that surpasses knowledge, so that you may be filled with all the fullness of God. (vv. 18–19)

John 6:1–21

Then Jesus took the loaves, and when he had given thanks, he distributed them to those who were seated; so also the fish, as much as they wanted. (v. 11)

⤗ MONDAY ⤖

2 Kings 4:42–44

REFLECTION

There is an absurdity to this text that cannot be overlooked. What we have received is a message that is countercultural to the rules of our world. The words of the servant live in the midst of our lives every day. "How can I set this before a hundred people?" We budget our resources and our time with a careful eye to the limitations we see present. We tell ourselves "there are only so many hours in the day" and "a penny saved is a penny earned." When we design our church budgets we are very careful to be prudent and make sure we can afford to pay for any program that is proposed. We would never put Elisha in charge of deciding how much food is necessary for a potluck supper or deciding what we can afford to do as a congregation. We very carefully do what we know we can do with the tangible resources before us. A character such as Elisha in our midst would appear to be reaching beyond the appropriate bounds of the resources before us and the expectations of what we believe we can accomplish.

DOUGLAS T. KING

RESPONSE

Meditate on this reflection in connection with your congregation. In what ways is the budgeting of time and resources connected to the consideration of limitations rather than possibilities?

PRAYER

God, your bread is always enough to feed hungry bodies and hungry souls. I sometimes forget this, and forget that there is always some left. Amen.

✦ TUESDAY ✦

2 Kings 4:42–44

REFLECTION

What we fail to see is that Elisha is being prudent as well. He too is carefully measuring the resources before him when he instructs the servant to feed one hundred people with twenty loaves. He views another element in the equation that we often overlook. Elisha is able to recognize the presence and will of God as a resource upon which we can draw to respond to the needs of the people of God. Of course it is a specific gift of the prophet to see when and where God's blessing will come to bear. But we are challenged to put on the eyes of the prophet. We are called to reach beyond the common-sense measurements of the world. We are given the opportunity to recognize how God's abundant blessings are at work in the world, or could be, and how we can participate in them. If we bring our first fruits before the Lord, recognize the needs of the people, and keep a close watch on God's movement in our midst, who knows what will happen? God's abundant blessings just might burst in upon us, bringing more before us than we ever previously imagined possible.   DOUGLAS T. KING

RESPONSE

Where might the eyes of the prophet be used in your church, in your community? How might this text be used in church committees as a meditation before planning their work?

PRAYER

Open my eyes to the many ways that your abundant blessings are present in the world around me. Amen.

✢ WEDNESDAY ✢

Psalm 145:10–18

REFLECTION

To repeat the *Tehillah* (Hebrew word for hymn of praise) every day requires the children of God to give voice to praise on the days of richest blessing as well as the days of journey in the dark valley. Particularly when we have fallen or the powers of the world have bowed us down and we hunger for a life that nourishes the soul, praise uttered in these harsh times does not fall to the floor as empty words, but rests in the ears and heart of the Sovereign One. The psalmist promises, "The LORD is near to all who call on him." My God the King says, "Tell me where you are; I will be right there." In the presence of the King, God's children know they are children of the world to come.

TOM ARE JR.

RESPONSE

Take time to repeat part of this *Tehillah* at different times during the day. What comfort does it offer? What challenge does it invite for your life of faith?

PRAYER

Thank you for being near when I call on you, Lord of my life. Amen.

✦ THURSDAY ✦

Ephesians 3:14–21

REFLECTION

The issue is letting Christ in to change us. Having Christ dwell
in our hearts is akin to having a new person move into your
household. If they're just visiting, it is all rather easy; you
simply offer hospitality and try to practice good manners. But
if someone moves in to stay, everything changes. At first you
might try to hold on to your familiar patterns and routines,
and the new member may work hard to accommodate you
and stay out of the way. But eventually they make their mark.
Conversations change. Relationships realign. Household tasks
increase and responsibilities shift. So it is when Christ moves
in to the hearts of Christians. This isn't merely tweaking old
patterns; everything changes. KAREN CHAKOIAN

RESPONSE

Consider the family of God of which you are a part. For whom
are you praying today?

PRAYER

Root me in your love. May Christ dwell in my heart. Fill me
with all your fullness, O God. Amen.

✦ FRIDAY ✦

John 6:1–21

REFLECTION

The Gospel of John is all about knowledge as power. It is
about the way, the truth, and the life. It is controlled. It is
not a knowledge that entertains or provides a satisfying
experience. Rather, it is knowledge of a different kind, one that
is expressly relational and deeply passionate. It is a knowledge
that grounds the knowing event in the triune life as revealed
in the incarnation of Jesus. . . . The feeding of the multitude
as portrayed in the Gospel of John addresses the temptation
to shrug one's shoulders in the face of human need. It shows
the finitude of human knowledge and points toward "the
incarnation that lives." Here is a paralyzing situation. There
is overwhelming need and few resources. Surveying the great
crowd, Jesus asks a question that tests the limits of the disciples'
knowledge: "Where are we to buy bread for these people to
eat?" . . . In the "prayers of the people," we place before the Lord
the great needs of humanity. We may find echoing back the
words, "What do you have?" Whatever we have is not enough.
Yet, as this text points out, the "not enough" is not the final
answer. When placed in the hands of Jesus, human weakness
and finitude become more than enough. CHERYL BRIDGES JOHNS

RESPONSE

Read this text from the point of view of someone in the story,
such as the boy, someone in the crowd, a disciple. What do you
bring? What do you need?

PRAYER

On some days I do believe I have enough to share with others,
enough love, enough compassion, enough vision. On other
days, I am hungry and know my need is great. In both my
bounty and my need, you are there. Amen.

✣ SATURDAY ✣

John 6:1–21

REFLECTION

All around us are those with knowledge of human need but
with few resources. There are countless small congregations.
There are people on limited incomes. There are those with
physical or mental handicaps. In the face of it, all these
resources are like a drop in the bucket. Yet, as this passage
vividly portrays, in the hands of Jesus, little can become much,
the few can become the many, and the weak can become strong.
This text closes with a couple of incidents that give warning to
those who wish to control the world or manipulate this power.
Jesus' refusal to "be taken" by force and made king and his
refusal to allow the disciples to take him into the boat make
clear that Jesus is not a concept that "works" for humanity,
but an incarnation that lives among us. This incarnation will
not be co-opted by human desire, no matter how sincere or
lofty the goals.   CHERYL BRIDGES JOHNS

RESPONSE

What evidence do you see of the "incarnation that lives
among us"?

PRAYER

Human need seems so great and overwhelming at times. Yet
I know and experience your incarnating presence in my life,
loving God. Remind me not to be afraid. Remind me of the
power of response embodied in communities of faith in my
community. Amen.

✦ SUNDAY ✦

2 Kings 4:42–44

REFLECTION

God will not leave us without a witness. When one prophet
passes from the scene, God will raise up another. Through the
prophets, God will be at work for the people's good in the midst
of the common realities, although this work may not appear
obvious at first. God's will for us is trust and abundance. We
will have what we truly need and more besides. Second, in a
world where the temptation to worship other powers is strong,
God will reveal in the ordinary course of daily events that God
is faithful to the covenant promises and that our faithfulness to
the covenant will bring us blessing.   KAREN C. SAPIO

Psalm 145:10–18

REFLECTION

Psalm 145 is a hymn of praise (in Hebrew, *tehillah*). . . . To
repeat the hymn of praise every day requires giving voice to
such praise on the best of days as well as in the darkest hours.
On the days filled with blessing, praise easily rises up from the
people of God carried by gratitude for God's faithfulness (v. 13),
mercy, and steadfast love (v. 8). Yet, the psalm is not a psalm for
these rich days of blessing only. The psalm is stitched together
with the word "all." It is also composed in an acrostic, an artistic
structure that begins the first line of the poem with *aleph* (the
first letter in the Hebrew alphabet) and each subsequent line
with the next letter in the alphabet. The intention is clear. The
praise of the faithful is to be offered not simply in the best
of times, but in all times and circumstances, because God is
faithful in all times.   TOM ARE JR.

Ephesians 3:14–21

The heart has its reasons the mind does not fathom, or as Ephesians puts it, for those in whom Christ dwells there is a "power at work within us . . . able to accomplish abundantly far more than all we can ask or imagine" (v. 20). It is in response to this One who is not only at work within us, but also at work in the breadth and length and height and depth of creation, that Christians are driven to their knees in worship.

GEORGE W. STROUP

John 6:1–21

REFLECTION

There was a time when knowledge was power. It was assumed that if a person had the right data and the correct information, he or she could "objectively" use that knowledge to make the world a better place. During the age we call modernity, knowledge was the solution to all the problems that plagued humankind. It provided power over the world—and when used "objectively"—this power seemed limitless. Now there is another reality, namely that of knowledge as powerlessness. What a strange irony that with the advent of the information age, wherein knowledge is everywhere, passivity is pervasive.

CHERYL BRIDGES JOHNS

RESPONSE

What prophets is God raising up today? As you look around you in your community of faith and in the larger community of faith in your city or town, what witnesses to God's love, mercy, and justice are in evidence?

PRAYER

I open my heart and my soul to your Spirit so that Christ's indwelling will root and ground me in love. Amen.

🌿 *Proper 13* 🌿

Exodus 16:2–4, 9–15

Then Moses said to Aaron, "Say to the whole congregation
of the Israelites, 'Draw near to the LORD, for he has heard
your complaining.'" And as Aaron spoke to the whole congregation
of the Israelites, they looked toward the wilderness, and the glory
of the LORD appeared in the cloud. The LORD spoke to Moses
and said, "I have heard the complaining of the Israelites; say
to them, 'At twilight you shall eat meat, and in the morning
you shall have your fill of bread; then you shall know that
I am the LORD your God.'" (vv. 9–12)

Psalm 78:23–29

Yet he commanded the skies above,
    and opened the doors of heaven;
he rained down on them manna to eat,
    and gave them the grain of heaven. (vv. 23–24)

Ephesians 4:1–16

I therefore, the prisoner in the Lord, beg you to lead a life
worthy of the calling to which you have been called, with
all humility and gentleness, with patience, bearing with one
another in love, making every effort to maintain the unity
of the Spirit in the bond of peace. (vv. 1–3)

John 6:24–35

"Do not work for the food that perishes, but for the food that
endures for eternal life, which the Son of Man will give you. For it
is on him that God the Father has set his seal." (v. 27)

✣ MONDAY ✣

Exodus 16:2–4, 9–15

REFLECTION

God hears the prayers and interrupts the misery of the chosen
people to provide even for those who neither expect it nor
recognize it for what it is. If the new Pharaoh does not know
Joseph, God still does. If stammering Moses is an exile—and
justifiably so—God is free to call even this murderer and
coward to become a mighty instrument of divine freedom and
justice. If Pharaoh's hard heart leads him to say, arrogantly,
"They are astray in the land; the wilderness has closed in on
them" (14:3 Tanakh), the alternative proclamation is that the
wilderness is a table prepared for the elect, a track wide enough
for pilgrimage. Today we stand at the end of the beginning, in
between the exodus itself and Sinai—which is to say, between
the deliverance of the people and the constitution of the nation.
We find ourselves, then, in a kind of wilderness within the
wilderness. If the theological affirmation is God's provision,
the corresponding anthropological confession is that those
for whom provision is provided are often petulant and rarely
satisfied.   THOMAS R. STEAGALD

RESPONSE

What wilderness wanderings have you experienced? What
provisions of God sustained you?

PRAYER

Like the Israelites in the wilderness, I complain loudly and
under my breath. I fail to recognize the bread you have put in
front of me, sustaining God. Thank you for this bread of life
that feeds my hungers. Amen.

✧ TUESDAY ✧

Psalm 78:23–29

REFLECTION

Once again, memory, experience, and expectation ground Israel's faith, yet Israel fails to trust, due to its narrow, immediate outlook. Mission trips to unfamiliar settings—places often described as "deficient," "lacking," or "undeveloped"—have a way of revitalizing the faith of many church people, who often respond to these experiences by saying, "I love the passion of those Christians" or "I've been blessed more than I have blessed." Such words point to a vitality of faith discovered in these new places. Though many who go on mission trips struggle to be open to those whom they serve, they often falsely see the places of mission as "backward" and their own environment as "progressive." They discover, however, that the faith of the Christians in the "backward" setting can actually be a fountain of hope. . . . Missioners often find their own capacity for awe, mystery, and enchantment revitalized. When they return home, they want to kindle this fire. Perhaps what they have experienced is not so much the simplicity of the faith of the people they have come to serve as the tangible cosmic presence of God in those people's lives—in their closeness to nature, in the reciprocity between nature and the human community. Suddenly, the cosmic has become an intrinsic dimension of their own faith. CARLOS F. CARDOZA-ORLANDI

RESPONSE

Can you recall a recent experience when the cosmic mystery of God has broken into the ordinary of your life?

PRAYER

Thanks be to you, O God, for the abundance of food you place before me, within me, and behind me. Amen.

✢ WEDNESDAY ✦

Ephesians 4:1–16

REFLECTION

The exhortation of the passage, therefore, is to encourage the listeners to accept their calling willingly, aware of the sacrifice that such a calling entails. They are called to "lead a life worthy of the calling to which you have been called" (v. 1) by "bearing with one another in love" (v. 2). To bear with one another is to sacrifice for the other. It is to help carry the other's burdens. Love is not an emotion; love is an act of the will. Paul is not calling for the early Christians to feel warmly toward one another, but to act according to their calling. They are to do love by serving one another. The church is called to be a new community based not on the divisions inherent in the existing social order but on the new humanity in Christ. The social hierarchy has been replaced by the body of Christ. In this new order, all members are essential, and all members are connected. Love, therefore, is neither theoretical nor abstract but is the glue of community; it is what knits the body together.

G. PORTER TAYLOR

RESPONSE

Which members of the body in your church do some consider not essential? Whose baptism is not recognized or welcomed in this body?

PRAYER

Continue to support my faith community, reminding us of the acts required of this one body—humility, gentleness, patience, love, and peace. Amen.

✦ THURSDAY ✦

Ephesians 4:1–16

REFLECTION

The tools for this body are humility, gentleness, and patience.
Humility keeps us grounded in the reality of who we are as
creatures formed from the dust by God. Gentleness reminds
us of our corporate identity. Because we are essentially part of
the body, we are called to build up the body by attending to
one another. Finally, we are patient because we live in time.
The kingdom of God is a gift from God, not a work achieved
by humans. The Christian life is one of expectation for the
new Jerusalem which gives us hope in the here and now.
Jesus' yoke is easy because he bears it with us and because
as we take it upon us and bear one another's burdens, we come
closer to him.   G. PORTER TAYLOR

RESPONSE

Whose burdens are you bearing this day? Include them in your
prayers.

PRAYER

God of *kairos*, help me to be more patient as I receive your gifts
and consider how I can use them. Amen.

✦ FRIDAY ✦

John 6:24–35

REFLECTION

In the Gospel of John, people come to Jesus again and again,
seeking to understand him. The question of his identity,
who he is and where he came from, is the central theme. No
other document in the New Testament is more explicit in its
answers to that question, yet those answers remain ironic or
paradoxical, as often repelling as persuading the men and
women with whom Jesus speaks. In the sixth chapter we see
first "the crowd," then the disciples, trying to grasp the enigma
of Jesus by using the best tools their religion supplies: the
evidence of miracles, tradition, and Scripture. Yet each of these
tools shatters when confronted with this One who seems to
belong to another world. Miracles, in the Fourth Gospel, do
not easily bring faith to those who witness them, but more
often confusion, division, and hostility. This Gospel calls them
"signs," but if they are symbolic markers pointing toward truth,
it is by a winding and ambiguous path. When this Gospel retells
one of the stories of Jesus' miraculous acts that were so rich a
part of the lore about him, it does so only to set the stage for
Jesus to talk about himself in words that are often puzzling and
challenging—to the characters in the story and to ourselves.

WAYNE A. MEEKS

RESPONSE

What questions of faith has your heart articulated recently—
either your own or those of people with whom you have been
in conversation?

PRAYER

I am not alone in praying for miracles. I offer my prayers to
you knowing that all hungers and thirsts are satisfied in your
abiding presence. You are indeed the bread of my life. Amen.

✣ SATURDAY ✣

John 6:24–35

REFLECTION

Too often, we forget how to pursue what really matters. We are accustomed to inviting people into the community of faith for all the wrong reasons: for the "right" kind of worship; for political engagement on behalf of the poor and downtrodden; for the sake of a Christian America; for a strong youth and family ministry; for the opportunity to practice mission in a downtown location, or to go on mission trips to Africa or Central America. Yet what we have to offer—in Christ and by Christ and because of Christ—first and foremost is "soul food," which lasts forever and does not change with the changing circumstances of the church or the world. It is soul food that we desire, and soul food in which we will rejoice, long after our bellies are full of rice and our lives know justice in a free society. We North American Christians have preached a broken, truncated gospel. We have been good marketers rather than true witnesses. We have bought into a culture that rewards consumers and addresses their needs, instead of proclaiming a gospel that offers us faith in the only begotten Son, who gave his life for the sins of the world—and who is lifted up so that all who believe in him have everlasting life. He is the bread of life. Those who come to him will never be hungry, and those who put their trust in him will never thirst.   O. BENJAMIN SPARKS

RESPONSE

Do you agree or disagree that we are guilty of preaching a "broken, truncated gospel"? What is that gospel? What gospel should be preached?

PRAYER

As I seek to be a faithful disciple, constantly remind me that what you need from me is the faithful witness of my life. Amen.

✤ SUNDAY ✤

Exodus 16:2–4, 9–15

REFLECTION

If God's provision for the sojourners is apparent day by day, whether in daily bread or daily work (the gathering of the quail, the harvesting and preparing of the manna, constitute the nation's first vocation on the other side of slavery), God's presence is more mysterious. As the Israelites "turned toward the wilderness, there, in a cloud, appeared the Presence of the Lord" (16:10 Tanakh). This lection leads us to the familiar unknown—to the grace and giving, to the guidance and demand—to the mysterious presence of the God whose gifts are not limited to meat and bread.   THOMAS R. STEAGALD

Psalm 78:23–29

REFLECTION

Time is a continuum of interrelated events and experiences that reveal to us the eschatological character of the Judeo-Christian tradition, of God's activity in the universe and for God's people. This text is a reminder, an exercise in memory, of God's wondrous deeds in the cosmos— in creation and beyond what our senses register.   CARLOS F. CARDOZA-ORLANDI

Ephesians 4:1–16

REFLECTION

The fractious church's need to hear grace notes and exhortations on the themes of unity and diversity is acute, as is its hunger for doxology and direction. The human community is in desperate need of communities of faith where belief and practice are congruous. The text appointed for today lies at the heart of an expansive vision for Christian community as

expressed in this widely circulated communiqué from a devoted
disciple of the apostle Paul.   RICHARD F. WARD

John 6:24–35

REFLECTION

Jesus, at least in this pericope, risks ambiguity, metaphor, and
"thick" communication. He is not trying to obfuscate the truth
but rather to reveal a difficult, counterintuitive, countercultural
truth. "Faith," as the word is used here, means more than
clarity about the facts, belief in a set of propositions. Faith
means encounter with a person, one who is "the way, and the
truth, and the life" (14:6). The one who speaks to us in this
peculiarly metaphorical way is the one who desires not only
that we think about him but that we feed on him, ingest him,
implying that we could starve to death without him. The truth
being communicated here is so peculiar that mere surface
comprehension, mere intellectual assent, is inadequate to the
truth under consideration. Therefore our speech in interpreting
Jesus' speech ought to be metaphorical, assertive, declarative,
rather than analytical. When John Calvin was asked to explain
the Eucharist, he said that he would "rather experience it than
to understand it." Actually to feed upon the truth who is Jesus
Christ, to find primary sustenance in him, is better even than to
understand him.   WILLIAM H. WILLIMON

RESPONSE

As you read over these selections for Sabbath, what connections
do you make among them? What images capture the dominant
themes?

PRAYER

Thank you, God, for journeying with us. Help us in community
to live faithfully as "vibrant cobelievers, and imaginative
innovators." Amen.

THE WEEK LEADING UP TO

Proper 14

1 Kings 19:4–8

But he himself went a day's journey into the wilderness, and came and sat down under a solitary broom tree. He asked that he might die: "It is enough; now, O Lord, take away my life, for I am no better than my ancestors." Then he lay down under the broom tree and fell asleep. Suddenly an angel touched him and said to him, "Get up and eat." (vv. 4–5)

Psalm 34:1–8

O magnify the Lord with me,
 and let us exalt his name together. (v. 3)

Ephesians 4:25–5:2

Therefore be imitators of God, as
beloved children, and live in love, as Christ loved
us and gave himself up for us, a fragrant offering
and sacrifice to God. (5:1–2)

John 6:35, 41–51

Jesus said to them, "I am the bread of life. Whoever comes to me will never be hungry, and whoever believes in me will never be thirsty." (v. 35)

⇝ MONDAY ⇜

1 Kings 19:4–8

REFLECTION

The backdrop of our lesson, so much like the stories of the
exodus, is the ongoing war of God through the persons and
work of the prophets against idolatrous royalty and their
minions. If the plagues are the weapons of choice of God
and Moses in the protracted battle against Pharaoh, then
apocalyptic fireworks win the day against Ahab and, more
particularly, against Jezebel and her imported priests of Baal. In
each battle God humiliates the usurpers and pretenders—there
is, quite evidently, no God but God. But if at the Reed Sea and
on Mount Carmel God is fighting against "other gods," in the
wilderness stories that follow these victories, God is contending
for the hearts of the faithful. The latter battles are not won by
plagues or dramatic demonstrations of power—nor, as it turns
out, by fire, wind, or earthquake—but rather by the ministry of
angels, the gift of food, and the still, small voice. In the lesson
before us we see the aftermath of the first battle (God against
Baal) and the first engagements of the second (God for Elijah).

THOMAS R. STEAGALD

RESPONSE

Consider your own experiences of running from that which
you most fear. What food sustained your ability to face the fear?
How was God most present to you, in a still voice or in the
sound of silence?

PRAYER

Sometimes the journey I face is difficult, and all I want to do is
run away, retreat, lie down, escape from that which is in front of
me. Touch me, wake me, remind me to eat. Then I know I can
eat and drink in the strength of your abiding presence, and it
will be enough to get me through. Amen.

✦ TUESDAY ✦

1 Kings 19:4–8

REFLECTION

The "wilderness" is a place of both giving and testing, a season of provision and obedience, a time of physical weakness and even despair, but also an occasion of spiritual strengthening and vocational redefinition. The words of God, as much as manna or cakes, are a feast for the famished faithful and a means for reinterpreting their experience so that the battle against idolatry and presumption, whether it occurs in the palace, on the mountain, or in the heart, may continue.

THOMAS R. STEAGALD

RESPONSE

Consider your own experience of wilderness. How were you challenged in the wilderness? In what ways was your spirit strengthened, your vocation redefined? What words of God fed you?

PRAYER

You feed me in ways that I cannot even begin to imagine—through the words of a friend, the touch on my hand, the offer of hospitality, the prayers that surround me. I am fed and am thankful. Amen.

✦ WEDNESDAY ✦

Psalm 34:1–8

REFLECTION

There are many communities of faith today held together more by what they condemn together than by what they bless together. Is your community one that condemns together or one that blesses together? "Let us exalt his name together," is the hope of Psalm 34. When the psalmist declares, "Look to him and be radiant," the images hearken back to the radiance of Moses. It was Moses whose face shone with glory after he had been in the presence of God. Can the preacher describe a radiant face she has seen lately? In particular, however, the hearer is urged to "look to him" in order to be radiant. The Lord might be rather like the sun, our star, after all. It shines forth light that is then reflected. Those who look to God actually reflect God. The one who sees God is rather like the moon, then, or a planet, reflecting the light of the sun. Even if each of us reflects that light at a different angle, or with perhaps a slightly different hue, the light itself is the light of deliverance (vv. 4 and 6).
SAM CANDLER

RESPONSE

Read this psalm. What goodness of God have you seen reflected this day?

PRAYER

I will bless you, my Lord and my God. I have tasted and know that you are God and the radiance of your love shines in my face. Amen.

✦ THURSDAY ✦

Psalm 34:1–8

REFLECTION

A distinguished Brazilian theologian was shot during a robbery
in downtown São Paulo. After several days in the hospital, a
fellow priest assured him that he was praying that God would
deliver the theologian from his terrible pain. The theologian
replied, "Do not pray for me. Pray for those whose lives are
in constant peril in the *favelas* [poorer neighborhoods] of our
city, suffering from the oppression and despair of lack of food,
health care, housing—basic human needs." His fellow priest
inquired, "But why should I not pray for you? You have suffered
a tragedy, and you have been close to death." "My esteemed
brother," the theologian tenderly answered, "do not confuse
the realities of life with the realities of a life strangled. I praise
God for all God has given me, but I don't need to be delivered
from this pain, because it nourishes my solidarity with those
who suffer for no reason in this world." As those in the Judeo-
Christian tradition discover the character of God, they also
discover the answer to the question "Who are we?" "My soul
makes its boast in the LORD; let the humble hear and be glad. O
magnify the LORD with me, and let us exalt his name together"
(vv. 2–3). As we witness and testify to God's deliverance, we
are launched to live our true human vocation. We are agents of
praise—no less, no more.   CARLOS F. CARDOZA-ORLANDI

RESPONSE

From what has God delivered you? Out of this deliverance,
what new thing is emerging in your human vocation?

PRAYER

Show me the ways that I can be an agent of your praise in this
world. Amen.

✦ FRIDAY ✦

Ephesians 4:25–5:2

REFLECTION

Here a bold statement, a command really, rises off the page and into our hearing: "Be imitators of God." What? "Imitating God" means putting our focus on the actions that flow from God's character. Teachers in the world that the writer of this epistle inhabited thought human beings to be mimetic beings, that is, those creatures who felt the urge to imitate their vision of the real through their actions in art and culture. "Real life" was that which was being "shown forth" in all of its dimensions through the "actions" of the poets, the playwrights, the orators, and the actors. Actions deemed worthy of imitation were "grand" ones by noble, even heroic individuals played out on stages in front of the gods and the gathered community for the instruction of all. The writer of Ephesians sees such an action performed by God in the person and work of Jesus Christ. It is a grand gesture of love played out on the stage of Creation for the instruction of the human community. Those who are baptized are called to be imitators of that action, not just in the sanctuaries we find ourselves in, but on the stage of a global village and on the front lines of human relationships. RICHARD F. WARD

RESPONSE

What does it mean for you to imitate Christ? Whom is Christ asking you to forgive?

PRAYER

I pray, O God, that you will take away all the bitterness and anger in my heart. Replace it with a heart that is tender and forgiving, a heart like yours. Amen.

⤞ SATURDAY ⤝

John 6:35, 41–51

REFLECTION

Here, standing before us, in the flesh, is the fullness of God. If
you have ever wondered just what God looks like, or how God
acts, or how God talks, then wonder no more. In this faith, we
do not have to climb up to the divine; God discloses, unveils,
climbs down to us. . . .

Let's admit it. There is something within us that likes our
gods high and lifted up, distant, exclusively in heaven. We so
want religion to be something spiritual, rather than something
that is uncomfortably incarnational. Yet here we are with God-
in-the flesh before us saying, "I'm your bread; feed on me!"

Our hungers are so deep. We are dying of thirst. We are
bundles of seemingly insatiable need, rushing here and there in
a vain attempt to assuage our emptiness. Our culture is a vast
supermarket of desire. Can it be that our bread, our wine, our
fulfillment stands before us in the presence of this crucified,
resurrected Jew? Can it be that many of our desires are, in the
eternal scheme of things, pointless? Might it be true that he
is the bread we need, even though he is rarely the bread we
seek? Is it true that God has come to us, miraculously with us,
before us, like manna that is miraculously dropped into our
wilderness?   WILLIAM H. WILLIMON

RESPONSE

For what do you hunger? For what are you thirsty? How is God
feeding you?

PRAYER

I offer you my life and my belief. I set my heart in you, God,
you who satisfy all hungers. Amen.

⊱ SUNDAY ⊰

1 Kings 19:4–8

REFLECTION

God's ministry of angels takes a variety of contemporary forms, of course, from loving friends to specially trained therapists. Fortunately, Elijah demonstrates strength as he cries out to the Lord, the one who listens. He also allows himself to be cared for. Elijah refuses to life a live of quiet desperation. Another way to shape the sermon might be to stress the need for time away, because, as Alice Walker writes, "wisdom requests a pause." Flight from all that is death dealing is needed to reorder our lives in communion with God. Elijah had to pause and let go of his fear before he could embrace the transition to what was next in his life.

DEAN MCDONALD

Psalm 34:1–8

REFLECTION

According to Lawrence Sullivan in his book *Ichanchu's Drum*, religion has four main aspects: cosmogony (where does creation come from?), cosmology (what is the nature of creation?), anthropology (who are human beings?), and terminology or eschatology (where is life going?). This psalm text is about anthropology, and in particular it offers us a window into Judeo-Christian anthropology. Although at first the text seems to speak about God and God's character, it also points to the human condition of those who believe in God. The psalmist invites readers to exuberant praise for God. . . . For those who wonder about the community's imperative, the psalmist highlights the nature and character of God as one who creates in the human being an imperative for praise and glory. Therefore praise is also a testimony, a biographical narrative of God's merciful acts in the life of the community.

CARLOS F. CARDOZA-ORLANDI

Daily Feast, Year B

Ephesians 4:25–5:2

REFLECTION

There is no doubt that intimacy will involve hurt; hence, the necessity for forgiveness. This theme runs through Scripture like a red thread. No meaningful relationship can function without it. Why should we forgive? We could make a list of possible psychological and sociological benefits, but it comes down to the fact that this is what God does in Christ (4:32). As God's "beloved children" (5:1), we do not just love God, praise God, worship God, thank God. We also aim to imitate God (5:1), minding and then closing the gap between God's behavior and our own. To imitate God, only one thing is needful: kenotic love (5:2), love that sacrifices for the good of others. If we get that, we get it all.   JAIME CLARK-SOLES

John 6:35, 41–51

REFLECTION

Whatever we need to comprehend Jesus, to come to Jesus, to see who he is and what he means, must come to us as a divine gift, through revelation, not through our earnest effort. . . . As Jesus says elsewhere in the Fourth Gospel, "The Spirit blows where it chooses" (John 3:8). Revelation is not containable, controllable by us, not programmed or predicted by us.

WILLIAM H. WILLIMON

RESPONSE

What contemporary forms has God's ministry of angels taken in your life?

PRAYER

Your Spirit does blow where it chooses. Sustain my breath so that I may live in response to your presence. Amen.

❧ *Proper 15* ❦

Proverbs 9:1–6

Wisdom has built her house.
. . . .
   she calls from the highest places in the town,
"You that are simple, turn in here!"
   To those without sense she says,
"Come, eat of my bread
   and drink of the wine I have mixed.
Lay aside immaturity, and live,
   and walk in the way of insight." (vv. 1, 3–6)

Psalm 34:9–14

Depart from evil, and do good;
   seek peace, and pursue it. (v. 14)

Ephesians 5:15–20

Be careful then how you live, not as unwise people
but as wise, making the most of the time, because the
days are evil. So do not be foolish, but understand
what the will of the Lord is. (vv. 15–17)

John 6:51–58

"I am the living bread that came down from heaven.
Whoever eats of this bread will live forever; and the bread that
I will give for the life of the world is my flesh." (v. 51)

✤ MONDAY ✦

Proverbs 9:1–6

REFLECTION

The wise woman has a well-kept house, built with a divine support structure. Her servants work faithfully to do her bidding. She is known in the city and prepares a great feast for all who come to her home. The personification of wisdom in Proverbs is not unlike a grandmother who keeps her house in order and offers a sumptuous feast that is familiar and welcoming to her young ones. She knows well the individual likes and dislikes of her grandchildren and can direct the attention of the youth to that which is most suitable for the building of faith and character. Ultimately, she offers the unconditional love of God. A grandmother's love and wise guidance have a firm grasp on the mind of the young. As children grow up to face various trials, hers is the voice of wisdom that surfaces from deep within. Focusing on the power and importance of God's way of love, rather than lifting up the negative choices that need to be avoided, is the work of the one who preaches on this passage. SUSAN E. VANDE KAPPELLE

RESPONSE

Where have you seen this kind of wisdom exemplified most recently?

PRAYER

You surround me with wisdom, O God. It is visible in the hug of a child, a conversation with a teenager, a meal shared in a home. The voice of wisdom and the acts of the wise sustain me as I walk in the ways of insight. Amen.

✦ TUESDAY ✦

Proverbs 9:1–6

REFLECTION

What is most important is the acknowledgment that here with
Lady Wisdom, as with the host mentioned by Jesus, all of us can
choose whether or not we will respond to God's invitation for a
fulfilling, blessed life. This life is not one of faithful drudgery or
morbid asceticism, but one of great satisfaction and happiness.
God intends an abundant life for us. The wine at Wisdom's
party is for enjoying, just like the new, improved wine Jesus
provides when prompted by his mother Mary— another wise
woman—at the wedding at Cana. To some hearers, this will be
a surprise. Their assumption is that the Christian life is one of
somber responsibility, with no time for enjoyment. Preached
toward the end of summer, the preacher could encourage
workaholics to take time off before the fall start-up, or a visiting
preacher could bless the priest/pastor on her well-deserved
vacation. But at a deeper level, before the eve of Labor Day is a
good time for all to self-reflect, asking, "Am I pursuing the life
of wisdom, or am I squandering my life on that which does not
satisfy?" This fallow period near the end of summer can provide
the time for self-assessment and recommitment to wise living,
to choose to accept Wisdom's invitation into her wonderful
home to feast at her rich table.   DEAN MCDONALD

RESPONSE

Focus on the question raised in this reflection: "Am I pursuing
the life of wisdom, or am I squandering my life on that which
does not satisfy?"

PRAYER

Thank you for an abundant life. In times of relaxation and in
times of work, help me to live wisely in your world. Amen.

✣ WEDNESDAY ✣

Psalm 34:9–14

REFLECTION

A pastor in a Puerto Rican country barrio, or neighborhood, was called by her denomination to help out a church experiencing deep conflict, much of it over the nature of proper worship. A group of very spiritually oriented men invited her to climb a hill in back of the church with them to pray and to discern the will of God for their congregation. She recognized that these faithful men had a passion for worship and a desire to be in solitude in the beauty of nature, but she decided to invite them to have a different kind of experience.

"After we descend from the hill and before we share our experiences with the congregation, let's visit the capital's medical center so that we can serve those who are sick and suffering," she said. The men stared at her, puzzled. They ended up refusing her invitation, in fact not even ascending the hill to pray. They shied away from praise, thereby losing the opportunity to rediscover something of what it means to be human. Our humanity means that we must praise God, but this praise must heal, building a community that "has no want."

CARLOS F. CARDOZA-ORLANDI

RESPONSE

How is the balance of praising God by doing good evidenced in the life of your congregation?

PRAYER

Show me new ways that I can do good and work for peace. Show me the places where evil is at work, and the work of my hands and heart are needed. Amen.

✧ THURSDAY ✧

Ephesians 5:15–20

REFLECTION

Living Christianly does not come naturally. Its features
require discernment and wisdom, because Christians live in a
world ruled by Satan, powers, and principalities, all of which
constantly aim to trip us up if not fell us (2:2; 4:27; 6:10ff.).
Since the author commands the reader to understand God's
will, it follows that God's will is discernible. Traditionally, it is
the role of Lady Wisdom to reveal God's will to human beings.
Proverbs 8 lucidly exemplifies her destiny. She cocreates the
world with God; she offers human beings wisdom. Some
accept it and thrive; others refuse her offer with calamitous
effects. Christian wisdom is tricky business, however, because
it is counterintuitive. Paul already noted this eloquently in
1 Corinthians 1:18–25: God's wisdom appears foolish to human
beings, but it is the world's so-called wisdom that turns out
to be moronic. According to Ephesians, we are susceptible
to powers that cloud our vision and deceive us into thinking
wrongly. Life in a well-defined Christian community, regular
worship, training in the church's tradition, and the indwelling of
the Spirit bulwark the church against such forces and train her
up in the ways of Lady Wisdom.   JAIME CLARK-SOLES

RESPONSE

How have your experiences in a faith community contributed
to your formation as a Christian? What recent experience
stands out for you as an example of the foolishness of God's
wisdom?

PRAYER

I pray that the melody of my life offers praise and thanks to you.
Amen.

✣ FRIDAY ✣

John 6:51–58

REFLECTION

Here we are again, one more time with Jesus as the bread of life, the eternal bread come down from heaven (6:51). John's repetitiveness can best be seen as a sign that what is being said is important. It is also a sign of the difficulty of what is being communicated. It is as if, in this sixth chapter, Jesus knows that what he is talking about is against our natural inclinations, against our accustomed means of making sense, so much so that he must be redundant and repetitive, in order to keep hammering upon our cognitive defenses until we comprehend that when he says "bread," he is not talking about flour, water, and yeast; he is talking about something that has "come down from heaven" (v. 51). Jesus always has more to say in John's Gospel as he beckons us toward a thick, multilayered world where there is always more than meets the eye. As modern people, we are conditioned to live in a flattened, demystified world that is only what we can see or touch. The modern world loves "this is only . . ." statements: this is only bread, this is just another day at the office, this is only a Jew from Nazareth. The Fourth Gospel tries to train us limited, modern people in the expectation that now the Word has become flesh, we may expect more.   WILLIAM H. WILLIMON

RESPONSE

What new thing do you hear or experience as you read this text and reflection?

PRAYER

I do live in the middle of a "flattened, demystified world." Expand my awareness of that which is mystical and deep, that which calls forth rich metaphorical language that can connect me with the living bread. Amen.

✦ SATURDAY ✦

John 6:51–58

REFLECTION

Ah, wouldn't the Christian faith be easier if it were a matter of mere belief or intellectual assent! No, today's rather scandalously carnal, incarnational gospel reminds us that Jesus intends to have all of us, body and soul. His truth wants to burrow deep within us, to consume us as we consume him, to flow through our veins, to be digested, to nourish every nook and cranny of our being.

I have a friend who teaches theology at Oxford. He says that his toughest task is to ask and answer the question, "What is theology about?" His students tend to respond that theology is about spiritual matters, or about religion, or deeper meaning in life, et cetera. No, he instructs them, theology (at least Christian, incarnational theology, theology in the mode of the sixth chapter of the Fourth Gospel) is about everything. Jesus has come down from heaven with the intention of taking it all back. He wants all of us, and he wants us to have all of him. This God is so scandalously, intimately available to us. Whoever knows this, knows how to live forever.   WILLIAM H. WILLIMON

RESPONSE

Recall encounters and conversations you have had this week. How do you think the people you met would answer the question, "What is theology about?" How would you answer it?

PRAYER

All you want of me is everything that I am. And all you want is for your creation to have all of you. The intimacy of your availability sustains my life. Amen.

✢ SUNDAY ✢

Proverbs 9:1–6

REFLECTION

In Proverbs, as in the rest of Scripture, we understand that God is one, God alone. And yet Wisdom is portrayed in Proverbs as God's consort and companion. Wisdom is God's first creation (8:25), who stands with and beside God as the balance of the world is created. . . .

Wisdom is both grace and faith. She is the gift of God to God's children, inviting them to learn her ways of life and peace. Wisdom is God's "torah" for all people, but she is also the pattern of faithful response to God. Wisdom, therefore, has both objective and subjective aspects, eternal dimensions that are at the same time quite temporal. Wisdom is, in sum, relational. It is a call and a way of relating to the world.

THOMAS R. STEAGALD

Psalm 34:9–14

REFLECTION

Jews and Christians believe that to be human is to live a life engaged in the praise of God. The human condition is transformed when it focuses on praise to the one true God. We shift our priorities from selfish human acquisition to compassionate simple lifestyles that help us be faithful to God. All of our actions and all of our thoughts—that is, our whole beings—seek to praise God. This condition of praise makes the worshiping community one that "has no want."

CARLOS F. CARDOZA-ORLANDI

Ephesians 5:15–20

REFLECTION

"Formation" is a word enjoying currency in both the church and the seminary. It is usually paired with the word "spiritual" to describe a way to live, move, and have our being within a Christian identity. . . . Many fear that in all the push toward "formation," the church is "in retreat" all right, but in flight from its responsibilities to offer a prophetic word in the marketplace. But for others, spiritual formation describes an integrated religious life, with balance between contemplation and action, firmly rooted in God's vision for all humanity, and particularly for those who are "in Christ." RICHARD F. WARD

John 6:51–58

REFLECTION

Jesus' claim that he is the "bread that comes down from heaven" is provocative enough. Now he puts the claim even more outrageously: "The bread that I will give for the life of the world is my flesh" (v. 51). . . .

Of course Jesus is not speaking literally of eating his flesh and drinking his blood; he refers, first of all, to the bread and wine of the Eucharist. The Gospel of John is written for insiders, for the beleaguered little group of believers whose allegiance to Jesus has brought them to the crisis of separation from their neighbors and families, "the Jews" who now hate them. When these believers hear this Gospel read to them, they know the story well. They have heard the echoes of the liturgy of the Lord's Supper from the beginning of chapter 6, echoes that are found in all four Gospels' accounts of the miraculous feeding. WAYNE A. MEEKS

RESPONSE

What themes speak to your own spiritual formation?

PRAYER

As I examine my life this week, remind me of my patterns of faithful response to you, O God. Remind me also of the places where my lack of faithful response to others is evident. I offer both to you. Amen.

❧ *Proper 16* ❧

Joshua 24:1–2a, 14–18

Now if you are unwilling to serve the LORD, choose this day
whom you will serve, whether the gods your ancestors served
in the region beyond the River or the gods of the Amorites in
whose land you are living; but as for me and my household, we
will serve the LORD." (v. 15)

Psalm 34:15–22

The eyes of the LORD are on the righteous,
 and his ears are open to their cry.
The face of the LORD is against evildoers,
 to cut off the remembrance of them from the earth. (vv. 15–16)

Ephesians 6:10–20

Therefore take up the whole armor of God,
 so that you may be able to withstand on that evil day,
and having done everything, to stand firm. Stand therefore,
 and fasten the belt of truth around your waist, and put
 on the breastplate of righteousness. (vv. 13–14)

John 6:56–69

"Those who eat my flesh and drink my blood abide in me,
and I in them. Just as the living Father sent me, and I live
because of the Father, so whoever eats me will live because of
me. This is the bread that came down from heaven, not like that
which your ancestors ate, and they died. But the one who eats
this bread will live forever." (vv. 56–58)

✦ MONDAY ✦

Joshua 24:1–2a, 14–18

REFLECTION

The covenant with YHWH is different from the worship of the ancestral gods. This one God is not simply a god of the land, of place, of prosperity. This one God is a God who travels with God's people. YHWH is not tied to the land, to any place or sanctuary. This God makes a different kind of promise to the people. This God promises to accompany the covenant people no matter where they go. This God will be with them not only in their prosperity but also in their suffering and in their trials. This God does promise security and abundance. This God promises to be present through all that life brings.

For a battle-worn, world-weary, wandering community, this is a different kind of promise from a different kind of God. Through it, they glimpse the one God who is present with them in birth, in death, in humiliation, in joy, in wandering, and in arrival. This God delights in the people and desires more than safety and plenty for them. This God desires for them new life.

The invitation to this covenant requires that these people will be loyal and faithful to this God who is with them. This covenant requires loyal relationship through all the vicissitudes of life, instead of looking for the god who will deliver the best benefits.

SUSAN HENRY-CROWE

RESPONSE

Consider the lives of those in the congregation of which you are a part. How can you affirm God's presence with you—in birth, death, humiliation, joy, wandering, and arrival?

PRAYER

In all humbleness and strength, in all joy and sadness, in times of certainty and times of questions, your covenant of love is written on my heart and in my life. Amen.

⁑ TUESDAY ⁌

Psalm 34:15–22

REFLECTION

The terms we use to label the "good" and the "bad" in our world are quite different from the terms of righteousness and wickedness identified in Psalm 34. The righteous are those who seek the Lord and fear God, who do good, speak truthfully, and seek peace. The wicked are those who do evil, hate the righteous, and cut themselves off from God. It is not our selves, our merits, or the other's demerits that are central to our identity, but God—God's care, God's purposes, and God's presence. Furthermore, the presence of God outlined in the final third of Psalm 34 is far more tender than any human self-righteousness we might extend to one another.

Here, in the poetry of the Psalms, God takes on human form in its most nurturing capacities. God's eyes gaze upon the righteous; God's ears are open to their cry. The face of the Lord, God's presence, shuns evil and spares our memories its mark. Hearing the righteous cry, God delivers them from their troubles. Those whose spirits are crushed, and the brokenhearted—for these God cares and tends. God keeps every bone of our bodies safe and ransoms the life of each servant. God hears, rescues, saves, and delivers. God's nurture is tender, loving care of our bodies as much as of our minds and souls. God's presence uplifts our spirits.   ALLISON READ

RESPONSE

Sit with Psalm 34 and this reflection. What affirmation of God do you most need to hear this day?

PRAYER

Be especially near to those who this day are brokenhearted and crushed in spirit. Lead your faithful children to their side. Amen.

✦ WEDNESDAY ✦

Psalm 34:15–22

REFLECTION

Psalm 34 presents an intimate portrait of God's goodness, care, and justice experienced on a very personal level. This is a level at which God's people can extend care to one another, but it is not a level at which we may assume that everyone has experienced a relationship with God. On one hand, someone in recovery from addiction might identify so closely with this hymn of personal thanksgiving that its words and its spirit of grateful redemption might as well be their very own. On the other hand, a newcomer to the church who grapples with the evening news of genocide, civil wars, widespread disease, and political corruption might distrust the psalmist entirely, seeing no evidence that God keeps safe all our bones. As with any personal thanksgiving, Psalm 34 will neither articulate the experience of everyone nor satisfy the observations of all people who seek God. Some pastoral imagination, or even evangelical sensitivity, may open the pastor's heart and the people's ears to hear God's call, feel God's presence, and see God's purposes, just as we are seen and heard by God.   ALLISON READ

RESPONSE

Think about people you know who exemplify both relationships with God described in this reflection. What in you is God calling forth as you are with those persons who see no evidence that God is keeping all of their bones safe?

PRAYER

As I live and move in your world this day, open my eyes and ears to the presence of those around me—to both those who see evidence of you in their life and those who do not. Amen.

→ THURSDAY ←

Ephesians 6:10–20

REFLECTION

"I am too blessed to be stressed," are words that some of the faithful have used. Paul's words, "put on the whole armor," prepare us for struggle. Stress and anxiety come when one prepares to engage things that really matter. No one in his or her right mind prepares for struggle without forethought. We want to know what we are up against so that we can prepare appropriately and engage the struggle successfully. Standing firm gives the struggle purpose and us meaning. In the midst of controversy we may ask, "Is the price to be paid worth the struggle?" Sometimes, in the midst of struggle and fatigue, we may find our strength renewed. We may find ourselves assessing and reassessing our situations and coming to new resolve. Surely, during the twenty-seven years of his incarceration, Nelson Mandela became discouraged. But he found strength to hope. He stood firm in his convictions. Such spiritual struggle requires discipline. We must prepare ourselves inwardly and prayerfully for the outer struggle. The outer struggle, the struggle against the principalities and powers, will test again and again our inner resolve. God never ceases to offer fresh opportunities to assess our situation, to grow and deepen our sense of commitment in community. Struggle can be part of the process of faith development where spiritual growth, deepening into a mature faith, is valued.   ARCHIE SMITH JR.

RESPONSE

What struggles in faith have you experienced most recently? In what ways has your faith been a shield for you?

PRAYER

I know that your Spirit surrounds my being, praying with me, providing peace. Amen.

John 6:56–69

REFLECTION

What John wants us to consider are our misunderstood ways of consumption. We "eat up" the world without appreciating how God has infused creation with the Spirit; thus we use and discard it in crude and materialist ways. The ethical imperative at the heart of John's incarnational theology of the Eucharist is clear. Will we treat the world around us as incarnational or simply as material? To do the former requires faith. Keeping the flesh together with the spirit requires us to live deeply, appreciating our interdependence and interconnectedness with the Creator, the creation, and our fellow creatures. By inviting us to eat and drink of his whole person, Jesus challenges us to risk living incarnationally, becoming whole in both flesh and spirit, as the means of our salvation.   LOYE BRADLEY ASHTON

RESPONSE

Spend some time with this text from John and with this reflection. Consider both the literal and metaphorical meanings. How are you living faithfully in response to the ethical imperatives of John's incarnational theology?

PRAYER

This life of incarnational living that you call me to is risky, for sure. Becoming whole in both flesh and spirit is a lifelong process. I join the disciples in affirming that I have come to believe and know that you are the Holy One of God. Amen.

☀ SATURDAY ☀

John 6:56–69

REFLECTION

This text provides a means of seeing the faithful life as a spiritual practice of "incarnational abiding." John's eucharistic theology is offered as means of helping to draw the believer into deeper relationship with Jesus and thus also with God the Creator through a spirituality of abiding, or being with/in. This then raises even more difficult practical questions for the believer: what does it actually look like to abide? John suggests that we abide with God by abiding with Christ, and we abide with Christ by truly abiding with ourselves, in other words, by not separating our flesh and spirit from each other. . . .

Just as Jesus is the incarnation of God, so we as believers are invited to be part of that divine body, to be the incarnation of Christ in and to the world. Perhaps then there is a vocational reading of Jesus' language regarding "abiding": to choose, by the gift of faith given by God, to accept God's call to become part of the divine life as it is in its eternal fullness, both body and Spirit.

LOYE BRADLEY ASHTON

RESPONSE

How are you and the congregation of which you are a part incarnating Christ in the world?

PRAYER

I accept your call to my life. I accept the gift of faith you give me. Renew me this day for the ministry to which you are calling me. Amen.

✦ SUNDAY ✦

Joshua 24:1–2a, 14–18

REFLECTION

We all need to rediscover Joshua's way of single-minded loyalty to the Lord, the obedient refusal to give ourselves over to the temptations of compromise with the great wealth, powers, and fears that enthrall most people and all nations today.

CHARLES E. RAYNAL

Psalm 34:15–22

REFLECTION

In the language of the psalmist, we are asked about our place of refuge. We are asked about our place of safety, of hiding, of restoration. We are asked to identify where we go when all of life is against us. In the language of the psalmist, we are told that God rescues us and keeps our very bones. The part of us that is our physical foundation—needed twenty-four hours each day of our lives—is undergirded by God's continuous holding.

The psalm at first glance could seem like an incendiary for name-calling and pointing fingers. Instead it brings grace and a question: . . . whom will we serve this day? JENNIFER L. LORD

Ephesians 6:10–20

REFLECTION

There is a difference between being stubborn and standing firm. Paul is not asking us to be stubborn, wedded to an opinion, rooted in prejudice, or closed-minded. But he is asking us to stand in something that is not transient, something that is transcendent and renewing. . . .

Standing firm means that one is willing to debate, listen, and consider alternatives in order to reach a beneficial goal, while at the same time not sacrificing basic principles. Martin Luther King Jr. stood firm on nonviolence. Margaret Sanger, the twentieth-century suffragette, stood firm on women's rights. Nelson Mandela stood firm and resolute against apartheid. . . . All stood firm against injustice. The lesson we draw from them is that to have a strong ego, a concern for justice and compassion, is to be grounded in the convictions of the community and open to critical evaluation. This is how we stand firm, as Paul counsels.   ARCHIE SMITH JR.

John 6:56–69

REFLECTION

In the moment that we choose to eat Jesus' flesh and drink Jesus' blood—and we truly abide in him and he in us—we choose life. We give up the notion that we are in control. Fear truly no longer has the upper hand. We understand that we are no better than any other child of God because of our denomination, our skin color, our gender, our job. We turn over to God that which we fear most, trusting that we are loved. When we can accept the love of God that is pure grace, love flows from us and we love others. We do forgive our pew mate for his addiction. We stop in real conversation with the homeless woman on the street corner. We value the baby fussing during worship. We suddenly prefer God to religion.

                    AMY C. HOWE

RESPONSE

What questions are raised in these texts and these reflections? What grace is being offered?

PRAYER

When the world offers no safety or hope, I turn to you. Your continuous holding of my life restores my hope and returns me to the world where you call me to be a witness. Amen.

Song of Solomon 2:8–13

My beloved speaks and says to me:
  "Arise, my love, my fair one,
    and come away;
  for now the winter is past,
    the rain is over and gone.
  The flowers appear on the earth;
    the time of singing has come,
  and the voice of the turtledove
    is heard in our land." (vv. 10–12)

Psalm 45:1–2, 6–9

My heart overflows with a goodly theme;
  I address my verses to the king;
    my tongue is like the pen of a ready scribe. (v. 1)

James 1:17–27

But be doers of the word, and not merely
hearers who deceive themselves. (v. 22)

Mark 7:1–8, 14–15, 21–23

Then he called the crowd again and said to them, "Listen to me,
all of you, and understand: there is nothing outside a person
that by going in can defile, but the things that come out are
what defile. . . . For it is from within, from the human heart,
that evil intentions come: fornication, theft, murder, adultery,
avarice, wickedness, deceit, licentiousness, envy, slander, pride,
folly. All these evil things come from within, and they defile a
person." (vv. 14–15, 21–23)

✣ MONDAY ✣

Song of Solomon 2:8–13

REFLECTION

Whether it is a love story about two human beings or an allegory about God's love for God's people, the sense of delight in today's text is striking. The author of the Song of Solomon poetically alludes to the transformative power of love. The lovers are each (and all) transformed by love.

SUSAN T. HENRY-CROWE

While we have human sexuality freely accessible, our free access does not automatically include our responsible, much less joyful, honoring of the goodness of God's intention. Sexual practice is often exploitive, especially of women and children. The accessibility of human sexuality becomes yet another means of objectifying and manipulating human beings, created in God's image for the Lord's own purposes. Moreover, global markets make human sexuality into a commodity for the promotion and sale of goods and services. Treating human sexuality as a commodity is parasitic on the goodness of God's intended mutuality. Commercialization devalues and subordinates human sexuality for the sake of economic gain, instead of honoring and respecting God's intended gift and joy.

CHARLES E. RAYNAL

RESPONSE

If love is transforming, why do you think that so many relationships are problematic and dysfunctional?

PRAYER

Transform me by the power of your love in Christ. Amen.

✣ TUESDAY ✣

Psalm 45:1–2, 6–9

REFLECTION

The exercise of power in any realm—politics, a household, the workplace, or society—produces evidence of tyranny as well as benevolence and can be considered for its semblance to the power of the kingdom of God.   ALLISON READ

The images in the psalm are alien at a certain level. Yet the recognition of beauty, the use of the senses, and the value of the body are familiar to us. But familiarity with images and methods of description does not mean comfort with them. Because of our consumer-driven ethos we can celebrate and enjoy the human body well past the point of faithful stewardship, to reclusive and demeaning addictions instead. Or, despite the witness of Scripture, we can continue to cling to our discomfort with valuing the body. A gnostic distaste for the body permeates attitudes in the church. We are content to hear about the dangers of celebrating or enjoying the body. We are happy to define death as a time to escape the trapping of the earthly body. At the point of death, we think, the true self will live on.   JENNIFER L. LORD

RESPONSE

When can you trust the rhetoric of public speech?

PRAYER

My heart overflows with a goodly theme; my tongue is like the pen of a ready scribe (Ps. 45:1). Amen.

→ WEDNESDAY ←

James 1:17–27

REFLECTION

In the Christian universe, every Christian receives this gift equally and not according to his or her rank in the hierarchy. The supreme gift that Christians receive is "birth by the word of truth" (v. 18).   HARUKO NAWATA WARD

Throughout history, in all Christian traditions and world religions, women have proven to be doers of the word, daily serving the poor. The majority of the poor also continue to be women and children. How can the church be better doers, not merely hearers, of the word in today's world?

HARUKO NAWATA WARD

Destructive anger can poison our own lives and that of the community as well. It cannot give new meaning to life or inspire creativity. Words that serve such anger are worthless. Destructive acts can never be the means for illuminating God's presence or making room for divine goodness in our lives. They cannot produce God's righteousness.   ARCHIE SMITH JR.

RESPONSE

"Sticks and stones may break my bones, but words will never hurt me." In what ways is that statement true? In what ways is it false?

PRAYER

May my words and my actions be acceptable in your sight, God our Redeemer. Amen.

✦ THURSDAY ✦

James 1:17–27

REFLECTION

James was a keen observer of human nature, and he paid close attention to the details of everyday living. He noticed the generous acts, the small gifts, the gestures and the words we use. He knew that such small acts are the nuts and bolts of everyday life, holding together the scaffold on which we build community and the social order. Why was he especially concerned with the way we use words? Because they can make a big difference in the way we relate to one another. He knew that our words reveal something about our motivation, intention, belief, and emotional life. Our emotional life grows from our earliest relationships with others and with the God who is Other. It also emerges from our relationship with our selves. Anger, for example, is an emotion that can be destructive. It can also be an emotion that alerts us to wrongdoing. Thus anger can be channeled in ways that lead to protest and improvement, so that we must make a decision about its meaning in our lives. James knows this and shows us his concern.

ARCHIE SMITH JR.

RESPONSE

Do all actions speak louder than words?

PRAYER

Before I speak or act in haste, give me pause to consider the effect of my words and deeds. Amen.

✧ FRIDAY ✦

Mark 7:1–8, 14–15, 21–23

REFLECTION

Hypocrisy is a negation of authentic life: it is life acted out to
fool others, a role that we take on and pretend to be, that is
not really us. It is a denial of our authentic self in favor of the
fabricated persona that we wish to be. Religious hypocrisy,
in particular, is a most destructive kind in that it uses sacred
teachings about Truth itself to elevate self-deception. It makes
our pretending both a distortion of Truth and a substitute for it.

LOYE BRADLEY ASHTON

Welcoming all into God's kingdom is important. We want to
focus on the mundane because facing the sins that stain our
own hands is so painful. However, when we face those sins,
letting go of that which is unimportant, and turn to God, we are
welcome in the sanctuary and at the table.   AMY C. HOWE

RESPONSE

When has an act of hypocrisy damaged your trust, and when
have you yourself promoted hypocrisy?

PRAYER

I face my sins, and release them into your forgiving hands.
Amen.

✦ SATURDAY ✦

Mark 7:1–8, 14–15, 21–23

REFLECTION

What makes Israel acceptable to God is not correct
performance of ritual acts but ethical behavior. Similarly, Jesus
declares that it is not scrupulous observance of the food laws
that makes Israel holy, but morality.   DOUGLAS R. A. HARE

Jesus' main point is perfectly clear: what really renders a person
"unclean" in God's sight is what comes out of him or her. It is
not what we eat but what we do that really counts with God.
                                               DOUGLAS R. A. HARE

The contrast between what goes into the mouth and what
comes out leads the reader to expect that Jesus will emphasize
sins of the mouth, such as lying, foul language, slander, and
false promises. In the list of immoral acts in verses 21–22, only
deceit and slander are sins of the mouth. Instead, attention
shifts from the mouth to the heart, from which "evil intentions"
(NRSV) or "evil thoughts" (NIV, REB, CEV) come. Jesus here
stresses that the thought is father to the deed. We think a sin
before we do it.   DOUGLAS R. A. HARE

RESPONSE

What is the true "moral of the story"?

PRAYER

Cleanse my words and my actions, so that I can praise you with
a clean heart. Amen.

✢ SUNDAY ✢

Song of Solomon 2:8–13

REFLECTION

The erotic love that opens the hearts and minds of the man and the woman in today's passage from the Song of Solomon does not stop with their openness to one another. It also opens them to the hearts and minds of other people. Discovering their solidarity with one another, they discover their solidarity with all other human beings as well. Whether the Song is read as a love story between two people or as an allegory about God's love for all creation, its beauty is that it invites all humankind to play as if life and love depended upon it (as they do).

SUSAN T. HENRY-CROWE

Psalm 45:1–2, 6–9

REFLECTION

Individuals, local congregations, and the wider Christian community exercise citizenship in multiple realms at once. The fact that it is God's throne that endures for ever and ever (v. 6) may be both a source of fear and disappointment for those enjoying power and a source of hope and gratification for those enduring powerlessness.

ALLISON READ

Christ occupies the eternal throne of God, toppling the powers of sin and death, securing justice, bringing down the rulers of this world and raising up the righteous. To be wedded to Christ is to be wedded to freedom from iniquity, to receive and share God's blessing of righteousness, and to extend his reign in this world. Where leadership serves God and God's purposes, we bless and are blessed; where it confuses divinity with its representatives, we serve kings other than the one whom God blessed for ever.

ALLISON READ

James 1:17–27

REFLECTION

One not doing the Word is deceiving him/herself. This is like a person who looks into a mirror and then goes away unmindful of his or her faith. What is this deception about? On a practical level, someone might say, "I really believe in Jesus; I really believe in the resurrection," but then give no evidence of such faith in dealing with his or her neighbor (2:18–19).

AARON L. UITTI

Mark 7:1–8, 14–15, 21–23

REFLECTION

What is at the heart of our own religious faith and traditions? Jesus uses the word "heart" three times in 7:1–23, and with each reference we sense the importance of the human heart for religious faith and practice. Since the heart was thought to be the center of one's will and decision-making abilities, to turn one's heart away from God (7:6b) or to have it filled with evil intentions (7:21) was a grievous sin. Passages such as 3:5; 6:52; and 8:17 also remind us that hardness of heart is among the most damning of spiritual conditions, revealing a lack of compassion toward others. In these and other verses, Christ urges us to examine our own defiled hearts rather than our neighbors' dirty hands.

DAWN OTTONI WILHELM

RESPONSE

How have acts of true compassion changed your heart?

PRAYER

Thank you for those who show compassion for others, for those whose kindnesses have changed my life for the better. Amen.

Proper 18

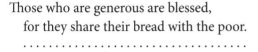

Proverbs 22:1–2, 8–9, 22–23

Those who are generous are blessed,
  for they share their bread with the poor.
. . . .
Do not rob the poor because they are poor,
  or crush the afflicted at the gate;
for the LORD pleads their cause
  and despoils of life those who despoil them. (vv. 9, 22–23)

Psalm 125

Do good, O LORD, to those who are good,
  and to those who are upright in their hearts. (v. 4)

James 2:1–10 (11–13), 14–17

What good is it, my brothers and sisters, if you say you have faith
  but do not have works? Can faith save you? If a brother or sister
is naked and lacks daily food, and one of you says to them, "Go in
peace; keep warm and eat your fill," and yet you do not supply their
  bodily needs, what is the good of that? So faith by itself,
    if it has no works, is dead. (vv. 14–17)

Mark 7:24–37

Now the woman was a Gentile, of Syrophoenician origin. She
  begged [Jesus] to cast the demon out of her daughter. He said
to her, "Let the children be fed first, for it is not fair to take the
children's food and throw it to the dogs." But she answered him,
"Sir, even the dogs under the table eat the children's crumbs." Then
he said to her, "For saying that, you may go—the demon has left
  your daughter." So she went home, found the child lying on the
    bed, and the demon gone. (vv. 26–30)

✢ MONDAY ✢

Proverbs 22:1–2, 8–9, 22–23

REFLECTION

We are fools if we do not address the widening gap between
rich and poor. Terrorism will continue to exploit it, and military
power alone will not quell it. The rich nations, as matters of
wise policy, will come to address the injustice of the punishing
gap between rich and poor. CHARLES E. RAYNAL

Today's appointed proverbs offer wisdom on matters of
relationships, generosity, and justice. They remind the gathered
community of the significance of seeing, understanding, and
relating to the poor. The weight of theological grounding for
this section is found in verse 2. "The rich and the poor have this
in common: the LORD is the maker of them all." In God there
are no distinctions. SUSAN T. HENRY-CROWE

RESPONSE

How is your congregation responsive to the unjust gaps
between the rich and the poor?

PRAYER

You are the maker of all; and we are equal in your sight. Amen.

✦ TUESDAY ✦

Psalm 125

REFLECTION

The Psalter is not only the "prayer book" of the Bible; it is also a deep and rich "theology text." The magnitude of God and the constancy of God's faithfulness to God's people is affirmed in confident terms. God's protective care is as obvious and as solid as the ring of mountains that surround Jerusalem.

LEANNE VAN DYK

The righteous long for God's goodness as surely as the hungry long for nourishment. God's goodness is the sustaining grace of all those who are "upright in their hearts" (v. 4).

LEANNE VAN DYK

RESPONSE

How do you reconcile the image of a God of protection with the disasters that happen in the world?

PRAYER

Even though the wicked often prosper, that is not your will, nor should it be ours. Amen.

→ WEDNESDAY ←

Psalm 125

REFLECTION

Patterns of oppression and injustice are not permanent. In its firm voice that evil rulers will not reign indefinitely, the psalm fully acknowledges the depth and variety of evil and shows an awareness that evil inevitably corrupts. The voice of the psalm in general makes clear that God opposes evil. Brokenness, sin, and evil are real in this world, in both individuals and institutions, but this is not the last word. God's relationship to evil is one of resistance, judgment, and, ultimately, victory.

LEANNE VAN DYK

The relationship of solidarity between people and God is based on God's goodness, God's immovability, God's righteousness, and God's reign. It is our relationship with God that bears safety and security in the promise and power of God to do good and bring forth righteousness. ALLISON READ

RESPONSE

Rather than being overwhelmed by the injustice in the world, in what small ways can you make a difference?

PRAYER

Every one of us can make a difference in bringing your kingdom into the world. Do not let us forget this! Amen.

✧ THURSDAY ✦

James 2:1–10 (11–13), 14–17

REFLECTION

James's challenge is radical in that he calls all Christians,
rich and poor, to show no partiality. He calls us to merge our
differing self-understandings into a new, enlarged, and richer
unity of identity as faithful followers of "our Lord Jesus Christ,
the Lord of glory."   ARCHIE SMITH JR.

The text speaks not only to the profound issue of acceptance but
potentially to the inclusion of the uncool. New people, whatever
their social rank, need to be stitched into the social fabric of the
church, not merely formally received as new members.

PETER RHEA JONES

RESPONSE

Is it possible to be impartial when it comes to the people you
love most?

PRAYER

Let me not show favoritism, but strive to love even the
unlovable, as you would do. Amen.

Mark 7:24–37

REFLECTION

Is it possible to be "fully human" and without sin? In connecting this passage with the admonition about hypocrisy that precedes it, perhaps Jesus here faces his own hypocrisy and struggles to find his own center in God, moving through his own pain of self-integration. In other words, Mark is showing us that the incarnation is not a cakewalk.

LOYE BRADLEY ASHTON

We do not sense the diminishment of Jesus' power through this exchange but the expansion of it, as he blesses her heart's desire and heals her daughter. However unsettling this exchange may be, its resolution reveals that God is not unchanging or unresponsive but compassionate and merciful.

DAWN OTTONI WILHELM

RESPONSE

The story from this week's Gospel is troubling in many ways. How do we reconcile Jesus' response to the woman with our belief in a God who loves all equally?

PRAYER

Your mercy and love never run out. Your blessings are more than enough. Amen.

⤳ SATURDAY ⤷

Mark 7:24–37

REFLECTION

When Jesus healed people, he not only corrected their physical problems. He also restored them to community. Jesus sees beyond this man's infirmity. He sees his value as a child of God.

AMY C. HOWE

Human beings suffer from a deep insecurity that pushes us to create rules that give status and value to some while denigrating others.

AMY C. HOWE

Most of us are reluctant to share our faith with others and we find very good reasons to keep quiet: we may believe that our actions speak more loudly than our words, we may be afraid of the inadequacy of our speech, or we may fear that we will make a mistake and alienate those to whom we are speaking.

DAWN OTTONI WILHELM

RESPONSE

Does the woman's response to Jesus raise feelings of admiration or indignation?

PRAYER

Give us boldness in the face of loss to claim the promises you offer. Amen.

⤞ SUNDAY ⤝

Proverbs 22:1–2, 8–9, 22–23

REFLECTION

As a unit, these passages challenge the common wisdom that wealth is of ultimate value, but they do not suggest that poverty can or should be eliminated. Perhaps in keeping with the privileged circles in which the book likely was written, they suggest an attitude of charity, rather than one of challenge, to the disparities between poor and rich. Some contemporary readers may conclude that these proverbs do not go far enough in acknowledging the structural dimensions of poverty and that additional discussion of poverty and its causes is needed.

JULIA M. O'BRIEN

Psalm 125

REFLECTION

This psalm is for the purpose of instilling trust in the pilgrims who make their way to the holy city Jerusalem. It is for the purpose of shaping them to trust, not only during that journey, but to trust God at all times, even in the face of foreign threats to nation and community. It is a call to trust God and not be persuaded by those who follow their own "crooked ways" (v. 5). Perhaps our act of trust as pilgrims on the journey of faith is to take account of how we have turned to our own crooked ways. This would be an act of trust—calling on God to set us right again as we honestly confess the ways that we are the foreign domination and the ways that we ignore the hurtful divisions in our own land.

JENNIFER L. LORD

James 2:1–10 (11–13), 14–17

REFLECTION

God, who gives to all generously (1:5), raises the lowly (1:9). If the poor are rich in faith and love God, God promises them the kingdom (2:5). Christians live out their faith in this God through works of mercy for the poor. Christian faith and good works are integrated and not separate (2:14). If faith is to produce fruit, it cannot remain dead in empty words. Faithful Christians supply "bodily needs" of the poor (2:15–17).

HARUKO NAWATA WARD

As we strive to follow the royal law, we must ask how the churches in wealthier places might act justly and mercifully toward the churches in economically disadvantaged places today.

HARUKO NAWATA WARD

Mark 7:24–37

REFLECTION

Jesus' ministry affirms and anticipates the church's need to share God's gifts of grace, peace, and healing with all people. The persons who are healed do not approach Jesus alone but are aided by others. The young girl is freed of demon possession because her mother pleads on her behalf. The deaf man is brought to Jesus by friends who beg for his healing. In these stories it is not the faith of the disabled persons that brings about their healing but the active faith of their companions. Their stories remind us to approach Christ on behalf of others and actively seek the well-being of those who need help and care.

DAWN OTTONI WILHELM

RESPONSE

What gives you the boldness to bring your petitions before the Lord?

PRAYER

Your mercy is from everlasting to everlasting. Praise the name of the Lord! Amen.

❧ *Proper 19* ☙

Proverbs 1:20–33

Wisdom cries out in the street;
    in the squares she raises her voice.
At the busiest corner she cries out;
    at the entrance of the city gates she speaks:
"How long, O simple ones, will you love being simple?
How long will scoffers delight in their scoffing
    and fools hate knowledge?
Give heed to my reproof;
I will pour out my thoughts to you;
    I will make my words known to you." (vv. 20–23)

Psalm 19

The heavens are telling the glory of God;
    and the firmament proclaims his handiwork.
Day to day pours forth speech,
    and night to night declares knowledge. (vv. 1–2)

James 3:1–12

Not many of you should become teachers, my brothers and sisters,
for you know that we who teach will be judged with greater
strictness. For all of us make many mistakes. (v. 2)

Mark 8:27–38

He called the crowd with his disciples, and said to them, "If any
want to become my followers, let them deny themselves and take
up their cross and follow me. For those who want to save their life
will lose it, and those who lose their life for my sake, and for the
sake of the gospel, will save it." (vv. 34–35)

✦ MONDAY ✦

Proverbs 1:20–33

REFLECTION

Fools do not become wise through persuasion, let alone
sympathy, but through the gift of a new mind. Only through
conversion and new creation will our words and thoughts
become acceptable to our rock and redeemer (Ps. 19:14).

TELFORD WORK

[Wisdom] demands attention in the streets, in the squares, at
the busiest corner, at the entrance of the city gate. These are the
sites of communal life, of the bustling relationships of daily life.
This is where Wisdom demands to be heard, not in the privacy
of homes, the sacredness of the temple, or even the quiet
recesses of souls. She calls for allegiance smack in the thick of
work and play, at busy intersections where people gather, and
at the city gates, where legal and commercial deals take place.
Ordinary life with its drama and busy social exchanges, with its
joys and disappointments, is Wisdom's domain. In this passage
and in the Wisdom literature in general, mundane human
life is the hallowed place, the sacred ground where one may
encounter Wisdom herself, if one is attentive.

KATHLEEN M. O'CONNOR

RESPONSE

Think of a time when insensitivity has jarred you into an
appropriate action.

PRAYER

Let the words of my mouth and the meditation of my heart be
acceptable in thy sight, O Lord, my rock and my redeemer (Ps.
19:14 RSV). Amen.

⤖ TUESDAY ⤛

Proverbs 1:20–33

REFLECTION

"Fear of the LORD" does not mean sniveling terror before God. The phrase is an ancient code for the proper behavior of the religious person in relation to God and creation. It involves awe, respect, and obedience; it summarizes righteous living. People who fear the Lord have their feet planted on the ground, see around them truthfully, and live in harmony with God and world.
                                                KATHLEEN M. O'CONNOR

Whether or not Wisdom is God in this text, she reveals herself like God, makes demands like God, and promises freedom and life to her followers like God. Whoever she is, her appearance destabilizes complacency, closed-heartedness, and death-dealing behavior that comes from ignorance, hatred of knowledge, and refusal to commit to the way of Wisdom. Wisdom invites everyone to a life of harmonious balance in the midst of daily life.
                                                KATHLEEN M. O'CONNOR

RESPONSE

Do you consider yourself to be a person of wisdom? What does it mean to be wise?

PRAYER

When I forget your ways, jog my memory, and rally me to attention. Amen.

✦ WEDNESDAY ✦

Psalm 19

REFLECTION

Silently the whole world testifies aloud, and the observer must give his or her attention to the natural world. Then even what is inanimate testifies.   SUSAN B. W. JOHNSON

The glory of God is not always comprehended, but to miss it is not to be missed by it. Like the sun's illumination and its inexorable heat, nothing is exempt, nothing can hide, nothing can escape.   SUSAN B. W. JOHNSON

If the whole realm of nature constantly proclaims God's glory in a continuous, ecstatic pouring forth of spiritual knowledge (v. 1), then what might be the spiritual ramifications of living sequestered from nature in office cubicles, in shopping malls, or in front of our home entertainment centers?   RUTH L. BOLING

RESPONSE

Recall a time and place where the distance between God and earth felt very small.

PRAYER

The world is full of thin places, where heaven and earth meet. Thank you for being no farther than a breath away. Amen.

✢ THURSDAY ✢

James 3:1–12

REFLECTION

What makes language so powerful? Or, to use James's phraseology, what makes it possible for a member of the body as small as the tongue to boast of such great exploits? James lays out two reasons for its power. First, language acts as a kind of representational catalyst: it is a small and even ephemeral thing that makes big things possible. Second, language can be a wild thing (wilder, even, than any animal species): it does great good and great harm and therein reveals how much it is caught up in the evil of human sinfulness.   MARK DOUGLAS

Perhaps becoming wise means, at least in part, learning how to use language in ways that are both increasingly playful and increasingly pure, both admitting our many mistakes and resisting the many temptations to make them.   MARK DOUGLAS

RESPONSE

Read a favorite poem, and enjoy language used well.

PRAYER

Creation came into being through your Word and your words. That alone is enough reason to cherish words as a means of bringing life into the world. Amen.

✣ FRIDAY ✣

James 3:1–12

REFLECTION

The most frequent reason given by those who steer clear of churches is the duplicity of Christians. Many of these people can tell you the exact details of how many times they have showed up at springs marked "Fresh Water" with cups in hand, only to end up with mouths full of salt water. You can remind them that no one is perfect. You can tell them that churches are made up of human beings, after all, and that there is always room for one more hypocrite. They still have a point. James knows they have a point. If God's word does not show up in the flesh of a congregation—if those who hear the word do not also incarnate the word—then the tongue has worked a wicked spell on them. "Why do you call me 'Lord, Lord,' and do not do what I tell you?" (Luke 6:46). In this same vein, tongue toxin is at work when people of faith indulge in glib speech, making what is difficult sound easy, or what is mysterious sound plain. Churches worried sick about waning membership can sometimes make the gospel sound like the South Beach diet: try it and see how good it makes you feel. This is the language of the world, not the church.   BARBARA BROWN TAYLOR

RESPONSE

Think about a person who has made a difference in your life for the better. What made this teacher so effective?

PRAYER

Teach me your ways, O Lord, that I may be always faithful to you. Amen.

✦ SATURDAY ✦

Mark 8:27–38

REFLECTION

An alternate way of interpreting Jesus' insistence that the Son of Man "must undergo great suffering" is that he needs to endure the depth of human pain in order to reconcile humanity with God. For Jesus Christ to bring full humanity into communion with God, he must bear the fullness of human experience, including suffering and death.   MARTHA L. MOORE-KEISH

There are limits to how much we can know about another person. In everyone there are secrets of the heart that will not be revealed or that cannot be discerned. Even two people who have lived together in a wonderfully shared marriage for half a century and more will find there are surprises in the other, and ever new insights to be gained. It is the wonder of life in human community that people are endlessly fascinating as they express in attitude and word and deed who they are.   HARRY B. ADAMS

On the basis of our relationship with Jesus, on the basis of what we have come to know of him in the biblical witness and in the life of the Christian community, we make our own assessment and judgment about who he is. There are many titles or descriptions that we can use. We too can call him Christ or Messiah. We can call him Lord, Savior, Master, Friend, Teacher, Prophet, Son of God, Redeemer, Exemplar.   HARRY B. ADAMS

RESPONSE

Make it your quest to be positively curious about the people closest to you.

PRAYER

Give me a healthy curiosity about the people who mean the most to me. Amen.

⟶ SUNDAY ⟵

Proverbs 1:20–33

REFLECTION

We are overwhelmed with options, choices, and advice. At the same time, we often sense that guidance is offered to those who have little interest in amendment of life, not unlike an all-you-can-eat buffet prepared for those who have already eaten. In discouragement the church has often abandoned the tradition of practical wisdom, and into the vacuum have come the therapist and the manager, each of whom speaks clearly and confidently, often with the use of spiritual language and even religious authorization.   KENNETH H. CARTER JR.

Psalm 19

REFLECTION

Sabbath keeping . . . is not primarily about the list of things we are prohibited from doing one day a week but about the discipline of making time in our busy lives to be still and know that God is God, a time for loving both God and neighbor.

RICHARD M. SIMPSON

It is not enough to talk about God and leave it at that. We do not praise God as unbiased observers but as creatures who, in pondering the magnificence of our Creator, come to terms with who we are in the cosmos.   RUTH L. BOLING

James 3:1–12

REFLECTION

Whether we mean to or not, we construct worlds with speech. Describing the world we see, we mistake it for the whole world. Making meaning of what we see, we conflate this with

God's meaning. Then we behave according to the world we have constructed with our speech, even when that causes us to dismiss or harm those who construe the world differently.

BARBARA BROWN TAYLOR

We praise God when we remember each other in prayer, when we lift our voices in song, when we affirm those who are learning. We bless God when we read the words of Scripture. Calling our children by name, welcoming a stranger, and speaking the truth in love are other ways that our tongues bless God. KATHY L. DAWSON

Mark 8:27–38

REFLECTION

"Picking up one's cross" is not accepting just any burden, but rather being prepared to put one's life on the line for the sake of Jesus and the gospel. The disciples are indeed called to be prepared to share in the fate of the one they follow, and to recognize that it is there that true life is found.

SHARON H. RINGE

Although we should be, no one is really shocked by Peter's confession or Jesus' description of the true meaning of being the Messiah. The domestication of Jesus as the Christ makes it hard to renew the shock of Peter's declaration and Jesus' teaching about the nature of the Messiah and the meaning of discipleship. NATHAN G. JENNINGS

RESPONSE

What values are of most importance to you?

PRAYER

The heavens are telling the glory of God; and the firmament proclaims God's handiwork. Day to day pours forth speech, and night to night declares knowledge (Ps. 19:1–2). Amen.

✢ *Proper 20* ✣

Proverbs 31:10–31

Strength and dignity are her clothing,
   and she laughs at the time to come.
She opens her mouth with wisdom,
   and the teaching of kindness is on her tongue. (vv. 25–26)

Psalm 1

Happy are those
   who do not follow the advice of the wicked,
or take the path that sinners tread,
   or sit in the seat of scoffers;
but their delight is in the law of the LORD,
   and on his law they meditate day and night. (vv. 1–2)

James 3:13–4:3, 7–8a

But the wisdom from above is first pure, then peaceable, gentle,
willing to yield, full of mercy and good fruits, without a trace of
partiality or hypocrisy. And a harvest of righteousness is sown in
peace for those who make peace. (3:17–18)

Mark 9:30–37

[Jesus] sat down, called the twelve, and said to them,
"Whoever wants to be first must be last of all and servant of all."
Then he took a little child and put it among them; and taking it
in his arms, he said to them, "Whoever welcomes one such
child in my name welcomes me, and whoever welcomes me
welcomes not me but the one who sent me." (vv. 35–37)

Proverbs 31:10–31

REFLECTION

This passage portrays a marriage that is neither egalitarian nor inegalitarian. This is because it is not interested in comparing husband and wife to one another. Comparison, whether of equals or of unequals, implies a kind of opposition; but what characterizes the relationship here is mutual support. Generous and empowering, it flows from each to the other and overflows into blessings on the family, the marketplace, and the whole city.

TELFORD WORK

Yet there is also good news here. How a story (or a biblical book) concludes is never accidental, and it is significant that the Proverbs find their consummation in these words about wisdom. Further, it is not accidental that wisdom is portrayed as a woman. Embedded in these words are the values that sustain our lives, our minds, our bodies, our souls: trust and integrity in personal relationships, sacrifice, going the extra mile, providing for our children, opening our hands to the poor, doing whatever needs to be done—and yet doing it with a sense of humor, because, really, what is the alternative?

KENNETH H. CARTER JR.

RESPONSE

When you read this passage from Proverbs, what is your first reaction to the relationship portrayed? That it is one of mutual support? That it depicts an overachiever vs. an underachiever? That it is a reason for tears and for laughter?

PRAYER

Let me open my mouth with kindness, and with the teaching of kindness on my tongue. Amen.

✣ TUESDAY ✣

Proverbs 31:10–31

REFLECTION

Because Wisdom has provided for the needs of all, no tragedy can disturb the equanimity of her family. She speaks wisely and persistently "looks well to the ways of her household" (v. 27). Rather than the woman praising her family, her family praises her, thus reversing gender expectations of the ancient world. She surpasses other women because she embodies the right attitude at the heart of religion.　　KATHLEEN M. O'CONNOR

This text is not just for Mother's Day, memorial services, and women's retreats. It is for communities that are struggling to come to grips with the roles for women that justice demands, Scripture portrays, and God expects.　　H. JAMES HOPKINS

The reverence in this proverb is not for women. Women do not need to be placed on pedestals. The expectations there are exhausting, and the fall from grace is destructive. The reverence, the fear of the Lord, is for God. This is the beginning, or the better part of wisdom.　　KENNETH H. CARTER JR.

RESPONSE

In what ways does your congregation stand up for justice for women?

PRAYER

Mother God, let your wisdom flow through me like a stream of living water. Amen.

✢ WEDNESDAY ✦

Psalm 1

REFLECTION

Psalm 1 presents a contrast between two attitudes toward life with God: righteousness or wickedness. It is not a legalistic decision, but, for the psalmist, it is a binary choice. "Happy are those," the Scripture says, who do not follow the ways of wickedness, but set their hearts on life with God.

SUSAN B.W. JOHNSON

[The psalm] does not condemn the people who surround us, or even the company we may invite to sit with us; it is about the way we allow their company to affect us. The righteous do not follow the advice of those who should not be advisors; the righteous do not take the path they already understand leads to destruction. The righteous do not comfort themselves with the perspectives of those who only express contempt and tear down.

SUSAN B.W. JOHNSON

So the community that gathers around this psalm knows that it is not the last word. But it is the first word, a word that invites the baptized community to orient their lives to the One who has come that we might have life, and have it abundantly.

RICHARD M. SIMPSON

RESPONSE

What does this passage say to people who let the opinions of others determine their self-worth?

PRAYER

My delight is in your laws, O Lord, but I confess that I do not meditate upon them nearly enough. Amen.

✣ THURSDAY ✣

James 3:13–4:3, 7–8a

REFLECTION

The conflicts we face are those that come from within us—from
disordered and conflicting desires that, when they come into
contact with the disordered desires of others, lead to disputes
and conflicts. The true battle is for self-awareness, self-control,
and enough self-mastery to know that we ought not take on
the task of trying to be masters of our own fates. The battle, in
short, is for heavenly wisdom.   MARK DOUGLAS

Within any relationship, family, or community, there will be
times of disagreement. James looks at these conflicts and sees
at their core the attitude or sin of envy (3:16; 4:1–3). He may
call it different things—selfish ambition (3:16), cravings (4:1),
coveting (4:2)—but it really comes down to desiring what
another has.   KATHY L. DAWSON

For James, wisdom is not in the head but in the behavior. It is a
way of life, not a way of thinking or believing.

BARBARA BROWN TAYLOR

RESPONSE

How would you define "heavenly wise"?

PRAYER

This day, may I see the mundane and routine as gifts and not
obligations. Amen.

✦ FRIDAY ✦

Mark 9:30–37

REFLECTION

Jesus first calls the disciples to emulate the child, thus
renouncing social status; he then calls them to welcome the
child, to make space for those with no social status, since to do
so is to welcome Jesus himself—and the One who sent him.
According to this story, a child enables God to be known as
one who overturns social hierarchies, welcoming the lowly into
God's embrace. The "gift of children" is thus not only about
the delight and wonder that children embody, but also about
the way that children draw Jesus' followers into resisting all
imperial powers of our time, struggling against all that opposes
the "kin-dom of God." MARTHA L. MOORE-KEISH

There are times when we are silent because we do not want to
hear what we fear we might hear. It is easier to keep quiet, to
pretend that we do not understand, than to ask and run the risk
of hearing something we might not like. HARRY B. ADAMS

RESPONSE

In a time of silence, turn your thoughts to God, trusting that
God already knows what is on your mind. Find comfort in
this belief.

PRAYER

O God, you know what is on my mind and in my heart. I offer
all that I am to you. Amen.

✦ SATURDAY ✦

Mark 9:30–37

REFLECTION

The word of Jesus—that those who would be first must be last, that those who would find status before God will do so as they serve the needy—comes as a liberating word rather than an onerous demand. HARRY B. ADAMS

Not only is Jesus himself said to honor and welcome a mere child (v. 36), but the saying in verse 37 equates one's welcome of such a child with welcoming Jesus himself—and even more, with welcoming the God who sent him. This passage, then, is far from a saccharine scene in which Jesus cuddles sweet little children and welcomes them to Sunday school, as it is often misrepresented. Instead, it is a powerful and even shocking depiction of the paradoxical values of God's will and reign, which confront the dominant values of human societies and assign worth and importance to every person. SHARON H. RINGE

RESPONSE

In our culture, where children are cherished and valued, who are the ones that we try and keep from the presence of Jesus?

PRAYER

Do not let me hinder anyone from coming into your presence; for yours is the kingdom and the glory. Amen.

✣ SUNDAY ✣

Proverbs 31:10–31

REFLECTION

Wisdom may be defined as a life well lived, a life that matters.
Wisdom in the Bible is not enlightenment. Rather, wisdom
is a lifetime of obedience to God, discipline honed in daily
decisions. Wisdom in the Bible is never mere knowledge. In our
culture, knowledge is a form of control, exercised for the benefit
of the one in possession of learning acquired through privilege
and maintained through credentialing. In Scripture, wisdom
is a way of life that includes justice, righteousness, humility,
compassion, and fairness.   KENNETH H. CARTER JR.

Psalm 1

REFLECTION

Psalm 1 does not tell us what to do in any given situation, but it
offers us a process in which we take our cues for living from our
understanding of who God is and what God intends for human
life on this planet. Delighting in God's word and meditating on
it are dynamic processes that continually inform our choices,
turning us toward the good and rooting us in pleasant places
where God's grace and God's blessings are accessible.

RUTH L. BOLING

James 3:13–4:3, 7–8a

REFLECTION

God is yearning and searching for the human spirit that mirrors
God's own image. Therefore, in choosing to draw near to God,
we are throwing off the power that earthly wisdom has over
us. . . . Gentleness—or humility or considerateness, as the word
is sometimes translated—marks those who know that God is

the source of their wisdom rather than presume to have made
themselves wise.   E. ELIZABETH JOHNSON

One must choose to serve God or the world; no middle
ground is possible. Only God's righteousness can make people
righteous and ensure their harmonious life together.

                                               E. ELIZABETH JOHNSON

Mark 9:30–37

REFLECTION

The disciples' lives will mirror the one to whom they are
committed. Instead of leaping immediately to examples of
Jesus' glory and power as their models, however, they need
to recognize that Jesus is first and foremost anointed to
suffer at the hands of the world's powers. In accepting such
a life contrary to the world's wisdom, they will share in the
resurrection that is God's final word on Jesus' life.

                                               SHARON H. RINGE

This is one of many Gospel texts that show that leadership
and authority among the Christian community is based upon
service and humility. . . . Radical servant leadership is not just
for the church; it is also the witness of the church to the world.

                                               NATHAN G. JENNINGS

RESPONSE

If you were writing the job description of a Messiah, what
would you include?

PRAYER

Make me your servant, and bless me with your wisdom and
grace. Amen.

🌿 *Proper 21* 🌿

Esther 7:1–6, 9–10; 9:20–22

On the second day, as they were drinking wine, the king
again said to Esther, "What is your petition, Queen Esther? It
shall be granted you. And what is your request? Even to the half
of my kingdom, it shall be fulfilled." Then Queen Esther answered,
"If I have won your favor, O king, and if it pleases the king, let
my life be given me—that is my petition—and the lives of
my people—that is my request." (7:2–3)

Psalm 124

Blessed be the Lord,
　　who has not given us
　　as prey to their teeth.
We have escaped like a bird
　　from the snare of the fowlers;
the snare is broken,
　　and we have escaped. (vv. 6–7)

James 5:13–20

My brothers and sisters, if anyone among you wanders from
the truth and is brought back by another, you should know that
whoever brings back a sinner from wandering will save the sinner's
soul from death and will cover a multitude of sins. (vv. 19–20)

Mark 9:38–50

But Jesus said, ". . . Whoever is not against us is for us.
For truly I tell you, whoever gives you a cup of water to
drink because you bear the name of Christ will by
no means lose the reward." (vv. 39a, 40–41)

⤷ MONDAY ⤶

Esther 7:1–6, 9–10; 9:20–22

REFLECTION

God is present and active in the life of Esther. . . consider
the lives of other women in which God is present and active,
women such as Hannah and Mary the mother of Jesus. In
the prayers of Hannah in the Hebrew Scriptures and Mary in
Christian Scriptures the belief is expressed that God is in the
business of lifting up the oppressed and bringing down the
oppressor. As she prepares to leave her young son in the care
of Eli the priest, Hannah prays, "The LORD makes poor and
makes rich; he brings low, he also exalts. He raises up the poor
from the dust; he lifts up the needy from the ash heap" (1 Sam.
2:7–8a). As she anticipates the birth of Jesus, the Son of the
Most High, Mary prays, "He has brought down the powerful
from their thrones, and lifted up the lowly; he has filled the
hungry with good things, and sent the rich away empty" (Luke
1:52–53). Certainly these prayers tell us that if we are looking
for evidence of God's presence, we do well to consider those
times and places when there are great reversals and dramatic
changes of fortune.   H. JAMES HOPKINS

RESPONSE

Who are some present-day women in whom you recognize
God as present and active?

PRAYER

Loving God, there are those who are not free to name your
name. Be known to them. Be known to them as you made
yourself known in Esther's time—remembering the forgotten
and saving those who were pawns in the games of the powerful.
Amen.   H. JAMES HOPKINS

→ TUESDAY ←

Psalm 124

REFLECTION

Psalm 124 is a stunning fusion of communal theological reflection and personal emotional response. Liturgical in form, the psalm calls for collective affirmation of God's protection and care upon deliverance from grave crisis, even certain death; yet the psalm also conveys in very powerful terms the breathless terror one experiences in the face of calamity. A relatively brief psalm, composed of just eight verses, it is the collective voice of the people of God, who affirm the active presence of God in crisis. But it is also the voice of one who is only just on the other side of sheer panic and fear.

SUSAN B.W. JOHNSON

Through the power of the Holy Spirit, God's saving grace remains at work in the world, undergirding the fabric of human life, supporting the powerless in times of trouble, and surprising the faithful with unexpected blessings.

RUTH L. BOLING

RESPONSE

When can we count on God to help us, and when does God expect us to use our own God-given talents and resources to help ourselves? Are we ever beyond help?   RUTH L. BOLING

PRAYER

In the midst of impending disaster, your hope gives us the strength to carry on. Amen.

✤ WEDNESDAY ✤

Psalm 124

REFLECTION

Our help is in the name of the Lord, and so it is our mission
to help others. How hard do we try to be helpful? If God is
by nature grace-full, do we as the people of God act in ways
that mirror God's grace? How well are we doing at aligning
our priorities with God's priorities? How ready are we to take
up the cause of those who are powerless in the face of evil?
How willing are we to work to change systems that perpetuate
imbalances of power?   RUTH L. BOLING

The psalm closes with a statement of confidence. For the
community, their help—their deliverance—is in the "name"
of the Lord who is the creator of heaven and earth, the creator
of the cosmos. For the community and for the psalmist, God's
name has redemptive power (Pss. 20:1; 54:1; cf. 1 Sam. 17:45).
Thus this psalm celebrates a God who cares for those who are
in need. It also provides a glimpse into the faith of the Jewish
people, who now have reason to sing and proclaim, "If it had
not been the LORD who was on our side. . . ."

                                            CAROL J. DEMPSEY, OP

RESPONSE

How, when, where, in what settings and circumstances have
you experienced God's saving grace? What difference would
it make if we put more of ourselves and our personal histories
into the worship event?   RUTH L. BOLING

PRAYER

My help is in the name of the LORD, who made heaven and
earth (Ps. 124:8). Amen.

✦ THURSDAY ✦

James 5:13–20

REFLECTION

That both those who suffer and those who are cheerful are encouraged to pray (songs of praise being a form of prayer) makes sense only if prayer can effect change, and prayer can effect change only if God hears and responds to prayer.

MARK DOUGLAS

But, it is not just for ourselves that we pray. We pray for others that we know personally who are in need and those whose needs are known to us in the wider world. This allows us to see the image of God embodied in others, to share in their suffering, and to add our voice in God's hearing for the good of the world. We can do this on our own, but the power of prayer is seen most clearly in the praying community of the church as these concerns are voiced aloud in worship and other gatherings of God's people.

KATHY L. DAWSON

RESPONSE

For whom have you prayed recently? Who has prayed for you?

PRAYER

Our help is in the name of the LORD, who made heaven and earth (Ps. 124:8). Amen.

✦ FRIDAY ✦

James 5:13–20

REFLECTION

When we praise God in our personal prayers, it is often linked
with thanksgiving for what God has given us. This is true
whenever we say grace before a meal, bless the beauty of God's
creation, or appreciate the returned health of a loved one. It is
a test of faith whether we can still adore or thank God in the
midst of suffering and illness. KATHY L. DAWSON

It is often in our brokenness that we can hear most clearly God's
reply to our prayers. When we are too broken to speak our
prayers, it is often through remembered hymns and spiritual
songs of praise from our youth that we are able to continue the
conversation with God. KATHY L. DAWSON

RESPONSE

Which hymns are your favorites; and which ones strengthen
your spirit in times of stress and sorrow?

PRAYER

I sing to the Lord a new song; and I sing an old one, too. Amen.

Mark 9:38–50

REFLECTION

If we reduce demons to figments of primitive imagination, then we miss the point that casting out demons is a significant "deed of power," and that it is Jesus' name that accomplishes this deed.

MARTHA L. MOORE-KEISH

What is the significance of the name of Jesus Christ? Some theologians have argued that to act in the name of Jesus Christ is simply to act in a manner consistent with his character. Others suggest that to act in Jesus' name means to act on behalf of Christ. Still others have insisted that the name "Jesus" itself is powerful, conveying the grace it signifies in a sacramental manner.

MARTHA L. MOORE-KEISH

This passage, in the end, may be less about the power of demons and more about the power of language itself to change the speaker and to shape the identity of the community.

MARTHA L. MOORE-KEISH

We can resist God's love in Christ, and such resistance bears its own consequences, but separation from God is neither God's will nor the focus of Christian proclamation.

MARTHA L. MOORE-KEISH

RESPONSE

What is the significance of the name of Jesus Christ?

PRAYER

In your holy name I pray. Amen.

✣ SUNDAY ✣

Esther 7:1–6, 9–10; 9:20–22

REFLECTION

That God does not appear in the Hebrew version of this text has created challenges to interpretation, but God's presence may be deduced from the loyalty, goodness, and triumph of the weak. It may be surmised from the reversals of fortune where the good triumph over the wicked, despite all expectation to the contrary. And God's presence is suggested by the liturgical feast of Purim, where food is shared, community strengthened, and the poor invited to the table. For Christians, the feast of Purim calls to mind eucharistic feasts and, in the context of Esther, serves as strong warning against social systems that benefit the powerful and harm others.   KATHLEEN M. O'CONNOR

Psalm 124

REFLECTION

Our help comes from God. It is one thing to discover (or rediscover) after hitting some bumps in the road that "Jesus loves me." But it is a richer and more mature faith that is able to claim God's love for us. This psalm articulates what it is like for a community to go through an ordeal and come out on the other side, not as a collection of isolated individuals, but as a community of faith.   RICHARD M. SIMPSON

James 5:13–20

REFLECTION

The prayers of the community shape the congregation and allow the people to become more nearly the body of Christ.
                              KATHY L. DAWSON

Even if the list is short, listeners may not have thought of the ways in which something as routine as a Wednesday night supper offers chances to pray with the suffering and sing songs of praise with the cheerful. Does someone routinely take plates from such suppers to those who are too sick to attend? Why not send an elder or two along for the ride? Whether or not they take oil, the point is for the community to go in search of those at risk of being lost to it. The point is to go to them when they cannot or will not come to you.   BARBARA BROWN TAYLOR

Mark 9:38–50

REFLECTION

There is a constant tension between being inclusive and being exclusive, with serious questions to be faced. How far should a community go in relating to other people who are different, and how far should it go in excluding those who have different standards and values and customs? How far must a community go in isolating itself from outsiders to keep its values? How does a community keep its identity if it recognizes the validity of differing ways and structures of other communities? How do people in a community fellowship with others without losing their defining distinctiveness?   HARRY B. ADAMS

RESPONSE

Ponder the questions in today's reflection from Mark regarding community.

PRAYER

Lord, bless us and keep us in community with the Holy Spirit and one another. Amen.

THE WEEK LEADING UP TO
❧ *Proper 22* ☙

Job 1:1; 2:1–10

Then his wife said to him, "Do you still persist in your integrity? Curse God, and die." But he said to her, "You speak as any foolish woman would speak. Shall we receive the good at the hand of God, and not receive the bad?" In all this Job did not sin with his lips. (2:9–10)

Psalm 26

But as for me, I walk in my integrity;
    redeem me, and be gracious to me.
My foot stands on level ground;
    in the great congregation I will bless the LORD. (vv. 11–12)

Hebrews 1:1–4; 2:5–12

Long ago God spoke to our ancestors in many and various ways by the prophets, but in these last days he has spoken to us by a Son, whom he appointed heir of all things, through whom he also created the worlds. He is the reflection of God's glory and the exact imprint of God's very being, and he sustains all things by his powerful word. (1:1–3)

Mark 10:2–16

"Truly I tell you, whoever does not receive the kingdom of God as a little child will never enter it." And he took them up in his arms, laid his hands on them, and blessed them. (vv. 15–16)

Job 1:1; 2:1–10

REFLECTION

Theologically considered, the issue is how we understand our place in the universe in relation to the rest of God's creation. Do we see ourselves as being in the center of things? Did God make the world for the sake of humanity? Has God designed the world in such a fashion that persons always get what they deserve? If not, then human happiness is not the end for which God created the world. Does this not suggest that our concern for salvation, however conceived, needs to be subordinated to that of discerning our appropriate place within the whole of creation?

PAUL E. CAPETZ

In the world as designed by God, suffering is not always the consequence of one's sin and virtue does not always entail happiness.

PAUL E. CAPETZ

RESPONSE

Why be religious at all? Can we truly serve God for God's sake alone, apart from reference to the self?

PAUL E. CAPETZ

PRAYER

I do not always understand the suffering in the world; but in my lack of understanding, may my trust be ever in you. Amen.

✴ TUESDAY ✦

Job 1:1; 2:1–10

REFLECTION

Find a way to let Job know that you realize the real dishonor here: that he has been reduced to a stand-in for everybody's illusions about their own righteous aspirations, that he is a stick figure in somebody else's melodrama, that he has not even been granted the dignity of the truth. Because what good is it, really, to be faithful to a God who jerks you around like a puppet on strings and does not have the good grace even to tell you what is really going on? Tell Job that God is not like that. Hang in there. Wait. There is more about God than this tale reveals.

THOMAS EDWARD FRANK

The book of Job is a complex work, exploring the intricate intersection of divine sovereignty, human faith, and innocent suffering. It is also a troubling work—troubling for the unsettling questions it poses to a neatly arranged, tidy faith.

J. S. RANDOLPH HARRIS

RESPONSE

In a world of both blessing and suffering, why is there faith at all? What good is faith? If persons of faith suffer as much as any other, then what's the use? J. S. RANDOLPH HARRIS

PRAYER

I hold in my heart those who suffer this day, some whom I know by name (name them here) and others whom only you know. Hear my prayer. Amen.

✦ WEDNESDAY ✦

Psalm 26

REFLECTION

The psalmist continually turns to God for affirmation and
for direction. He is confident in his faith, but only to a point.
Without God to validate his thoughts and actions, he is
unsteady. The faith that has been unwavering up until now can
easily unravel, and he knows it. . . . Like a sea captain looking
to the stars for bearing, so the faithful keep turning to God to
be sure that both our motivations and intentions are springing
from a desire to please God, and God alone.

KATHLEEN BOSTROM

At the heart of Psalm 26, the psalmist desires to please God,
and that in itself is pleasing to God. God loves an earnest
believer! God is not an impossible-to-please prima donna. God
seeks our affection, and delights in our devotion. It is with our
seeking to please God, not being piously perfect, that God is
indeed pleased. If our heart is in the right place, God knows.

KATHLEEN BOSTROM

RESPONSE

What does integrity mean to you?

PRAYER

Your steadfast love is before my eyes, and I walk in faithfulness
to you. Amen.

✥ THURSDAY ✥

Psalm 26

REFLECTION

The psalm is an "envelope" of "integrity" at the beginning and end that celebrates genuine, obedient, practical faith.

WALTER BRUEGGEMANN

When one calls upon God for judgment and vindication, an important line divides those who genuinely suffer from false testimony against their integrity from those who are deluded that they live forthrightly and steadfastly.

STEPHEN BUTLER MURRAY

RESPONSE

In what ways, large and small, do you contribute to making your church home a welcoming place?

PRAYER

Prove me, O Lord, and try me; test my heart and mind. Amen.

Hebrews 1:1–4; 2:5–12

REFLECTION

God's work in Christ does not float above the world or disregard its pain and brokenness. On the contrary, faith in Christ drives the believer into history and the world.

JOHN P. BURGESS

Jesus is the real thing—the authentic pioneer of God-drenched living, reflecting the glory of God in the flesh-and-blood experiences of earthly life. SUSAN R. ANDREWS

"Perfection" does not mean an excellence out of reach of ordinary human experience. Perfection, in a gospel sense, means "completeness"—fully carrying out the purpose for which we have been created—clearing out the clutter and corruption of our living so that the "imprint of God's very being," which is in each one of us, can be fully revealed.

SUSAN R. ANDREWS

RESPONSE

How do you view perfection in Christ as different from perfection the way society defines it?

PRAYER

May I carry your imprint upon my soul. Amen.

✦ SATURDAY ✦

Mark 10:2–16

REFLECTION

How then are we to receive and enter the kingdom of God? Not as those who try to justify ourselves, but as those who accept God's grace, like children who with purity of heart accept the grace of their parents.   JAMES J. THOMPSON

What may sound to our ears as relentlessly harsh assumes a different tenor when we understand that Jesus' intent is the protection and honor of the spouse as a child created in God's image, not as chattel to be discarded on selfish whim. The latter would be utterly incongruent with discipleship that cares for the vulnerable (Mark 9:42–50; 10:13–16).   C. CLIFTON BLACK

RESPONSE

Have you ever suffered at the hands of an unyielding opinion? How did you deal with that?

PRAYER

You are a God of justice and compassion; let your will be done on earth as it is in heaven. Amen.

✦ SUNDAY ✦

Job 1:1; 2:1–10

REFLECTION

What is the relationship between blessing and faith? Do persons believe in order to be blessed? Or is faith instead an expression of gratitude because we have been blessed? For many it is, but what constitutes that blessing? (And what happens to faith when those blessings are no longer perceived to be present?) Why is there suffering, and what effect might it have on faith?

J. S. RANDOLPH HARRIS

The reality is that sometimes faithfulness does indeed yield blessing; but sometimes faithfulness yields only suffering. Such ambiguity surely tests faith! J. S. RANDOLPH HARRIS

Psalm 26

REFLECTION

The church is always full of sinners, thank you very much, and if it is not, you and I do not deserve to be part of it either.

JASON BYASSEE

The rest of the psalm must be read in this light: as praise not of our goodness, but of God's—"borrowed" or on loan from God as it were—and only so is it ours. JASON BYASSEE

Hebrews 1:1–4; 2:5–12

REFLECTION

It is as if we are afflicted by the spiritual version of chronic fatigue syndrome—out of sync with the culture around us, weary of serving, and unable to muster either the discipline or the delight that daily discipleship can offer us. The electricity of Hebrews can reignite our faith, reminding us of the amazing grace of God's very imprint in Jesus and in us, and assuring us that endurance through suffering—as well as joy—is the power of God in us for others.   SUSAN R. ANDREWS

This is not a moralizing text. We are not told what to do to get right with God or our neighbor. We are overwhelmed in this proclaimed word by the power and presence of God.

MICHAEL G. HEGEMAN

Mark 10:2–16

REFLECTION

Jesus was declaring the beginning of a new era in which relationships could work if each party approached the other with mutual respect and concern. It was now possible to go beyond what was just permissible to what was kingdom enhanced. Unfortunately, then and now, not everyone chooses to live out the ethics of God's kingdom. Abuse and neglect are substituted for respect and concern.   DAVID B. HOWELL

We are always being told what to think and how to feel. Each day brings a torrent of advertisements for products and services of every kind, mostly in the form of moral tales of salvation bottled for a minibar. I failed to watch my kid, but here's a towel that can wipe up any spill. I can't sleep for thinking about my falling out with my best friend, but here is a pill that will carry me off to the land of Nod. There's a ready answer for everything and a right solution to every situation.   THOMAS EDWARD FRANK

RESPONSE

There are so many people telling us who to be and what to do. Take a few moments to just *be*.

PRAYER

I will proclaim your name to my brothers and sisters, in the midst of the congregation I will praise you. Amen.

❧ *Proper 23* ❧

Job 23:1–9, 16–17

"God has made my heart faint;
  the Almighty has terrified me;
If only I could vanish in darkness,
  and thick darkness would cover my face!" (vv. 16–17)

Psalm 22:1–15

My God, my God, why have you forsaken me?
  Why are you so far from helping me, from the
    words of my groaning?
O my God, I cry by day, but you do not answer;
  and by night, but find no rest. (vv. 1–2)

Hebrews 4:12–16

For we do not have a high priest who is unable to sympathize
with our weaknesses, but we have one who in every respect has
been tested as we are, yet without sin. Let us therefore approach
the throne of grace with boldness, so that we may receive mercy
and find grace to help in time of need. (vv. 15–16)

Mark 10:17–31

Jesus said, "Truly I tell you, there is no one who has left house
or brothers or sisters or mother or father or children or fields, for
my sake and for the sake of the good news, who will not receive
a hundredfold now in this age—houses, brothers and sisters,
mothers and children, and fields, with persecutions—and in the
age to come eternal life. But many who are first will be last,
and the last will be first." (vv. 29–31)

✦ MONDAY ✦

Job 23:1–9, 16–17

REFLECTION

The assumption that evil can be sufficiently explained as the just punishment of God upon the wicked is radically called into question by the experience of all the faithful persons throughout history who had every reason to think that the magnitude of the evil inflicted upon them was completely out of proportion to any calculation of sin and punishment. For that reason, Job articulates and symbolizes their legitimate protest against God and the presumption that God rules the world with justice.

PAUL E. CAPETZ

We must not assume that such doubt is an expression of sinful pride; rather, as Job's example shows, willingness to wrestle with God is the supreme test of whether piety or faith is adequate to our lived human experience in the world. Paradoxically, even a loss of faith may reflect a more genuine engagement with God than a faith that refuses to allow itself to be so tested.

PAUL E. CAPETZ

RESPONSE

Reflect on this excerpt: "Speaking the darkness of faith is a daring, and faithful, act."

J. S. RANDOLPH HARRIS

PRAYER

Even the powers of darkness cannot quench your light,
O Christ! Amen.

✦ TUESDAY ✦

Job 23:1–9, 16–17

REFLECTION

Too often have folk simply given in, resigning themselves to
their misfortune: "It must be the Lord's will; I guess we will just
have to accept it." Or . . . they abandon faith in God altogether.
Job offers a third way: he is unwilling to accept suffering
passively, but he also refuses to abandon his faith!

J. S. RANDOLPH HARRIS

Arguing with God is an act of deep faith—deeper, perhaps,
than a passive acceptance of whatever happens as God's will,
or a carefully articulated theological rationalization for why
things are.

J. S. RANDOLPH HARRIS

Job too is well acquainted with suffering, but his faith
endures. His mouth is full of arguments, but they are
arguments with God.

J. S. RANDOLPH HARRIS

RESPONSE

What is there for the church to say as the congregation stands
between human suffering and the seeming silence of God?

J. S. RANDOLPH HARRIS

PRAYER

Life can bring such anguish and pain! Give comfort and hope to
all who struggle this day. Amen.

✤ WEDNESDAY ✤

Psalm 22:1–15

REFLECTION

Intermittently the psalmist remembers God's holiness and past mercy—to Israel's ancestors (v. 4) and to himself at his mother's breast (vv. 9–10), but these memories do not dull the present pain. Indeed, such memories seem only to enhance the pain. Where is the God who is mighty to save and gentle in nursing us into a faithful life?   JASON BYASSEE

The writer's back-and-forth proclamations of devotion and despair swing from one end of the arc of the pendulum of faith to the other, and his agony is visible for all the world to see. The flames of destitution are fanned by the cruel mockery of outsiders. "You were so certain of God's love! Where is your God now?" The shame of being abandoned by God in a way that everyone else can see rubs salt into the raw and bleeding gashes of the psalmist's wounded spirit. If this is how God treats God's friends, then who needs enemies?   KATHLEEN BOSTROM

RESPONSE

Where in the world—literally—is God?

PRAYER

On you I was cast from my birth, and since my mother bore me, you have been my God. Amen.

✣ THURSDAY ✣

Psalm 22:1–15

REFLECTION

Yet suffering can also have the opposite effect. Our suffering can draw us into an awareness of and connection with the suffering of others. The heart of the mother who grieves over the death of her child is bound to the hearts of all the mothers who have ever buried a daughter or a son. The victim of a violent crime reads the newspaper with a keener eye to the plight of the other innocents whose lives are changed in an instant, forever. The employee whose job is "downsized" has a new sensitivity to those who have lost their jobs through no fault of their own. Shared suffering connects us to a larger world at the very time we are most at risk to feel isolated and alone. We are able to tap into the hope for healing and resurrection that resides in the life of that community.   KATHLEEN BOSTROM

The voice of the pray-er is of someone in dire straits who has no time for the luxury of conventional piety.

                                    WALTER BRUEGGEMANN

RESPONSE

Have you ever felt completely abandoned by God?

PRAYER

My God, my God, why have you forsaken me? Why are you so far from helping me, from the words of my groaning? (Ps. 22:1) Amen.

✢ FRIDAY ✢

Hebrews 4:12–16

REFLECTION

The Bible is the word of God—not because it is correct in every historical or scientific detail, but rather because it witnesses to what God has done and continues to do in Christ. In John Calvin's famous analogy, the Scriptures are like spectacles for weak, failing eyes. Without Scripture, we see only a world in chaos, driven by human ambition and failure. God's plans and purposes are blurry and hardly detectable. But if we put on the Scriptures and really look through them, allowing them to refocus our vision, God's saving work in Christ becomes crystal clear. We no longer see a world abandoned to its own devices, but see, rather, God's transforming love, which brings good out of evil and hope out of despair.   JOHN P. BURGESS

If we do not keep our own Bibles open, our own hearts unlocked, our own minds ready for God's deft sword, we may miss that liberating moment when the dis-ease of our life is cut away by the healing wisdom of a living word.

                                        SUSAN R. ANDREWS

RESPONSE

How old were you when you received your first Bible? Do you still have it?

PRAYER

Your word is a lamp to my feet, a lamp to my path, and a light to the world! Amen.

Mark 10:17–31

REFLECTION

What then are the relationships between faith and reward, or virtue and wealth? Why must this man give up his riches in order to follow Jesus? What will he get in return? A standard answer is that there is nothing wrong with wealth itself. The problem is not wealth per se but our attitude toward it. As we accumulate riches, we are tempted to trust in our possessions and our powers of acquiring them, rather than in God, for our ultimate security and comfort. Even honestly acquired and generously shared wealth can thus lead to pride. This is why it is easier for a camel to go through the eye of a needle than for a rich person to enter the kingdom of God. It is hard to let go of the immediate basis of our security and comfort—and the more we have, the harder it gets.   JAMES J. THOMPSON

Rather than receiving the kingdom in complete dependence as a little child, the rich man wants to know what he can do to inherit eternal life. Indeed, this tension is present even in his question. One can rarely do anything for an inheritance; by definition, an inheritance is something a person can only be given.   CHARLES L. CAMPBELL

RESPONSE

Who can live a kingdom life? How can I change? How can I take the necessary first steps?   DAVID B. HOWELL

PRAYER

When I am weak, your strength is all the more evident in my life. Thank you for allowing me to glorify you! Amen.

✢ SUNDAY ✢

Job 23:1–9, 16–17

REFLECTION

Job's problem is not with God's attributes; Job's problem is with God's absence. . . . This painful situation pulls Job in two directions. On the one hand, he remains confident in his belief that if God would only hear his case, he would be acquitted. On the other hand, Job is terrified (v. 16) that God's absence means that God's power will be exercised autocratically.

MARK A. THRONTVEIT

Psalm 22:1–15

REFLECTION

The psalmist questions the absence of God while at the same time affirming the divine presence. There is never any doubt that God exists, even when God's seeming abandonment brings desperation and ridicule. The history of God's people gives context to our anguish and affirms that our trials and tribulations are not personal attacks wrought by an abusive God. Rather, it is God who gives the strength, courage, and hope to see us through the darkest of days. KATHLEEN BOSTROM

In a form of address rarely found in the biblical text God is referred to as "my God." Not "O God," or even just "God," but "*My* God." The pure and abiding trust that the writer has in God conveys his despair at being abandoned by the One who elicits that faith. God, who once seemed as close and life giving as the person's own breath, is now distant and removed. The one who has felt the security of God's proximity feels even more keenly the shattering devastation of the Almighty's presumed absence.

KATHLEEN BOSTROM

Hebrews 4:12–16

REFLECTION

Where God speaks, Christ is present, who has entered fully into our human condition, yet without sin. The God who places us under judgment is the very God who loves us and sympathizes with us in every respect. JOHN P. BURGESS

In the author's heart, Jesus' perfection is not about power or purity, but about endurance. This Lord meets us in the places of temptation and weakness, experiencing all the human foibles that separate us from God. Yet Jesus is able to endure in ways we cannot—to endure to the end, to endure the darkness until it is completely transformed by light. SUSAN R. ANDREWS

Mark 10:17–31

REFLECTION

Jesus holds out the hope that, with God, change and first steps are not only possible but are already happening. DAVID B. HOWELL

Not once in Mark do we see the Twelve in prayer. Doubtless that accounts for their infidelity to Jesus on the night he was betrayed (14:27–31, 50–52, 66–72). Yet, unlike the rich man, they have left everything to follow him (1:16–20; 2:13–14), which Peter asserts and Jesus does not deny (10:28–29). Their reward for such obedience is an abundant new family to replace that relinquished by acceptance of Jesus' call (10:29–30). C. CLIFTON BLACK

RESPONSE

Have you ever had to go without food, shelter, or clothing because of a lack of resources?

PRAYER

Thank you for enfolding us all into your family. Amen.

❧ *Proper 24* ❧

Job 38:1–7 (34–41)

"Where were you when I laid the foundation of the earth?
    Tell me, if you have understanding.
Who determined its measurements—surely you know!
    Or who stretched the line upon it?
On what were its bases sunk,
    or who laid its cornerstone
when the morning stars sang together
    and all the heavenly beings shouted for joy?" (vv. 4–7)

Psalm 104:1–9, 24, 35c

You stretch out the heavens like a tent,
    you set the beams of your chambers on the waters,
you make the clouds your chariot,
    you ride on the wings of the wind,
you make the winds your messengers,
    fire and flame your ministers. (vv. 2b–4)

Hebrews 5:1–10

Although he was a Son, he learned obedience through what he
suffered; and having been made perfect, he became the source of
eternal salvation for all who obey him. (vv. 8–9)

Mark 10:35–45

"But whoever wishes to become great among you must be
your servant, and whoever wishes to be first among you must be
slave of all. For the Son of Man came not to be served but to serve,
and to give his life a ransom for many." (vv. 43–45)

✣ MONDAY ✣

Job 38:1–7 (34–41)

REFLECTION

Job has spent much of the thirty-seven previous chapters asking why, in one form or another, and his friends have expended many words trying to say why. Now God takes an enormous risk that Job will never want anything to do with God again, by responding, not about Job's "why" but about the grandeur, beauty, and order of the creation.   THOMAS EDWARD FRANK

Job's friends argued exhaustively, but logically backwards, that since Job was suffering he must have sinned. But when God speaks, contrary to the expectations of the friends, there is nary a word of condemnation or chastisement.

MARK A. THRONTVEIT

Job may indeed be God's special servant, as is made clear in the prologue; but that special status does not mean that the distance between Creator and creature has been overcome. God's sovereign love extends to the whole of creation.

J. S. RANDOLPH HARRIS

RESPONSE

What is the worst advice anyone ever gave you?

PRAYER

When there seems to be no answer to the question "Why?" grant me a view of a larger picture that allows me to see your greatness and your grace. Amen.

✦ TUESDAY ✦

Psalm 104:1–9, 24, 35c

REFLECTION

Psalm 104 gives us some visual imagery for God that is even more arresting than Michelangelo's and our attempts to visualize God using human characteristics and experiences. God's clothes: light, majesty, honor. God's world: stretched out as easily as we do a tent. God's transportation: chariot, with the "wings of the wind" as charioteers. God's creation: an earth that shall never be moved. The psalm's image of God is an impressive image. . . . It is as though the psalmist were saying: "Imagine something more unimaginable than you have ever imagined. You cannot? Good, you are starting to get it."

JASON BYASSEE

The psalm invites the very self of the speaker to come face to face with the wonder of creation and with the creator God who orders and guarantees that life-giving wonder.

WALTER BRUEGGEMANN

The uses of the divine name in verses 1 and 24 form an envelope whereby the wonder of the creator holds the many wonders of creation. The poem does not flinch from the awed conviction that the creation is indeed revelatory of the creator!

WALTER BRUEGGEMANN

RESPONSE

Do you have a favorite image of God as depicted in art?

PRAYER

O Lord, how manifold are your works! In wisdom you have made them all (Ps. 104:24). Amen.

✦ WEDNESDAY ✦

Psalm 104:1–9, 24, 35c

REFLECTION

Imagine a world where all creation lives in perfect harmony: a world of sparkling, clean water and unpolluted air; of majestic mountains whose surfaces are not scraped and scarred by bulldozers and asphalt; a world where the womb of the earth is not gutted by mines of any kind; where forests never tremble to the sounds of chain saws. Imagine a world where "litter" refers to the birthing of animals that leap, crawl, and sleep with no fear of cages and steel-toothed traps; a world where birds are not plucked for their plumage, and fishing nets are nonexistent. Imagine a world of complete compatibility, peace, and untarnished beauty. KATHLEEN BOSTROM

Other psalms sing praise to God for creation, but no other psalm quite portrays the synthesis of the natural world void of human intervention. Surprise! Human beings are not the center of the universe, which actually functions quite nicely without us. KATHLEEN BOSTROM

RESPONSE

Read through the psalm several times, writing down the words and images that capture your attention.

PRAYER

Bless the LORD, O my soul. O LORD my God, you are very great (Ps. 104:1). Amen.

✣ THURSDAY ✤

Hebrews 5:1–10

REFLECTION

Although the atonement is at the heart of the Christian faith, it is so deep in meaning and mystery that no one theory can exhaust it. The Scriptures offer us, instead, several images of atonement, each of which opens us more profoundly to God's gracious, transformative work on the cross.   JOHN P. BURGESS

For Hebrews, Christ's death results not in death but in eternal salvation and victory over death. Those who were unable to approach God on their own now have a high priest who acts on their behalf. The One who struggled within his very self to give himself completely to God now moves us to intervene morally on behalf of the weak and the wayward (v. 2; also, see Heb. 13:1–3).We see here aspects of all three theories of atonement. But what is more fundamental is the mystery of the cross itself, a mystery that we can only contemplate, and that fills us with awe and gratitude.   JOHN P. BURGESS

RESPONSE

The next time you are in a sanctuary, spend some time observing the cross, and thinking about what God has done for you in Christ.

PRAYER

When I survey the wondrous cross upon which you died, O Christ, I can only bow in praise and awe. Amen.

✦ FRIDAY ✦

Hebrews 5:1–10

REFLECTION

In some traditions, pastors tend to make ordination days into coronations—with long, wordy services filled with pomp, power, and prestige. This is a far cry from the only ordination Jesus ever received—that muddy baptismal bath in the shallows of the River Jordan, presided over by a locust-eating hippie. Much more appropriate are the ordination services that Presbyterians celebrate for lay leaders, when a whole host of humble servants kneel—many of them wondering if they are worthy for the task—while half the congregation, previously ordained, lays hands upon them, a reminder that ministry is something we all share as the people of God.

SUSAN R. ANDREWS

The earthly reality pales in the light of who God is and what God does on humanity's behalf. What happens here on earth is never "just as" what happens in heaven.   MICHAEL G. HEGEMAN

RESPONSE

Take time to gaze at the night sky, and glory in the wonder of God's creation and God's love for the whole world.

PRAYER

How grateful I am for your love for me and for all creation. Amen.

Mark 10:35–45

REFLECTION

The central liturgical practices of the church challenge all fear-driven quests for security, and call the church into the alternative way of Jesus—the way of servanthood. . . . This call, as it is issued to James, John, and the church, brings with it a promise: "The cup that I drink you will drink; and with the baptism with which I am baptized, you will be baptized" (v. 39). Sometimes these words are read as a threat or warning from Jesus: "James and John, you too will be crucified." However, in the larger context of the story, Jesus' words may also be read as an extraordinary promise: "You will not always be driven by your fears and your need for security. Rather, you will be empowered to take up your cross and follow me. You will be faithful disciples even to the end." Here is the great promise for the church. We need not always live in fear; we need not continually seek our own security. Rather, we have Jesus' promise that we can and will live as faithful disciples as we seek to follow him. It is an extraordinary promise made to such a fumbling, bumbling group of disciples—then and now!

CHARLES L. CAMPBELL

RESPONSE

Are you comfortable with the concept of servanthood?

PRAYER

Deliver me from self-serving tendencies; glean from me my better self. Amen.

Job 38:1–7 (34–41)

REFLECTION

In a very literal sense, the book of Job raises more questions than it answers. At the very least, however, we are assured that God is God, and we are not; and that we are human beings who struggle with things we cannot understand. Nevertheless our hope is tied to the firm conviction that this same God will take care of that which we do not understand, as we see in the created world around us.   MARK A. THRONTVEIT

Psalm 104:1–9, 24, 35c

REFLECTION

The psalmist speaks in the present tense, invoking God's activity and agency in bringing the elements to bear, taming that which otherwise might be wild and dangerous into God's employment and demeanor. The waters, skies, earth, and fire become the very implements of God's residence with us on the earth.

STEPHEN BUTLER MURRAY

Hebrews 5:1–10

REFLECTION

As baptized "priests" we are given all the power, vision, and grace to be who we are called to be—not because we are perfect, but because God's grace is made perfect in us. We can be "bridge people": standing in the middle of red state/blue state politics, standing in the middle of violent conflicts, standing in the middle of broken relationships, standing in the middle of theological skirmishes, standing in the middle of the enormous gaps between rich and poor, black and white, immigrant and bigot—standing in the middle, between God's vision of shalom and the disharmony of contemporary life. Yes, as "priest," each of us is called to stretch out our arms to embrace all that is dissident, becoming a dwelling place of reconciliation where all of creation finds a harmonious home in God's heart.

SUSAN R. ANDREWS

Mark 10:35–45

REFLECTION

Maybe Jesus' ominous predictions of his passion have become clear to them. Maybe they do understand what lies ahead. And being afraid, they seek the promise of a secure future. James and John may not just be power hungry; they may rather be acting quite naturally on their fears.

CHARLES L. CAMPBELL

Jesus' rebuke of the disciples is not meant, however, to be a counsel of cynicism or despair. His rebuke is a reminder to us that we should be cautious about expecting too much of mere humans. We should be careful, for example, not to pin our hopes for salvation on those who cannot bear the weight of our expectations. Any human being who is a self-appointed savior is likely to be a disappointment. But to recognize that even the best and most committed leaders among us are subject to vanity and ambition does not imply that we should become detached misanthropes, or simply surrender to the ways of the world and aim to get ahead as best we can.

JAMES J. THOMPSON

RESPONSE

What is your definition of a servant-leader?

PRAYER

I am not sure that I can drink the cup that you drink; but I pray for the willingness to try. Amen.

❧ *Proper 25* ❧

Job 42:1–6, 10–17

Then Job answered the LORD:
"I know that you can do all things,
    and that no purpose of yours can be thwarted.
'Who is this that hides counsel without knowledge?'
Therefore I have uttered what I did not understand,
    things too wonderful for me, which I did not know." (vv. 1–3)

Psalm 34:1–8 (19–22)

I sought the LORD, and he answered me,
        and delivered me from all my fears.
. . . .
This poor soul cried, and was heard by the LORD,
        and was saved from every trouble.
The angel of the LORD encamps
        around those who fear him, and delivers them.
O taste and see that the LORD is good;
        happy are those who take refuge in him. (vv. 4, 6–8)

Hebrews 7:23–28

Consequently [Jesus] is able for all time to save
those who approach God through him, since he always
        lives to make intercession for them. (v. 25)

Mark 10:46–52

Then Jesus said to him, "What do you want me to do for you?" The
blind man said to him, "My teacher, let me see again." Jesus said to
him, "Go; your faith has made you well." Immediately he regained
        his sight and followed him on the way. (vv. 51–52)

✦ MONDAY ✦

Job 42:1–6, 10–17

REFLECTION

In the midst of his dark night, he dares to tell the truth of his life to his Creator. By lamenting, complaining, and shouting his discontent to the God he believes to be attacking him, he keeps his relationship with God alive.   KATHLEEN M. O'CONNOR

Now Job meets God in his own life, on his own recognizance, in the thick of the storm that is his life. Instead of being forced into submission, Job speaks of firsthand experience, a personal meeting, a kind of seeing that surpasses known speech about God. From Job's viewpoint, this encounter overwhelms and honors him and transforms his life. The encounter in the storm calls Job to a new kind of theological knowledge; it summons him beyond himself to a heightened sense of divine presence in his life and in the world.   KATHLEEN M. O'CONNOR

RESPONSE

Are you comfortable with having an argument with God?

PRAYER

Thank you for loving me enough to argue with and confront me! Amen.

→ TUESDAY ←

Psalm 34:1–8 (19–22)

REFLECTION

Christian hope in the fulfillment of God's kingdom in the
resurrection has traditionally grounded hope for deliverance in
the long term. Short-term divine deliverance is not guaranteed.
God often relies upon human cooperation in establishing
justice.   LISA D. MAUGANS DRIVER

God does not accept current struggles as an excuse to languish
in idle self-pity, but encourages suffering to become a vehicle to
address the suffering of others.   LISA D. MAUGANS DRIVER

The psalmist teaches us that amid the challenges over the
course of our lives God will answer our prayers, dwell with us
in our fear and loneliness, and give to the faithful every good
thing.   MICHAEL MORGAN

RESPONSE

Is it true that those who seek God lack no good thing (v. 10)?
What are good things? Do we not know of those in the past
who have taken refuge in God and who have known great
condemnation (v. 22)?   MARY DONOVAN TURNER

PRAYER

I sought the LORD, and the LORD answered me, and delivered
me from all my fears (Ps. 34:4). Amen.

✣ WEDNESDAY ✣

Psalm 34:1-8 (19–22)

REFLECTION

The psalmist invites us to open ourselves to receive the goodness of the Lord—opening not only our mouths to taste, but our minds to learn and our hearts to love. It is not enough to accept that invitation for ourselves alone, but through our lives to teach others how rich and bountiful is the feast of God's blessing for all who will faithfully receive it.

MICHAEL MORGAN

What would it mean to be delivered from "all fears," the fears of hunger or poverty, physical harm or decline, ridicule, injury, or loneliness? Is this possible? There are no guarantees against finitude, decline, or death. Does fear serve any constructive purposes? Is the challenge to learn to live creatively with all our fears, so that they do not paralyze us but prompt us to be vigilant and caring for others and ourselves?

MARY DONOVAN TURNER

RESPONSE

Why should we endeavor to be the obedient children of God if we are not promised the instant gratification of a "good life," free from conflict and rich in blessing? MICHAEL MORGAN

PRAYER

O taste and see that the LORD is good; happy are those who take refuge in God! (Ps. 34:8) Amen.

→ THURSDAY ←

Hebrews 7:23–28

REFLECTION

Sacrifice is something of a two-edged sword. On the one hand, we praise those who are willing to defer, or perhaps to give up entirely, instant experiences of gratification for the sake of some future good; such sacrifices are considered particularly praiseworthy if they are for the sake of another. . . . On the other hand, we also recognize that the concept of sacrifice can be easily abused.   DAVID S. CUNNINGHAM

Verse 25 offers the logical consequence of the continuous priesthood of Jesus: he is always able to save those who approach God through him. . . . The theological affirmation of the eternal priesthood of Christ translates into a sense of security.   DAVID CORTÉS-FUENTES

In contrast to other priests, he does not need to offer repetitive sacrifices, and he does not need to offer sacrifices for his own sins. Jesus offered himself, once and forever.

DAVID CORTÉS-FUENTES

RESPONSE

In what ways is the living Christ present in our worship and practice? How is the Christ "for all time" manifest in our lives today? How can we as individuals and as a church express our awareness of Christ's living presence to those around us?

GINGER GRAB

PRAYER

Therefore I have uttered what I did not understand, things too wonderful for me, which I did not know (Job 42:3). Amen.

✦ FRIDAY ✦

Mark 10:46–52

REFLECTION

Not even the blindness of his closest followers can impede the work of Christ in the world. VICTOR MCCRACKEN

Thus, while Bartimaeus sees that Jesus is the Messiah, the prevailing assumptions about the role that the Messiah was to play in the life of Israel continue to blind him to Jesus' true mission. Like the disciples, Bartimaeus sees, but only in part. VICTOR MCCRACKEN

Those who thought that they could truly see Jesus will discover in Jesus' death that they did not see after all. VICTOR MCCRACKEN

This story invites us to consider our own ministry to the outsider, the voice silenced by institutional pronouncements, the so-called reprobate whose cry stands us still in our tracks. CYNTHIA A. JARVIS

RESPONSE

What do you ask Jesus to do for you?

PRAYER

In the midst of my asking you for what I need, let me also ask what you need me to do. Amen.

✦ SATURDAY ✦

Mark 10:46–52

REFLECTION

In the healing of Bartimaeus, Mark gently affirms Jesus' identity as the anointed Son, but Jesus accepts that role by helping a noisy beggar. Together, the healer and the beggar recognize in one another more than the distracting, misguided crowd (or the imperial forces, or the temple establishment) understands: that regal authority comes to divine expression in deliverance, in persistence, in fulfilling the vocation of recognizing and strengthening one another.   A. K. M. ADAM

The blind man is portrayed as a model of Christian discipleship. He comes to Jesus and does so by casting aside his cloak. It is quite reasonable to regard his cloak as representing his most treasured possession. It has kept him warm through the cold nights. It may also hold the meager spoils of his begging. In his act of throwing off his cloak, we see the image of one who leaves his former life behind.   LINCOLN E. GALLOWAY

RESPONSE

Put yourself in Bartimaeus's shoes (or sandals!) and imagine how he might have felt.

PRAYER

Let me take heart in the gentleness and power of your presence. Amen.

✦ SUNDAY ✦

Job 42:1–6, 10–17

REFLECTION

His deepened experience of God summons him to new
perceptions, leads him outside of himself, and creates of him
a new being in the midst of his community, where he bestows
inheritance even upon his daughters.   KATHLEEN M. O'CONNOR

The encounter with God itself transforms us while yet in the
midst of suffering. God's inbreaking empowers us to transcend
suffering. God's restoration empowers us to seek a more just
way of living that overcomes the injustice of suffering.

DALE P. ANDREWS

Psalm 34:1–8 (19–22)

REFLECTION

Grateful praise, however, can hardly be self-contained, so the
psalmist invites the "humble" to join the festive throng. The
"humble" are those within the community who are at risk and
ever aware of their own limitations (i.e., "the afflicted" as in
the NIV). The circle of joy is complete only when those at the
margins participate fully in the celebration of praise.

LOUIS STULMAN

Tasting is not a passive verb, but one that requires action. To
taste anything, we must first open our mouths!

MICHAEL MORGAN

Hebrews 7:23–28

REFLECTION

A major predicament of the human condition is that ordinary
and necessary human actions inevitably lead to a chaos of
unintended and irreversible consequences. It is the nature of

human beings to act, and it is the nature of action to unleash the unforeseeable and the irreversible. Without the possibility of forgiveness, . . . we would be trapped forever in the consequences of a single action.

GINGER GRAB

Sin cripples us because it traps us in the past; never-ending resentment and guilt can shut down our natural vitality and inhibit our growth, both individually and corporately.

GINGER GRAB

Mark 10:46–52

REFLECTION

Jesus' inattention to the crowd is noteworthy. Other than commanding them to call the outsider to his side, he simply lets them be. He does not upbraid them for their blindness to human need, nor does he call their faithfulness into question. Rather, in his command to "Call him here" he is also commanding the gathered crowd to become the disciples they would not be without this very specific act of obedience. Given that in Jesus the blind receive their sight, the lame walk, and the lepers are cleansed, those who simply want to be near him will find themselves in the company his love commands them to keep.

CYNTHIA A. JARVIS

Bartimaeus refuses to be defined by his circumstances or by the expectations of those who are able to see, who appear to be close to Jesus, and who assume the right to speak on his behalf. He ensures that his call will be heard by Jesus.

LINCOLN E. GALLOWAY

RESPONSE

What is your experience of repentance?

PRAYER

May I have the courage to come forward when you call to me. Amen.

✸ *All Saints' Day* ✸

Wisdom of Solomon 3:1–9

But the souls of the righteous are in the hand of God,
and no torment will ever touch them.
. . . .
In the time of their visitation they will shine forth,
and will run like sparks through the stubble.
They will govern nations and rule over peoples,
and the Lord will reign over them forever.
Those who trust in him will understand truth,
and the faithful will abide with him in love,
because grace and mercy are upon his holy ones,
and he watches over his elect. (vv. 1, 7–9)

REFLECTION

The justice of God is not always visible. God's justice extends
beyond human seeing into the invisible world of eternity,
where the righteous receive justice at last, justice so strong and
desirable that it vindicates them, gives them peace, and assures
them of life with God as well as continued communion with the
living. KATHLEEN M. O'CONNOR

This text speaks not just a final word of assurance about "all
the saints who from their labors rest"; it also encourages wise
and courageous daily living for individual believers and the
community of faith, as "God watches over God's elect" (v. 9).
For the people of God to know that "the faithful abide with God
in love" (v. 9) is to know what Paul would later declare: nothing
"will be able to separate us from the love of God" (Rom. 8:39).
This is more than a comforting assurance of things eternal. This
assurance is a powerful motivator for the church to "trust in
God" (v. 9), to live with the courage of conviction in any setting,
in any age. GARY W. CHARLES

The Wisdom of Solomon does not speak of resurrection from the dead in the same ways Christians understand it, but the passage stammers in that direction, anticipates it, and makes theological space for it. Because the martyrs have died in persecution and seemingly in shame and tragedy, human reflection can perceive only the successful reign of evil and injustice. But the holy ones, the righteous ones who endured their travails, now live with God. As God's elect, their souls survive and continue to be present to God and in "communion" with the living.   KATHLEEN M. O'CONNOR

Psalm 24

Who shall ascend the hill of the LORD?
    And who shall stand in his holy place?
Those who have clean hands and pure hearts,
    who do not lift up their souls to what is false,
    and do not swear deceitfully.
They will receive blessing from the LORD,
    and vindication from the God of their salvation.
Such is the company of those who seek him,
    who seek the face of the God of Jacob. *Selah* (vv. 3–6)

REFLECTION

The barriers to paradise, like the stone rolled away from the empty tomb in the garden, have been pushed aside to give us unfettered access to behold the smiling face of a gracious and accepting God, whose mercy, rather than our own merits, enables us to pass through the open door.   MICHAEL MORGAN

The church is a community of grace where temptations can be overcome and the faithful may be lovingly prepared for immortality. When souls look to the eternal and allow themselves to be shaped by divine stability and simplicity, actions of like kind radiate toward neighbors.   LISA D. MAUGANS DRIVER

The psalm begins with a joyful acknowledgment that "the earth and all that dwell therein"—including us and every member of the family of humanity—were created by God and belong to God. The fullness of the earth is not ours, but belongs to God. The blessings of our lives—indeed, our lives themselves—are gifts from God, given for a time, but eventually repossessed by the One who lends them to us. This is the past we all share and celebrate as the heirs and stewards of creation.

MICHAEL MORGAN

Revelation 21:1–6a

Then I saw a new heaven and a new earth; for the first heaven and the first earth had passed away, and the sea was no more. And I saw the holy city, the new Jerusalem, coming down out of heaven from God, prepared as a bride adorned for her husband. And I heard a loud voice from the throne saying,

"See, the home of God is among mortals.
    He will dwell with them;
    they will be his peoples,
    and God himself will be with them;
    he will wipe every tear from their eyes.
    Death will be no more;
    mourning and crying and pain will be no more,
    for the first things have passed away." (vv. 1–4)

REFLECTION

So, just as a story of origin offers us more than just a descriptive play-by-play account of events that led up to our present moment, so do "stories of destination" provide more than a sequence of future events. Rather, they answer the question "Where are you going?" in a much broader sense: Where are you headed? In what direction is your life taking you? What is your true destination?   DAVID S. CUNNINGHAM

To hear this reading on All Saints' Day is to hear a summons to solidarity with all those who have suffered in their witness to Christ—whether in the farthest reaches of the first-century Roman Empire or in the drug-ridden streets of an American slum; whether on an abandoned road in Central America or in the faceless precincts of a Burmese prison. When a part of the body suffers, all suffer—their tribulation is ours, and so is their hope.   ROGER A. FERLO

God is making everything new and that God will dwell with the people. God's direct statement interprets the visions and the messages of the loud voice as God's action. The creation of a new community in communion with God is not the result of history but the purpose of history.   DAVID CORTES-FUENTES

John's visions lift him out of everyday life to a heavenly realm where he can view earthly existence from God's perspective. We who read John's visions can likewise be transported. We can be put in the position of suddenly seeing our own day-to-day lives from God's point of view.   GINGER GRAB

John 11:32–44

When Mary came where Jesus was and saw him, she knelt at his feet and said to him, "Lord, if you had been here, my brother [Lazarus] would not have died." When Jesus saw her weeping, and the Jews who came with her also weeping, he was greatly disturbed in spirit and deeply moved. He said, "Where have you laid him?" They said to him, "Lord, come and see." Jesus began to weep. So the Jews said, "See how he loved him!" But some of them said, "Could not he who opened the eyes of the blind man have kept this man from dying?" (vv. 32–37)

REFLECTION

The God of the church, embodied in the triune relationship of Father, Son, and Spirit, is not unaffected by the suffering and loss of the world. . . . The good news of this text is that in Christ God freely enters into this suffering.   VICTOR MCCRACKEN

Though she repeats, word for word, the speech of her sister, it is Mary's grief that renders God's Word silent. Jesus weeps, his tears constituting the only conscionable theological response we often can make when called to the side of the grieving.

CYNTHIA A. JARVIS

Jesus does not stand outside of the moment as an observer. He participates in the moment and takes within himself the experience of loss that shapes and clothes that moment. In taking upon himself the sorrow and pain of those whom he loves, Jesus reveals the promise available to all (3:16).

LINCOLN E. GALLOWAY

When Jesus calls Lazarus out of the tomb, he authenticates his claim to divine Sonship, his claim to embody life itself, and his superiority to the forces of decay and death. Death still affects those who turn to Jesus in faith, as it affected Lazarus and Jesus himself; but John deploys this story to show that even though disciples may still die, death does not end, but interrupts their life.   A. K. M. ADAM

RESPONSE

Does God hold the world in God's hands? What are the evidences that this is the case?   MARY DONOVAN TURNER

PRAYER

We shall receive blessing from the Lord, and vindication from the God of our salvation. Such is the company of those who seek your face, O God (based on Ps. 24:6). Amen.

❧ *Proper 26* ❧

Ruth 1:1–18

Ruth said,
"Do not press me to leave you
    or to turn back from following you!
Where you go, I will go;
    where you lodge, I will lodge;
your people shall be my people,
    and your God my God." (v. 16)

Psalm 146

I will sing praises to my God all my life long.
. . . .

The LORD sets the prisoners free;
the LORD opens the eyes of the blind. (vv. 2b, 7b–8a)

Hebrews 9:11–14

But when Christ came as a high priest of the good
things that have come, then through the greater and perfect
tent (not made with hands, that is, not of this creation), he
entered once for all into the Holy Place. (vv. 11–12b)

Mark 12:28–34

"Which commandment is the first of all?" Jesus answered, "The
first is, 'Hear, O Israel: the Lord our God, the Lord is one; you shall
love the Lord your God with all your heart, and with all your soul,
and with all your mind, and with all your strength.' The second is
this, 'You shall love your neighbor as yourself.' There is no other
commandment greater than these." (vv. 28b-31)

✦ MONDAY ✦

Ruth 1:1–18

REFLECTION

In essence, Ruth is willing to die to her past so that her mother-in-law and she may live anew. In doing so, she finds God's people and God. Without her willingness to move, she would not have found God or Boaz, her kinsman redeemer.

JOHN AHN

Through their relationships the women already begin to break the bondage of tragedy. The various struggles in these relationships focus on how the women will be with one another. They struggle to give to each other, to act in each other's best interest.

DALE P. ANDREWS

The God for whom Ruth abandons everything is the God of the lowly, the widow, the stranger, and the enemy.

KATHLEEN M. O'CONNOR

RESPONSE

What are the marks of a true friend?

PRAYER

Thank you, dear God, for the people I call friend. I am so blessed by them! Amen.

✦ TUESDAY ✦

Psalm 146

REFLECTION

Imitating divine justice and love shapes believers through encountering God in others. Likewise, worship ensures that they remain bound to God, who is especially present to transform the faithful. When humans turn from God in sin or in apathy, their self-chosen distance weakens access to the source of life and uproots their attempts at justice.

LISA D. MAUGANS DRIVER

Christians struggle with consistency in belief and action. Often the struggle spins around the fallen desire to be in control, even if it is intellectually obvious that such a desire is impossible. Yet humans continue to be crushed and resentful when their plans are thwarted, when those on whom they depended fail, and especially when death yanks down the polite curtain of denial with which they try to hide it. LISA D. MAUGANS DRIVER

God does not promise in every instance to change things for us; sometimes we are changed for things. And a large part of our faithfulness is the wisdom to perceive the difference!

MICHAEL MORGAN

RESPONSE

What are the names you use for God?

PRAYER

I will praise the LORD as long as I live; I will sing praises to my God all my life long (Ps. 146:2). Amen.

✦ WEDNESDAY ✦

Psalm 146

REFLECTION

Psalm 146 is one of the Alleluia Psalms, exhorting us to praise God—a common thread throughout the book. But here the psalmist not only gives the imperative to the listeners, "Praise the Lord!" but echoes the words internally, "Praise the Lord, O my soul!" How can we command others to do what we ourselves are not willing to do?   MICHAEL MORGAN

Accordingly, praise is more than an isolated act that takes place quickly and over a very short time. It is durative and continuous, and envelops the continuum of life. To be sure, praise of God is a fundamental commitment of life, no less essential to the faithful than oxygen is to the lungs.

LOUIS STULMAN

At its core the psalm is a meditation on what it means to praise God throughout life. It addresses sustaining life commitments that shape attitude, behavior, worldview, and character; in other words, it attends to the building blocks of spirituality.

LOUIS STULMAN

RESPONSE

Breathe slowly in, breathe slowly out; remembering that the same Greek word means "Spirit" and "breath."

PRAYER

(Breath prayer, repeated several times as you breathe in and out) Praise the Lord! Praise the Lord, O my soul! (Ps. 146:1) Amen.

✢ THURSDAY ✢

Hebrews 9:11–14

REFLECTION

The ritual of sacrifice was a means of enshrining, within a highly structured practice, a broader theological concept with which we are all familiar: the idea that everything ultimately belongs to God. When we return to God some small portion of what we have (whether it be grain or animals or time or money), we are underscoring our belief that what we have is not actually ours. It already belongs to God, and we return a portion of it to God as a sign and reminder of that reality.

DAVID S. CUNNINGHAM

As a repeated and habitual action on the part of worshipers, sacrifice is not necessarily a bad thing. Our sacrifices today do not make use of the blood of goats and the ashes of a heifer; but just as those were valuable assets in an agricultural economy, so do we do something similar when we sacrifice time, money, and energy in order to reach out to those in need—or when we offer up our "sacrifice of thanksgiving and praise" in worship.

DAVID S. CUNNINGHAM

RESPONSE

How are we challenged to respond to the pressing needs of the world around us? As a church and as a nation, what are our responsibilities to the rest of the world? GINGER GRAB

PRAYER

O LORD, our Sovereign, how majestic is your name in all the earth! (Ps. 8:1) Amen.

✦ FRIDAY ✦

Hebrews 9:11–14

REFLECTION

A mark of Christian life is this ongoing creative tension
between love of holy places and the conviction that, in the end,
place doesn't matter. ROGER A. FERLO

If our holy places become centers of pilgrimage, it is not
because they are intrinsically holy. These places are holy—
whether a grand basilica in Rome or a storefront church in
Poughkeepsie—because of what happened in them and what
continues to happen in them. ROGER A. FERLO

RESPONSE

Are we as Christians required, for example, to make sacrifices
to alleviate the injustice caused by massive extreme poverty?
If so, what would such sacrifices look like, and how might we
make them? GINGER GRAB

PRAYER

Holy, holy, holy, Lord God Almighty, early in the morning, and
late into the night, my song of praise shall rise to thee! Amen.

✦ SATURDAY ✦

Mark 12:28–34

REFLECTION

To love the neighbor cannot mean that one gives all of oneself to the neighbor; to do so would be an act of idolatry. The priority of the first command places appropriate limits on what neighbor love can require of us. Moreover, neighbor love is fundamentally disinterested and, unlike erotic love and friendship, does not depend on the admirable traits of or my personal relationship with my neighbor.   VICTOR MCCRACKEN

The scribe, in attempting to love God with heart and soul, with mind and strength, loves religion less. For the moment and in Jesus' presence, he has put his whole trust in the unity of the God revealed in Scripture's greatest commandment, rather than in the religious practices and pronouncements prescribed by human authorities that divide.   CYNTHIA A. JARVIS

RESPONSE

Name a way you love God with your heart, and with your soul, and with your might, and with your mind.

PRAYER

I love you, God, with my heart, my soul, my might, and my mind. Amen.

✤ SUNDAY ✦

Ruth 1:1–18

REFLECTION

For a Moabite—and one who had been a part of a mixed marriage with a Hebrew man—to set foot in Bethlehem would have been to set off all the cultural, social, and religious detectors of the time. Leaving Moab, Ruth would face not only a language barrier, a food barrier, a social etiquette barrier, and a religious practice barrier; she would also face the constant subtle and not-so-subtle reminders that she was "not one of us."

GARY W. CHARLES

Psalm 146

REFLECTION

The God who reaches out to the most vulnerable in society (oppressed, hungry, prisoners, blind, bowed down, strangers, widows, and orphans) insists that people follow this example. Jesus assured doubters of his divine mandate by appealing to these very signs within his ministry (e.g., Matt. 11:2–6).

LISA D. MAUGANS DRIVER

God, the creator and ever creating Lord, is alone worthy of our soul's trust and gratitude. This God, in whom we live, move, and have our being, is the source of our life and deepest sense of joy.

MARY DONOVAN TURNER

Hebrews 9:11–14

REFLECTION

God in Christ can now be worshiped anywhere and anytime—whenever Christians gather at table, break bread, pour wine, all in remembrance of him.

ROGER A. FERLO

The result of Christ's sacrifice is the purification of the conscience "from dead works" to "worship the living God." The inner effect in the conscience can be seen as a result of the forgiveness of sins. The purification of the conscience opens the door to free and authentic worship of the living God. Christians do not worship in order to have freedom or to clean their consciences. They worship because these gifts have already been granted them by God's grace in Christ's giving of himself.

DAVID CORTÉS-FUENTES

Mark 12:28–34

REFLECTION

Mark (and Leviticus) does not put special emphasis on "loving oneself" in a therapeutic sense. He expects, in a common-sense way, that everyone begins with loving himself or herself. While he would frown on self-loathing, he here accentuates the love of neighbor, introducing "oneself" as a comparative measure for "how much one should love one's neighbor."

A. K. M. ADAM

The words that in ancient Israel called forth love and compassion for the widow, orphan, foreigner, poor, or slave are the words of the Gospel, proclaimed today to call forth love for migrants, poor and homeless people, the victims of ecological and economic injustice, and those ravaged by disease, war, and violence.

LINCOLN E. GALLOWAY

RESPONSE

Recall a time when you ate a meal with people you loved and you recognized it as a holy time.

PRAYER

This is the day that you have made. I rejoice and am very glad in it! Amen.

❧ *Proper 27* ❦

Ruth 3:1–5; 4:13–17

Then the women said to Naomi, "Blessed be the LORD, who has not left you this day without next-of-kin; and may his name be renowned in Israel! He shall be to you a restorer of life and a nourisher of your old age; . . . The women of the neighborhood gave him a name, saying, "A son has been born to Naomi." They named him Obed; he became the father of Jesse, the father of David. (4:14–15b, 17)

Psalm 127

Unless the LORD builds the house,
    those who build it labor in vain.
Unless the LORD guards the city,
    the guard keeps watch in vain. (v. 1)

Hebrews 9:24–28

But as it is, he has appeared once for all at the end of the age to remove sin by the sacrifice of himself. And just as it is appointed for mortals to die once, and after that the judgment, so Christ, having been offered once to bear the sins of many, will appear a second time, not to deal with sin, but to save those who are eagerly waiting for him. (vv. 26b–28)

Mark 12:38–44

As he taught, [Jesus] said, "Beware of the scribes, who like to walk around in long robes, and to be greeted with respect in the marketplaces, and to have the best seats in the synagogues and places of honor at banquets! They devour widows' houses and for the sake of appearance say long prayers. They will receive the greater condemnation." (vv. 38–40)

✣ MONDAY ✣

Ruth 3:1–5; 4:13–17

REFLECTION

Ruth is able to find inclusion. She is able to be seen, embraced, and provided for in a system that she approached as an outsider. . . . Ruth is also a model of a way of life, which is what allows her a way in and a way toward acceptance in the covenant community. This way of life is reflected in its ideal as one of loyalty and trust, connection, and interdependence.

MARCIA MOUNT SHOOP

Normally, we associate hospitality with being able to offer something tangible, like food or shelter. But Ruth is destitute. She has no food or shelter to offer. So she offers the only thing she has left—her own continued presence.

MARTIN B. COPENHAVER

God never intervenes directly in the book of Ruth. Though God's hand is behind the plot, the narrator chooses to tell this story through the faithful actions of the story's characters.

FRANK M. YAMADA

RESPONSE

Where is the Holy in happy endings or in the rich human tapestry that displays our best visions? How is God unseen but never absent? In what ways is God full of surprises down the road, the keeper of ultimate promises? G. MALCOLM SINCLAIR

PRAYER

You are a God of surprises, and grace. You keep us ever guessing, yet your promise is ever sure. Amen.

✣ TUESDAY ✣

Ruth 3:1–5; 4:13–17

REFLECTION

In following Naomi, Ruth is not making a heroic choice as much as she is simply living out her fidelity to the one who has been given to her. Naomi keeps trying to reason with Ruth. But for Ruth there is nothing to talk about, because she does not approach this as a decision. This theme returns again in the concluding verses as Naomi and Ruth—who are, after all, unrelated—care for one another with the fidelity usually reserved for family. MARTIN B. COPENHAVER

The family and the church are both places where we have opportunity to learn to live with people we did not choose. Our fidelity to those we are stuck with can be a reflection of the fidelity of a God who is stuck with us all. . . . God's fidelity is beyond a choice. Such fidelity simply is an expression of who God is. MARTIN B. COPENHAVER

RESPONSE

Where is God in times of upheaval? What is sacred in tragedy and reversal of fortune? How does the Deity speak through unshakable loyalties, gut feelings, and canny decisions? G. MALCOLM SINCLAIR

PRAYER

Give me a heart faithful to those whose lives I impact, and to you, O God! Amen.

→ WEDNESDAY ←

Psalm 127

REFLECTION

It doesn't make a difference if we find a way to squeeze more time out of our day by staying up later to get work done, or rising early in the morning to start the day before the sun is up. . . . Our work is first God's work. We are merely instruments of God's work, which started long before we were born, and which will continue long after we are gone.

KATE FOSTER CONNORS

A people whose faith is capable of generating new life will remain confident in times of trouble. . . . All our worship, work, and witness, all our service, ministry, and mission efforts are in vain unless God is always and already at work.

MICHAEL PASQUARELLO III

First, God builds the house. Second, God watches over the city. Third, God provides while God's people sleep. The psalm effects what it claims by situating its singers in ordinary life, recalling the goodness of God's providential activity while acknowledging the primary place of God's working. It is God who ultimately builds, protects, and provides in, beneath, and through all human work and effort. MICHAEL PASQUARELLO III

RESPONSE

If you consider that your work is God's work, and God's work is your work, how does that change the way you go about your daily responsibilities?

PRAYER

You are greater than anything that threatens me at any time in any way. May I always remember this truth. Amen.

✧ THURSDAY ✧

Hebrews 9:24–28

REFLECTION

The second coming is not a day of judgment to be feared, but a day of salvation, again because of the "once for all" nature of Jesus' reconciling work.   JANE E. FAHEY

Christ has blazed a path for those who would follow him into the very presence of God. Not only that, but Christ enters into that holy space to intercede for us. We now have a champion in heaven, someone to advocate for us in the highest court.

ELIZABETH B. FORNEY

Sin is still a reality, but so now is forgiveness. We no longer belong to a fear-based community. Instead, we find that confession becomes a regular part of our life together, because revenge and punishment need no longer be feared. Just as the child who is certain of a parent's love will come forward in trust and security rather than hide in shame, so we move toward one another and God. Forgiveness engenders intimacy between both God and neighbor.   ELIZABETH B. FORNEY

RESPONSE

Our relationship with God is no longer an issue with God; it's an eternal reality—so why should it be an issue with us?

PETER M. WALLACE

PRAYER

In Christ's presence, I am brought into the holiest place of worship, no matter where I am. How marvelous this is! Amen.

✢ FRIDAY ✢

Mark 12:38–44

REFLECTION

Sacrifice is a dangerous notion. It is dangerous because we often ask those who are the most vulnerable to give the most.

EMILIE M. TOWNES

At times, it seems that sacrifice is best when someone else is doing it. We marvel at such figures as Mother Teresa, the families of slain or injured soldiers, and teachers in tough inner-city schools. We lift them high on the pedestal with the poor widow, keeping them distinct and distant from our daily lives. The focus is on their giving and the inadequacy of ours— but nothing changes. This is one of the problems of things we put on pedestals. We do not imagine ourselves alongside them because what they represent for us is often more than we can give or more than we can imagine we are capable of giving.

EMILIE M. TOWNES

RESPONSE

As you think through this passage, what ideas, images, stories, concepts come to mind when you think of offering as being personal?

EMILIE M. TOWNES

PRAYER

I honor those who give their entire selves to you, our Savior; and I long to be one who does this in my own life. Amen.

✣ SATURDAY ✣

Mark 12:38–44

REFLECTION

Jesus does not condemn only those who are aware of how they benefit from systems of violence and oppression. Jesus condemns any who benefit from such systems, whether they are aware or not. Ignorance is no excuse here.

RODGER Y. NISHIOKA

Reflection alone is not enough. Reflection must lead to specific and sustained action by engaging spiritual practices that challenge political and economic systems in the church, the nation, and the world. Feeding the hungry and providing clothing are important spiritual practices, but the church must come to view these practices as more than programs. The church must come to understand these practices as the very life flowing out of its worship. RODGER Y. NISHIOKA

RESPONSE

Could it reinforce the call of Christ to the church to give the whole of its life for the sake of those who do not deserve such a gift? PETE PEERY

PRAYER

Forgive me for the times I have held back that which already belongs to you. Amen.

→ SUNDAY ←

Ruth 3:1–5; 4:13–17

REFLECTION

The Ruth story is a firebreak between the lush, green aspirations of the whole tribe and the consuming flames of the powerful few. It calls for us to remember that God works every day. God labors on the ground, in the heart, among the folk, and through life circumstances. God weaves simple gestures, feelings, decisions, and actions in ways that bring good things. All this arises despite loss and trouble, opposition and tyranny, displacement and pain. That is huge. It shakes the powerful. It undermines the chain of command. It short-circuits the big plans of the few. It elevates the tender and dirt-real lives of the many.   G. MALCOLM SINCLAIR

Psalm 127

REFLECTION

Just as the psalmist makes it clear that our work is, in actuality, not our work at all, but God's work, the psalmist also seems to be trying to underscore that God is sovereign even in matters as seemingly personal as childbearing. The parts of our lives that are the most ordinary, and the parts of our lives that are the most extraordinary, are indeed a matter of God's concern.

KATE FOSTER CONNORS

Hebrews 9:24–28

REFLECTION

Looming over much religion is the idea of judgment, that people must ultimately stand before God and account for themselves. A great deal of religious energy, therefore, is spent figuring out how to make ourselves acceptable to God in the coming judgment. In this part of the passage, the writer of Hebrews indicates that the offering of Christ makes this obsession with judgment moot. In Christ, sin has already been extinguished, and lasting forgiveness has been granted. So Christians do not have to dread the future, watching fearfully for God the judge. God's future is one of salvation and redemption.   THOMAS G. LONG

Mark 12:38–44

REFLECTION

The widow's offering demonstrates her total trust in God.
                                                ROBERT A. BRYANT

Does Jesus point to the poor widow who gives her last two coins to the temple as a model for giving? Or does Jesus point to her because she is a tragic example of how religious institutions suck the life out of people?   PETE PEERY

This widow offers a glimpse into what Jesus is about. He is on the way to giving "the whole of his life" for something that is corrupt and condemned: all of humanity, the whole world. Jesus calls the disciples, the church, to himself and points out this poor widow and her manner of giving. Watching her will not lead to unvarnished support for religious institutions.
                                                        PETE PEERY

RESPONSE

Aside from the place where you worship in a congregation, where are the sanctuaries where you are brought into the presence of God?

PRAYER

Lord, prepare me to be a place of sanctuary for your Spirit. Amen.

❦ *Proper 28* ❦

1 Samuel 1:4–20

But Hannah answered, "No, my lord, I am a woman
deeply troubled; I have drunk neither wine nor strong drink,
but I have been pouring out my soul before the LORD. Do not
regard your servant as a worthless woman, for I have been
speaking out of my great anxiety and vexation all this time."
Then Eli answered, "Go in peace; the God of Israel grant
the petition you have made to him." (vv. 15–17)

1 Samuel 2:1–10
(The Song of Hannah)

Hannah prayed and said,
"My heart exults in the LORD;
my strength is exalted in my God.
My mouth derides my enemies,
because I rejoice in my victory.
There is no Holy One like the LORD." (vv. 1–2a)

Hebrews 10:11–14 (15–18), 19–25

Let us hold fast to the confession of our hope without wavering,
for he who has promised is faithful. And let us consider how to
provoke one another to love and good deeds, not neglecting to meet
together, as is the habit of some, but encouraging one another, and
all the more as you see the Day approaching. (vv. 23–25)

Mark 13:1–8

Then Jesus began to say to them, "Beware that no one leads you
astray. Many will come in my name and say, 'I am he!' and they
will lead many astray." (vv. 5–6)

✣ MONDAY ✣

1 Samuel 1:4–20

REFLECTION

When Hannah seeks out God's presence in this state of anguish, her prayer signals that she is aware of a divine concern for those who are of questionable cultural worth. She does not just come to God with formal petition. She does not come with traditional sacrifice. She comes in loneliness, isolation, and despair. She lays bare all the emotion and all the pain. Her disposition of prayer is a remarkable image of piety. Her "prayer of groaning" makes her an icon not simply of the mother of a son who is prophetic and powerful, but of a human being who knows herself to be known and loved by God.   MARCIA MOUNT SHOOP

That Hannah is inscribed with God's grace and love is embedded in the fact that she does not just ask and promise in her prayer; she also grieves, meditates, murmurs, and stands silent. She is there as her whole self—cultural baggage, broken dreams, audacious hope, and all.   MARCIA MOUNT SHOOP

The divine response to Hannah's distress points to God's compassion for those who suffer unjustly at the hands of others.

FRANK M. YAMADA

RESPONSE

How is Hannah's cry an act of faith?

PRAYER

I pray today for the unnamed women of the world who struggle with the despair of infertility. Amen.

✦ TUESDAY ✦

1 Samuel 2:1–10

REFLECTION

In every situation God's power is specifically guided by God's gracious wisdom and God's creative purposes. God acts powerfully in relation to every creature according to its nature and circumstances. With respect to the struggles of history, this means God acts in power to establish human freedom and nourish moral responsibility, as well as to maintain accountability for our use of power. THOMAS D. PARKER

In this text, the very personal story of a previously childless woman bearing a child becomes a symbol of hope for the entire community. In congregations too, the personal routinely becomes a matter of public concern. Grief following the death of a child or the unexpected death of an adult can develop into a call to the congregation to take action in the community (fighting cancer, eradicating gang violence, supporting and treating substance abusers, etc.). Births are routinely celebrated in congregations and can become symbols of new life for the entire community. The challenge—and the opportunity—for churches is to find ways in the liturgical life of the congregation to honor the personal and name the ways personal experiences of those in the congregation become symbolic for the entire community. KATE FOSTER CONNORS

RESPONSE

What does God's stand for the oppressed mean for those of us in a nation perceived by many other nations as the oppressor? KATE FOSTER CONNORS

PRAYER

When I see an act of oppression, give me the courage to speak up, and to speak out. Amen.

Hebrews 10:11–14 (15–18), 19–25

REFLECTION

As baptized and forgiven people, believers need not be crippled by guilt or fear, but can live before God with confidence.

JANE E. FAHEY

The people must gather for mutual encouragement and support. The gift of Christ is not one that we receive and keep to ourselves. It is meant for the building of the whole body.

ELIZABETH B. FORNEY

The writer shows how completely Christ accomplished eternal atonement "by a single sacrifice for sins" by picturing Christ as sitting down and waiting. One can almost see the Lord dusting his hands with an attitude of "mission accomplished" (in this case rightly so) and slumping into an easy chair with a satisfied sigh.

PETER M. WALLACE

RESPONSE

Have you ever been selfish with sharing the good news of Jesus Christ by keeping it to yourself?

PRAYER

If I can encourage someone today, give me eyes and ears to be aware of who that is. Amen.

✦ THURSDAY ✦

Hebrews 10:11–14 (15–18), 19–25

REFLECTION

Jesus walked right into the fire of human pain, and while
ordinary human beings allow the trouble of life to twist and
distort them—into victims, oppressors, or a combination of the
two—Jesus' suffering shaped him into a perfect offering.

THOMAS G. LONG

Worshipers do not need to slink into the sanctuary as guilty and
unworthy sinners. In baptism, their bodies were washed clean
and their hearts were made new (v. 22), and by the sacrifice of
Christ they have become blood brothers and sisters of Jesus.
They can therefore walk into church confidently, knowing that
to the eye of God they appear as pure and sinless as the Christ
who claims them as his own (vv. 19–22).   THOMAS G. LONG

RESPONSE

Do you feel confident in the belief that Christ sees you as pure
and sinless? If not, what holds you back?

PRAYER

Free me from the doubt I have in my own worthiness. Amen.

✢ FRIDAY ✢

Mark 13:1–8

REFLECTION

Salvation is a process of repentance, forgiveness, and new birth, and not a static event in our lives. EMILIE M. TOWNES

Think through the many ways those who will hear this passage experience the need, the yearning, for God's grace through salvation as they face incredible—and what can often feel like (and may actually be) insurmountable—obstacles that seem to make the freedom of salvation a utopian pipe dream, rather than an act of radical witness and faithfulness.

EMILIE M. TOWNES

Evil is rampant in the world, it affects the earth itself, and it produces its own terror. But God's judgment and rescue are sure. ROBERT A. BRYANT

RESPONSE

Define "salvation" in your own words.

PRAYER

Lead me through the valleys of the shadows in times of trial. Amen.

☙ SATURDAY ❧

Mark 13:1–8

REFLECTION

Towering buildings are not supposed to crumble to the ground.
Oceans are not supposed to leap out of their seabeds and
flood miles inland. The ground is not supposed to shake and
undulate. The sky is not supposed to form a funnel cloud and
destroy a town. Yet all who have watched the World Trade
Towers collapse, seen a tsunami flood a nation, experienced
an earthquake, or suffered through the power of a tornado
know that such events happen. Those who provide care for the
victims report that all express a profound sense of loss. Not
only have they lost loved ones and property, but in a deep and
abiding sense they have lost their innocence. They now know
that something they once believed to be sure—that a towering
structure would stand forever, for instance, or that the ocean
would stay securely in its seabed—is no longer trustworthy.
They have lost a foundational belief upon which they once built
their lives. No longer will they be able to step on the ground
without wondering, if only for a moment, whether the ground
is going to remain stable. No longer will they be able to look up
into a darkening sky without wondering if a destructive storm
is on its way.   RODGER Y. NISHIOKA

RESPONSE

Which historical catastrophes have caused you to wonder about
the ways of God in the world?

PRAYER

When it seems the world has fallen into pieces, help me find my
center in you. Amen.

1 Samuel 1:4–20

REFLECTION

At church, strange seeds are planted in the soul. As they germinate, their hosts begin to look forward, beyond one life span, beyond one set of preoccupations, beyond one political agenda, beyond personal laundry lists of hopes and fears. Promised children wait in the wings of tomorrow. They are pressing to be born. They will need witnesses, nurses, and midwives. They will require protectors, singers of songs, keepers of their story, advocates to the broader community, and companions for the hills and valleys that are sure to come.

G. MALCOLM SINCLAIR

1 Samuel 2:1–10

REFLECTION

God's people live out of the past and into the future, a future that has been promised but is yet to be fully realized. We always need to offer thanks and praise to God, to acknowledge gifts graciously given, and to hope in God's continuing and surprising provision for the future.   MICHAEL PASQUARELLO III

Hebrews 10:11–14 (15–18), 19–25

REFLECTION

Let us enter into and experience God's presence fully, honestly, authentically—knowing we are wholly clean and pure and accepted and even desired (v. 22). Let us luxuriate in God's loving, accepting presence, soaking it up. But let us not get stuck there. . . . Let us believe and exercise our faith boldly, following the example of Christ, who will be faithful to his promises (v. 23). . . . Let us be creative in provoking and encouraging and pushing and pulling all those in our family of faith to "love and good deeds" (v. 24). This is all about participating in the body of Christ, working with and for and through others in the family of faith. This point speaks more directly to the gospel of Christ as our model and mentor. We are not mere spectators of God's work or simple recipients of God's grace: we are active participants in the saving work of God in the world, as we follow Christ's ultimate example of sacrificial giving, serving, and loving until the very end.

PETER M. WALLACE

Mark 13:1–8

REFLECTION

So how does one survive the devastation of an aggressive cancer diagnosis or other illness, the crashing down of a building, or the aftermath of a natural disaster? How does one survive the loss of innocence? How does one live in the midst of competing voices, all full of passionate intensity, claiming that these are signs of the end of the age? Our focus must not be on the signs themselves, but rather on the one who is to come—the one who enables us to look up after such devastation and claim the certainty of blessing. Things may seem to have fallen apart. It may appear that anarchy has been loosed on the world. Nevertheless, the center will hold and—much to our amazement—we will discover that we have much faithful work to do.

RODGER Y. NISHIOKA

RESPONSE

How do you respond to this verse in Hebrews: "And let us consider how to provoke one another to love and good deeds, not neglecting to meet together, as is the habit of some, but encouraging one another"?

PRAYER

There is no Holy One like the LORD, no one besides you; there is no Rock like our God (1 Sam. 2:2). Amen.

❧ *Proper 29* ❦

(Reign of Christ)

2 Samuel 23:1–7

Is not my house like this with God?
    For he has made with me an everlasting covenant,
    ordered in all things and secure. (v. 5)

Psalm 132:1–12 (13–18)

For the LORD has chosen Zion;
    he has desired it for his habitation:
"This is my resting place forever;
    here I will reside, for I have desired it.
I will abundantly bless its provisions;
    I will satisfy its poor with bread." (vv. 13–15)

Revelation 1:4b–8

"I am the Alpha and the Omega," says the Lord God, who is
and who was and who is to come, the Almighty. (v. 8)

John 18:33–37

Jesus answered, "My kingdom is not from this world. If my
kingdom were from this world, my followers would be fighting
to keep me from being handed over to the Jews. But as it is, my
kingdom is not from here." Pilate asked him, "So you are a king?"
Jesus answered, "You say that I am a king. For this I was born, and
for this I came into the world, to testify to the truth. Everyone who
belongs to the truth listens to my voice." (vv. 36–37)

⇥ MONDAY ⇤

2 Samuel 23:1–7

REFLECTION

On the cusp of a new church year it seems fitting to utter the
best words we can, those truest, noblest, cleanest, and closest to
the heart. Such words are wide and hold open the door to the
wideness of the mystery being born.   G. MALCOLM SINCLAIR

This song indicates the character of God-conscious rule when
it is true to its proper or created nature—and its proper nature
is characterized by the kind of justice and mercy that God so
freely pours out on God's people.   MARCIA MOUNT SHOOP

Might does not make right in God's kingdom, but justice and
mercy and love abound.   MARCIA MOUNT SHOOP

When one sees one's gifts as issuing from God, as David clearly
does, then celebrating them is not an act of pride as much as it
is an expression of gratitude and praise.

MARTIN B. COPENHAVER

RESPONSE

How else can we leave those we care about, unless we entrust
them to the care of God? That is, after all, what the word "good-
bye" means—"God be with you." What else can be said in
parting that does not simply wither and fall at our feet as soon
as it is said?   MARTIN B. COPENHAVER

PRAYER

Help us in our good-byes, both to mourn and to hope at the
same time. Amen.

✦ TUESDAY ✦

Psalm 132:1–12 (13–18)

REFLECTION

The "house of God" was a location, not a limitation.

THOMAS D. PARKER

Where in the world is God? Both the synagogue and the church answer, everywhere! This is the first thing. God is omnipresent. The power and wisdom of God are active in everything that is, bringing it to being and sustaining it during its time, upholding the unfolding universe, lending it beauty and meaning. "The whole earth is full of his glory" (Isa. 6:3). Everything speaks in voices without words.

THOMAS D. PARKER

On this day of Christ the King, the One whose glory illumines all our days, the church is prompted to praise God for God's great faithfulness, to claim God's promises, and to proclaim the blessings of God's rule for the whole creation.

MICHAEL PASQUARELLO III

RESPONSE

What images come to mind when you hear the words "the house of God"?

PRAYER

O Lord, remember in our favor all that we have endured, and give us relief when it is most needed. Amen.

Psalm 132:1–12 (13–18)

REFLECTION

Where on earth does God dwell? The psalm identifies the dwelling place of God in the city of Jerusalem, perched on the lip of western Asia. It is a sacred place, a place people have found access to unsurpassable spiritual power and meaning. Are these places closer to God than others, or is it that in these places some have felt themselves touched by a divine power and love beyond the ordinary?   THOMAS D. PARKER

God cannot be confined to one exclusive location, but insists on being "God with us" in whatever exile we find ourselves in.

CAROL M. BECHTEL

RESPONSE

What do [your] patterns of behavior suggest about what/whom [you] worship as lord?   JANE E. FAHEY

PRAYER

I will not give sleep to my eyes or slumber to my eyelids, until I find a place for you, O Lord. Amen.

✢ THURSDAY ✢

Revelation 1:4b–8

REFLECTION

The worship life of the Christian community becomes part of
the work through which God is continuing to transform the
world. Message and medium merge.   JANE E. FAHEY

God's rule over the powers of sin and death in the world is
an "already" through the Christ event. By his death Jesus has
liberated believers from sin (v. 5b). The community experiences
the risen Christ's love in the present ("loves us" in v. 5b). And
as the "firstborn of the dead" (v. 5a), Jesus has inaugurated a
new creation. The "new earth" (21:1) is already on the way. But
God's rule is also a "not yet." There is more to come.

     JANE E. FAHEY

RESPONSE

What does it mean to be a "faithful witness" in a time of
alarming evidence of the destructive impact of human behavior
on God's creation?   JANE E. FAHEY

PRAYER

Let my first thought of the day and last thought at night be of
you, our Alpha and Omega. Amen.

✦ FRIDAY ✦

Revelation 1:4b–8

REFLECTION

This is a God who is served by a complete ensemble of spirits (again the number seven; see also 4:5 and 5:6) and who holds all time—past, present, and future—in the divine hand. To know that this God rules eternally provides reassurance and confidence for those who have fallen under the wheel of a seemingly indifferent history.   THOMAS G. LONG

After asking readers to look up into the heavenly realm, John next asks them to look forward into the future: "Look! He is coming with the clouds; every eye will see him" (1:7–8).What is now visible only to the eyes of faith—that Christ is the Alpha and Omega of human history and the Lord of all—will one day be known by the whole cosmos, saint and foe alike.
                                    THOMAS G. LONG

We reflect within our everyday spheres John's threefold description of Christ: (1) we follow Christ's example as a faithful witness; (2) we seek ardently to understand his will for us, to deny ourselves, and take up our crosses and serve others sacrificially; and (3) we make it our life's goal to bring others into his reign of love and praise, which will last forever.
                                    PETER M. WALLACE

RESPONSE

So, how do we live under the reign of Christ the King? How do we operate as priests who serve God?   PETER M. WALLACE

PRAYER

I seek to be one who both lives and conveys your truth. Amen.

✣ SATURDAY ✣

John 18:33–37

REFLECTION

Though important in helping establish and maintain many social norms, intellectual truth does not fill all of our needs. We are compelled to go beyond merely understanding and making sense and order in our world. We must seek to know God and live as active witnesses on this journey into God. Jesus' life and mission is a model of this for us. In Jesus, we learn that truth is a stimulant for faithful living and witness, rather than only a matter for contemplation. It is something we do.

EMILIE M. TOWNES

Freedom, change, and spontaneity coalesce so that we not only accept responsibility for the world round us but seek to be a part of God's transformation of the world.   EMILIE M. TOWNES

RESPONSE

What is right and what is wrong in your attitudes about yourself and others?

PRAYER

Continue your work of healing and restoration, and use me to be an encourager of your kingdom. Amen.

2 Samuel 23:1–7

REFLECTION

This passage encapsulates the nature of divine power in the way David meditates on his life. God has not determined everything that has happened in his life, but has urged David in the best possible direction. When human intention and action can cooperate with that goad toward divine justice and love, then God's Spirit shines more clearly, with the beautiful gleam "from the rain on the grassy land" (v. 4). God promised to work with David, to stay close to him as he made his way in the world. In that proximity of relationship is the potential for all of humanity to be sanctified in its purpose and best potential. David's walk through life is full of flaws, but God's promise is everlasting.   MARCIA MOUNT SHOOP

Psalm 132:1–12 (13–18)

REFLECTION

The ongoing activity of God in the world, ever life-giving, ever challenging, ever leading to a future of hope and promise, does not cease. The faithful trust that God is still there for them.

THOMAS D. PARKER

Revelation 1:4b–8

REFLECTION

Today's passage from Revelation invites us to reflect more deeply on just what we expect of Christ's return. Often we hear it spoken of in great anticipation. In the final page of this book John himself prays, "Come, Lord Jesus" (Rev. 22:20). John gives voice to a longing to be in the real presence of Christ, having no longer to survive on faith alone—even if that presence is one

that causes us to wail as we are transformed into the likeness of
Christ.   ELIZABETH B. FORNEY

John 18:33–37

REFLECTION

On this Sunday, the church proclaims Christ the King. The
church announces that it bows only to Jesus the Christ. The
church declares that it does not give allegiance to any other
person, principality, or power claiming to be sovereign. Yet
will the church live out its profession? Forever fearful in this
increasingly post-Christian era of losing members and thus
losing influence in the community, does the church temper
its message and its mission in a desperate effort to maintain
position?   PETE PEERY

By looking deeply, we must look at what is right and wrong in
our actions and attitudes toward others and within ourselves.
This means that we challenge ourselves to look beyond what
we think to the truth found in God as represented by Jesus. The
truth that Jesus represents is found in God, who is love and
grace.   EMILIE M. TOWNES

RESPONSE

In your opinion, has the church lived out its profession? What
new venues must congregations take in order to meet changing
society?

PRAYER

In a world that continues to need the truth, let your Truth set
our hearts free. Amen.

Contributors

Numbers in italic are page numbers on which each contributor's refelection can be found.

Charles L. Aaron Jr., Pastor, First United Methodist Church, Farmersville, Texas; *8, 12, 174.* **A. K. M. Adam**, Professor of New Testament, Seabury-Western Theological Seminary, Evanston, Illinois; *516, 523, 532.* **Harry B. Adams**, Professor Emeritus, Yale Divinity School, Hamden, Connecticut; *462, 470, 471, 482.* **Marilyn McCord Adams**, Canon, Christ Church Cathedral, and Regius Professor of Divinity, Oxford University, Oxford, United Kingdom; *163.* **Stephen P. Ahearne-Kroll**, Associate Professor of New Testament, Methodist Theological School in Ohio, Delaware, Ohio; *365.* **John Ahn**, Assistant Professor of Old Testament, Austin Presbyterian Theological Seminary, Austin, Texas; *525.* **Ronald J. Allen**, Nettie Sweeney and Hugh Th. Miller Professor of Preaching and New Testament, Christian Theological Seminary, Indianapolis, Indiana; *163, 171.* **Wm. Loyd Allen**, Professor of Church History and Spiritual Formation, McAfee School of Theology, Atlanta, Georgia; *156, 162.* **Carmelo Álvarez**, Affiliate Professor of Church History and Theology, Christian Theological Seminary, Indianapolis, Indiana; *272, 273, 284, 291, 293.* **Dale P. Andrews**, Martin Luther King Jr. Professor of Homiletics and Pastoral Theology, Boston University School of Theology, Boston, Massachusetts; *517, 525.* **Susan R. Andrews**, Executive Presbyter, Hudson River Presbytery, Scarborough, New York; *488, 491, 497, 500, 506, 509.* **Anne H. K. Apple**, Parish Associate, Idlewild Presbyterian Church, Memphis, Tennessee; *104, 109, 113, 114, 121, 122.* **Tom Are Jr.**, Pastor, Village Presbyterian Church, Prairie Village, Kansas; *378, 382, 386, 387, 396, 400.* **Talitha Arnold**, Senior Minister, United Church of Santa Fe, New Mexico; *8, 12, 13, 17, 21, 22.* **William V. Arnold**, Pastor to Senior Adults, Bryn Mawr Presbyterian Church, Bryn Mawr, Pennsylvania; *52, 64, 70, 71.* **Loye Bradley Ashton**, Assistant Professor of Religious Studies, Tougaloo College, Tougaloo, Mississippi; *434, 435, 443, 452.*

Scott Bader-Saye, Associate Professor, University of Scranton, Scranton, Pennsylvania; *8, 20, 26.* **Randall C. Bailey**, Andrew W. Mellon Professor of Hebrew Bible, Interdenominational Theological Center, Atlanta, Georgia; *31.* **Lee Barrett**, Mary B. and Henry P. Stager Professor of Theology, Lancaster Theological Seminary, Lancaster, Pennsylvania; *79, 88, 97.* **David L. Bartlett**, Professor of New Testament, Columbia Theological Seminary, Decatur, Georgia; *14, 18, 25, 27, 132, 154, 253.* **Woody Bartlett**, Episcopal Diocese of Atlanta, Atlanta, Georgia; *210.* **Jouette M. Bassler**, Professor Emerita of New Testament, Perkins School of Theology, Southern Methodist University, Dallas, Texas; *193, 202.* **Michael Battle**, Rector, Church of Our Savior, San Gabriel, California; *215, 221.* **Eugene C. Bay**, President, Colgate Rochester Crozer Divinity School, Rochester, New York; *29, 35 38.* **Timothy A. Beach-Verhey**, Copastor, Faison Presbyterian Church, Faison, North Carolina; *77, 85, 94, 99.* **Carol M. Bechtel**, Professor of Old Testament, Western Theological Seminary, Holland, Michigan; *554.* **Dianne Bergant, CSA**, Professor of Old Testament Studies, Catholic Theological Union, Chicago, Illinois; *162, 165.* **Jon L. Berquist**, President, Disciples Seminary Foundation, Claremont, California; *220.* **C. Clifton Black**, Otto A. Piper Professor of Biblical Theology, Princeton Theological Seminary, Princeton, New Jersey; *489, 500.* **Nancy R. Blakely**, Chaplain, Hospice of the Upstate, Pelzer, South Carolina; *245, 246, 263, 264.* **Dave Bland**, Professor of Homiletics, Harding University Graduate School of Religion, Memphis, Tennessee; *81, 90, 95, 99.* **Ruth L. Boling**, Minister of Word and Sacrament, Presbyterian Church (U.S.A.), Forest Hills, New York; *459, 463, 472, 476, 477.* **Donald Booz**, District Executive, Church of the Brethren, Mid-Atlantic District, Ellicott City, Maryland; *3, 160.* **Kathleen Bostrom**,

Copastor, Wildwood Presbyterian Church, Grayslake, Illinois; *486, 495, 496, 499, 504.* **Lee W. Bowman**, Senior Pastor, First Presbyterian Church, Lexington, Kentucky; *24.* **Richard Boyce**, Associate Professor of Preaching and Pastoral Leadership, Union Presbyterian Seminary, Charlotte, North Carolina; *76, 81, 93, 99.* **Paul D. Brassey**, Director of Music Ministries, St. Mark Lutheran Church, Lacey, Washington; *4, 13.* **Christina Braudaway-Bauman**, Associate for New Clergy Development for the Massachusetts Conference, United Church of Christ, and Pastoral Residency Coordinator at Wellesley Congregational Church (United Church of Christ), Wellesley, Massachusetts; *227.* **William Brosend**, Associate Professor of Homiletics, School of Theology, Sewanee, the University of the South, Sewanee, Tennessee; *23, 24, 27.* **Elton W. Brown**, Pastor, Aurora/Hoyt Lakes United Methodist Parish, Aurora, Minnesota; *79, 80, 88, 89, 98, 100.* **Sally A. Brown**, Elizabeth M. Engle Associate Professor of Preaching and Worship, Princeton Theological Seminary, Princeton, New Jersey; *32.* **William P. Brown**, Professor of Old Testament, Columbia Theological Seminary, Decatur, Georgia; *3.* **Walter Brueggemann**, Professor Emeritus of Old Testament, Columbia Theological Seminary, Decatur, Georgia; *355, 374, 487, 496, 503.* **Robert A. Bryant**, Associate Professor of Religion, Presbyterian College, Clinton, South Carolina; *541, 547.* **John P. Burgess**, James Henry Snowden Professor of Systematic Theology, Pittsburgh Theological Seminary, Pittsburgh, Pennsylvania; *488, 497, 500, 505.* **Eberhard Busch**, Professor for Reformed Theology, University of Göttingen, Germany; *320.* **Jason Byassee**, Executive Director of Leadership Education at Duke Divinity and Director of the Center for Theology, Writing, and Media, Duke Divinity School, Durham, North Carolina; *490, 495, 503.*

Katherine C. Calore, Pastor, St. Stephen's Episcopal Church, Monett, Missouri; *48, 57, 72.* **Charles L. Campbell**, Professor of Homiletics, Duke University Divinity School, Durham, North Carolina; *5, 6, 208, 209, 211, 498, 507, 509.* **Cynthia M. Campbell**, President, McCormick Theological Seminary, Chicago, Illinois; *229, 238.* **Sam Candler**, Dean, The Cathedral of St. Philip, Atlanta, Georgia; *414.* **Paul E. Capetz**, Associate Professor of Historical Theology, United Theological Seminary of the Twin Cities, New Brighton, Minnesota; *484, 493.* **Carlos F. Cardoza-Orlandi**, Professor of Global Christianities and Mission Studies, Perkins School of Theology, Southern Methodist University, Dallas, Texas; *9, 129, 147, 148, 153, 404, 409, 415, 418, 423, 427.* **William J. Carl III**, President and Professor of Homiletics, Pittsburgh Theological Seminary, Pittsburgh, Pennsylvania; *102, 112, 120.* **Kenneth H. Carter Jr.**, Pastor, Providence United Methodist Church, Charlotte, North Carolina; *463, 466, 467, 472.* **Karen Chakoian**, Pastor, First Presbyterian Church, Granville, Ohio; *379, 392, 397.* **Gary W. Charles**, Pastor, Central Presbyterian Church, Atlanta, Georgia; *25, 107, 127, 136, 519, 531.* **Linda Lee Clader**, Dean of Academic Affairs and Professor of Homiletics, Church Divinity School of the Pacific, Berkeley, California; *38, 43.* **Jaime Clark-Soles**, Associate Professor of New Testament, Perkins School of Theology, Southern Methodist University, Dallas, Texas; *419, 424.* **Kimberly L. Clayton**, Director of Contextual Education, Columbia Theological Seminary, Decatur, Georgia; *49, 50, 58, 64.* **Ashley Cook Cleere**, Chaplain, Piedmont College, Demorest, Georgia; *34, 41, 46.* **Ronald Cole-Turner**, H. Parker Sharp Professor of Theology and Ethics, Pittsburgh Theological Seminary, Pittsburgh, Pennsylvania; *243, 244, 257, 262, 266.* **Elizabeth Conde-Frazier**, Associate Professor of Religious Education, Claremont School of Theology, Claremont, California; *229, 238.* **Andrew Foster Connors**, Pastor, Brown Memorial Park Avenue Presbyterian Church, Baltimore, Maryland; *349, 350, 364, 367, 368.* **Kate Foster Connors**, Parish Associate and Youth Director, Brown Memorial Park Avenue Presbyterian Church, Baltimore, Maryland; *536, 540, 544.* **Stephen A. Cooper**, Professor of Religious Studies, Franklin and Marshall College, Lancaster, Pennsylvania; *257.* **Shelley D. B. Copeland**, Executive Director, The Capitol Region Conference of Churches, Hartford, Connecticut; *53, 55, 61, 62, 73.* **Martin B.**

Copenhaver, Pastor, Wellesley Congregational Church, United Church of Christ, Wellesley, Massachusetts; *7, 9, 15, 16, 18, 534, 535, 552*. **David Cortés-Fuentes**, Associate Professor of New Testament, San Francisco Theological Seminary, Pasadena, California; *514, 522, 532*. **Charles B. Cousar**, Professor Emeritus, Columbia Theological Seminary, Decatur, Georgia; *230*. **David S. Cunningham**, Professor of Religion and Director, The Crossroads Project, Hope College, Holland, Michigan; *275, 281, 514, 521, 528*.

MaryAnn McKibben Dana, Associate Pastor, Burke Presbyterian Church, Springfield, Virginia; *156, 162*. **Lillian Daniel**, Senior Minister, First Congregational Church, United Church of Christ, Glen Ellyn, Illinois; *9, 15, 18*. **Kathy L. Dawson**, Associate Professor of Christian Education, Columbia Theological Seminary, Decatur, Georgia; *464, 469, 478, 479, 481*. **Patricia E. de Jong**, Senior Minister, First Congregational Church of Berkeley, Berkeley, California; *2, 8*. **Carol J. Dempsey, OP**, Professor of Theology (Biblical Studies), University of Portland, Oregon; *477*. **Richard S. Dietrich**, Minister, First Presbyterian Church, Staunton, Virginia; *301*. **Mark Douglas**, Associate Professor of Christian Ethics and Director of the MATS Program, Columbia Theological Seminary, Decatur, Georgia; *29, 38, 460, 469, 478*. **Lisa D. Maugans Driver**, Associate Professor of Theology, Valparaiso University, Valparaiso, Indiana; *512, 520, 526, 531*. **James O. Duke**, Professor of History of Christianity and History of Christian Thought, Brite Divinity School, Fort Worth, Texas; *332*.

Adam E. Eckhart, Associate Pastor, First United Church of Christ, Milford, Connecticut; *184, 193, 197, 198*. **Mark D. W. Edington**, Rector, St. Dunstan's Church, Dover, Massachusetts; *356, 363, 374*. **Stephen Edmondson**, Rector, St. Thomas Episcopal Church, McLean, Virginia; *391*. **Mark Barger Elliott**, Senior Minister, Mayflower Congregational Church, Grand Rapids, Michigan; *329, 338*. **P. C. Enniss**, Theologian in Residence, Trinity Presbyterian Church, Atlanta, Georgia; *109, 116, 124*. **Brian Erickson**, University Chaplain, University of Evansville, Evansville, Indiana; *158, 169*. **Noel Leo Erskine**, Professor of Theology and Ethics, Candler School of Theology, Emory University, Atlanta, Georgia; *292*. **Barbara J. Essex**, Minister for Higher Education and Theological Education, United Church of Christ, Cleveland, Ohio; *248, 255, 266, 270, 278, 279*.

Jane E. Fahey, Pastor, Druid Hills Presbyterian Church, Atlanta, Georgia; *537, 545, 554, 555*. **Clyde Fant**, Professor Emeritus, Religious Studies, Stetson University, DeLand, Florida; *96*. **Margaret A. Farley**, Gilbert L. Stark Professor Emerita of Christian Ethics, Yale Divinity School, New Haven, Connecticut; *220*. **Wendy Farley**, Professor, Department of Religion, Emory University, Atlanta, Georgia; *338, 345*. **Stephen Farris**, Dean, St. Andrew's Hall, and Professor of Homiletics, Vancouver School of Theology, Vancouver, British Columbia, Canada; *54, 67*. **Jane Anne Ferguson**, Associate Minister, First Plymouth Congregational Church, United Church of Christ, Englewood, Colorado; *168, 174*. **Roger A. Ferlo**, Associate Dean and Director for the Institute for Christian Formation and Leadership, Virginia Theological Seminary, Alexandria, Virginia; *522, 529, 531*. **Richard Floyd**, Pastor, Crystal Lake Presbyterian Church, Crystal Lake, Florida; *204, 216, 217*. **Margaret Ann Fohl**, Associate Pastor, Bryn Mawr Presbyterian Church, Bryn Mawr, Pennsylvania; *225*. **David Forney**, Pastor, First Presbyterian Church, Clarksville, Tennessee; *108, 111, 117, 120*. **Elizabeth B. Forney**, Minister of Word and Sacrament, Presbyterian Church (U.S.A.), Clarksville, Tennessee; *537, 545, 559*. **Thomas Edward Frank**, Professor of Religious Leadership and Administration and Director of Methodist Studies, Candler School of Theology, Emory University, Atlanta, Georgia; *485, 491, 502*. **Kent M. French**, Archie C. Epps Fellow, The Memorial Church–Harvard University, Cambridge, Massachusetts; *247, 256, 265*.

Lincoln E. Galloway, Associate Professor of Homiletics, Claremont School of Theology, Claremont, California; *516, 518, 523, 532*. **Ismael García**, Professor of Christian Ethics, Austin Presbyterian Theological Seminary, Austin, Texas; *274*. **Susan R. Garrett**, Professor of New Testament, Louisville Presbyterian Theological Seminary, Louisville, Kentucky; *33, 40, 45*. **Beverly Roberts Gaventa**, Helen H. P. Manson Professor of New Testament Literature and Exegesis, Princeton Theological Seminary, Princeton, New Jersey; *237*. **W. Hulitt Gloer**, Professor of Preaching, George W. Truett Theological Seminary, Waco, Texas; *181, 190*. **Ginger Grab**, Chaplain, Bard College, Tivoli, New York; *514, 518, 522, 528, 529*. **Mike Graves**, Wm. K. McElvaney Professor of Preaching, Saint Paul School of Theology, Kansas City, Missouri; *106, 107, 116, 118, 125*. **Garrett Green**, Professor Emeritus of Religious Studies, Connecticut College, New London, Connecticut; *360*.

Douglas John Hall, Professor Emeritus of Christian Theology, McGill University, Montreal, Quebec, Canada; *392*. **Paul L. Hammer**, Professor of New Testament (retired), Colgate Rochester Crozer Divinity School, Rochester, New York; *311, 320*. **Douglas R. A. Hare**, Wm. F. Orr Professor of New Testament Emeritus, Pittsburgh Theological Seminary, Pittsburgh, Pennsylvania; *444*. **J. S. Randolph Harris**, Pastor, Highland Presbyterian Church, Winston-Salem, North Carolina; *485, 490, 493, 494, 502*. **J. Barney Hawkins IV**, Executive Director of the Center for Anglican Communion Studies and Professor of Parish Ministry, Virginia Theological Seminary, Alexandria, Virginia; *299, 306*. **Christopher B. Hays**, D. Wilson Moore Assistant Professor of Ancient Near Eastern Studies, Fuller Theological Seminary, Pasadena, California; *57, 66*. **Michael G. Hegeman**, Coordinator of the Engle Institute of Preaching, Princeton Theological Seminary, Princeton, New Jersey; *491, 506*. **Susan T. Henry-Crowe**, Dean of Cannon Chapel and Religious Life, Emory University, Atlanta, Georgia; *430, 439, 445, 448*. **William R. Herzog II**, Dean of Faculty, Professor of New Testament, Andover Newton Theological School, Newton Centre, Massachusetts; *62, 71*. **Claudia Highbaugh**, Dean of Religious and Spiritual Life, Connecticut College, New London, Connecticut; *248, 254*. **Allen R. Hilton**, Minister of Faith and Learning, Wayzata Community Church, Wayzata, Minnesota; *54*. **Geoffrey M. St. J. Hoare**, Rector, All Saints' Episcopal Church, Atlanta, Georgia; *157, 163*. **John C. Holbert**, Lois Craddock Perkins Professor of Homiletics, Perkins School of Theology, Southern Methodist University, Dallas, Texas; *284, 287, 288*. **Ruthanna B. Hooke**, Assistant Professor of Homiletics, Virginia Theological Seminary, Alexandria, Virginia; *78, 87, 91, 96, 100*. **Paul K. Hooker**, Executive Presbyter, Presbytery of St. Augustine, Presbyterian Church (U.S.A.), Jacksonville, Florida; *58*. **H. James Hopkins**, Pastor, Lakeshore Avenue Baptist Church, Oakland, California; *467, 475*. **Leslie J. Hoppe**, Adjunct Old Testament Studies Professor, Catholic Theological Union, Franklin, Wisconsin; *82, 91, 98*. **Amy C. Howe**, Parish Associate, Evergreen Presbyterian Church, Memphis, Tennessee; *437, 443, 453*. **David B. Howell**, Editor of Lectionary Homiletics, Midlothian, Virginia; *491, 498, 500*. **James C. Howell**, Pastor, Myers Park United Methodist Church, Charlotte, North Carolina; *52, 55, 61, 62, 70*. **Mary Lin Hudson**, Professor of Homiletics and Liturgics, Memphis Theological Seminary, Memphis, Tennessee; *142, 145, 150, 151*. **Rodney J. Hunter**, Professor of Pastoral Theology Emeritus, Candler School of Theology, Emory University, Atlanta, Georgia; *160, 161, 172*. **Christopher R. Hutson**, Associate Professor of New Testament, Abilene Christian University, Abilene, Texas; *18*.

Jerry Irish, McLean Professor of Religion and Religious Studies, Pomona College, Claremont, California; *133, 143, 152*.

Cynthia A. Jarvis, Minister and Head of Staff, The Presbyterian Church of Chestnut Hill, Philadelphia, Pennsylvania; *11, 515, 518, 523, 530*. **Nathan G. Jennings**, Assistant

Professor of Liturgics and Anglican Studies, Episcopal Theological Seminary of the Southwest, Austin, Texas; *464, 473.* **Willie James Jennings**, Assistant Research Professor of Theology and Black Church Studies, Duke University Divinity School, Durham, North Carolina; *289, 293.* **Michael Jinkins**, Academic Dean and Professor of Pastoral Theology, Austin Presbyterian Theological Seminary, Austin, Texas; *382.* **Cheryl Bridges Johns**, Copastor, New Covenant Church of God, Cleveland, Tennessee; *380, 381, 398, 399, 401.* **E. Elizabeth Johnson**, J. Davison Philips Professor of New Testament, Columbia Theological Seminary, Decatur, Georgia; *5, 6, 473.* **Susan B. W. Johnson**, Minister, Hyde Park Union Church, Chicago, Illinois; *459, 468, 476.* **Peter Rhea Jones**, Professor of Preaching and New Testament, James and Carolyn McAfee School of Theology, Mercer University, Atlanta, Georgia; *451.* **Serene Jones**, President, Union Theological Seminary, New York, New York; *230, 239.* **Verity A. Jones**, Publisher and Editor, Disciples World, Indianapolis, Indiana; *108, 111, 117, 126.*

Eunjoo Mary Kim, Associate Professor of Homiletics, The Iliff School of Theology, Denver, Colorado; *133, 134, 145, 152.* **Douglas T. King**, Associate Pastor, Brick Presbyterian Church, New York, New York; *376, 377, 385, 394, 395.* **Michael D. Kirby**, Pastor, Good Shepherd Presbyterian Church, Chicago, Illinois; *234.* **Cynthia Briggs Kitteredge**, Ernest J. Villavaso Jr. Associate Professor of New Testament, Episcopal Theological Seminary of the Southwest, Austin, Texas; *325.* **Elizabeth C. Knowlton**, Canon for Prayer and Mission, The Cathedral of St. Philip, Atlanta, Georgia; *117, 126.* **Craig Kocher**, Associate Dean of the Chapel and Director of Religious Life, Duke University, Durham, North Carolina; *177, 183.* **Steven J. Kraftchick**, Associate Professor of the Practice of New Testament Interpretation, Candler School of Theology, Emory University, Atlanta, Georgia; *118, 123.*

Emmanuel Y. Lartey, Professor of Pastoral Theology, Care and Counseling, Candler School of Theology, Emory University, Atlanta, Georgia; *318.* **Gregory Ledbetter**, Pastor, Shell Ridge Community Church (American Baptist),Walnut Creek, California; *226.* **Michael L. Lindvall**, Senior Minister, Brick Presbyterian Church, New York, New York; *354, 372.* **Kimberly Bracken Long**, Assistant Professor of Worship, Columbia Theological Seminary, Decatur, Georgia; *36, 41, 46.* **Thomas G. Long**, Bandy Professor of Preaching, Candler School of Theology, Emory University, Atlanta, Georgia; *250, 256, 265, 541, 546, 556.* **Jennifer L. Lord**, Associate Professor of Homiletics, Austin Presbyterian Theological Seminary, Austin, Texas; *436, 440, 454.* **David J. Lose**, Marbury E. Anderson Chair in Biblical Preaching, Luther Seminary, St. Paul, Minnesota; *166.* **Barbara K. Lundblad**, Joe R. Engle Professor of Preaching, Union Theological Seminary, New York, New York; *277, 283.* **Dwight M. Lundgren**, Director of Reconciliation Ministries, American Baptist Churches USA, Valley Forge, Pennsylvania; *49, 58, 67, 72.*

Ross Mackenzie, Historian Emeritus, Chautauqua Institution, Richmond, Virginia; *135, 138, 153.* **W. Eugene March**, A. B. Rhodes Professor of Old Testament Emeritus, Louisville Presbyterian Theological Seminary, Louisville, Kentucky; *201.* **Ian S. Markham**, President and Dean, Virginia Theological Seminary, Alexandra, Virginia; *189, 202.* **Bert Marshall**, Regional Director, Church World Service, Ludlow, Massachusetts; *322, 323, 331, 337, 340.* **Al Masters**, Pastor, St. Andrews Presbyterian Church, Taylors, South Carolina; *134, 136, 143, 154.* **Victor McCracken**, Ph.D. Candidate, Emory University, Atlanta, Georgia; *515, 523, 530.* **David W. McCreery**, Professor, Department of Religious Studies, Willamette University, Salem, Oregon; *346.* **Judith M. McDaniel**, Howard Chandler Robbins Professor of Homiletics, Virginia Theological Seminary, Alexandria, Virginia; *300, 302, 308, 309, 317.* **Dean McDonald**, Cathedral College of Preachers, Washington, D.C; *418, 422.* **John**

T. **McFadden**, Chaplain, Goodwill Industries of North Central Wisconsin, Appleton, Wisconsin; *352, 356, 361, 370, 374*. **Donald K. McKim**, Executive Editor for Theology and Reference, Westminster John Knox Press, Germantown, Tennessee; *295, 319*. **Allen C. McSween Jr.**, Pastor, Fourth Presbyterian Church, Greenville, South Carolina; *86, 94, 95*. **James W. McTyre**, Pastor, Lake Hills Presbyterian Church, Knoxville, Tennessee; *51, 59, 68, 69, 73*. **Wayne A. Meeks**, Woolsey Professor Emeritus of Biblical Studies, Yale University, New Haven, Connecticut; *407, 428*. **Deborah Anne Meister**, Rector, Christ Church, New Brunswick, New Jersey; *328, 333, 342*. **Bonnie J. Miller-McLemore**, E. Rhodes and Leona B. Carpenter Professor of Pastoral Theology, Vanderbilt University Divinity School, Nashville, Tennessee; *271, 280*. **Mark Miller-McLemore**, Assistant Professor, Practice of Ministry, Vanderbilt University Divinity School, Nashville, Tennessee; *298, 305, 315*. **Shawnthea Monroe-Mueller**, Senior Minister, Plymouth United Church of Christ, Shaker Heights, Ohio; *159, 175*. **Stephen R. Montgomery**, Pastor, Idlewild Presbyterian Church, Memphis, Tennessee; *210, 214*. **Joseph Monti**, Professor of Christian Ethics and Moral Theology, The School of Theology, The University of the South, Sewanee, Tennessee; *130, 144, 149*. **Martha L. Moore-Keish**, Assistant Professor of Theology, Columbia Theological Seminary, Decatur, Georgia; *211, 219, 462, 470, 480*. **Michael Morgan**, Seminary Musician, Columbia Theological Seminary, Decatur, Georgia, and Organist, Central Presbyterian Church, Atlanta, Georgia; *512, 513, 517, 520, 521, 526, 527*. **D. Cameron Murchison**, Dean of Faculty, Columbia Theological Seminary, Decatur, Georgia; *337, 341*. **Stephen Butler Murray**, Senior Pastor, The First Baptist Church of Boston, Massachusetts, and College Chaplain and Associate Professor of Religion, Endicott College, Beverly, Massachusetts; *487, 508*. **Donald W. Musser**, Hal S. Marchman Professor of Civic and Social Responsibility Emeritus, Stetson University, DeLand, Florida; *32, 39, 45*.

Andrew Nagy-Benson, Senior Minister, Spring Glen Church, United Church of Christ, Hamden, Connecticut; *54, 63, 66*. **Rodger Y. Nishioka**, Benton Family Associate Professor of Christian Education, Columbia Theological Seminary, Decatur, Georgia; *539, 548, 550*.

Julia M. O'Brien, Professor of Old Testament, Lancaster Theological Seminary, Lancaster, Pennsylvania; *454*. **Kathleen M. O'Connor**, William Marcellus McPheeters Professor of Old Testament, Columbia Theological Seminary, Decatur, Georgia; *11, 17, 457, 458, 467, 481, 511, 517, 519, 520, 525*. **Gail R. O'Day**, Associate Dean of Faculty and Academic Affairs and A. H. Shatford Professor of Preaching and New Testament, Candler School of Theology, Emory University, Atlanta, Georgia; *236*. **Ofelia Ortega**, Professor of Theological Ethics, Evangelical Theological Seminary, Matanzas, Cuba; *106, 107, 116, 118, 124, 125, 127*. **Douglas F. Ottati**, Craig Family Professor of Reformed Theology and Justice Ministry, Davidson College, Davidson, North Carolina; *78, 87*.

Alan G. Padgett, Professor of Systematic Theology, Luther Seminary, St. Paul, Minnesota; *233*. **Eugene Eung-Chun Park**, Dornsife Professor of New Testament, San Francisco Theological Seminary, San Anselmo, California; *82*. **Thomas D. Parker**, Emeritus Professor of Systematic Christian Theology, McCormick Theological Seminary, Chicago, Illinois; *103, 108, 113, 117, 121, 122, 126, 544, 553, 554, 558*. **Jeff Paschal**, Pastor, First Presbyterian Church, Wooster, Ohio; *180*. **Michael Pasquarello III**, Granger E. and Ann A. Fisher Professor of Preaching, Asbury Theological Seminary, Wilmore, Kentucky; *536, 549, 553*. **Pete Peery**, Pastor, First Presbyterian Church, Asheville, North Carolina; *539, 541, 559*. **David L. Petersen**, Professor of Old Testament, Candler School of Theology, Emory University, Atlanta, Georgia; *223*. **Jeffrey D. Peterson-Davis**, Copastor, Pioneer Memorial Presbyterian Church, Solon, Ohio; *268, 269, 274, 286*. **Joseph L. Price**, Genevieve S. Connick

Professor of Religious Studies, Whittier College, Whittier, California; *75, 90, 93*. **Robert Warden Prim**, Pastor, Nacoochee Presbyterian Church, Sautee-Nacoochee, Georgia; *314*. **Neta Lindsay Pringle**, Minister of Word and Sacrament, Presbyterian Church (U.S.A.), Wilmington, Delaware; *351, 364, 369*. **Richard A. Puckett**, Director of Public Relations and Development, United Methodist Children's Home, Decatur, Georgia; *102, 112, 126*. **Andrew Purves**, Professor of Reformed Theology, Pittsburgh Theological Seminary, Pittsburgh, Pennsylvania; *30, 39, 44*.

Charles Quaintance, Assistant Professor of Homiletics, Hanover College, Hanover, Indiana; *157, 158*.

G. Lee Ramsey Jr., Professor of Pastoral Theology and Homiletics, Memphis Theological Seminary, Memphis, Tennessee; *301*. **Charles E. Raynal**, Associate Professor Emeritus of Theology, Columbia Theological Seminary, Decatur, Georgia; *436, 439, 448*. **Allison Read**, Assistant Rector, Christ Church in Short Hills, Short Hills, New Jersey; *431, 432, 440, 445, 450*. **Leanne Pearce Reed**, Pastor, Montevallo Presbyterian Church, Montevallo, Alabama; *358*. **André Resner Jr.**, Professor of Homiletics and Church Worship, Hood Theological Seminary, Salisbury, North Carolina; *232*. **Gail A. Ricciuti**, Associate Professor of Homiletics, Colgate Rochester Crozer Divinity School, Rochester, New York; *39, 44*. **Cynthia L. Rigby**, W. C. Brown Professor of Theology, Austin Presbyterian Theological Seminary, Austin, Texas; *34, 40, 46*. **V. Bruce Rigdon**, President Emeritus, Ecumenical Theological Seminary, Detroit, Michigan; *105, 109, 115, 118, 123, 127*. **John W. Riggs**, Professor of Historical Theology and Church History, Eden Theological Seminary, St. Louis, Missouri; *132, 136, 141, 150, 154*. **Marcia Y. Riggs**, J. Erskine Love Professor of Christian Ethics, Columbia Theological Seminary, Decatur, Georgia; *27, 138, 147*. **Matthew S. Rindge**, PhD Candidate in New Testament, Graduate Division of Religion, Emory University, Atlanta, Georgia; *302*. **Sharon H. Ringe**, Professor of New Testament, Wesley Theological Seminary, Washington, D.C; *464, 471, 473*. **Luis R. Rivera**, Associate Professor of Theology, McCormick Theological Seminary, Chicago, Illinois; *64, 69*. **Vernon K. Robbins**, Professor of New Testament, Emory University, Atlanta, Georgia; *105, 123*. **John Rollefson**, Pastor, Lutheran Church of the Master, Los Angeles, California; *328*. **Dale Rosenberger**, Senior Pastor, Dennis Union Church United Church of Christ, Dennis, Massachusetts; *131, 135, 139, 149*. **Iwan Russell-Jones**, Television Producer, Cardiff, United Kingdom; *297, 310, 320*.

Kristin Emery Saldine, Assistant Professor of Homiletics, Austin Presbyterian Theological Seminary, Austin, Texas; *296, 304, 310, 313*. **Don E. Saliers**, William R. Cannon Professor Emeritus of Theology and Worship, Candler School of Theology, Emory University, Atlanta, Georgia; *329, 347*. **Karen C. Sapio**, Pastor, Claremont Presbyterian Church, Claremont, California; *400*. **Stanley P. Saunders**, Associate Professor of New Testament, Columbia Theological Seminary, Decatur, Georgia; *161, 175*. **Donna Schaper**, Senior Minister, Judson Memorial Church, New York, New York; *75, 76, 84, 93*. **David J. Schlafer**, Homiletics Consultant, Author, and Conference Leader, Bethesda, Maryland; *275, 284*. **Clayton J. Schmit**, Arthur DeKruyter/Christ Church Oak Brook Professor of Preaching and Academic Director of the Brehm Center for Worship, Theology, and the Arts, Fuller Theological Seminary, Pasadena, California; *307, 311, 316*. **Donald Senior**, President, Catholic Theological Union, Chicago, Illinois; *221*. **Trisha Lyons Senterfitt**, Associate Pastor, First Presbyterian Church, Atlanta, Georgia; *30, 31, 36, 39, 44*. **Marcia Mount Shoop**, Minister of Word and Sacrament, Presbyterian Church (U.S.A.), Chapel Hill, North Carolina; *534, 543, 552, 558*. **Paul C. Shupe**, Pastor, Lake Edge United Church of Christ, Madison, Wisconsin; *182, 191, 199, 200*. **Judy Yates Siker**, Dean of Faculty and Associate Professor of New Testament, American Baptist Seminary of the West and The Graduate Theological Union, Berkeley, California; *9, 16.* **Gary V. Simpson**, Senior Pastor, The Concord Baptist Church of Christ, Brooklyn, New York; *242, 251, 252, 260, 261.* **Richard M. Simpson**, Rector, St. Francis Episcopal Church, Holden, Massachusetts; *463, 468, 481.* **G. Malcolm Sinclair**, Preaching Minister, Metropolitan United Church, Toronto, Ontario, Canada; *48, 63, 534, 535, 540, 549, 552.* **Joseph D. Small**, Director, Office of Theology and Worship, Presbyterian Church (U.S.A.), Louisville, Kentucky; *184, 202.* **Archie Smith Jr.**, James and Clarice Foster Professor of Pastoral Psychology and Counseling, Pacific School of Religion, Berkeley, California; *433, 437, 441, 442, 451.* **Susan Marie Smith**, Assistant Professor of Preaching and Worship, Saint Paul School of Theology, Kansas City, Missouri; *188, 201.* **Ted A. Smith**, Assistant Professor of Ethics and Society, Vanderbilt Divinity School, Nashville, Tennessee; *80, 82, 91, 97, 98, 100.* **Richard E. Spalding**, Chaplain to the College, Williams College, Williamstown, Massachusetts; *207, 218.* **O. Benjamin Sparks**, Presbyterian Church (U.S.A.) Pastor, Retired, Nashville, Tennessee; *408.* **Mark E. Stanger**, Canon Precentor and Associate Pastor, Grace Cathedral, San Francisco, California; *183, 196.* **Thomas R. Steagald,** Pastor, Lafayette Street United Methodist Church, Shelby, North Carolina; *55, 59, 60, 69, 403, 409, 412, 413, 427.* **John K. Stendahl**, Pastor, Lutheran Church of the Newtons, Newton, Massachusetts; *343.* **Martha Sterne**, Associate Rector, Holy Innocents' Episcopal Church, Atlanta, Georgia; *136, 141, 142, 145, 150, 151.* **Chandler Brown Stokes**, Pastor, First Presbyterian Church, Oakland, California; *359.* **George W. Stroup**, J. B. Green Professor of Theology, Columbia Theological Seminary, Decatur, Georgia; *17, 192, 235, 239, 383, 388, 389, 401.* **Nibs Stroupe**, Pastor, Oakhurst Presbyterian Church, Decatur, Georgia; *326, 327, 335, 336, 344.* **Louis Stulman**, Professor of Religious Studies, University of Findlay, Findlay, Ohio; *517, 527.*

Beth Laneel Tanner, Associate Professor of Old Testament, New Brunswick Theological Seminary, New Brunswick, New Jersey; *35, 43.* **Barbara Brown Taylor**, Butman Professor of Religion, Piedmont College, Demorest, Georgia; *169, 170, 173, 178, 186, 187, 195, 241, 259, 461, 464, 469, 482.* **G. Porter Taylor**, Bishop, Episcopal Diocese of Western North Carolina, Asheville, North Carolina; *405, 406.* **Eugene TeSelle**, Professor Emeritus, Vanderbilt University Divinity School, Nashville, Tennessee; *334, 347.* **James J. Thompson**, Assistant Professor of Philosophy, Presbyterian College, Clinton, South Carolina; *489, 498, 509.* **Mark A. Throntveit**, Professor of Old Testament, Luther Seminary, St. Paul, Minnesota; *499, 502, 508.* **Emilie M. Townes**, Associate Dean of Academic Affairs, Andrew W. Mellon Professor of African American Religion and Theology, Yale Divinity School, New Haven, Connecticut; *538, 547, 557, 559.* **Thomas H. Troeger**, J. Edward and Ruth Cox Lantz Professor of Christian Communication, Yale Divinity School, New Haven, Connecticut; *282, 290.* **Steven S. Tuell**, Associate Professor of Old Testament, Pittsburgh Theological Seminary, Pittsburgh, Pennsylvania; *129, 135, 144, 153.* **Mary Donovan Turner**, Vice President and Dean, Pacific School of Religion, Berkeley, California; *512, 513, 523, 531.* **Mary Douglas Turner**, Associate Rector, Bruton Parish Episcopal Church, Williamsburg, Virginia; *324, 346.* **W. C. Turner**, Associate Professor for the Practice of Homiletics, Duke University Divinity School, Durham, North Carolina; *18, 23.*

Aaron L. Uitti, Rector, Episcopal Church of Saints Peter and Paul, Marietta, Georgia; *446.*

Susan E. Vande Kappelle, Pastor, Fourth Presbyterian Church, Washington, Pennsylvania; *421.* **Edwin Chr. Van Driel**, Assistant Professor of Theology, Pittsburgh Theological Seminary, Pittsburgh, Pennsylvania; *391.* **Leanne Van Dyk**, Dean and Vice President of Academic Affairs, Western Theological Seminary, Holland, Michigan; *449, 450.*

G. Oliver Wagner, Pastor, Montoursville Presbyterian Church, Montoursville, Pennsylvania; *159*. **Paul W. Walaskay**, Professor Emeritus of Biblical Studies, Union Presbyterian Seminary, Richmond, Virginia; *247*. **Peter M. Wallace**, Vice President and Dean, Alliance for Christian Media, Atlanta, Georgia, and Producer and Host, "Day 1" Radio Program; *537, 545, 550, 556*. **Haruko Nawata Ward**, Associate Professor of Church History, Columbia Theological Seminary, Decatur, Georgia; *441, 455*. **Richard F. Ward**, Fred B. Craddock Chair in Preaching and Worship, Phillips Theological Seminary, Tulsa, Oklahoma; *11, 17, 410, 416, 428*. **Jo Bailey Wells**, Associate Professor of the Practice of Christian Ministry and Bible and Director of Anglican Studies, Duke University Divinity School, Durham, North Carolina; *355, 373*. **Audrey West**, Adjunct Professor of New Testament, Lutheran School of Theology at Chicago, Illinois; *205, 206, 220, 221*. **Charles A. Wiley**, Associate for Theology, Office of Theology and Worship, Presbyterian Church (U.S.A.), Louisville, Kentucky; *179, 192, 201*. **Marsha M. Wilfong**, Pastor, First Presbyterian Church, Bellevue, Iowa; *77, 86*. **Dawn Ottoni Wilhelm**, Associate Professor of Preaching and Worship, Bethany Theological Seminary, Richmond, Indiana; *446, 452, 453, 455*. **William H. Willimon**, Bishop, North Alabama United Methodist Church, Birmingham, Alabama; *410, 417, 419, 425, 426*. **Patrick J. Willson**, Pastor, Williamsburg Presbyterian Church, Williamsburg, Virginia; *140, 153*. **Robert R. Wilson**, Hoober Professor of Religious Studies and Professor of Old Testament, Yale Divinity School, New Haven, Connecticut; *144, 149*. **J. Philip Wogaman**, Professor of Christian Ethics Emeritus,Wesley Theological Seminary, Washington, DC; *222*. **Charles M. Wood**, Lehman Professor of Christian Doctrine and Director, Graduate Program in Religious Studies, Perkins School of Theology, Southern Methodist University, Dallas, Texas; *8, 17, 21, 26*. **Lawrence Wood**, Pastor, Fremont United Methodist Church, Fremont, Michigan; *81, 99*. **Telford Work**, Associate Professor of Theology, Westmont College, Santa Barbara, California; *224, 457, 466*.

Frank M. Yamada, Director of the Center for Asian American Ministries and Associate Professor of Hebrew Bible, McCormick Theological Seminary, Chicago, Illinois; *534, 543*. **Christine Roy Yoder**, Associate Professor of Old Testament, Columbia Theological Seminary, Decatur, Georgia; *104*. **Cathy F. Young**, Retired Pastor, Presbyterian Church (U.S.A.), Waterloo, Iowa; *33, 36, 40, 45*. **Sakena Young-Scaggs**, Associate Dean, Marsh Chapel, Boston University, Boston, Massachusetts; *292*. **Karen Marie Yust**, Associate Professor of Christian Education, Union Seminary–Presbyterian School of Christian Education, Richmond, Virginia; *383, 390*.

Beverly Zink-Sawyer, Professor of Preaching and Worship, Union Seminary–Presbyterian School of Christian Education, Richmond, Virginia; *353, 362, 365, 371*.

Scripture Index

Genesis 1:1–5	74	Psalm 34:15–22	429
Genesis 3:8–15	330	Psalm 41	128
Genesis 9:8–17	164	Psalm 45:1–2, 6–9	438
Genesis 17:1–7, 15–16	176	Psalm 47	276
Exodus 16:2–4, 9–15	402	Psalm 50:1–6	155
Exodus 20:1–17	185	Psalm 51:1–17	167
Numbers 21:4–9	194	Psalm 62:5–12	92
Deuteronomy 5:12–15	146	Psalm 70	224
Deuteronomy 18:15–20	101	Psalm 72:1–7, 10–14	65
Joshua 24:1–2a, 14–18	429	Psalm 78:23–29	402
Ruth 1:1–18	524	Psalm 80:1–7, 17–19	1
Ruth 3:1–5; 4:13–17	533	Psalm 81:1–10	146
1 Samuel 1:4–20	542	Psalm 85:1–2, 8–13	10
1 Samuel 2:1–10	542	Psalm 85:8–13	375
1 Samuel 3:1–10 (11–20)	83, 321	Psalm 92:1–4, 12–15	339
2 Samuel 7:1–11, 16	28	Psalm 96	37
2 Samuel 23:1–7	551	Psalm 98	42, 267
1 Kings 19:4–8	411	Psalm 103:1–13, 22	137, 312
2 Kings 2:1–12	155	Psalm 104:1–9, 24, 35c	501
2 Kings 4:42–44	393	Psalm 104:24–34, 35b	294
2 Kings 5:1–14	119	Psalm 107:1–3, 17–22	194
Esther 7:1–6, 9–10; 9:20–22	474	Psalm 107:1–3, 23–32	348
Job 1:1; 2:1–10	483	Psalm 111	101
Job 14:1–14	227	Psalm 116:1–2, 12–19	225
Job 23:1–9, 16–17	492	Psalm 118:1–2, 14–24	228
Job 38:1–7 (34–41)	501	Psalm 118:1–2, 19–29	212
Job 38:1–11	348	Psalm 119:9–16	203
Job 42:1–6, 10–17	510	Psalm 123	366
Psalm 1	285, 465	Psalm 124	474
Psalm 4	240	Psalm 125	447
Psalm 19	185, 456	Psalm 126	19
Psalm 22:1–15	492	Psalm 127	533
Psalm 22:23–31	176	Psalm 130	330
Psalm 22:25–31	258	Psalm 132:1–12 (13–18)	551
Psalm 23	249, 384	Psalm 133	231
Psalm 24	520	Psalm 139:1–6, 13–18	83, 321
Psalm 25:1–10	164	Psalm 145:10–18	393
Psalm 26	483	Psalm 146	524
Psalm 29	74, 303	Psalm 147:1–11, 20c	110
Psalm 30	119, 357	Psalm 147:12–20	56
Psalm 31:9–16	213	Psalm 148	47
Psalm 34:1–8	411	Proverbs 1:20–33	456
Psalm 34:1–8 (19–22)	510	Proverbs 9:1–6	420
Psalm 34:9–14	420	Proverbs 22:1–2, 8–9, 22–23	447

Proverbs 31:10–31	465	Mark 8:27–38	456
Song of Solomon 2:8–13	438	Mark 8:31–38	176
Isaiah 6:1–8	303	Mark 9:2–9	155
Isaiah 9:2–7	37	Mark 9:30–37	465
Isaiah 25:6–9	228	Mark 9:38–50	474
Isaiah 40:1–11	10	Mark 10:2–16	483
Isaiah 40:21–31	110	Mark 10:17–31	492
Isaiah 42:1–9	222	Mark 10:35–45	501
Isaiah 43:18–25	128	Mark 10:46–52	510
Isaiah 49:1–7	223	Mark 11:1–11	212
Isaiah 50:4–9a	213	Mark 12:28–34	524
Isaiah 52:7–10	42	Mark 12:38–44	533
Isaiah 52:13–53:12	226	Mark 13:1–8	542
Isaiah 60:1–6	65	Mark 13:24–37	1
Isaiah 61:1–4, 8–11	19	Mark 14:1–15:47	213
Isaiah 61:10–62:3	47	Luke 1:26–38	28
Isaiah 64:1–9	1	Luke 1:47–55	28
Jeremiah 23:1–6	384	Luke 2:1–14	37
Jeremiah 31:7–14	56	Luke 2:22–40	47
Jeremiah 31:31–34	203	Luke 24:36b–48	240
Ezekiel 2:1–5	366	Luke 24:44–53	276
Ezekiel 17:22–24	339	John 1:(1–9) 10–18	56
Hosea 2:14–20	137, 312	John 1:1–14	42
Joel 2:1–2, 12–17	167	John 1:6–8, 19–28	19
Amos 7:7–15	375	John 1:43–51	83
Jonah 3:1–5, 10	92	John 2:13–22	185
Wisdom of Solomon		John 3:1–17	303
1:13–15; 2:23–24	357	John 3:14–21	194
Wisdom of Solomon 3:1–9	519	John 6:1–21	393
Matthew 2:1–12	65	John 6:24–35	402
Matthew 6:1–6, 16–21	167	John 6:35, 41–51	411
Mark 1:1–8	10	John 6:51–58	420
Mark 1:4–11	74	John 6:56–69	429
Mark 1:9–15	164	John 10:11–18	249
Mark 1:14–20	92	John 11:32–44	522
Mark 1:21–28	101	John 12:20–33	203
Mark 1:29–39	110	John 15:1–8	258
Mark 1:40–45	119	John 15:9–17	267
Mark 2:1–12	128	John 15:26–27; 16:4b–15	294
Mark 2:13–22	137, 312	John 17:6–19	285
Mark 2:23–3:6	146, 321	John 18:33–37	551
Mark 3:20–35	330	John 20:1–18	228
Mark 4:26–34	339	John 20:19–31	231
Mark 4:35–41	348	Acts 1:1–11	276
Mark 5:21–43	357	Acts 1:15–17, 21–26	285
Mark 6:1–13	366	Acts 2:1–21	294
Mark 6:14–29	375	Acts 3:12–19	240
Mark 6:30–34, 53–56	384	Acts 4:5–12	249
Mark 7:1–8, 14–15, 21–23	438	Acts 4:32–35	231
Mark 7:24–37	447	Acts 8:26–40	258

Acts 10:34–43	228	Ephesians 4:1–16	402
Acts 10:44–48	267	Ephesians 4:25–5:2	411
Acts 19:1–7	74	Ephesians 5:15–20	420
Romans 4:13–25	176	Ephesians 6:10–20	429
Romans 8:12–17	303	Philippians 2:5–11	213
Romans 8:22–27	294	1 Thessalonians 5:16–24	19
Romans 16:25–27	28	Titus 2:11–14	37
1 Corinthians 1:3–9	1	Hebrews 1:1–4 (5–12)	42
1 Corinthians 1:18–25	185	Hebrews 1:1–4; 2:5–12	483
1 Corinthians 6:12–20	83	Hebrews 4:12–16	492
1 Corinthians 7:29–31	92	Hebrews 5:1–10	501
1 Corinthians 8:1–13	101	Hebrews 5:5–10	203
1 Corinthians 9:16–23	110	Hebrews 7:23–28	510
1 Corinthians 9:24–27	119	Hebrews 9:11–14	524
2 Corinthians 1:18–22	128	Hebrews 9:24–28	533
2 Corinthians 3:1–6	137, 312	Hebrews 10:11–14	
2 Corinthians 4:3–6	155	(15–18), 19–25	542
2 Corinthians 4:5–12	146, 321	James 1:17–27	438
2 Corinthians 4:13–5:1	330	James 2:1–10 (11–13), 14–17	447
2 Corinthians 5:6–10		James 3:1–12	456
(11–13), 14–17	339	James 3:13–4:3, 7–8a	465
2 Corinthians 5:20b–6:10	167	James 5:13–20	474
2 Corinthians 6:1–13	348	1 Peter 3:18–22	164
2 Corinthians 8:7–15	357	2 Peter 3:8–15a	10
2 Corinthians 12:2–10	366	1 John 1:1–2:2	231
Galatians 4:4–7	47	1 John 3:1–7	240
Ephesians 1:3–14	56, 375	1 John 3:16–24	249
Ephesians 1:15–23	276	1 John 4:7–21	258
Ephesians 2:1–10	194	1 John 5:1–6	267
Ephesians 2:11–22	384	1 John 5:9–13	285
Ephesians 3:1–12	65	Revelation 1:4b–8	551
Ephesians 3:14–21	393	Revelation 21:1–6a	521